INCOME OF THE
AMERICAN PEOPLE

A VOLUME IN THE CENSUS MONOGRAPH SERIES

INCOME OF THE
AMERICAN PEOPLE

by

HERMAN P. MILLER

U. S. Bureau of the Census

for the
SOCIAL SCIENCE RESEARCH COUNCIL
in cooperation with the
U. S. DEPARTMENT OF COMMERCE
BUREAU OF THE CENSUS

JOHN WILEY & SONS, INC., NEW YORK
CHAPMAN & HALL, LIMITED, LONDON

Library of Congress Catalog Card Number: 55–9613

PRINTED IN THE UNITED STATES OF AMERICA

FOREWORD

The statistical results compiled by the Bureau of the Census constitute a tremendous mass of detailed information about the population of the United States and its characteristics and economic activities. To meet the requirements of government agencies, business concerns, and investigators of social problems and to satisfy the needs of individual citizens, facts must be gathered and published, showing the distribution of the population in each large and small political unit with respect to age, sex, color, marital status, occupation, income, education, national origin, and other characteristics. This information provides the basis for apportionment of representatives in Congress, for answering many questions by direct reference, and for formulating many plans, at least in preliminary form.

It is the first business of the Bureau to the Census to put into print the census results that directly answer as many such questions as possible. Along with these results, similar data from one or two previous censuses are usually included. Limitations of time, space, and money prevent any extensive statement of the relations between particular results, the long-term trends of significant totals and subtotals, the shifting proportions of the people belonging to different categories, various interesting and important relations such as those between income, occupation, and age. It is not that the Bureau of the Census fails in any sense to appreciate the value and need for such analyses, but rather that it must concentrate on its basic concern with the summary statistics that constitute its unique contribution to knowledge.

When plans for the 1950 Census were made, the need for more extensive analysis was recognized and a series of census monographs similar to those issued after the 1920 Census was proposed. Because of the pressures caused by the depression in the early 1930's and by defense and war in the early 1940's, plans for monographs based on those censuses could not be carried out. Late in the 1940's interested persons from business, research, and government agencies expressed the need for a series that would provide analyses of the most significant results of the 1950 Census. The Social Science Research Council, with the assistance of Russell Sage Foundation, took the lead in stimulating the formulation of suitable plans and in June 1950 appointed a Committee on Census Monographs to cooperate with the Bureau in organizing this project. The members of the Comittee are:

Ralph G. Hurlin, Russell Sage Foundation (Chairman)

Robert W. Burgess, formerly Western Electric Company, since February 1953 Director of the Bureau of the Census

John D. Durand, United Nations

Ernest M. Fisher, Columbia University

F. F. Hill, Cornell University

Fredrick F. Stephan, Princeton University

Conrad Taeuber, Bureau of the Census

Ralph J. Watkins, Dun & Bradstreet, Inc.

Paul Webbink, Social Science Research Council

J. Fredrick Dewhurst, Twentieth Century Fund, and William F. Ogburn, University of Chicago, were members of the Committee during the first year and a half.

It is essential in any sound census monograph program to obtain the cooperation of authors with a broad understanding not only of the statistical information provided by the regular tabulations of the current census but also of the results of earlier censuses and other relevant knowledge and points of view from other sources and even from other countries. The preparation of a monograph should include broad exploration of new questions suggested by ·the new information, as well as narrowing the elements of doubt and controversy on old questions. The Social Science Research Council Committee early undertook, in consultation with leading figures in various professional fields, to develop a suggggested list of monograph titles and authors and persuaded experts in the subject areas selected to undertake the preparation of memoranda outlining and discussing the topics proposed. Then, in 1951, arrangements were made for continuing cooperation between the Committee and the Bureau concerning the selection of topics, proposals of authors and consultants, and editorial supervision.

Throughout the conduct of the project there has been close collaboration with a number of interested Federal agencies and with universities and research organizations, which provided staff and facilities to help bring the project to completion. They and the Council, which also obtained necessary funds from the Rockefeller and Russell Sage Foundations, provided assistance without which the monographs could not have been prepared.

The task of preparing monographs is an essential part of the broad function of making the information secured by censuses fully available to satisfy the needs and interests of the community and to constitute a broad base for further studies in the social sciences. As Director of the Census and President of the Social Science Research Council, respectively, we wish to record our full approval of the monograph project. It is not implied, of course, that the views expressed in these reports are necessarily those of the Bureau of the Census, the Department of Commerce, or the

Social Science Research Council.   The views are those of the individual authors, each of whom has been given the freedom to interpret available materials in the light of his technical knowledge and competence.   This freedom of the individual authors is an essential element in making the most useful analyses and interpretations generally available to the community.

ROBERT W. BURGESS, DIRECTOR
BUREAU OF THE CENSUS
PENDLETON HERRING, PRESIDENT
SOCIAL SCIENCE RESEARCH COUNCIL

1955

PREFACE

Too frequently, statisticians become so involved in the intricacies of their analysis that they fail to highlight their major findings. Whatever other errors I have made, I have tried to avoid this one. The purpose, scope, and results of this study are briefly summarized in the very first chapter. Therefore, there is little need to retrace these steps here. Readers who are interested in obtaining a broad view of the problems which are considered and the conclusions which are reached in this book, are referred to Chapter 1. Here, in the preface, I shall merely state, as the title indicates, that this is a book about people and income. It is a statistical analysis based largely on data obtained in two national censuses and in numerous sample surveys of the population. The primary aim of the study is to indicate the relation between the amount of income received by individuals and certain social and economic characteristics like geographic location, occupation, color, education, etc. The study also includes an analysis of the changes in income distribution which have taken place in the United States since the depression of the thirties, as well as an evaluation of the data which provide the basis for the findings.

During the past eight years, it has been my good fortune to be associated with the collection of income data at the Bureau of the Census. Serving in various capacities, first as a member of the Consumer Income Unit of that Bureau, and then as the head of that Unit, I participated in the 1950 Census of Population and in numerous sample surveys in which income data were collected. These surveys took us into the homes of the American people where we were cordially received. The typical housewife was usually less annoyed by the questions we asked than by the fact that we came unexpectedly and sometimes interrupted her household chores. Indeed, one of the things which has impressed me most in my experience with household surveys is the cooperativeness and the frankness of the American people in their relations with government representatives. It is my hope that this monograph, and others in this series, will provide in some small way a return to the people for the patience, honesty, and trust they have shown by answering our questions.

I am grateful beyond words to the Bureau of the Census and to the Social Science Research Council for providing me with the opportunity to work on this study. The entire manuscript was critically reviewed by Dr. Conrad Taeuber of the Bureau of the Census, and Dr. Ralph Hurlin of the Russell Sage Foundation. Their careful scrutiny eliminated many errors and improved the organization of the material considerably. The list of other people who read and criticized all or part of the manuscript is too long to reproduce here. However, I do feel especially indebted to Dr. Dorothy Brady of the U. S. Department of Labor, to Professor Frank Hanna of Duke University, and to various members of the faculty of the American University of Washington, D. C., for the comments and advice which I received from them. I alone, of course, accept full responsibility for the shortcomings of the study.

Several members of the staff of the Census Bureau contributed materially to the completion of this study. Without the assistance of Dr. Joseph Daly, much of the derived data shown in tables C-1 to C-6 would have been seriously delayed or perhaps never produced. It was his nimble mind which set the giant electronic brain of UNIVAC into motion and produced in ten minutes a volume of work which would have taken about six months by conventional methods. I am also grateful to David Kaplan and Claire Casey for their invaluable advice with regard to the use of occupational data based on the 1940 and 1950 Censuses. I owe much to Edwin Goldfield for the patience with which he listened to my many statistical troubles and for the sound technical advice he gave so willingly, and to Leon Paley for his direct contributions to this monograph and for the able way in which he relieved me of many official duties while it was in preparation. Finally, I should like to express my gratitude to my wife, Elaine, who is a member of the Census Bureau staff in spirit, if not in fact, for the many hours she spent reviewing drafts of the manuscript and helping me to explain my ideas in nontechnical terms.

CONTENTS

INTRODUCTION

The importance of statistics on income distribution is attested by the inclusion of information on income in the Population Censuses of 1940 and 1950 and, annually, in the Current Population Surveys since 1944. Of the many topics that compete for a place in census inquiries, only a limited list can be finally chosen for the collection of data. The selection of topics depends on evidence of extensive need for the particular facts on a broad population base. The question on income was added to the 1940 Census upon the recommendation of scholars and research analysts representing many different fields of study which require information on the distribution of income. The diversity in the amount of information required among the various fields of study was then, and still remains, so great that only a census or a large sample from the census could supply the basic facts. The decision to include a question on income in the 1940 Census was made shortly after an inventory of existing information on income distribution had revealed that the fragmentary, inconsistent, and inadequate information compiled from scattered surveys could not possibly serve the growing needs for data on income distribution. The income data provided as a by-product of sample survey investigations on various subjects did not cover a sufficient number of localities for market analysis and studies of housing, education and other topics which must be related to the individual locality. It was not possible to collate information on the income distribution at different dates for use in the analysis of population trends and of changes in the characteristics of the labor force. Very little knowledge of the incomes of specific population groups needed for the examination of problems of social welfare could be gleaned from the scattered sample survey data.

The evaluation of administrative records as a source of information on income distribution was equally discouraging in 1939. Tax statistics did not provide adequate data for the lower income brackets; social insurance records did not supply information on the higher income brackets. Neither source provided the information on family incomes which is necessary for the study of consumer behavior. The lowering of income tax exemptions has contributed to the generality of tax statistics, but otherwise the situation has not changed since 1939. Data from administrative records can supply information on only a part of the income distribution.

The income information in the 1940 Census was limited to wages and salaries, chiefly for reasons of feasibility. At that time little was known about the inaccuracies of income reported in interviews and about the public's willingness to divulge income information to a census interviewer. The restriction, in the 1940 Census, to wages and salaries was based on the presumption that the most regular and chief source of income for the greater part of the population would be less affected by reporting error than the income from unincorporated business, rent, interest, dividends, and other sources. This argument has not yet been refuted by evidence showing the effect of reporting errors on the form of the income distribution.

The sample surveys made between 1940 and 1950 proved that it was possible to collect credible and usable information on all types of income in the census interview. The uses for facts on income had multiplied so much after the data from the 1940 Census became available that there was little debate among technicians about the inclusion of a question on total income in the Census of 1950. The information on income distribution offered by the 1950 Census has not been paralleled in this country for any other date or matched in any other country with as much diversity in the population. A great number and a great variety of studies can be based on the information provided in the statistical tables already published or planned for publication. This monograph concentrates on a study of the factors that account for the variation in the incomes of individuals in a given year. The 1950 Census data on incomes constitute the first collection of information in this country that permits an investigation of the total structure of the income distribution. Estimates of the income distribution for earlier years, based either on compilations of data from diverse sources or on extensions of small sample surveys, could not offer information on the incomes of individuals in particular population classes that is necessary for understanding the relative importance of the elements associated with the variation in incomes. The analysis in this monograph of the sources of variation in incomes of individuals will contribute ultimately to our knowledge of the changes in the income distribution over time and to our understanding of the connection between the income distribution and the behavior of the population in a whole range of economic, social, and political activities.

An important immediate consequence of this analysis will come through the light it sheds on the question of the validity of the income data. The reliability of statistical analyses and of the inferences drawn from them depends in part on the sources of the systematic errors in reported incomes. The systematic errors in income surveys usually result in a net understatement of aggregate income for all types of income. The most valid hypothesis about the distribution of the total error in reporting among population groups and within population groups by income classes cannot be constructed before analyzing the reported incomes of these groups and classes. The observed differences between groups in the income reported to the census interviewers can eventually be compared with information from many sources, and the observed association between income and such factors as education and age can be checked for correspondence with the results of other investigations. Such a study of the distribution of the systematic errors in reported income is a research program in itself and must follow, not precede, the analysis of income as reported. The analysis of the income data as reported operates on the assumption that the aggregate error is proportionately distributed among all groups and classes in the population. If this assumption were proved invalid, the results of analyses of the type undertaken in this monograph would be inaccurate only with respect to the magnitudes of the observed differences, but not with respect to their direction. The concentration of the greater part of the discrepancy between the aggregate income reported in field surveys, and other estimates of the national aggregate in a few groups in the population, can be ruled out as a plausible assumption by simple comparisons with tax and other administrative records. Some comparisons of this kind are shown in this volume. No extreme inequality in the distribution of reporting errors has been indicated by any tests based on such comparisons. The general structure of the distribution of the income as reported must accordingly be an accurate description of the prevailing relations between the incomes of various groups in the population.

The interpretation of an income distribution for a single year has been a matter of controversy ever since the publication of "Consumer Incomes in the United States, 1935–36," by the National Resources Committee. It is now generally recognized that the incomes of individuals and families in a particular year may deviate considerably from the average over a number of years. The distribution for one year includes individuals with incomes below their average in the lower part of the income range and individuals with incomes above their average in the higher income brackets. Although there have been a number of statistical studies of income information for the same individuals over a period of years, there is still no sound basis for estimating the extent to which the chance variations in individual incomes affects the distribution data for a single year. The effect of these chance fluctuations in individual incomes on the shape of the income distribution is often ignored and the data are misinterpreted as representative of longer time spans.

This monograph suggests a statistical basis for identifying the more permanent core of the distribution. The main factors associated with the level of income, such as occupation and age, define groups that are relatively homogeneous with respect to those factors and also with respect to the chance influences on individual incomes. If the classification of individuals by a number of factors results in normal distributions of incomes within groups, it is reasonable to assume that these group distributions provide a measure of the chance elements operating on the incomes for a particular year. The distribution of the mean incomes of such homogeneous groups under these circumstances provides a measure of the systematic part of the income distribution in that year. The analysis in this monograph shows that such a distribution would have a significantly lower dispersion than the distribution of individual incomes.

It has long been known that the correlation of income with outlay and other activities varies among socio-economic groups living in the same community at the same time. While such differences have been interpreted as a reflection of different living standards, their nature has yet to be given a completely satisfactory empirical explanation. The differences in the dispersion of income from group to group shown in this monograph suggest an association between the chance factor in income distribution and the observed differences in the correlations of income with consumer expenditures or other variables. This study of income may show how classes of the population with similar patterns of behavior in relation to income can be defined.

Such an integration of the analyses of income distribution and of individual or family behavior in relation to income might ultimately contribute to an understanding of the aggregative data for the same variables. The most important final use of cross-section data will eventually come from the contribution that such analyses make towards an explanation of the changes in the aggregates for large communities or for the Nation.

DOROTHY S. BRADY
U.S. Bureau of Labor Statistics

C H A P T E R   1

SUMMARY

This study presents an analysis of the distribution of personal income in the United States. During the early 1950's, over one-quarter of a *trillion* dollars was paid out annually to the American people. The total is astronomical. The amount received by the average person, however, was not very high by most standards. In 1950, for example, one-half of the income receivers got less than $2,000. The range of incomes about this average was enormous. It extended from substantial losses to incomes of several million dollars. Over 200 tax returns were filed for incomes of $1,000,000 or more received in 1950. What factors account for the wide range of incomes? What has happened to the range of incomes in the United States since the depression of the 1930's? These are two of the basic questions that this book sets out to answer.

Income distribution is the result of the interplay of many forces. No single study can hope to include all the factors that are related to that distribution. Indeed, the role of certain significant, if not basic, factors such as health, intelligence, ambition, and even family connections, cannot be readily measured. These factors have, therefore, been excluded from the present study. Instead, the analysis focuses on several social and economic characteristics of individuals that can be measured and that are believed to play a basic role in the establishment of income differentials. In general, an attempt has been made to describe the variability of income among persons in terms of geographic location, occupational differentials, and various social and demographic factors such as age, sex, marital status, educational attainment, and color.

1. The data used in this analysis were derived largely from the 1940 and 1950 Censuses of Population and from the income surveys that have been conducted annually by the Bureau of the Census since 1944. The information was obtained by census enumerators in direct interviews with households. The income questions asked by these enumerators were quite simple, and the answers obtained were generally based on memory rather than on records. Despite these shortcomings, the results are reasonable and useful for many types of analysis. There is some evidence of a greater unwillingness or inability on the part of the public to respond to the income questions as compared with other inquiries on the census questionnaire. The differences, however, are not great, and the over-all nonresponse rate

1

to the income questions is so small as to preclude the possibility that it had any serious impact on the quality of the data.

These conclusions are stressed at the outset because they have bearing on an extended public controversy that took place prior to both the 1940 and 1950 Censuses. The announcement of the inclusion of income questions in these censuses brought a wave of protest directed at the Bureau of the Census. One outspoken critic in 1940 charged in a nationwide radio address to the American people that "these census questions demanding you to divulge your income manifestly violate your constitutional rights." [1] He also said that these questions "constitute an unwarranted prying into your personal affairs, they open up personal information to people in your own community who have been politically appointed as enumerators, and they are an invasion of the natural right of privacy of every citizen." Similar charges were made before the 1950 Census. It should be clear from the experience obtained in two national censuses and in many smaller surveys that the general public does not share the alarmist views that have so frequently been expressed with respect to household surveys in which income information is obtained. Moreover, the fact that this information was collected without a single reported incident of unlawful disclosure should convince even the most cautious individual that the rights of citizens are not jeopardized when they cooperate with their government by providing information that materially assists in the efficient operation of the economy.

2. Philosophers of all ages have speculated about reasons for the inequality of incomes. Various explanations have been offered. Some have stressed ability, others chance, and still others institutional factors that give the children of the wealthy an undue advantage over the children of the poor. In general, theories of personal income distribution can be classified as either "natural" (i.e., the result of factors that are beyond the control of the economic system) or "institutional." In this study an attempt is made to relate the empirical evidence to the theoretical systems, and the results are generally inconclusive. The data that are presented do not conclusively support or refute either group of theories. Much of the "inequality" of income (or the dispersion of income, which is a less colorful but a technically more accurate description) can be explained without reference to institutional factors such as the advantages bestowed by inheritance. The inclusion of women in the income distribution adds considerably to the lopsidedness (skewness) of the income curve; however, the difference between income distributions for men and women has little to do with chance, ability, or the possession of great wealth. Even for men, there is more symmetry in income distribution than most analysts have

---

[1] Radio address by Senator Charles Tobey on February 19, 1940, as reported in *Hearings Before a Subcommittee of the Committee on Commerce on S. Res. 231*, 76th Congress, 3rd Session, February 1940, p. 63.

recognized. The income distributions for the three groups of occupations that together include about three-fourths of employed men were found to be quite symmetrical when analyzed separately.

Although much of the asymmetry of the income curve can be explained statistically in terms of the merging of symmetrical curves for nonhomogeneous groups, the fact remains that there are great differences in the level of income among these groups. It was found, for example, that about three-fourths of the highest income recipients among men are independent professionals (doctors, dentists, lawyers, etc.), businessmen, or managerial workers. The facts regarding freedom of entry into these high-paid occupations are not now adequately known. The absence of such information makes it difficult to draw definitive conclusions about the underlying reasons for the skewness of the over-all income curve.

Once the statistical factors that largely account for the skewness of personal income distribution in the United States are identified, it immediately becomes apparent that the skewness of income distribution for other times and places may have resulted from an entirely different set of factors. In less industrialized societies, the landed aristocracy would undoubtedly replace the professional and managerial groups as the upper income class. Therefore, two societies may have the same degree of inequality for different reasons. Ethical judgments regarding the same degree of inequality could therefore be different depending upon the factors that create that inequality.

3. Geographic location affects both the level and the source of income. Income comparisons between farm and nonfarm residents cannot be made adequately on the basis of this study because the data used did not include noncash receipts in the definition of income. The study does show, however, that a substantial proportion of the farm population derives its income from nonfarm sources. In 1950, for example, about one-third of the farm families received more cash earnings from nonfarm work than from farming. It is evident that the farm population has become, to a large extent, dependent upon income received from nonfarm sources and that the once typical farm-operator household that lived and worked exclusively on the family farm no longer represents the majority of the farm population.

The analysis of regional differentials in income largely resolves itself into an investigation of the factors that differentiate the South from the rest of the Nation. The major conclusion suggested by the regional analysis is that, even when the data are properly controlled with respect to color, sex, residence, and size of community, there is an income differential between the South and the other regions. This differential does not appear to be related to the occupational composition of the southern labor force. It is tentatively concluded that other factors such as the pay-and-price structure, the industrial structure, differences in productivity, or perhaps even imperfections in the competitiveness of the labor market may account for the income differential between the South and the rest of the Nation.

The analysis of the relationship between income and size of place in this study, as in several earlier studies, indicates a positive correlation between these two variables. In other words, incomes tend to increase with size of place. For certain "disadvantaged" groups in the labor force, such as female workers and nonwhite men, the variation in income by size of place is quite pronounced and appears to be related to the limited nature of the occupational opportunities available to these groups in the smaller cities. However, even for white men, whose occupational opportunities do not appear to differ markedly by size of place, there is a tendency for average income to be lower in the smaller cities.

4. The regional analysis led to an investigation of income differences between whites and nonwhites. The evidence shows that in all regions of the United States the income of whites is considerably higher, on the average, than that of nonwhites, even when such factors as age, sex, education, and size of place are taken into account. In the northern and western parts of the United States as well as in the South, the nonwhite college graduate earns less on the average than the white who did not complete his high-school training. The concentration of nonwhites with relatively high educational attainment in low-paid jobs indicates that even when the nonwhite worker has succeeded in obtaining an education, his increased productive capacity is not fully utilized. There was some improvement in the kinds of jobs available to the nonwhite population between 1940 and 1950; however, the fact remains that the nonwhite industrial worker is still generally restricted to the lower paid jobs in our economy.

5. Despite the many changes in both labor market demands and practices that took place between 1939 and 1949, there were comparatively few changes in the relative income position of occupations dominated by wage or salary workers. With very few exceptions, the occupations studied retained their same relative position when ranked by income in 1939 and 1949. Only the comparatively fixed-income occupations like firemen and policemen experienced a marked drop in relative income position.

Some occupations like mail carriers, railroad conductors, and baggagemen, which are not generally regarded as high paid, were near the top of the income scale in both 1939 and 1949. In contrast, occupations like masons, plasterers, and other construction trades, which are among the highest paid on an hourly basis, are much nearer to the middle of the distribution when ranked by annual income. The latter occupations had the same relative income position during the depression of the 1930's as they had during the prosperous 1940's. The stability of the occupational structure in terms of income during the past decade lends some support to the thesis that wage structures tend to change relatively little over time.

6. The occupational structure shows less stability when ranked with respect to dispersion (the spread of incomes within a group) than when ranked by level of income. However, the data show conclusively that occupations do form a reasonably stable pattern with respect to dispersion.

The great majority of occupations retained about the same relative position with respect to dispersion in 1939 and 1949. Occupations characterized by regularity of employment and a narrow income range, such as mail carriers, policemen, firemen, and railroad workers, showed the least income dispersion. They were also among the highest paid occupations. In contrast, the occupations in which income dispersion was relatively great included those that ranked high on the income scale (such as real estate brokers and salaried managers or officials of manufacturing plants) as well as those that paid very little (such as messengers, parking lot attendants, and certain types of laborers).

7. There was a marked change in the distribution of wage or salary income in the United States between 1940 and 1950. Although the average income rose considerably in all occupations, the increase was by no means uniform. The greatest relative gains were made by the lowest paid occupations, and the smallest relative gains were made by the highest paid occupations. This narrowing of the gap between high-paid and low-paid occupations was in part responsible for the over-all diminution in the spread of incomes over the decade.

Also important in the explanation of the diminution of the inequality of incomes is the fact that there was a significant narrowing of the income gap between high-paid and low-paid workers within occupations. About four-fifths of the occupations that were studied for men showed a decrease in income dispersion of 10 percent or more. This decrease was as great for full-year workers as it was for all workers, suggesting that the narrowing of the wage spread is closely related to a decrease in wage-rate differentials as well as to an increase in full-time employment during the period. The narrowing of wage differentials was not restricted to any particular group of occupations such as those dominated by strong unions or by production workers. On the contrary, it was a widespread phenomenon that affected the great majority of occupations in which men are employed.

8. Although the study has focused primarily on personal income, some attention has been paid to family income as well. The data indicate that the family head occupies a pivotal position in determining the economic status of his dependents. At the same time, however, the financial contribution of working wives has been growing in importance. During the decade between 1940 and 1950, the proportion of working wives nearly doubled. Worker rates increased among married women of all ages and at all income levels during this period. The importance of the working wife's contribution to family income is suggested by the fact that the chances that a family had an income of $5,000 or more in 1951 were twice as great if the wife worked than if she stayed at home. The working wife has become an important part of the American economy. Any development that would seriously reduce worker rates among married women would also adversely affect the incomes and purchasing power of millions of families.

An attempt was made in the study to determine the proportion of families with incomes insufficient to maintain an "adequate standard of living." Although the estimates are very rough, they indicate that in 1946 and 1947, about one-fourth of the "city-worker" families had incomes that were insufficient to purchase a budget that would provide "a modest but adequate standard of living."

CHAPTER 2

BACKGROUND

Purpose of the study

Income distribution has well been characterized as the "point where the functioning of the economy impinges on the lives of the millions." [1] Indeed, in the light of the basic philosophy of democracy, there is probably no other single statistical measure that so well appraises the extent to which the masses of the population are sharing in the fruits of our remarkable industrial progress. Information relating to the volume of output has been available for some time, and a well-established and, what is more important, a well-digested literature on this subject already exists. However, it is only recently, and with considerable opposition to their collection, [2] that any extensive body of data relating to the distribution of that output among the population has begun to emerge. It is the purpose of this monograph to analyze these data, particularly those from the 1950 Census of Population and from the annual sample surveys conducted by the Bureau of the Census, with a view toward more clearly defining the factors that determine the personal distribution of income.

Historically, there has been a great deal of interest in the problem of income distribution; and there is no evidence of any abatement in this interest in the modern age. In a recent book, the historian, Toynbee, asks

[1] Simon Kuznets, *National Income: A Summary of Findings*, National Bureau of Economic Research, New York, 1946, p. 30.

[2] Questions relating to personal income were included in a national census for the first time in 1940. At that time hearings were held before the Senate Committee on Commerce seeking the removal of these questions from the census schedule. Witnesses appearing before this committee charged that the questions represented bureaucratic snooping and that they were evidence of a whittling away of American liberties. Fortunately, the income questions were not stricken from the census questionnaire in 1940, for a very useful body of statistical data emerged. The same storm arose at the time of the 1950 Census, and once again the results showed that the public reaction to income questions is not basically different from what it is to other census questions.

Controversy over the contents of censuses are by no means new or unique to the United States. In 1753 there was a discussion in the English Parliament regarding a proposal for a census to be taken the following year. One of the critics of this proposal is reported to have said, "I cannot believe that the motives from which they [the proposers] are pleased to assign are those from which they act; the hope of some advantage to themselves can only urge them to perpetuate such evil to others. . . ." He also regarded this act as "totally subversive of the last remains of English liberty" and proclaimed that if any interviewer tried to get information regarding the "number or circumstances of my family, I would refuse it; and if he persisted in the affront, I would order my servants to give him the discipline of the horse-pond." (The above quotations are excerpts from an article by D. V. Glass, "Population Controversy in Eighteenth-Century England," *Population Studies*, Vol. 6, July 1952, pp. 80, 81.)

whether, in view of the notable advances in the minimum standard of living which have resulted from technological improvements, we can "not look forward to seeing this rapidly rising minimum standard raised to so high a level, and enjoyed by so large a percentage of human beings, that the even greater riches of a still more highly favored minority will cease to be a cause of heartburning." [3]   He very wisely answers this question in the negative and points out that "however high the minimum standard of [man's] material living may be raised, that will not cure his soul of demanding social justice; and the unequal distribution of the world's goods between a privileged minority and an underprivileged majority has been transformed from an unavoidable evil into an intolerable injustice by the technological inventions of western man." [4]

Each age has had apologists and critics of its income distribution. [5]   Too often, however, this problem has been approached as an emotional outlet rather than as a subject for study.   It has been pointed out that much of the literature on this subject has "ranged from apologetic justification of income inequality in our society to discussion of principles of welfare economics with socialistic implications." [6]   Bias is apparently difficult to avoid in this emotionally laden field; and the careful reader will undoubtedly discover that, despite all efforts to the contrary, it has not been completely eliminated from the present study.   However, the aim of the study is to present, as objectively as possible, an analysis of the factors that bear on income distribution, using as a benchmark the data obtained in the various income surveys conducted by the Bureau of the Census.

A broad view of the problem

In the United States, as in other countries, there are great variations in the incomes received by individuals during a given year.   In April 1952 there were about 151½ million persons residing in the United States.   An examination of the distribution of these people by their own incomes (table 1 and figure 1) indicates that the income curve is very much as Pigou has described it, "humped and lopsided." [7]   The very striking fact demonstrated by figure 1 is that about one-half of the people in the United States received no cash income at all during the calendar year 1951.   If persons who did unpaid work on a family farm or business were included as income recipients, the proportion without income would be reduced only

---

[3] Arnold J. Toynbee, *Civilization on Trial*, Oxford University Press, 1948, p. 25.

[4] *Ibid.*, p. 25.

[5] Dorothy Brady has noted that "perhaps no other area of research presents a comparable volume of attempts at statistical generalization."   See her article "Research on the Size Distribution of Income," *Studies in Income and Wealth*, Vol. 13, National Bureau of Economic Research, New York, 1951, p. 5.

[6] George Garvy, "Inequality of Income: Causes and Measurements," *Studies in Income and Wealth*, Vol. 15, National Bureau of Economic Research, New York, 1952, p. 31.

[7] A. C. Pigou, *Economics of Welfare*, third edition, Macmillan and Company, London, 1929, p. 648.

slightly since the maximum number of people who were so employed during any given month in that year was less than 2½ million.[8]   The proportion without income may be somewhat overstated because of the difficulty of correctly allocating the income within a household and because of the tendency for people to forget to report small amounts of interest, dividends, and similar types of income to interviewers.   However, even if all the imperfections of measurement could be eliminated, it is doubtful that the conclusion that one-half of the population in this country works and invests to support the other half would have to be changed significantly.

TABLE 1.—INCOME OF ALL PERSONS IN 1951

Total money income in 1951	Number of persons[1] (thousands)	Percent distribution	Total money income in 1951	Number of persons[1] (thousands)	Percent distribution
Total..................	151,532	100.0	$3,000 to $3,499..........	6,959	4.6
Loss......................	287	0.2	$3,500 to $3,999..........	5,309	3.5
No income[2]...............	79,786	52.7	$4,000 to $4,499..........	3,946	2.6
$1 to $499................	11,553	7.6	$4,500 to $4,999..........	2,296	1.5
$500 to $999..............	8,968	5.9	$5,000 to $5,999..........	3,013	2.0
$1,000 to $1,499..........	5,955	3.9	$6,000 to $6,999..........	1,363	0.9
$1,500 to $1,999..........	6,314	4.2	$7,000 to $9,999..........	1,220	0.8
$2,000 to $2,499..........	7,246	4.8	$10,000 to $14,999........	502	0.3
$2,500 to $2,999..........	6,385	4.2	$15,000 and over..........	430	0.3

[1] The total population of the United States is shown in this table including persons under 14 years of age, institutional inmates, and members of the Armed Forces.   All subsequent tables based on the 1950 Census relate to persons 14 years of age and over, unless otherwise specified.   Tables based on the Current Population Survey (i.e., those derived from *Current Population Reports*) relate to the civilian noninstitutional population 14 years old and over plus a relatively small number of Armed Forces members living off post, unless otherwise specified.

[2] Includes the following groups:

Children under 14 years old..	42,204
Persons aged 14 to 19, most of whom were attending high school or college........	7,702
Housewives...	25,609
Persons aged 65 and over (excluding housewives)...........................	1,077
Other adults..	3,194

Source: Estimated population based on unpublished data of the Bureau of the Census.   Income distribution derived from the Bureau of the Census report, *Current Population Reports—Consumer Income*, Series P–60, No. 11, table 1.

There are some who will object to the presentation of the statistics as they are shown in figure 1.[9]   They will correctly point out that the 80 million people without income include 42 million children under 14 years

[8] U. S. Bureau of the Census, *Current Population Reports—Annual Report on the Labor Force*, Series P–50, No. 40, p. 23.
[9] It can be noted in figure 1 as well as in figures 2 to 9 that the curve for both extremes of the distribution has been fitted with a dashed line rather than with the solid one that has been used for the rest of the distribution.   The dashed line has been used to indicate that the data for this part of the curve represent only rough approximations.   For example, in figure 1, the only information available for the "loss" interval and the "$15,000 and over" interval is that they respectively include 0.2 percent and 0.3 percent of the civilian noninstitutional population.   Since these intervals comprise only a small area of most of the distributions for which data are presented, this liberty with the figures has the advantage of indicating the shape of the complete curve without significantly affecting any of the conclusions.

of age and 8 million additional persons 14 to 19 years old, most of whom are going to school. The figure also includes 26 million housewives and 1 million aged persons. Surely these groups should be treated separately if the aim is to understand the forces that shape income distribution. There is considerable dispute as to who should be included in a measure of income distribution. It has been argued that a measure of income inequality should refer to the entire population rather than to a segment of it.[10]

FIGURE 1.—INCOME OF ALL PERSONS IN 1951

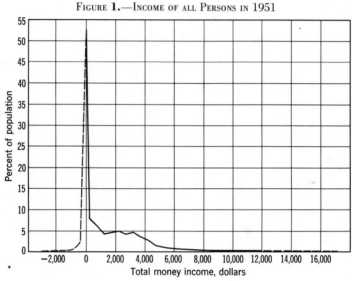

Note: Based on data in table 1.

Even if the analysis of income distribution is restricted to income recipients, it is apparent from figure 2 that the income curve remains much the way Pigou described it. Over one-fourth of the income recipients are clustered in the relatively narrow range of incomes between $1 and $1,000. If this range is doubled, nearly half of all income recipients can be accounted for.

A more direct view of the magnitude of income inequality may be obtained by considering the distribution of aggregate income rather than the frequency distribution of persons by income levels. Table 2 indicates that, although people who made less than $650 during 1951 represented 20 percent of the income recipients, they received less than 3 percent of

---

[10] "In brief, no group less extensive than the total population should be the base for studying changes in the inequality of incomes: Morris A. Copeland came to this conclusion in *Recent Economic Changes in the United States*, and Kuznets has stressed its logic in 'National Income,' *Encyclopedia of Social Sciences;* and *National Income: A Summary of Findings.*" The above quotation appears in an article by Dorothy S. Brady, "Research in the Size Distribution of Income," *Studies in Income and Wealth*, Vol. 13, National Bureau of Economic Research, New York, 1951, p. 10.

the aggregate income.   On the other hand, those who received more than $3,860 also represented 20 percent of the income recipients, but they received nearly half of the income.

FIGURE 2.—INCOME RECIPIENTS BY INCOME IN 1951

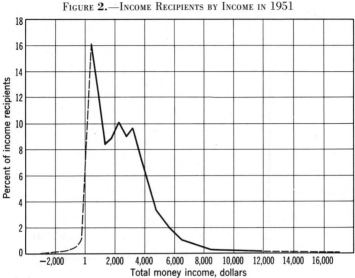

Note: Based on data in table 1.

TABLE 2.—PERCENT OF AGGREGATE INCOME RECEIVED BY EACH FIFTH OF INCOME RECIPIENTS RANKED BY INCOME IN 1951

Income recipients	Income range	Percent of total
Total......................	....	100.0
Lowest fifth.....................	Under $648........................	2.5
Second fifth.....................	$648 to $1,662....................	8.4
Middle fifth.....................	$1,663 to $2,720.................	16.7
Fourth fifth.....................	$2,721 to $3,859.................	24.7
Highest fifth....................	$3,860 and over.................	47.7

Source: U. S. Bureau of the Census, *Current Population Reports—Consumer Income*, Series P–60, No. 11, p. 9.

Here then, in broad outline, is a general view of the problem under consideration.   What factors account for the characteristic skewness of the over-all income curve?   Why is there so great a dispersion of incomes? Obviously, there is no simple answer to so complex a question.   Some of the factors that affect the receipt of income, such as health, intelligence, and ambition, cannot be readily measured.   However, there is another group of factors relating to the social and economic characteristics of individuals that can be measured and that are believed to play a basic role in the establishment of income differentials.   In general, the variability of income among persons may be described in terms of (*a*) the variation introduced by geographic location; (*b*) the factors accounting for differences among occupations; and (c) the social and demographic factors explaining differences among individuals. Each of these factors will be examined in some detail in this study.

Income distribution and public policy

To account for the structure of the income distribution as the end result of the operation of the economy, it is necessary to examine the elements responsible for variation in the earnings of individuals and for variation in the receipt of income from property and transfers. The task is to elicit through comparisons for one date some understanding, in quantitative, statistical form, of the variables that determine the form of the income distribution.

Income distribution, analyzed for an understanding of its "causes," refers to the incomes of individuals; for, in this country, income accrues, in general, to individuals. Income distribution, analyzed in terms of its influence on the future course of the economy, means "family" income; for, incomes are spent or saved by consumption units, the family, or the single individual living apart from family units. Income distribution, from the viewpoint of public policy, may refer to both individual and family incomes. Measures designed to alter the shape of the income distribution have been formulated and put into practice with little exact knowledge of the actual characteristics of the distribution. Empirical analysis of the determinants of income should contribute to an understanding of public policies directed towards equalization of the shares in the social product. The historic issues relating to poverty, inequality, and insecurity were debated without adequate support from facts and figures. The unique collection of data on income offered by the 1950 Census, supplemented by data available from the various field surveys of income conducted during recent years, has much to contribute in the clarification of the nature of those "social" problems that are associated with economic welfare and economic policy.

Some cautions and explanations [11]

Income, like most other economic concepts, can be defined in various ways depending upon the purpose one has in mind. An income concept that is suitable for measuring the ability to pay taxes may be quite different from one that measures the reward for employment, purchasing power, economic welfare, or any other characteristic of which income is thought to be an index. For example, if one is interested in measuring the reward

---

[11] In order to maintain continuity in the analysis, detailed descriptive materials such as definitions of the terms and measures of the reliability of the data have been included in appendixes. Appendix A contains definitions and explanations of the terms used in this report as well as data on the source and reliability of the estimates. Appendix B contains an appraisal of the quality of census income data.

for employment in different occupations, earnings before taxes would be more suitable than earnings after taxes because the latter may reflect factors that are not related to employment. On the other hand, income after taxes is a better measure of purchasing power than income before taxes. Similarly, capital gains are generally considered as income for tax purposes but are excluded from measures of purchasing power primarily because they are thought to be sporadic and not to function like recurring receipts in the formation of spending patterns. Without listing the many variations in the income concept that would be useful for different purposes, it should be apparent that there is no single income concept that would satisfy all needs.

In addition to the theoretical problems of defining income, there are many problems of a practical nature that arise when an enumerative technique is used. In the 1950 Census, as well as in the other field surveys of income from which data for this study have been obtained, the income and other information were obtained by direct interview in a door-to-door canvass of households. This method placed very rigid limitations on the types of data that could be included in the income concept. For example, the value of food produced and consumed in the home by farmers should be included in almost any definition of income. However, it would have required much more training time for interviewers, and much longer interviews to obtain such information with any degree of accuracy, than could be afforded with the funds allocated for taking the census. Similarly, for certain purposes it would have been more desirable to obtain income after taxes rather than before taxes. However, this too would have been very expensive to obtain with any degree of accuracy.

Income information in the 1950 Census was obtained from a 20-percent sample of the population. If a person came into the sample he was asked the following three questions about his cash income receipts during 1949: (a) the amount received from wages or salary; (b) the net amount received from the operation of a business, farm, or professional practice; and (c) the amount received from other income such as interest, dividends, veteran's allowances, pensions, and rents. If the sample person was a family head, these questions were repeated for his relatives in the household in order to obtain income information for the entire family group.[12]

Even this very brief description of the definition of income used in the

---

[12] Essentially the same procedure is used to collect income information in the annual supplements to the Current Population Survey of the Bureau of the Census, which have been used extensively in this study. For example, in April 1952, data on income were collected in the Current Population Survey from approximately 15,000 households in 68 sample areas located in 42 states and the District of Columbia. In this survey, income questions on the following points were asked for each person in the sample who was 14 years of age and over: (1) the amount of money wages or salary received in 1951; (2) the amount of net money income received from nonfarm self-employment in 1951; (3) the amount of net money income received from farm self-employment in 1951; and (4) the amount of other income received in 1951, such as interest, dividends, veterans' allowances, pensions, or rents.

1950 Census is sufficient to indicate some of the cautions that should be exercised in the interpretation of the data. First, income is defined to exclude noncash receipts (income "in kind"). Inasmuch as nonmoney income is an important part of farm receipts, this factor must be taken into consideration in comparing the income of farm and nonfarm residents.[13] Second, current income does not include money derived from the sale of assets or withdrawals from savings. Therefore, the income definition does not fully describe the financial position of the individual or the family group. Third, income represents the amount received during a given year and therefore may unduly reflect the effects of transient factors such as temporary illnesses, the establishment of a new business, a "good" or "bad" year, etc. Finally, income is measured in current prices. Therefore, in comparing the money income data for any year with those for other years, account should be taken of the fact that changes in money income were frequently accompanied by changes in prices.

The estimates of income distribution presented here are based on samples rather than on complete enumerations of the population. Therefore, they are subject to sampling variability. This means that the figures that are presented may be somewhat different from those that would have been obtained from a complete enumeration of the population. For example, the median income in 1949 of all persons reporting income in the census was $1,917. If a complete enumeration of the population had been made, the chances are two out of three that the median would have ranged between $1,916 and $1,918. Most of the estimates have a wider range of variability than this;[14] however, because of the large size and the representativeness of the sample used in the 1950 Census, the sampling variability is quite small and does not materially affect the analysis except where very small differences are concerned.

More important than sampling variation are the errors of response and nonreporting that exist in the data. Income information could not be obtained from about 6 percent of the persons in the 1950 Census sample. Data available from an intensive quality check of the census results indicate

---

[13] The following figures, adapted from the Department of Agriculture report, *How Families Use Their Incomes* (*Misc. Pub. 653*), indicate the importance of nonmoney income for farm families at different income levels:

Net money income level	Total income	Percent of total income, by source		
		Money income	Food, not purchased	Housing and other goods, not purchased
Low ($403)................	100.0	58.1	22.9	19.0
Medium ($833).............	100.0	69.5	14.8	15.7
High ($1,591).............	100.0	79.4	9.4	11.2

For a detailed discussion of nonmoney income and its impact on the size distribution of income, see Margaret G. Reid, "Distribution of Nonmoney Income," *Studies in Income and Wealth*, Vol. 13, National Bureau of Economic Research, New York, 1951, pp. 125–185.

[14] Appendix A contains a detailed discussion of the sampling variability of the estimates.

that there is very little likelihood that this group has introduced any bias in the data. In addition, however, there is some evidence that many of the persons who reported their income did not do so correctly. In most cases the income information was based on memory rather than on records; and in the majority of households on the memory or knowledge of one person, usually the wife of the family head. The memory factor produces an underestimate of income because of the tendency to forget minor or irregular sources of income. Other errors of reporting are due to misrepresentation or to misunderstanding of the income concept. Table 3 shows a comparison of the income aggregates estimated from the 1950 Census data with those prepared by the National Income Division of the Department of Commerce. This table emphasizes the well-established fact that data in all field surveys of income are subject to errors of response that produce underestimates of the level of income.[15] At the same time, however, the fact that the aggregate total income estimated from the 1950 Census data was 91 percent of the comparable estimate derived from national income accounts, which are prepared on an entirely independent basis, suggests that the census income data are sufficiently reliable for analytical use. Other checks on the quality of census income data, which are described in Appendix B, tend to confirm this conclusion.

TABLE 3.—ESTIMATES OF AGGREGATE INCOME IN 1949, BY TYPE, PREPARED FROM 1950 CENSUS DATA AND FROM NATIONAL INCOME ACCOUNTS

(In billions)

Type of income	1950 Census	National income accounts
Total income.............................	[1]$171.4	$187.6
Wage or salary income.........................	124.3	127.5
Self-employment income.....................	31.1	29.3
Income other than earnings..................	16.6	30.8

[1] The detail by type of income does not add to the total because each of the aggregates was estimated independently.

Source: Herman P. Miller, "An Appraisal of the 1950 Census Income Data," *Journal of the American Statistical Association*, Vol. 48, March 1953, p. 34.

---

[15] Virtually all analyses of income data obtained from household interviews show that this method produces an understatement of income. The most complete appraisal of the available data on the size distribution of income appears in Volume 13 of *Studies in Income and Wealth*, published by the National Bureau of Economic Research. The articles in this volume by Goldsmith; Mandel; and Wasson, Hurwitz, and Schweiger are particularly useful in this connection. The Bureau of Labor Statistics report, "Family Spending and Saving in Wartime," *Bull. 822*, contains a detailed appraisal of the income data obtained in the Survey of Family Spending and Saving in Wartime as well as brief indications of the extent of underreporting of income in other field surveys such as the Consumer Purchases Study, 1935–1936; Minnesota Income Study, 1938–1939; and the 1940 Census. The only detailed appraisal of the wage or salary income data obtained in the 1940 Census appears in an unpublished memorandum prepared by the staff of the Bureau of the Census. A recent report on income distribution in Great Britain (H. F. Lydall, "National Survey of Personal Incomes and Savings" *Bulletin of the Oxford University Institute of Statistics*, February and March 1953) indicates essentially the same type of understatement in British field surveys of income.

C H A P T E R 3

AN ANALYSIS OF THE OVER-ALL INCOME CURVE

Until the early part of this century, interest in income distribution centered almost exclusively on the rates of return to the factors of production. Very little was said about the determinants of share of aggregate income received by each of the factors, and the subject of income distribution among individuals was virtually ignored. In fact, we are told that before the publication of *Principles of Economics* by Taussig in 1911 "no systematic treatise on economic principles contained any attempt to answer, comprehensively and directly, the question: What are the causes of inequality of individual income?" [1]

This lamentable state of affairs was noted by several prominent economists before World War I. In 1905, Edwin Cannan wrote with respect to the functional distribution of income that "No intelligent person who has considered the subject for a moment can imagine that any investigation of the causes which determine wages per head, interest per cent, and rent per acre can provide directly an answer to the question: What regulates the proportions in which the produce is divided between wages, interest, and rent?" [2] Cannan was even more critical of the failure of economic theory to treat the problem of income distribution among individuals.[3]

Some theories regarding the income curve [4]

Numerous attempts have been made to construct theoretical systems that would account for the structure of income distribution among persons. These theories can be traced as far back as the latter part of the nineteenth century, and they persist with full vigor to the present day. In general, theories of the personal distribution of income can be classified as either "natural" or "institutional." The natural theories generally take a mathematical form, and they attempt to explain income distribution in terms of

---

[1] Hugh Dalton, *Some Aspects of the Inequality of Incomes in Modern Communities*, George Routledge and Sons, Ltd., London, 1920, p. 239.

[2] Edwin Cannan, "The Division of Income," *Quarterly Journal of Economics*, Vol. 19, May 1905, p. 352.

[3] *Ibid.*, pp. 343, 344.

[4] More detailed reference to the literature regarding theories of income distribution than is presented here may be found in the excellent article by George Garvy, "Inequality of Income: Causes and Measurement," *Studies in Income and Wealth*, Vol. 15, National Bureau of Economic Research, New York, 1952, pp. 25–47.

models that are generated by the theory of probability. Although some of these theories take institutional factors into account, the great majority regard income distributions as the result obtained by a play of natural forces outside the economic system; forces that would persist regardless of the particular form of economic organization. These theories range from a view of the income curve as a joint probability distribution of biological traits transmitted by heredity,[5] to the analysis of income distribution in terms of a game of chance played under certain specified conditions.[6]

In contrast to the natural theories, the institutionalist approach tends to be nonmathematical in nature. The theories based on this approach typically do not seek a model that can produce the observed income curve. Rather, they try by means of descriptive analysis to explain income inequality in terms of the institutional setting. These theories recognize the importance of certain natural phenomena like the distribution of ability, chance, etc. However, their unique stamp is the emphasis they give to institutional arrangements like the inheritance laws which they claim help to perpetuate inequality once it is established. Thus, for example, Taussig typifies this view when he attributes the origin of inequality to differences in innate ability and the perpetuation of inequality to "the influence of the inheritance both of property and of opportunity," as well as to the biological transmission of "native ability."[7] Pigou states the issues even more succinctly. In his *Economics of Welfare*, Pigou raises the following question:

> The essential characteristic of current income distribution is that the great bulk of incomes are massed together near the lower end of the income scale. This fact is significant for the following reason. There is clear evidence that the physical characters of human beings—and considerable evidence that their mental characters—are distributed on an altogether different plan. When, for instance, a curve is plotted out for the heights of any large group of men, the resulting picture will not, as with incomes, have a humped and lopsided appearance, but it will be a symmetrical curve shaped like a cocked hat. It will, in short—to use a technical term—be the characteristic Gaussian curve. . . . Now, on the face of things, we should expect that if, as there is reason to think, people's capacities are distributed on a plan of this kind, their incomes will be distributed in the same way. Why is not this expectation realized.[8]

Pigou thought he found the answer to this question. After considering the possibility that the skewed income curve largely reflected the merging of nonhomogeneous groups, each of which could be characterized by a nonskewed curve, Pigou discovered "a more important and more certain

[5] Carlos C. Classon, "Some Social Applications of the Doctrine of Probability," *Journal of Political Economy*, Vol. 7, March 1899, pp. 204–239.

[6] Maurice Fréchet, "Nouveaux essais d'explication de la répartition des revenus," *Revue de l'institut international de statistique*, Vol. 13, 1945, pp. 16–32.

[7] F. W. Taussig, *Principles of Economics*, second edition, Macmillan Company, New York, 1920, p. 246.

[8] A. C. Pigou, *Economics of Welfare*, third edition, Macmillan and Company, London, 1929, p. 648.

explanation"; namely, "Income depends not on capacity alone, whether manual or mental, but on a combination of capacity and inherited property. Inherited property is not distributed according to capacity, but is concentrated upon a small number of persons." [9]   Pigou thus attributed the major explanation for the shape of the income curve to institutional factors that bestow an undue advantage upon the wealthier classes in society.   This conclusion was undoubtedly influenced by the English social setting at the time Pigou wrote.   It may in fact be an adequate explanation for the causes of income inequality in that country at that time.   However, the evidence presented below for the United States suggests that the income curve reflects the interplay of many forces and that it would be unwise and perhaps incorrect to overstress the importance of any single factor.   This is not to say that the statistical evidence either supports or contradicts Pigou's conclusions.   Like all statistics, these data are subject to interpretation and they can be read in such a way as to find them consistent with either the natural or the institutional theories.   Perhaps the chief value of the empirical evidence is that it focuses attention on the characteristics associated with the component parts of the income curve and permits the formulation of more specific hypotheses regarding the controlling factors in the determination of personal income distribution.

Component parts of the income curve

The skewed income curve is composed of many heterogeneous elements. Therefore, it is extremely important to consider the parts before generalizing about the whole.   One of the most important sources of heterogeneity in the income curve is the inclusion of both men and women in the same distribution.   It is desirable for several reasons to show income distributions separately for each sex.   Although income from employment represents the most important source of receipts for both men and women, the labor force behavior of women is markedly different from that of men.   In our society it is customary for the man to provide for his own support and that of his family.   Accordingly, practically all able-bodied men in the productive age groups become full-time workers and develop permanent attachments to the labor force.   In contrast, it is customary for women to have the primary responsibility for home management.   During any given month, roughly three-fourths of the married women do not engage in any paid economic activity and only one-fourth are in the labor force as either paid workers or unpaid workers in their family farm or business.[10]   Nevertheless, married women comprise about one-half of the female labor force.[11] This means among other things that the majority of women workers can typically accept only intermittent employment and at jobs that interfere

---

[9] *Ibid.*, p. 649.
[10] U. S. Bureau of the Census, *Current Population Reports—Labor Force*, Series P–50, No. 39, table 1.
[11] *Ibid.*, table 1.

least with the fulfillment of their prime responsibility. Moreover, even when the working woman is not a housewife, she frequently limits herself to certain types of jobs. For these and many other reasons, it is important in the analysis of income distribution that the data for men and women be studied separately.

Table 4 and figure 3 present the separate income distributions for men and women. It will be noted that both curves are skewed and show a pronounced tendency toward bimodality. Neither curve resembles the "cocked hat" which Pigou sought. In terms of the problem that Pigou set out to analyze, it should be noted that the skewness of the income curve for women can largely be explained in terms of the factors noted above rather than by reference to inheritance.

TABLE 4.—INCOME IN 1951 OF PERSONS, BY SEX

Total money income of civilians in 1951	Both sexes	Male	Female	Total money income of civilians in 1951	Both sexes	Male	Female
Number of persons with income....thousands..	71,746	46,572	25,174	$2,500 to $2,999........	8.9	9.8	7.2
				$3,000 to $3,499........	9.7	12.4	4.9
				$3,500 to $3,999........	7.4	10.3	2.2
Percent.............	100.0	100.0	100.0	$4,000 to $4,499........	5.5	8.1	0.9
				$4,500 to $4,999........	3.2	4.8	0.5
Loss....................	0.4	0.4	0.2				
$1 to $499..............	16.1	8.9	29.2	$5,000 to $5,999........	4.2	6.3	0.5
$500 to $999............	12.5	8.5	19.6	$6,000 to $6,999........	1.9	2.8	0.2
$1,000 to $1,499........	8.3	6.8	10.9	$7,000 to $9,999........	1.7	2.5	0.2
$1,500 to $1,999........	8.8	6.8	12.3	$10,000 to $14,999......	0.7	1.1	0.1
$2,000 to $2,499........	10.1	9.6	11.0	$15,000 and over........	0.6	0.9	0.1

Note: To facilitate graphic presentation, all percents shown in figure 3 are based on the total of both sexes (71,746) rather than on the individual column totals used in this table.

Source: Derived from U. S. Bureau of the Census, *Current Population Reports—Consumer Income*, Series P–60, No. 11, table 4.

FIGURE 3.—INCOME IN 1951 OF PERSONS BY SEX

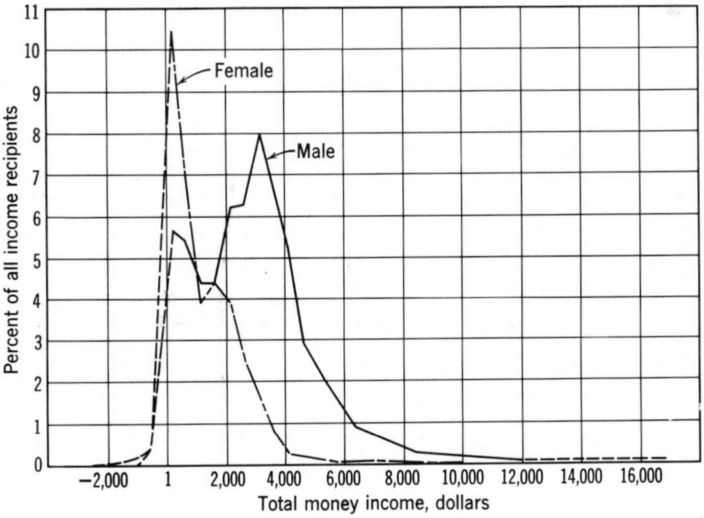

Note: Based on data in table 4.

One important fact to note about female income recipients is that when the distributions for full-year workers are separated from the distributions for women without work experience or for women who worked only part of the year, two unimodal curves appear (table 5 and figure 4). The arithmetic mean and the median of the curve for the full-year workers

TABLE 5.—INCOME IN 1949 OF WOMEN, BY EXTENT OF EMPLOYMENT

Total money income in 1949	Worked 50 weeks or more in 1949	Worked less than 50 weeks or did not work at all in 1949		
		Total	Worked 1 to 49 weeks	Did not work
Number of women with income..thousands..	7,981	14,291	9,348	4,943
Percent.............................	100.0	100.0	100.0	100.0
$1 to $499 or loss.........................	6.0	43.8	42.0	47.9
$500 to $999.............................	9.3	24.0	21.9	27.8
$1,000 to $1,499.........................	14.5	12.5	14.2	9.2
$1,500 to $1,999.........................	21.1	7.6	9.2	4.5
$2,000 to $2,499.........................	22.1	5.0	5.9	3.2
$2,500 to $2,999.........................	12.7	2.4	2.9	1.5
$3,000 to $3,499.........................	7.1	1.6	1.7	1.4
$3,500 to $3,999.........................	2.8	0.8	0.8	0.7
$4,000 to $4,499.........................	1.5	0.6	0.5	0.7
$4,500 to $4,999.........................	0.8	0.3	0.3	0.3
$5,000 to $5,999.........................	0.9	0.5	0.3	0.8
$6,000 to $6,999.........................	0.4	0.2	0.1	0.4
$7,000 to $9,999.........................	0.4	0.3	0.1	0.6
$10,000 and over.........................	0.4	0.4	0.1	1.0

Note: To facilitate graphic presentation, all percents shown in figure 4 are based on all female income recipients (22,272) rather than on the individual column totals used in this table.

Source: U. S. Bureau of the Census, *U. S. Census of Population: 1950*, Vol. II, *Characteristics of the Population*, Part I, U. S. Summary, table 141.

FIGURE 4.—INCOME IN 1949 OF WOMEN BY EXTENT OF EMPLOYMENT

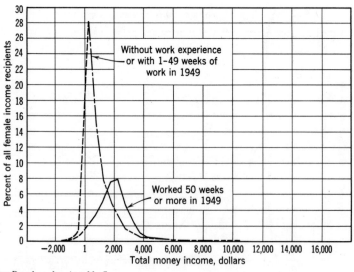

Note: Based on data in table 5.

differ by only $100,[12] and an examination of the relationship between the quartiles and the median, which is a rough measure of the symmetry of a distribution, indicates only moderate skewness.[13] The curve for the non-workers and the part-year workers is considerably more skewed than the curve for the full-year workers. The quartiles in this distribution are not symmetrical about the median,[14] and the mean is about $400 higher than the median indicating a concentration of people in the lower part of the distribution.[15] This distribution resembles the type of income curve that Pigou had in mind. Much of the asymmetry of the curve for nonworkers and part-year workers can be explained in terms of the combination of dissimilar groups such as nonworkers, many of whom were living on transfer payments or on inherited property, and part-year workers whose periods of employment could have ranged anywhere from 1 week to 49 weeks. It is equally important to note, however, that the small absolute difference between the mean and the median indicates that the tail of the distribution carries relatively little weight. Therefore, from an analytical viewpoint, the essential feature of this distribution may well be the symmetry that characterizes it throughout most of its range.

The income curve for men in figure 3 retains some of the skewness and much of the bimodality that appeared in the distribution for all income recipients. Apparently, therefore, this curve may still contain elements of heterogeneity that are to be accounted for. The simple expedient of classifying income recipients as either full-year workers or as nonworkers or part-year workers, which was used for women, cannot be meaningfully employed for men. Although the nonworkers do represent a significantly different group from full-year workers, the same meaning cannot necessarily be ascribed to the part-year workers. A large proportion of the men who worked less than a full year may have either worked in industries like construction where pay scales are adjusted to account for the seasonality of the work, or else they experienced some temporary unemployment. As a first approximation, it is convenient to regard the income curve for men as a combination of the curves for two groups: (a) those who are employed; and (b) those who are not employed, which includes both those who were unemployed and those who were not in the labor force. Although separate data are available for the unemployed, they were combined with persons who were not in the labor force because of their relatively small numbers (table 6 and figure 5).

It is apparent from figure 5 that this dichotomy eliminates much of the bimodality from the income distribution for men. The income curve for men who were not employed in April 1952 is quite symmetrical. Although

---

[12] $\overline{X} = \$2,109$; median $= \$1,980$.

[13] $1 - \dfrac{Q1}{Q2} = 0.33; \dfrac{Q3}{Q2} - 1 = 0.30.$

[14] $1 - \dfrac{Q1}{Q2} = 0.55; \dfrac{Q3}{Q2} - 1 = 1.05.$

[15] $\overline{X} = \$1,025$; median $= \$628$.

TABLE **6.**—INCOME IN 1951 OF MEN, BY EMPLOYMENT STATUS

Total money income of civilians in 1951	Employed in April 1952	Not employed in April 1952		
		Total	Unemployed	Not in labor force
Number of men with income....thousands..	40,687	5,885	950	4,935
Percent.................................	100.0	100.0	100.0	100.0
Loss.....................................	0.5	0.2	0.4	0.2
$1 to $499..............................	5.1	33.7	21.7	36.0
$500 to $999............................	5.3	29.3	16.3	31.8
$1,000 to $1,499........................	6.0	12.6	14.1	12.3
$1,500 to $1,999........................	6.6	8.0	14.9	6.7
$2,000 to $2,499........................	10.4	4.7	9.4	3.9
$2,500 to $2,999........................	10.8	3.4	8.7	2.3
$3,000 to $3,499........................	13.9	2.5	5.4	1.9
$3,500 to $3,999........................	11.7	1.3	1.1	1.4
$4,000 to $4,499........................	9.1	1.1	4.0	0.6
$4,500 to $4,999........................	5.4	0.6	2.2	0.3
$5,000 to $5,999........................	7.1	0.9	0.7	0.9
$6,000 to $6,999........................	3.2	0.5	0.7	0.4
$7,000 to $9,999........................	2.8	0.8	0.4	0.8
$10,000 to $14,999......................	1.2	0.3	...	0.4
$15,000 and over........................	1.0	0.1	...	0.1

Note: To facilitate graphic presentation, all percents shown in figure 5 are based on all male income recipients (46,572) rather than on the individual column totals used in this table.

Source: U. S. Bureau of the Census, *Current Population Reports—Consumer Income*, Series P–60, No. 11, table 4.

FIGURE **5.**—INCOME IN 1951 OF MEN BY EMPLOYMENT STATUS

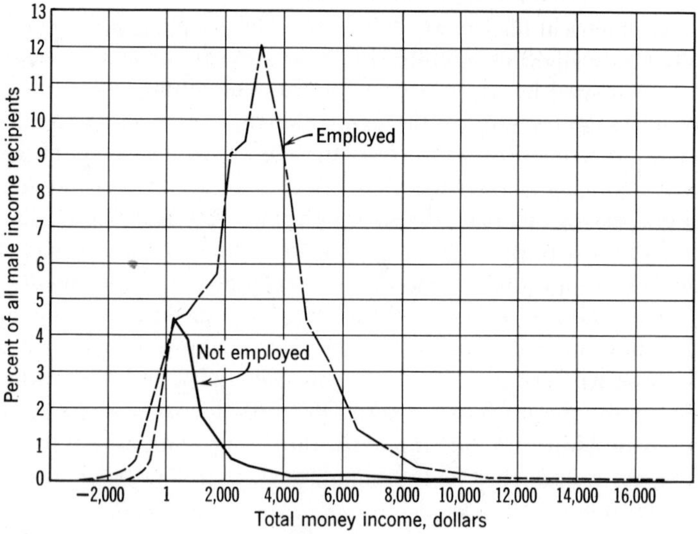

Note: Based on data in table 6.

the curve for employed men is more symmetrical than the curve for all men shown in figure 3, it apparently still contains some elements of heterogeneity. Note, for example, the pronounced bulge in the lower part of the distribution as well as the extended tail of the distribution in the direction of the higher values. In order to obtain a better understanding of the income distribution for employed men, it is necessary first to examine the distributions for the component occupation groups. In figure 6 (derived from table 7) the income distribution for employed men has been divided into three groups: (a) farmers and farm managers (9 percent of the total); (b) service workers and laborers (17 percent of the total); and (c) men employed in other occupations (74 percent of the total). It is apparent that the distributions for the first two groups are asymmetrical. The distribution for farmers and farm managers is skewed in the direction of the higher incomes; and the distribution for service workers and laborers has several modal groups. In contrast, there appears to be considerable symmetry in the income distribution for other employed men despite the fact that it is an amalgamation of many different occupation groups.

Considering first the occupation groups characterized by asymmetrical curves, it may be noted that the income curve for service workers and laborers is almost "box-like" in appearance. There are roughly equal proportions of workers in each of the income levels between $1 and $4,000, and virtually all the workers are concentrated in this narrow income range. The shape of this curve cannot be adequately explained in terms of the merging of dissimilar occupations because an analysis of the various occupations included in this group such as farm laborers, nonfarm laborers, and service workers indicates that each of these occupation groups has an asymmetrical distribution. The "box-like" appearance of the curve is changed only slightly if farm laborers, whose total incomes are not completely represented by the figures on cash income, are excluded; however, the income curves for nonfarm laborers and service workers are very similar.

There appear to be at least two factors involved in the explanation of the basic difference between the shape of the income curve for these occupations and for other occupations. In the first place, there appears to be a low upper limit to the amount of income received for this type of work so that the workers in these occupations are forced into a narrow income range. The workers are not symmetrically distributed within this income range because there is a much greater prevalence of part-time employment in these occupations than in others. For example, the 1950 Census data show that only about 50 percent of the laborers worked a full year (50 weeks or more) in 1949 as compared with about 60 percent of the operatives, 66 percent of the craftsmen, and about 75 percent of the clerical and sales workers.[16] In addition, a somewhat larger proportion of the full-year workers in these occupations have only regular part-time employment (i.e., they work regularly on a part-time basis). In 1950 about 6 percent of the men employed for 50 weeks or more in the service trades or as laborers had regular part-time jobs. The comparable proportion was only

---

[16] U. S. Bureau of the Census, *U. S. Census of Population: 1950*, Vol. II, *Characteristics of the Population*, Part 1, U. S. Summary, table 129.

TABLE 7.—INCOME IN 1951 OF EMPLOYED MEN, BY OCCUPATION GROUP

Total money income in 1951	Service workers and laborers	Farmers and farm managers	Occupation group of employed men in April 1952			
			Other employed men			
			Total	"White-collar" workers[1]	"Blue-collar" workers[2]	Independent profes-sionals, nonfarm proprietors, and managers and officials
Number of men with income...thousands..	6,915	3,795	29,977	7,540	16,962	5,475
Percent............	100.0	100.0	100.0	100.0	100.0	100.0
Loss....................	0.2	2.6	0.3	0.1	0.1	1.3
$1 to $499...............	10.6	16.5	2.4	3.7	1.8	2.6
$500 to $999............	10.0	15.7	2.9	3.3	2.9	2.2
$1,000 to $1,499.........	11.6	14.9	3.6	3.0	4.0	3.2
$1,500 to $1,999.........	12.5	11.1	4.7	3.6	5.7	3.0
$2,000 to $2,499.........	15.1	10.4	9.3	6.6	11.0	7.2
$2,500 to $2,999.........	11.7	6.7	11.1	9.6	12.6	8.1
$3,000 to $3,499.........	13.3	5.3	15.2	14.4	16.8	10.1
$3,500 to $3,999.........	7.2	2.9	13.8	14.7	14.7	9.4
$4,000 to $4,499.........	3.6	2.9	11.1	12.5	11.3	8.7
$4,500 to $4,999.........	2.3	1.3	6.6	7.0	6.5	6.3
$5,000 to $5,999.........	1.1	3.0	9.0	9.3	8.3	11.3
$6,000 to $6,999.........	0.2	1.6	4.1	5.5	3.0	5.8
$7,000 to $9,999.........	0.4	2.2	3.4	5.0	1.1	9.1
$10,000 to $14,999.......	...	1.2	1.4	1.1	0.2	6.2
$15,000 and over.........	0.2	1.9	1.1	0.6	...	5.5

Note: To facilitate graphic presentation, all percents shown in figure 6 are based on all employed males with income (40,687) and those in figure 9 are based on the total of "other" employed males (29,977) rather than on the individual column totals used in this table.

[1] Salaried professional and technical workers, clerical workers, and sales workers.

[2] Craftsmen, foremen, operatives, and kindred workers.

Source: U. S. Bureau of the Census, *Current Population Reports—Consumer Income*, Series P–60, No. 11, table 5.

FIGURE 6.—INCOME IN 1951 OF EMPLOYED MEN BY OCCUPATION GROUP

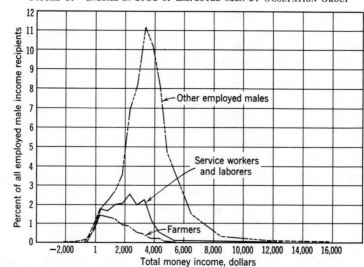

Note: Based on data in table 7.

TABLE **8.**—Self-Employment Income in 1949 of Self-Employed Men in Selected Occupations

Income from self-employment in 1949	Occupation in 1950								
	Farm opera-tors	Nonfarm proprietors				Independent professionals			
		Retail trade	Whole-sale trade	Manu-fac-turing	Con-struc-tion	Physi-cians and surgeons	Den-tists	Lawyers and judges	Engi-neers
Total with self-employment income....	100.0	100.0	100.0	100.0	100.0	100.0	100.0	100.0	100.0
Loss or $1 to $499........	21.4	5.7	6.0	4.8	4.4	2.1	1.2	2.7	6.0
$500 to $999.............	19.3	5.5	4.2	3.9	3.7	2.2	2.2	3.1	3.3
$1,000 to $1,499..........	14.7	7.5	5.3	5.1	5.2	2.3	2.4	3.8	3.7
$1,500 to $1,999..........	10.0	7.9	4.8	4.9	6.0	2.2	2.7	3.0	3.5
$2,000 to $2,499..........	9.4	10.8	6.9	7.0	8.4	2.7	3.7	4.6	5.5
$2,500 to $2,999..........	5.1	9.6	5.7	5.5	7.5	1.3	3.2	3.5	3.7
$3,000 to $3,499..........	5.5	11.1	8.2	8.7	10.4	3.8	5.1	5.8	4.9
$3,500 to $3,999..........	2.6	7.1	6.6	5.9	7.5	1.9	5.2	4.4	6.0
$4,000 to $4,499..........	2.8	6.6	6.5	5.4	7.1	3.6	4.9	5.6	6.0
$4,500 to $4,999..........	1.3	3.4	3.4	3.1	3.6	1.9	4.0	3.0	2.5
$5,000 to $5,999..........	2.6	8.2	9.9	10.9	8.8	6.6	13.8	11.1	9.4
$6,000 to $6,999..........	1.5	3.9	5.6	4.7	4.8	6.2	9.3	6.9	7.4
$7,000 to $9,999..........	2.1	5.1	7.9	8.2	8.2	13.0	18.9	11.9	12.1
$10,000 and over..........	1.8	7.6	19.0	21.9	14.4	50.1	23.4	30.6	26.1

Note: To facilitate graphic presentation, all the percents shown in figure 7 are based on the sum of the workers in all these occupations rather than on the individual column totals used in deriving this table.

Source: Unpublished data from 1950 Census of Population.

1 percent for craftsmen and about 3 percent for operatives and clerical workers.[17]

The asymmetry of the income curve for farm operators cannot be explained in the same way as the curve for service workers and laborers. In this case a different set of factors appears to be involved. Farmers are self-employed, and therefore the distinction between full-time and part-time employment, which is so important in an analysis of income from other types of employment, is rather nebulous for farming. Moreover, there is a much greater chance for the receipt of very high or very low (even negative) income in farming than in salaried employment. For these reasons, the asymmetry of the income curve for farmers can be understood only by comparison with the income curve for other self-employed workers. The data required for this comparison are shown in table 8 and figure 7. It may be noted from these data that there is a marked difference between the income distribution of farm operators and other self-employed workers. None of the other groups, even when examined in greater detail than is shown in this table, shows the peakedness that is exhibited by the farm group.

With regard to the factors that may account for the skewness of the income curve for farm operators, one important difference between farmers

---

[17] Derived from U. S. Bureau of the Census, *Current Population Reports—Labor Force*, Series P–50, No. 35, table 3, and from unpublished data of the Bureau of the Census.

FIGURE 7.—SELF-EMPLOYMENT INCOME IN 1949 OF SELF-EMPLOYED MEN IN
SELECTED OCCUPATIONS

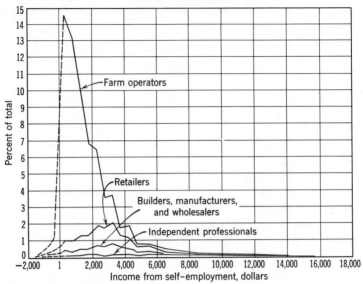

Note: Based on data in table 8.

TABLE 9.—VALUE OF PRODUCTS SOLD BY COMMERCIAL FARM OPERATORS, BY SELF-EMPLOYMENT
INCOME IN 1949

Income from self-employment in 1949	Total	Value of products sold in 1949				
		$10,000 and over	$5,000 to $9,999	$2,500 to $4,999	$1,200 to $2,499	$250 to $1,199[1]
Number with income from self-employment........	3,017,565	403,337	637,306	742,657	700,991	533,274
Percent...............	100	100	100	100	100	100
Under $500....................	18	3	4	12	24	46
$500 to $999...................	18	4	7	16	26	34
$1,000 to $1,499..............	16	5	12	21	22	12
$1,500 to $1,999..............	10	7	13	13	12	3
$2,000 to $2,499..............	10	12	17	11	9	2
$2,500 to $2,999..............	5	7	8	7	3	1
$3,000 to $3,499..............	6	9	11	8	2	...
$3,500 to $3,999..............	3	7	5	4	1	...
$4,000 to $4,499..............	3	8	4	4	1	...
$4,500 to $4,999..............	2	4	4	2	...	...
$5,000 to $5,999..............	3	8	6	1	1	...
$6,000 to $6,999..............	2	5	4	...	...	...
$7,000 to $9,999..............	2	9	5	...	...	...
$10,000 and over.............	2	12	1	...	...	...

Note: To facilitate graphic presentation, the percents shown in figure 8 are based on all commercial
farms (3,017,565) rather than on the individual column totals used in this table.

[1] Provided the farm operator worked off the farm less than 100 days and provided the income the
farm operator and members of his family received from nonfarm sources was less than the value of
all farm products sold.

Source: Joint report of the U. S. Departments of Commerce and Agriculture, *Farms and Farm People*, Washington, D. C., 1953, tables 6 and 7.

and other self-employed workers must be considered. When the receipts from a nonfarm business become too small to cover expenses, the owner is generally forced to sell out. For a while he may lower his living standards or try to make ends meet in other ways; however, when the fixed expenses like rent, utilities, and merchandise costs cannot be met, the business must be closed. In farming, many types of enterprises are continued even if they show no net gain to the farmer over a period of time. For example, a sharecropper may barely earn enough from farming to keep alive; however, if it is profitable for the landowner to keep the farm in operation, the sharecropper will stay "in business." In this connection it is important to observe that fully one-third of the low-production commercial farms (i.e., commercial farms with sales of farm products amounting to less than $2,500 in 1949) in the United States are operated by tenant farmers.[18] Most of them are probably southern Negro sharecroppers.[19] In view of this difference in the nature of farm and nonfarm self-employment, it appears likely that much of the asymmetry of the income curve for farm operators is attributable to the existence of a relatively large number of small low-production farms. This thesis can be supported by data shown in table 9 and figure 8. It can be noted that the 40 percent of the farms with sales under $2,500 in 1949 account for most of the peakedness of the over-all income curve for farm operators. Moreover, as the value of sales is increased, the income curve for farm operators increasingly takes on the shape of the curve for other self-employed workers. Indeed, there is a marked similarity between the income curve for farmers with sales of $5,000 or more and the income curve for various types of nonfarm businessmen shown in figure 7.

Returning once again to the consideration of the over-all income distribution for employed males shown in figure 5, it is apparent that the bulge in the lower part of the distribution is largely attributable to the inclusion of farmers, service workers, and laborers. Once these occupation groups are removed for separate analysis, the distribution for the remaining three-fourths of the employed males is quite symmetrical except for the fact that it retains a rather pronounced "tail" in the direction of the higher values. In order to achieve a better understanding of this distribution, it has been divided into three occupation groups: (a) "blue-collar" workers or operatives and craftsmen (57 percent of the total); (b) "white-collar" workers or salesmen, clerks, and salaried professionals (25 percent of the total); and (c) in-

---

[18] Joint report of the U. S. Departments of Commerce and Agriculture, *Farms and Farm People*, Washington, D. C., 1953, table 5.

[19] This inference is drawn from the following facts presented in *Farms and Farm People*, table 5. Out of a total of 548,277 low-production farms operated by tenants, 472,132 were in the South. The distribution of commercial low-production farms in the South by color and tenure is not given; however, 329,586 farms were operated by nonwhites (owners and tenants), the great majority of whom are tenants.

FIGURE 8.—VALUE OF PRODUCTS SOLD BY COMMERCIAL FARM OPERATORS, BY SELF-EMPLOYMENT
INCOME IN 1949

FIGURE 8.—VALUE OF PRODUCTS SOLD BY COMMERCIAL FARM OPERATORS, BY SELF-EMPLOYMENT
INCOME IN 1949

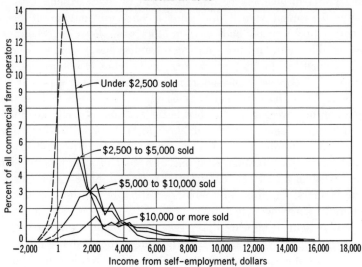

Note: Based on data in table 9.

FIGURE 9.—INCOME IN 1951 OF EMPLOYED MEN IN SELECTED OCCUPATION GROUPS

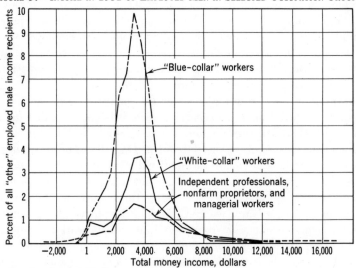

Note: Based on data in table 7.

dependent professionals, nonfarm proprietors, and managerial workers (18
percent of the total). In figure 9 it may be noted that the three distributions
are essentially symmetrical and appear to differ from each other primarily
with respect to level of income and income dispersion. The "tail" of the
over-all distribution is largely attributable to the independent professional,
business, and managerial group that contains about three-fourths of all men
with incomes over $10,000.

Some tentative conclusions

It is important to emphasize that the data that have been presented neither confirm nor refute the "natural" or the "institutional" views regarding the controlling forces in the determination of the income curve. However, they do suggest that, in some measure, the skewness of the over-all distribution of income can be explained without reference to special institutional factors such as the advantages bestowed by inheritance. Much of the skewness of the income curve is attributable to the inclusion of women in the distribution. Although the essential difference between the income curves for men and women may stem from the mores of our society, it has little to do with inheritance. Even for men, there is more symmetry in income distribution than most analysts have recognized. The income distributions for the three groups of occupations that together include about three-fourths of the employed men were found to be quite symmetrical when analyzed separately.

Of course, it can still be argued that, although the skewness of the income curve can be explained in terms of the merging of nonhomogeneous groups, the fact nevertheless remains that there are great variations in the incomes received for different kinds of work. Inheritance may be an important factor in explaining income inequality, in a number of obvious ways, including the restriction of entry into the better paying occupations. In 1951, only 2 percent of the men made over $10,000; but they received 12 percent of the income.[20] It is significant that only a very small proportion of these men can be classified as the "idle rich." For example, 99 out of every 100 of these men were in the labor force in April 1952,[21] and 70 out of every 100 derived their incomes entirely from earnings.[22] Only 2 percent of these men derived their incomes entirely from property or investments. Further analysis of the characteristics of the highest income recipients indicates that nearly three-fourths of them were either independent professionals, businessmen, or managerial workers.[23] If farmers are included, about 85 percent of the highest income group can be accounted for. It is apparent, therefore, that these occupations are the channels through which one can "hit the jackpot" in our society. If it can be shown that entry into the independent professions, business ownership, or managerial work is limited to persons reared in wealthy families, much of Pigou's analysis could be correct. However, if there is relatively free entry into these occupations, then it might well be that "a large part of the existing

---

[20] Estimated from the Bureau of the Census report, Series P–60, No. 11, table 1.

[21] Ibid., table 4.

[22] Ibid., table 7. Earnings as defined here include income received from wages or salaries or from the operation of a farm, business, or professional practice. It is undoubtedly true that in a broad philosophical sense this definition of earnings may include the receipts from property or investments in which work was performed only in a nominal way. However, it is impossible to determine the magnitude or the importance of such receipts from the data that are currently available.

[23] Ibid., table 5.

inequality of wealth can be regarded as produced by men to satisfy their tastes and preferences." [24] In other words, to the extent that all men have access to the professional and managerial occupations, and the numbers admitted to these occupations are sufficient to keep monopolistic practices at a minimum, the income differences between these occupations and others may merely reflect the payments by society for rare skills or risk-taking. As the figures indicate, mere entry into the higher paid occupations is no guarantee of financial success. There were proportionately as many of the professional and managerial group with incomes under $2,000 as there were with incomes over $10,000. Some of those at the lower income levels were undoubtedly trading income for leisure, or they were just starting a business or professional career and could hope for much higher rewards in the future. However, the largest proportion were businessmen who either had a bad year or a bad business. The data suggest that the entrant into these occupations frequently runs the risk of becoming a great success or a great failure; or, as a British writer recently observed in his summary of the National Survey of Personal Incomes and Savings in England: "to be one's own master is no guarantee of prosperity, though it may be a source of other satisfactions." [25] It has been demonstrated theoretically that choices involving risk tend to carry higher rewards,[26] and this may well be a factor in explaining the inequality of incomes.

It is important to observe that satisfactory conclusions regarding the accessibility of the higher paid occupations to all strata of society cannot be made on an *a priori* basis, as is so frequently done.

We are all only too familiar with the restrictions on entry into some of the higher paid occupations. To mention only a few, educational quotas restrict the entry of certain racial and religious groups into some types of occupations; great capital is required to finance and establish a professional practice or a business; and nepotism is advantageous to the sons and daughters of the wealthy. These restrictions on entry are balanced by several important factors. Access to a free higher education, with government subsistence payments while in attendance, has been made available to millions of former soldiers of this country. These same GI's have had access to capital loans on excellent terms for the establishment of a business. There has also been an increase in public education at all levels over the decades. Finally, anyone who has observed immigrant families is only too familiar with the process of "lifting one's self by the bootstraps" via the "mama-papa" store or by the self-denial of the parents for the sake

[24] Milton Friedman, "Choice, Chance, and the Personal Distribution of Income," *Journal of Political Economy*, Vol. 91, No. 4, August 1953, p. 290.

[25] H. F. Lydall, "National Survey of Personal Income and Savings," *Bulletin of the Oxford Institute of Statistics*, Vol. 15, February and March 1953, p. 47.

[26] Milton Friedman and L. J. Savage, "The Utility Analysis of Choices Involving Risk," *The Journal of Political Economy*, Vol. 56, No. 4, August 1948.

of the children. These are the kinds of considerations that must be examined, weighed, and balanced before ethical conclusions regarding the inequality of incomes are reached.

The factors involved in occupational mobility and occupational choice are basic to an understanding of income distribution. Yet, surprisingly little is known about such factors, and such data as are available are deficient in many respects.[27] One measure of occupational mobility is provided by the comparison of the occupations of fathers and sons to see to what extent occupational skills are handed down from one generation to the next. There are no nationwide data on this subject for the United States. However, a recent survey conducted in six American cities provides a fairly good picture of this type of mobility within these cities.[28] Some of the data from this survey are presented in tables 10 and 11. Ta-

TABLE 10.—LONGEST OCCUPATION OF FATHER BY OCCUPATION OF SON IN 1950, FOR SIX CITIES

Occupation of son in 1950[1]	Total	Longest occupation of father[2]								
		Professional, technical, and kindred wkrs.	Farmers and farm managers	Mgrs., off'ls, and propr's, except farm	Clerical and kindred wkrs.	Sales workers	Craftsmen, foremen, and kindred wkrs.	Operatives and kindred wkrs.	Service workers	Laborers, except mine
Number.............thousands..	2,246	141	367	384	59	96	553	356	119	172
Percent......................	100.0	100.0	100.0	100.0	100.0	100.0	100.0	100.0	100.0	100.0
Profess'l, techn'l, & kindred wkrs..	9.7	29.5	2.9	14.0	12.8	19.1	7.4	7.8	8.7	3.9
Farmers and farm managers...........	0.2	...	0.8	...	...	...	0.2	0.1	...	...
Mgrs., off'ls, & propr's, exc. farm.	15.8	22.4	12.3	31.4	14.1	17.4	14.1	7.9	13.4	6.5
Clerical and kindred workers........	7.9	6.4	4.3	6.2	27.0	13.2	8.1	10.2	8.0	6.4
Sales workers.......................	6.5	9.0	2.5	11.4	5.7	19.0	6.2	3.8	5.2	2.5
Craftsmen, foremen, & kindred wkrs..	22.7	14.3	21.0	13.7	18.8	10.5	32.2	27.1	18.7	24.1
Operatives and kindred workers......	21.5	9.2	25.8	12.1	13.0	11.8	20.6	31.9	21.1	33.3
Service workers.....................	9.0	5.9	14.4	8.1	5.9	6.5	6.5	6.4	20.6	9.9
Laborers, except mine...............	6.7	3.3	15.9	3.1	2.8	2.6	4.7	4.8	4.3	13.3

[1] Longest occupation of son in 1950.

[2] Longest occupation of father during his lifetime.

Source: Unpublished data from Occupational Mobility Survey.

---

[27] For example, Dewey Anderson could cite only one source that contained statistical data on occupational mobility in his testimony before the Subcommittee on Low-Income Families. That source was his own pioneer study, *Occupational Mobility in An American Community*, published in 1937. Beyond that he could refer only to studies that he characterized as "case studies, ranging from the Middletown Study, the Zimmerman study of rural populations, Sorokin's studies of mobility, the Taussig and Joslyn study." See testimony of Dewey Anderson in *Hearings Before the Subcommittee on Low Income Families*, Joint Committee on the Economic Report, 81st Congress, 1st Session, p. 508.

[28] Reference is made to the Occupational Mobility Survey which was conducted in January and February 1951 in six cities: Philadelphia, New Haven, San Francisco, Chicago, Los Angeles, and St. Paul. A representative sample of about 1,900 households in each city was interviewed by trained enumerators of the Bureau of the Census. The survey was sponsored by the Social Science Research Council in cooperation with six university research centers and the U. S. Department of the Air Force for the purpose of obtaining data on the occupational and industrial mobility of labor in these six cities. For detailed information regarding this survey see Gladys L. Palmer, *Labor Mobility in Six Cities*, Social Science Research Council, New York, 1954.

ble 10 stresses the occupation of the father and shows the kind of work done by the sons of men who pursued different occupations. Table 11 stresses the sons' occupations and shows the skills of parents of men doing different kinds of work at present. Of course, both tables merely show different views of the same set of facts, namely, the relationship between the occupations of fathers and their sons. There are several cautions that must be exercised in the interpretation of these data. In the first place, the occupational distribution of fathers differs from that of their sons because of the change in the industrial structure over the generations. The long-run trend in our economy away from the independent businessman and farmer to the salaried "white-collar" and "blue-collar" worker is reflected in the occupational distribution of the two generations. Thus, it may be noted that about 16 percent of the fathers worked as farmers at their longest jobs whereas a negligible proportion of the sons were engaged in these types of employment in 1950. Another caution relative to the use of the occupation data centers about the fact that because of changes in occupational classification the composition of each occupation group differs from one generation to the next. Finally, there are other factors that affect the results, such as age, the period covered by the occupation, and the fact that the current agricultural labor force is virtually excluded from the data. Despite these limitations, however, the data are of some value as a rough indication of the difference between fathers and sons in occupational skills.

TABLE 11.—OCCUPATION OF SON IN 1950 BY LONGEST OCCUPATION OF FATHER, FOR SIX CITIES

Occupation of son in 1950[1]	Total		Longest occupation of father[2]								
	Number (thousands)	Percent	Professional, technical, and kindred wkrs.	Farmers and farm managers	Mgrs., off'ls, and propr's, except farm	Clerical and kindred wkrs.	Sales workers	Craftsmen, foremen, and kindred wkrs.	Operatives and kindred wkrs.	Service workers	Laborers, except mine
Total......................	2,246	100.0	6.3	16.3	17.1	2.6	4.3	24.6	15.8	5.3	7.7
Profess'l, techn'l, & kindred wkrs..	218	100.0	19.0	4.9	24.7	3.4	8.4	18.8	12.8	4.8	3.1
Farmers and farm managers..........	4	100.0	(3)	(3)	(3)	(3)	(3)	(3)	(3)	(3)	(3)
Mgrs., off'ls, & propr's, exc. farm.	356	100.0	8.9	12.7	33.9	2.3	4.7	22.0	7.9	4.5	3.2
Clerical and kindred workers........	178	100.0	5.0	8.9	13.3	8.9	7.1	25.0	20.3	5.3	6.2
Sales workers......................	146	100.0	8.7	6.4	30.0	2.3	12.5	23.6	9.2	4.3	3.0
Craftsmen, foremen, & kindred wkrs..	509	100.0	4.0	15.2	10.3	2.2	2.0	35.0	18.9	4.4	8.2
Operatives and kindred workers......	483	100.0	2.7	19.6	9.6	1.6	2.3	23.6	23.5	5.2	11.9
Service workers....................	202	100.0	4.1	26.1	15.4	1.7	3.1	17.8	11.3	12.2	8.4
Laborers, except mine..............	150	100.0	3.0	38.9	8.0	1.1	1.7	17.3	11.3	3.4	15.2

[1] Longest occupation of son in 1950.

[2] Longest occupation of father during his lifetime.

[3] Number of sample cases too small to be shown separately.

Source: Unpublished data from Occupational Mobility Survey.

Table 10 clearly indicates that there is some tendency for sons to work in the same major occupation groups as their fathers; however, the importance of this tendency can easily be exaggerated. About one-third of the sons of men who were professional workers, managerial workers, craftsmen, and operatives were employed in the same major occupation groups as their fathers. This proportion drops to one-fourth for clerical workers, one-fifth for the sales and service workers, and one-seventh for the laborers. The data clearly suggest that men in such well-paid jobs as professional and managerial workers are more likely than are other workers to have their sons employed in these two high-paid occupation groups. About one-half of the sons of professional workers and about the same proportion of the sons of managerial workers were themselves professional or managerial workers. However, a rather large proportion of the sons of men employed in several other occupations also became professional or managerial workers. It can be noted that about 37 percent of the sons of sales workers were professional or managerial workers, as were 27 percent of the clerical workers and 22 percent of the craftsmen and service workers.

An examination of the kind of work done by the fathers of men employed in different occupations in 1950 (table 11) suggests that the extent of exposure of a man's family to urban life may be a significant factor in occupational choice. For example, less than 10 percent of the clerical, sales, and professional workers had fathers who were farmers as compared with 13 percent of the nonfarm managerial workers, 15 percent of the craftsmen, 20 percent of the operatives, 26 percent of the service workers, and 39 percent of the laborers. These figures suggest that about nine-tenths of the white-collar workers but only six-tenths of the laborers were reared in urban areas where they were exposed to better educational opportunities and more varied occupational experience.

CHAPTER 4

THE ROLE OF GEOGRAPHIC LOCATION AND COLOR

Urban-rural residence

Level of income. Residence affects income by limiting the type of work readily available to the individual. The residents of large metropolitan areas generally have a wide choice of industries in which they may readily seek employment. The choice is much more limited in the smaller towns and villages, and in the farming areas it is frequently restricted to the family farm or to neighboring farms. These differences in employment opportunities affect both the level and the source of personal income. They also affect the pattern of living in these areas. The incomes of many farm operators are not as regular or predictable as those of city workers. By the very nature of agricultural production, the work is seasonal and receipts are concentrated in a very short period. These factors, along with differences in the level of living operate to produce markedly different living patterns in farm and nonfarm areas.

Nonfarm residents have higher cash incomes than farm residents. This fact, however, does not necessarily connote greater economic well-being because the living costs in nonfarm areas tend to be higher. Moreover, as already indicated, a relatively large part of the observed differences between the incomes of farm and nonfarm residents stems from the exclusion of the value of farm produce consumed at home and other types of income "in kind" from the income measurement.

Comparing the incomes of men and women, it can be noted from table

TABLE **12.**—MEDIAN INCOME IN 1949 OF PERSONS, BY RESIDENCE, COLOR, AND SEX

Color and sex	Total	Urban	Rural nonfarm	Rural farm
TOTAL				
Male....................................	$2,434	$2,783	$2,072	$1,339
Female..................................	1,029	1,227	716	458
WHITE				
Male....................................	2,572	2,917	2,183	1,489
Female..................................	1,137	1,325	784	533
NONWHITE				
Male....................................	1,341	1,749	975	577
Female..................................	584	764	374	311

Source: U. S. Bureau of the Census, *U. S. Census of Population: 1950*, Vol. II, *Characteristics of the Population*, Part 1, U. S. Summary, table 138.

12 that within each residence group the median income of men was considerably greater than that of women.[1] In urban areas the median income of both white and nonwhite men was about twice that received by women; and in rural areas the relative difference in incomes between the sexes was even greater. Among rural whites, the relative income difference between the sexes was about the same for farm and nonfarm residents; however, among rural nonwhites, the relative differences between the sexes were greater in the nonfarm areas than on the farms. The small difference between the incomes of nonwhite men and women in farm areas largely reflects the poor economic status of nonwhite male farm residents, more than 90 percent of whom live in the South, largely as tenants on farms with small acreage and low production. White urban men had a median cash income that was about twice that received by white farm men; but for nonwhite men the median income of urban residents ($1,700) was about three times as great as that received by farm residents ($600). This, of course, is simply another way of saying that the income gap between farm and nonfarm residents is considerably greater for nonwhite men than for white men. The significance of this fact, aside from its reaffirmation of the low economic status of the nonwhite farmer and farm laborer, is that it provides some insight into a major population shift during the past decade.

Between 1940 and 1950 there was a large migration of farm households to nonfarm areas. This movement was particularly strong for the nonwhite population. Unfortunately, comparisons covering the whole 10-year period cannot be made accurately because of the change in the farm definition introduced in the 1950 Census of Population;[2] however, comparable fig-

---

[1] It is of some interest in this connection to refer to an earlier Bureau of the Census monograph on income that touched on this subject. In this monograph it was noted, "there is some evidence that the ratio of the average earnings of male workers to the average earnings of female workers is likely to remain fairly constant over considerable periods. The special census investigation of 1904 showed that, for all manufacturing industries combined, the ratio of men's average weekly earnings to women's was, for that year, 1.8. The National Bureau of Economic Research reports that 'a survey of a number of industries for which data are available for more recent years indicates that the ratio of the earnings of males to those of females, in the case of wage earners at least, has not changed materially since 1905.' It may well be, therefore, that for any period within which the proportions of the work force made up of men and women, respectively, do not materially change, the ratio of men's earnings to women's will remain practically constant." Paul F. Brissenden, *Earnings of Factory Workers 1899 to 1927*, Census Monographs, Vol. X, U. S. Government Printing Office, 1929.

In support of Dr. Brissenden's conclusion it is interesting to note that the ratios of the median annual wage or salary of men and women was 1.7 in 1939 and 2.2 in 1950. Of course, in 1950, women comprised a larger proportion of the labor force than in 1939. The increase in the proportion of women workers is largely attributable to the part-time employment of married women who tended to reduce the average wage for all women workers.

[2] "The farm population for 1950, as for 1940 and 1930, includes all persons living on farms without regard to occupation. In determining farm and nonfarm residence in the 1950 Census, however, certain special groups were classified otherwise than in earlier censuses. . . . For the United States as a whole, there is evidence from the Current Poplation Survey that the farm population in 1950 would have been about 9 percent larger had the 1940 procedure been used." U. S. Bureau of the Census, *U. S. Census of Population: 1950*, Vol. II, *Characteristics of the Population*, Part 1, U. S. Summary, p. VII.

ures covering the years 1940 and 1947 indicate that during this period the number of farm households decreased from 7.1 million to 6.7 million (6 percent), whereas the number of nonfarm households increased from 28.0 million to 32.5 million (16 percent).[3] About four-fifths of the decrease in the rural farm population can be accounted for by the movement of nonwhite households, mostly southern Negro sharecroppers and their families, from the farms to nonfarm areas.[4] Although there were undoubtedly many factors that stimulated this movement away from the farms, it is not at all unlikely that the attractiveness of the higher city incomes played a major role.

Source of income. Residence affects not only the level of income but the source of income as well. The data in table 13 tend to exaggerate the number of persons entirely dependent upon earnings, because of the failure of many persons to report small amounts of other income in addition to their earnings; however, the data clearly indicate the contrasting nature of the receipts of the farm and nonfarm population.

TABLE **13.**—SOURCE OF INCOME IN 1949 OF PERSONS, BY RESIDENCE, COLOR, AND SEX

Source of income in 1949	Male				Female			
	White		Nonwhite		White		Nonwhite	
	Nonfarm	Farm	Nonfarm	Farm	Nonfarm	Farm	Nonfarm	Farm
Total......................	100.0	100.0	100.0	100.0	100.0	100.0	100.0	100.0
Percent with income............	88.8	83.0	84.9	78.2	44.6	24.8	53.7	36.5
Percent without income.........	11.2	17.0	15.1	21.8	55.4	75.2	46.3	63.5
Total with income..........	100.0	100.0	100.0	100.0	100.0	100.0	100.0	100.0
Earnings only.................	74.0	77.1	82.5	86.3	70.0	69.0	80.9	83.1
Wages or salary only.........	64.3	31.0	77.2	36.0	65.9	52.3	77.4	59.9
Self-employment income only..	7.7	36.7	4.0	36.2	3.5	14.8	2.8	17.6
Wages or salary and self-employment income...........	2.0	9.4	1.4	14.0	0.6	1.9	0.7	5.5
Earnings and other income.....	19.0	17.2	10.5	8.7	9.3	7.7	6.0	4.4
Other income; no earnings......	7.1	5.7	7.0	5.0	20.7	23.3	13.1	12.5

Source: U. S. Bureau of the Census, *U. S. Census of Population: 1950*, Vol. II, *Characteristics of the Population*, Part 1, U. S. Summary, tables 142 and 143.

It is apparent that the vast majority of men are income recipients. Clearly, the most important source of income is earnings. About three-fourths of the white men and four-fifths of the nonwhite men derived all their income from this source. Only a very small proportion (about 6 percent) of each group depended entirely upon income other than earnings such as interest, dividends, rents, pensions, etc. The remainder (about one-fifth of the white men and one-tenth of the nonwhite men) received

---

[3] U. S. Bureau of the Census, *Current Population Reports—Population Characteristics*, Series P–20, No. 11, table 2.

[4] In 1940 there were 6.1 million white farm households and 1.0 million nonwhite farm households. In 1947 the comparable figures were 6.0 million for the whites and 0.7 million for the nonwhites (*ibid.*, table 2).

some income from both earnings and other sources. Farm and nonfarm men had roughly the same pattern of receipts with one important exception. Wage or salary income was the basic revenue provider for the nonfarm population (two-thirds of the whites and three-fourths of the nonwhites derived all their income from this source), whereas the farm population tended to depend much more upon receipts from the operation of a farm. However, as subsequent analysis will show, nonfarm activities provide a very important source of income for the farm population.

Women have a basically different source pattern of income than men. A much smaller proportion of women are income recipients. In 1949, only about two-fifths of the white women in nonfarm areas and about one-fourth of those in farm areas received some income. The corresponding proportions for nonwhite women were much higher. Earnings were the most important income source for women, just as they were for men. Roughly two-thirds of the white women and four-fifths of the nonwhite women derived all their income from this source. Unlike the men, however, a relatively large proportion of the women (one-fifth of the whites and one-eighth of the nonwhites) depended exclusively upon income other than earnings.

As suggested earlier, farm residence is by no means synonymous with dependence upon agriculture. On the contrary, a substantial proportion of the farm population find their primary source of income in nonfarm activities. This conclusion is supported by the following facts.[5] In 1950, about one-third of the 5.6 million farm families received more cash earnings from nonfarm sources than from farming (i.e., the operation of a farm or farm-wage work). About one-half of these families derived all their earnings from nonfarm sources and did not engage in any commercial farm activities. It may be presumed that most of these families were either operating "hobby" farms or else that they had only recently moved to the farm from a nonfarm area.

Only three-fifths of the farm families derived most of their earnings from farming; however, many of these families had income from nonfarm sources as well. Only one-third of the farm families derived all their earnings from farm operation. These facts have led one analyst to conclude that "out of all rural farm families, a third are what we once thought to be typical of families living on farms—the farm-operator family with no additional source of earnings."[6]

---

[5] Data were obtained from an article by Virginia Britton, "Sources of Earnings of Rural Farm Families," *Journal of Home Economics*, Vol. 45, May 1953. This article is based largely on a special tabulation of data from the April 1951 Current Population Survey prepared by the Bureau of the Census at the request of the Bureau of Human Nutrition and Home Economics.

[6] *Ibid.*, p. 313.

Size of place

Various studies have examined the relationship between income and size of place. In general, they all appear to indicate that there is a positive correlation between these two variables, or, stated differently, that incomes tend to increase with size of place. Thus, for example, Herbert Klarman found after analyzing the data from the Consumer Purchases Study for 1935–36 that "income differences among communities are correlated with differences in community size, not with regional location." [7] Similarly, Friedman and Kuznets in their analysis of the incomes of independent professionals concluded that "both the general character and the magnitude of the size of community differences in average income from independent professional practice in large part reflect similar differences in the average income of the public. The average income of nonrelief families decreases consistently with size of community. . . ." [8] Finally, in a more recent study, using data from the Current Population Survey of the Bureau of the Census for 1946 in addition to those previously analyzed by Klarman, D. Gale Johnson has concluded that regional differences in the United States are largely attributable to size of place. He says that for "white nonfarm families living in communities of the same size income does not differ appreciably regionally." [9]

In most major respects, the census data confirm the findings of the earlier studies. However, as a result of the detail that could be included in the census tabulations, these data provide some new insight into the manner in which size of place affects the income distribution. Table 14 shows the variation in income by size of place where the effects of age, sex, and color are eliminated.

It is apparent from these data that incomes tend to increase with size of place for both white and nonwhite men and women. The median income for all white men increased from $2,500 for residents of the smallest towns to $3,200 for those residing in the largest metropolitan areas. Approximately the same general relationships were found for white men 25 to 44 years old. For nonwhite men, the increase in the median by size of place was even more pronounced than for white men. For the nonwhites, the median income ranged from $1,100 in the smallest towns to $2,200 in the largest urban centers. Similarly, the median income for women, both white and nonwhite, varied by size of place to a much greater extent than for white men. For all white women the median ranged from $900

---

[7] Herbert E. Klarman, "A Statistical Study of Income Differences Among Communities," *Studies in Income and Wealth*, Vol. 6, National Bureau of Economic Research, New York, 1943, p. 218.

[8] Milton Friedman and Simon Kuznets, *Income From Independent Professional Practice*, National Bureau of Economic Research, New York, 1945, p. 183.

[9] D. Gale Johnson, "Some Effects of Region, Community Size, Color, and Occupation on Family and Individual Income," *Studies in Income and Wealth*, Vol. 15, National Bureau of Economic Research, New York, 1952, p. 54.

TABLE 14.—MEDIAN INCOME IN 1949 OF URBAN PERSONS, BY SIZE OF PLACE, AGE, COLOR, AND SEX

Age and size of place	Male			Female		
	Total	White	Nonwhite	Total	White	Nonwhite
ALL PERSONS						
Urbanized Areas						
3,000,000 or more.....................	$3,078	$3,184	$2,213	$1,603	$1,661	$1,278
1,000,000 to 3,000,000.................	3,026	3,166	2,226	1,471	1,544	1,072
250,000 to 1,000,000...................	2,779	2,947	1,695	1,215	1,330	723
Less than 250,000.....................	2,692	2,827	1,543	1,121	1,239	633
Urban Places Not in Urbanized Areas						
25,000 or more........................	2,554	2,682	1,407	1,003	1,125	569
10,000 to 25,000......................	2,484	2,609	1,275	926	1,018	469
2,500 to 10,000.......................	2,354	2,477	1,134	839	919	415
PERSONS 25 TO 44 YEARS OLD						
Urbanized Areas						
3,000,000 or more.....................	3,348	3,461	2,342	1,853	1,978	1,408
1,000,000 to 3,000,000.................	3,300	3,443	2,374	1,713	1,846	1,252
250,000 to 1,000,000...................	3,144	3,301	1,878	1,451	1,610	809
Less than 250,000.....................	3,061	3,201	1,722	1,356	1,503	719
Urban Places Not in Urbanized Areas						
25,000 or more........................	2,984	3,121	1,607	1,283	1,435	666
10,000 to 25,000......................	2,916	3,049	1,495	1,217	1,367	565
2,500 to 10,000.......................	2,811	2,923	1,411	1,081	1,229	487

Source: Derived from U. S. Bureau of the Census. *U. S. Census of Population: 1950*, Series P–E, No. 5A, *Characteristics by Size of Place*, tables 4 and 4a.

to $1,700, and for nonwhite women it ranged from $400 to $1,300. Here again, the control on age produced essentially the same relationships. At least two questions arise at this point. What factors account for the differentials by size of place? Why do these factors operate differently for each sex and color group?

Several factors are involved in the answer to these questions; however, one of the most important factors is undoubtedly the variations in occupational opportunities available to each group. As table 15 indicates, white men had the smallest relative differences in occupational distribution by size of place. Accordingly, it is not surprising to find that this group also showed the smallest relative difference in income. The 30 percent differential between the incomes of white men residing in the smallest towns and in the largest metropolitan centers may well be attributable to differences in the proportions of professional workers and laborers in these areas. The proportion of professional workers, the highest paid occupation group, decreased progressively from 11 percent in the largest cities to 8 percent in the smallest towns. At the same time, the proportion of laborers, one of the lowest paid occupation groups, increased progressively from 6 percent to 10 percent. Since the largest centers contain a somewhat larger proportion of professional workers and a significantly smaller proportion of laborers, it is likely that much of the over-all difference in

TABLE 15.—OCCUPATION GROUP OF EMPLOYED URBAN PERSONS, BY SIZE OF PLACE, COLOR, AND SEX: 1950

Major occupation group in 1950, color, and sex	Urbanized areas				Urban places not in urbanized areas		
	3,000,000 or more	1,000,000 to 3,000,000	250,000 to 1,000,000	Less than 250,000	25,000 or more	10,000 to 25,000	Less than 10,000
MALE							
White, employed......................	100.0	100.0	100.0	100.0	100.0	100.0	100.0
Professional, technical, and kindred wkrs..	11.4	11.3	10.0	9.2	9.2	8.8	8.3
Managers, officials, and proprietors.......	15.3	12.8	14.1	13.7	14.5	14.8	15.5
Clerical and sales workers................	19.0	18.7	19.2	17.7	17.1	15.6	14.1
Craftsmen, foremen, and kindred workers....	21.1	23.4	23.4	23.1	22.4	22.3	22.4
Operatives and kindred workers............	19.6	21.0	21.1	23.3	22.5	23.3	24.0
Service workers...........................	7.8	6.5	6.1	6.1	6.8	6.4	5.9
Laborers..................................	5.8	6.2	6.1	7.0	7.6	8.9	10.0
Nonwhite, employed...................	100.0	100.0	100.0	100.0	100.0	100.0	100.0
Professional, technical, and kindred wkrs..	3.5	2.8	2.6	2.8	3.4	3.8	3.4
Managers, officials, and proprietors.......	4.9	3.3	3.1	3.5	3.6	3.6	3.8
Clerical and sales workers................	11.6	9.4	5.2	4.0	2.9	3.0	2.4
Craftsmen, foremen, and kindred workers....	11.4	10.8	9.8	10.5	10.1	10.2	9.3
Operatives and kindred workers............	27.1	26.6	25.2	25.5	23.8	27.4	25.8
Service workers...........................	23.0	20.3	23.2	21.6	24.5	18.4	16.3
Laborers..................................	18.4	26.8	30.9	32.1	31.7	33.6	39.0
FEMALE							
White, employed......................	100.0	100.0	100.0	100.0	100.0	100.0	100.0
Professional, technical, and kindred wkrs..	12.9	13.6	13.2	13.6	15.1	14.6	14.5
Clerical workers..........................	38.2	40.2	37.5	32.4	29.3	27.0	24.6
Sales workers.............................	7.7	9.6	10.0	10.1	10.6	11.2	11.3
Operatives and kindred workers............	21.8	16.7	17.4	21.8	20.7	21.1	21.9
Private household workers.................	3.4	3.0	3.2	3.7	4.4	4.7	5.7
Service workers, except private household..	8.6	10.0	11.5	11.5	12.9	13.8	14.6
Other workers............................	7.4	7.0	7.3	7.0	7.0	7.7	7.5
Nonwhite, employed...................	100.0	100.0	100.0	100.0	100.0	100.0	100.0
Professional, technical, and kindred wkrs..	4.8	5.5	5.3	5.7	6.0	7.3	8.0
Clerical workers..........................	9.2	10.4	3.8	3.0	2.4	1.7	1.2
Sales workers.............................	1.8	1.9	1.7	1.2	1.2	1.8	1.2
Operatives and kindred workers............	31.9	18.8	13.7	13.4	10.9	11.0	9.2
Private household workers.................	32.3	35.4	43.2	48.1	50.9	53.3	56.4
Service workers, except private household..	15.1	23.4	27.9	24.5	24.4	19.5	17.1
Other workers............................	4.9	4.5	4.4	4.0	4.3	5.5	6.9

Source: Derived from U. S. Bureau of the Census, *U. S. Census of Population: 1950*, Series P–E, No. 5A, *Characteristics by Size of Place*, tables 5 and 5a.

the income of white men by size of place can be attributed to the occupational structure.

In the case of nonwhite men, the income differential by size of place is considerably greater than for white men. For nonwhite men, the average incomes in the largest cities are twice what they are in the smallest towns. However, the occupational variation by size of place is also much more pronounced for nonwhite men than for white men. In the largest urban centers only 18 percent of the nonwhite men were employed as laborers and 12 percent were employed in the white-collar field as clerical and sales workers. The proportion of laborers increased progressively, as size of place decreased, and reached a maximum of 39 percent in the smallest towns. At the same time there were fewer opportunities for the employment of nonwhite men in white-collar jobs in the smaller towns. Only 2

percent of the nonwhite men residing in the smallest towns worked as clerical or sales workers. The decrease by size of place in the proportion of
workers engaged in the clerical and sales field was much sharper for nonwhite men than for white men. About 19 percent of the white men in urbanized areas of 1,000,000 or more and roughly 16 percent of those residing in towns that were not parts of urbanized areas worked in these
occupation groups. The corresponding proportions for nonwhite men were
about 10 percent and 3 percent. These figures indicate that, although
there is only a slight diminution in the importance of clerical and sales
work in the smaller places, nonwhite men residing in these places are virtually excluded from these occupations and appear to be forced into the
laboring field.

Among women, as among men, the income differentials by size of place
are much sharper for nonwhites than for whites. White women residing
in the largest cities had an average income that was just less than twice
that of residents of the smallest towns, whereas the average income of nonwhite women residing in the largest cities was three times that received
by residents of the smallest towns. Here again, the variations in occupational structure were much more pronounced for nonwhites than for whites;
but, occupation appears to be a basic factor in the explanation of income
differentials by size of place for both groups. The proportion of white
women employed as professional workers, the highest paid occupation group
for women, and as operatives, also a relatively high-paid occupation group
for women, does not vary appreciably by size of place. However, the proportion employed as clerical workers, an occupation group that ranks very
close to professional workers in terms of average income, decreased from
38 percent in the largest places to 25 percent in the smallest towns. At
the same time, the proportion of white women employed in the service
trades, the lowest paid jobs for women, increased progressively from 12
percent in the largest places to 20 percent in the smallest places.

Nonwhite women in the smallest towns appear to have an even more
difficult time getting into well-paid jobs than their male brethren. Professional work is the only white-collar occupation in which nonwhite women
appear to any appreciable extent, and in this occupation they undoubtedly
are employed as relatively low-paid school teachers. The proportion of
nonwhite women employed as professional workers increased progressively
from 5 percent in the largest places to 8 percent in the smallest towns.
However, there were very sharp decreases in the proportions employed as
clerical workers and operatives. Nearly three-fourths of the nonwhite
women workers in the smallest towns were employed in the service trades.

Another factor in the analysis of size of place differentials among women,
which should be explicitly noted, relates to the martial status composition
of the female labor force. According to the 1950 Census, more than half
(54 percent) of the women in the labor force were either married women

or unmarried girls under 20 years of age.[10]   These workers typically were members of families in which the husband (or father) was the principal breadwinner and in which the female workers were supplementary earners. Because of the primary responsibility of the male worker, he can respond to shifts in the demand for labor by migrating.   In contrast, women workers typically have far less freedom of movement, and in a very large proportion of the cases are restricted to seek employment in the same area as their husbands (or fathers) despite the possibility of obtaining more lucrative offers elsewhere.   Women, by the very nature of their attachment to the labor force, may be less responsive than men to variations in the demands for their services.   Therefore, their incomes may be subject to relatively larger variations by size of place than the incomes of men.[11]

Region

The analysis of regional differences in income among men largely resolves itself into an investigation of the factors that differentiate the South from the rest of the Nation.   The median income of men in the South was only $1,800 as compared with $2,700 for each of the other regions.   How-

TABLE **16.**—MEDIAN INCOME IN 1949 OF PERSONS, BY COLOR AND SEX, BY REGIONS

Region	Male			Female		
	Total	White	Nonwhite	Total	White	Nonwhite
Northeast........................	$2,713	$2,759	$2,054	$1,384	$1,407	$1,165
North Central....................	2,681	2,721	2,187	1,072	1,086	931
South............................	1,775	2,065	1,033	755	947	440
West.............................	2,722	2,786	1,862	998	1,008	884

Source: Derived from U. S. Bureau of the Census, *U. S. Census of Population: 1950*, Vol. II, *Characteristics of the Population*, Part 1, U. S. Summary, table 162.

ever, among women, there appear to be rather striking regional income differentials.   The median income of women varied from $800 in the South to about $1,000 in the West and North Central States to $1,400 in the Northeast.   To some extent the differential between the South and the other

[10] U. S. Bureau of the Census, *U. S. Census of Population: 1950*, Vol. II, *Characteristics of the Population*, Part 1, U. S. Summary, table 121.

[11] The following interesting observation regarding the behavior of the female labor force appears in a recent monograph by Donald J. Bogue, *A Methodological Study of Migration and Labor Mobility*, Scripps Foundation Studies in Population Distribution, No. 4, June 1952, p. 98.

"At the present time the labor mobility of female workers is little understood. Because of the small number of mobile female workers in the sample, the present study was able to add comparatively little information.   The study does abound, however, with examples of the failure of female workers to respond to given combinations of factors in the same way as males.

"Because female workers are constituting an increasing proportion of the total labor force, and because the scope of their participation is steadily being broadened to include all industries and occupations, it will become increasingly necessary to cease using the male worker as a prototype in theorizing about the behavior of the labor force. This means that it will be necessary to stop regarding female workers as somewhat erratic members of the labor force and to undertake research studies which will yield adequate generalization about their mobility and other labor force behavior."

regions reflects the low economic status of the nonwhites in that region. However, even when regional income comparisons are made separately for each color group, it can be noted that the incomes of both whites and nonwhites are lower in the South than in any of the other regions. At the same time, the data also indicate that the differentials between the South and the other regions are much greater for nonwhites than for whites.

TABLE 17.—MEDIAN INCOME IN 1949 OF PERSONS, BY RESIDENCE, COLOR, AND SEX, BY REGIONS

Residence, color, and sex	Northeast	North Central	South	West
MALE				
White.....................................	$2,759	$2,721	$2,065	$2,786
Urban.....................................	2,877	3,056	2,652	3,030
Rural nonfarm.............................	2,417	2,302	1,857	2,349
Rural farm................................	1,817	1,818	1,120	1,987
Nonwhite..................................	2,054	2,187	1,033	1,862
Urban.....................................	2,078	2,252	1,420	2,122
Rural nonfarm.............................	1,587	1,039	942	1,164
Rural farm................................	1,320	766	554	993
FEMALE				
White.....................................	1,407	1,086	947	1,008
Urban.....................................	1,506	1,284	1,192	1,163
Rural nonfarm.............................	948	739	745	742
Rural farm................................	752	617	469	545
Nonwhite..................................	1,165	931	440	884
Urban.....................................	1,181	969	579	988
Rural nonfarm.............................	772	449	361	486
Rural farm................................	569	346	307	419

Source: Derived from U. S. Bureau of the Census, *U. S. Census of Population: 1950*, Vol. II, *Characteristics of the Population*, Part 1, U. S. Summary, table 162.

Since farming is of much greater importance in some regions than in others, it is important that the regional differences be examined separately for the farm and nonfarm population. The data required for this examination are shown in table 17. The major conclusion suggested by this table is that, even when the data are properly controlled with respect to color, sex, and residence, there appears to be an income differential between the South and the other regions. Among white men, the median income of farm residents was about three-fifths of that received by the comparable group in other regions, and the income of urban residents was about 10 percent below that received in the northern and western parts of the country. Among white women, the income of farm residents was also below that received in the other regions; however, urban residents had about the same average income as in the West. For nonwhites, the incomes of both male and female and farm and nonfarm residents in the South was far below that received in the other regions.

It has been suggested that much of the income differential between the South and the other regions can be explained by size of place and that the incomes of whites residing in communities of the same size are approximately the same in each region.[12] The available evidence does not entirely support this conclusion. Table 18 shows that when the effects of age are eliminated, white men residing in large cities in the South have higher average incomes than those residing in cities of the same size in the Northeastern part of the United States; and, those residing in smaller cities have about the same average income in both regions. However, incomes are lower in the South than in the North Central or the West for all city-size groups. The income differential between the South and the West was less than 10 percent in the largest cities, but it was about 15 percent in the smaller towns. Approximately the same differentials were found between the South and North Central States.

TABLE **18.**—MEDIAN INCOME IN 1949 OF WHITE URBAN MEN 25 TO 44 YEARS OLD, BY SIZE OF PLACE, BY REGIONS

Region	Urbanized areas		Urban places not in urbanized areas		
	250,000 to 1,000,000	Less than 250,000	25,000 or more	10,000 to 25,000	Less than 10,000
Northeast...........................	$3,047	$2,878	$2,881	$2,835	$2,874
North Central........................	3,374	3,407	3,274	3,135	3,022
South...............................	3,176	3,103	2,903	2,897	2,686
West................................	3,403	3,397	3,369	3,426	3,303

Source: Unpublished data of the Bureau of the Census derived from 1950 Census tabulations.

In the preceding section, the income differences by size of place were found to be largely attributable to variations in occupational structure. This explanation cannot be used to account for the lower incomes in the South. As table 19 shows, the occupational structure within each city-size group is much the same in the South as in the West. Nevertheless, there are substantial differences in the level of income within each city-size group for these regions. Similarly, the Northeast and North Central regions have similar occupational structures but different levels of income. These data suggest that other factors such as the pay-and-price structure, the industrial structure, differences in productivity, or perhaps even imperfections in the competitiveness of the labor market account for regional income differentials within the same city-size groups.

The above data, especially those in table 17, show very vividly the sharp differences between the incomes of whites and nonwhites that exist within each region. The differences are greatest in the South where the nonwhites, on the average, received only half the income of the whites within each residence and sex group; however, substantial differences between the in-

[12] D. Gale Johnson, "Some Effects of Region, Community Size, Color, and Occupation on Family and Individual Income," *Studies in Income and Wealth*, Vol. 15, National Bureau of Economic Research, New York, 1952, p. 57.

TABLE **19.**—OCCUPATION GROUP OF EMPLOYED WHITE URBAN MEN 25 TO 44 YEARS OLD, BY SIZE OF PLACE, BY REGIONS: 1950

Region and major occupation group in 1950	Urbanized areas		Urban places not in urbanized areas		
	250,000 to 1,000,000	Less than 250,000	25,000 or more	10,000 to 25,000	Less than 250,000
NORTHEAST					
Total employed..........................	100.0	100.0	100.0	100.0	100.0
Professional, technical, and kindred workers...	10.9	9.0	9.0	9.4	9.8
Managers, officials, and proprietors...........	10.5	10.5	11.0	10.6	11.2
Clerical and sales workers.....................	16.4	15.7	15.0	13.8	13.1
Craftsmen, foremen, and kindred workers.......	23.5	23.0	22.2	23.2	23.3
Operatives and kindred workers.................	27.2	29.2	29.9	31.0	29.6
Service workers................................	5.8	5.5	5.8	4.8	4.7
Laborers.......................................	5.6	7.2	7.2	7.4	8.2
NORTH CENTRAL					
Total employed..........................	100.0	100.0	100.0	100.0	100.0
Professional, technical, and kindred workers...	11.7	10.8	10.8	10.1	9.7
Managers, officials, and proprietors...........	11.4	12.3	13.2	13.8	14.7
Clerical and sales workers.....................	19.3	17.9	15.8	15.5	13.9
Craftsmen, foremen, and kindred workers.......	23.1	23.2	23.5	23.5	24.5
Operatives and kindred workers.................	25.2	26.5	26.1	25.9	25.8
Service workers................................	4.2	4.1	4.5	4.3	3.8
Laborers.......................................	5.1	5.3	6.0	7.0	7.6
SOUTH					
Total employed..........................	100.0	100.0	100.0	100.0	100.0
Professional, technical, and kindred workers...	11.5	12.0	11.4	10.0	9.6
Managers, officials, and proprietors...........	16.1	16.6	17.2	16.5	16.7
Clerical and sales workers.....................	21.6	20.7	18.6	17.2	14.0
Craftsmen, foremen, and kindred workers.......	23.8	23.7	24.0	24.4	24.2
Operatives and kindred workers.................	18.1	18.8	19.7	22.5	25.5
Service workers................................	4.6	4.2	4.4	3.7	3.4
Laborers.......................................	4.3	4.1	4.8	5.6	6.7
WEST					
Total employed..........................	100.0	100.0	100.0	100.0	100.0
Professional, technical, and kindred workers...	13.8	11.8	10.9	11.8	10.6
Managers, officials, and proprietors...........	16.0	15.1	15.7	16.6	15.2
Clerical and sales workers.....................	20.1	19.9	18.0	14.2	12.4
Craftsmen, foremen, and kindred workers.......	22.2	22.0	23.8	21.8	25.8
Operatives and kindred workers.................	15.9	17.8	17.4	20.3	20.7
Service workers................................	5.3	6.2	6.1	5.3	4.9
Laborers.......................................	6.7	7.2	8.1	10.0	10.4

Source: Unpublished data of the Bureau of the Census derived from 1950 Census tabulations.

comes of the whites and nonwhites were also found in the other regions as well. Since whites and nonwhites differ with respect to educational attainment, an attempt has been made (in table 20) to eliminate the effect of education and to show the median income of white and nonwhite males of the same age and educational attainment, within each region. Here again, some extremely interesting differences emerge.

Within each region and for each color group greater educational attainment is reflected in higher income. However, within each region, the income differential between whites and nonwhites tends to increase with education. In the South, the proportion by which the average income of whites exceeded that of nonwhites increased from 48 percent for grammar

TABLE **20.**—MEDIAN INCOME IN 1949 OF MEN 35 TO 44 YEARS OLD, BY YEARS OF SCHOOL
COMPLETED AND COLOR, BY REGIONS

Years of school completed	South			North and West		
	White	Nonwhite	Ratio of white to nonwhite	White	Nonwhite	Ratio of white to nonwhite
No schooling.....................	$1,120	$962	1.16	$2,221	$1,734	1.28
Elementary: 1 to 4 years...........	1,475	1,105	1.33	2,475	2,140	1.16
5 to 7 years...........	2,117	1,371	1.54	2,711	2,214	1.22
8 years................	2,378	1,607	1.48	2,971	2,285	1.30
High school: 1 to 3 years...........	2,906	1,725	1.68	3,342	2,425	1.38
4 years................	3,463	1,998	1.73	3,583	2,579	1.39
College: 1 to 3 years...........	3,963	2,048	1.94	4,048	2,778	1.46
4 years or more........	5,227	2,830	1.85	5,213	3,275	1.59

Source: Derived from U. S. Bureau of the Census, *U. S. Census of Population: 1950*, Series P–E,
No. 5B, *Education*, tables 12 and 13.

school graduates to 73 percent for high school graduates to 85 percent for
college graduates. Approximately the same general relationship prevailed,
but with narrower differentials, in the North and the West.

In view of the similarity of both groups in age, residence, and education, the differences in income can be explained primarily in terms of the
occupations in which these men were employed. Table 21 shows that in
the South a much larger proportion of nonwhites than whites in each education group were employed as either laborers or service workers, two of
the lowest paid occupations. For example, among high school graduates,
less than 10 percent of the whites but over one-third of the nonwhites
worked in these occupations. The corresponding proportions for elemen-
tary school graduates were one-eighth for the whites and one-half for the
nonwhites. Only among college graduates was a larger proportion of nonwhites than whites employed in a relatively high-paid occupation group
such as professional and technical workers. Even here, however, it is very
likely that the nonwhites in these occupations were largely employed as
school teachers, whose salaries are typically lower than those received by
other professional workers.

The evidence presented suggests that in all regions of the United States
whites are better able to capitalize on their education than nonwhites. In
the northern and western parts of the United States as well as in the South
the nonwhite who has invested four years of his life in a college education
earns less on the average than the white who did not complete his high
school training. This situation represents an improvement in the relative
position of the nonwhite over 1940 when a Negro college graduate earned
less, on the average, than the white who did not complete grammar school.[13]
Between 1940 and 1950 there was some improvement in the kinds of jobs
available to nonwhite men; however, the fact remains that the nonwhite

[13] Based on data shown in U. S. Bureau of the Census, Sixteenth Decennial Census of the United
States (1940), *Education: Educational Attainment by Economic Characteristics and Martial Status*,
tables 29 and 31.

TABLE **21.**—OCCUPATION GROUP OF EMPLOYED MEN 35 TO 44 YEARS OLD, BY YEARS OF SCHOOL COMPLETED AND COLOR, FOR THE SOUTH: 1950

Years of school completed and color	Total	Professional, techn'l, and kindred workers	Farmers and farm managers	Managers, officials, and proprietors, exc. farm	Clerical and sales workers	Craftsmen, foremen, and kindred workers	Operatives and kindred workers	Service workers	Laborers
WHITE									
Total employed..........	100.0	7.5	15.3	13.9	11.3	21.4	19.4	3.1	8.3
No schooling................	100.0	0.8	21.3	2.3	2.0	9.4	18.9	4.2	41.3
Elementary: 1 to 4 years....	100.0	0.7	26.3	3.9	2.6	15.1	27.1	2.6	21.5
5 to 7 years....	100.0	0.9	22.7	6.1	4.2	23.4	27.7	3.2	11.9
8 years.........	100.0	1.3	19.2	9.0	6.8	27.4	24.4	3.7	8.4
High school: 1 to 3 years....	100.0	2.5	13.1	15.0	12.6	27.6	20.4	3.5	5.0
4 years.........	100.0	6.5	7.8	22.7	21.7	22.9	12.4	3.4	2.6
College: 1 to 3 years....	100.0	16.5	5.4	31.7	25.5	11.9	6.0	1.6	1.4
4 years or more.	100.0	53.4	3.1	22.1	13.8	4.5	1.7	0.7	0.6
NONWHITE									
Total employed..........	100.0	2.5	19.7	1.9	2.7	7.5	21.5	11.1	33.2
No schooling................	100.0	0.2	26.1	0.8	0.6	4.7	17.8	4.2	45.6
Elementary: 1 to 4 years....	100.0	0.3	28.1	0.9	0.9	5.6	19.5	6.2	38.4
5 to 7 years....	100.0	0.5	19.2	1.8	1.6	8.3	23.5	11.6	33.5
8 years.........	100.0	1.1	11.4	2.3	2.9	8.1	27.2	18.1	29.0
High school: 1 to 3 years....	100.0	2.5	7.2	3.5	5.9	11.4	24.3	21.0	24.0
4 years.........	100.0	5.5	4.0	4.4	12.6	12.7	21.6	21.8	17.3
College: 1 to 3 years....	100.0	17.2	1.3	6.7	18.9	12.8	15.8	17.5	9.7
4 years or more.	100.0	65.3	1.4	6.2	10.3	3.8	3.5	5.7	3.8

Source: Derived from U. S. Bureau of the Census, *U. S. Census of Population: 1950*, Series P–E, No. 5B, *Education*, table 11.

industrial worker still finds himself generally restricted to the lower paid jobs in our economy. As table 22 clearly shows, there was no increase in the proportion of men employed in the highest paid occupation groups (professional and managerial workers) and only a small increase in the proportion employed as clerical workers and craftsmen. The marked change in employment patterns for nonwhite men was a movement out of the laboring and service trades and into the factory trades as operatives. The proportion of nonwhite industrial workers employed as laborers and service workers dropped from 58 percent to 48 percent, and the proportion employed as operatives increased from 21 percent to 28 percent. Nonetheless, the fact seems to be almost as true today as it was in 1940 that about one-half of the nonwhite male industrial workers are restricted to the lowest paid jobs. There was greater evidence of an increase in the diversification of job opportunities for nonwhite women. Even here, however, it is striking that in 1950 two-thirds of the nonwhite women employed at nonfarm jobs worked in the service trades, largely as private household workers.

The above conclusions for the country as a whole apply with even greater force for the South.[14] This fact is not demonstrated in census data only.

[14] See, U. S. Bureau of the Census, *1950 Census of Population—Preliminary Reports*, "Employment and Income in the United States, by Regions: 1950," Series PC–7, No. 2, table 6.

TABLE 22.—OCCUPATION GROUP OF NONWHITE PERSONS EMPLOYED IN NONFARM JOBS, BY SEX: 1950 AND 1940

Major occupation group	Male		Female	
	1950	1940	1950	1940
Total employed.................................	100.0	100.0	100.0	100.0
Professional, technical, and kindred workers...........	3.0	3.2	6.4	5.1
Managers, officials, and proprietors, except farm......	3.0	2.8	1.5	0.9
Clerical and kindred workers.........................	4.1	2.1	4.9	1.1
Sales workers.......................................	1.6	1.6	1.6	0.7
Craftsmen, foremen, and kindred workers...............	10.2	7.5	0.7	0.2
Operatives and kindred workers.......................	27.7	21.3	16.7	7.9
Private household workers............................	1.4	3.9	45.6	70.4
Service workers, except private household.............	17.9	21.1	20.9	12.5
Laborers, except farm and mine......................	30.9	36.5	1.7	1.0

Source: Data for 1950 derived from U. S. Bureau of the Census, *U. S. Census of Population: 1950*, Vol. II, *Characteristics of the Population*, Part 1, U. S. Summary, table 128. Data for 1940 are derived from U. S. Bureau of the Census, *1950 Census of Population—Preliminary Reports*, "Employment and Income of the United States, by Regions: 1950," Series PC–7, No. 2, table 6.

It also appears in a recent study of the National Planning Association conducted in 108 plants, employing 105,000 persons in four Southern States (Virginia, Kentucky, and North and South Carolina).[15] This study does not pretend to be representative of the South as a whole or even of the states studied. Nevertheless, the results are of interest. The following are some of the major conclusions:[16]

1. Negroes are totally excluded from white-collar employment in white-managed firms.

2. Negro workers have scarcely a toe-hold in supervisory jobs. Negro foremen were found in only three firms.

3. The mixed work group is not common.

4. In the plants surveyed, the racial division of labor has been remarkably stable over a long period of time.

---

[15] Donald Dewey, *Four Studies of Negro Employment in the Upper South*, National Planning Association, Washington, D. C., 1953.

[16] *Ibid.*, p. 205, 206.

C H A P T E R   5

INCOME DIFFERENCES ATTRIBUTABLE TO OCCUPATION

The most nearly dominant single influence in a man's life is probably his occupation. More than anything else, perhaps, a man's occupation determines his course and his contribution in life. And when life's span is ended, quite likely there is no other single set of facts that will tell so well the kind of man he was and the part he played in life as will a detailed and chronological statement of the occupations he pursued. Indeed, there is no other single characteristic that tells so much about a man and his status—social, intellectual, and economic—as does his occupation. A man's occupation not only tells, for each workday, what he does during one-half of his waking hours, but it indicates, with some degree of accuracy, his manner of life during the other half —the kind of associates he will have, the kind of clothes he will wear, the kind of house he will live in, and even, to some extent, the kind of food he will eat. [Alba M. Edwards, *Comparative Occupation Statistics for the United States, 1870 to 1940*, Government Printing Office, 1943, p. XI.]

The above paragraph effectively summarizes the importance of occupation to the individual. It indicates the dual nature of occupation as a way of life and as a way of making a living. Stated in economic terms, this paragraph describes the pivotal position of occupation in both the production and the distribution of the national output. An individual contributes his effort, time, and skill to the production process. In return he receives an income that can be saved or used to purchase goods. Income is thus the catalyst between people and jobs, production and distribution.

Studies of occupational wage differentials have generally been restricted to the analysis of hourly or weekly earnings of workers in selected occupations and industries for specific localities.[1] These studies have provided considerable insight into various factors associated with differences in occupational earnings. However, they have several important limitations, the most serious being the use of hourly or weekly earnings rather than annual earnings. For some types of analysis, particularly those concerned with comparative well-being, the longer time reference is preferable because it provides a more general view of the earnings in a particular occupation.

---

[1] Particular reference is made to the wage surveys conducted by the Bureau of Labor Statistics and summarized in the following articles in the *Monthly Labor Review:* "City Comparisons of Wage Levels and Skill Differentials" (June 1952); "Regional Wage Differentials, 1909–47" (April 1948); and "Occupational Wage Differentials, 1907–47" (August 1948).

Level of income for major occupation groups

The occupational distribution of the labor force in the United States has been characterized in the following way:

> The occupational world is shaped like a pyramid. The unskilled form a thick broad base largely hereditary in character, surmounted by another broad layer of semi-skilled, many of whose circumstances are not unlike the lowest level.   Then nearer the middle is a smaller block of skilled workers; above them the white-collar clerical and sales force; then the semiprofessional and lower administrative positions; and at the top a small group of professional and higher administrative persons. Farmers and farm laborers, who have dwindled from 15 to 18 percent of the total—depending on seasonal factors—are of such a diversity of occupational patterns, property, and income status as to range from the very top to the bottom of the occupational pyramid and are not easily described in relation to the rest of the working world.
>
> Associated with this pyramidal spread of designated occupations is some as yet un-measured exactingness or skill, a measurable succession of average incomes, ranging from a few hundred dollars for the mass at the bottom to many thousands for the few at the top. Other recognized attributes such as financial status, social and community prestige, standards of living, eminence, education, and culture, and even tested intelli-gence, correspond in considerable degree with rising levels in the occupational world.[2]

This description suggests that the bulk of the American labor force is employed at unskilled work; these unskilled workers stand little chance of rising to higher levels; and very wide income differentials exist among oc-cupation groups. Analysis of the statistical data will indicate that at least some of these points are not completely supported by the facts.

Table 23 shows the occupational distribution of employed persons by sex, as well as the mean and the median income received by persons in each occupation group. For reasons already given,[3] male and female workers will be considered separately. If the term "unskilled" is given its conventional meaning and is considered to be synonymous with the classification "laborers," it is apparent that about 11 percent of the em-ployed men are in this category. Semiskilled workers, who are frequently defined as operatives (largely factory workers) and service workers, repre-sent about 27 percent of the employed men. Therefore, these groups, which may be roughly described as the unskilled and semiskilled workers, comprise about two-fifths of the employed. The remaining 62 percent are divided as follows: 21 percent are craftsmen, 20 percent are professional or managerial workers, 12 percent are clerical and sales workers, and 9 percent are farmers. Although it could still be argued on the basis of these facts that the American labor force contains a "thick broad base of unskilled workers," it would appear that a more characteristic feature of the labor force is the great concentration of workers in the semiskilled, skilled, and "white-collar" occupations.

---

[2] Statement of Dewey Anderson quoted in *Hearings before the Subcommittee on Low-Income Fami-lies,* Joint Committee on the Economic Report, 81st Congress, 1st Session, p. 489.

[3] See p. 18.

There is a very large gap between the incomes of the highest paid workers like doctors and dentists and the lowest paid workers such as farm and nonfarm laborers. However, for most occupation groups, the income differentials are quite narrow. Nonfarm laborers, for example, had a median income of $2,300 in 1951 or about $44 per week. The corresponding median for service workers was only slightly higher ($2,500 or $48 per

TABLE 23.—PERCENT OF EMPLOYED PERSONS IN EACH OCCUPATION GROUP, AND PERCENT OF AGGREGATE INCOME IN 1951 RECEIVED BY EACH OCCUPATION GROUP, BY SEX

Major occupation group in April 1952	Male					Female				
	Income recipients		Income in 1951			Income recipients		Income in 1951		
	Number (thousands)	Percent	Percent of total	Median	Arithmetic mean	Number (thousands)	Percent	Percent of total	Median	Arithmetic mean
Total employed..........	40,687	100.0	100.0	$3,193	$3,640	15,529	100.0	100.0	$1,718	$1,802
NONFARM OCCUPATIONS										
Professional, technical, and kindred workers............	3,120	7.7	11.1	4,250	5,271	1,798	11.6	16.6	2,517	2,579
Self-employed[1]...........	517	1.3	2.9	6,167	8,390	74	0.5	0.6	(2)	(2)
Salaried.................	2,603	6.4	8.2	4,176	4,689	1,724	11.1	16.0	2,556	2,601
Managers, officials, and proprietors, exc. farm.........	4,958	12.2	19.8	4,100	5,915	841	5.4	6.9	2,070	2,309
Self-employed[1]...........	2,726	6.7	10.5	3,529	5,706	481	3.1	3.2	1,313	1,843
Salaried.................	2,232	5.5	9.3	4,547	6,148	360	2.3	3.7	(2)	(2)
Clerical and kindred workers..	2,763	6.8	6.4	3,424	3,424	4,743	30.5	36.5	2,165	2,152
Sales workers................	2,174	5.3	6.1	3,628	4,132	1,118	7.2	5.8	1,281	1,463
Craftsmen, foremen, and kindred workers............	8,419	20.7	21.5	3,656	3,783	233	1.5	1.6	(2)	(2)
Operatives and kindred wkrs...	8,543	21.0	17.9	3,108	3,101	3,161	20.4	19.6	1,758	1,739
Private household workers.....	38	0.1	0.1	(2)	(2)	1,472	9.5	3.3	492	622
Service workers, exc. private household..................	2,426	6.0	4.2	2,474	2,562	1,821	11.7	8.5	1,106	1,311
Laborers, exc. farm and mine..	3,363	8.3	5.2	2,281	2,272	111	0.7	0.5	(2)	(2)
FARM OCCUPATIONS										
Farmers and farm managers.....	3,795	9.3	6.7	1,518	2,626	148	1.0	0.4	(2)	(2)
Farm laborers and foremen.....	1,088	2.7	1.1	1,057	1,505	84	0.5	0.2	(2)	(2)

[1] Includes a very small number of unpaid family workers.

[2] Average not shown where there were fewer than 100 cases in the sample reporting with income.

Source: U. S. Bureau of the Census, *Current Population Reports—Consumer Income*, Series P–60, No. 11, table H. The arithmetic means and the distribution of the aggregates between self-employed and salaried workers within the professional and managerial groups were derived from table 5 of the same report.

week), and the median for operatives was $3,100 or $60 a week. The craftsmen, clerical workers, and sales workers each had median incomes ranging between $3,400 and $3,700 for the year or between $65 and $70 a week. The use of over-all averages based on the major occupation groups tends to conceal some differences; however, the subsequent analysis will show that the use of more refined occupation groups produces essentially the same results.

As indicated earlier, the labor force attachments of women in our society are basically different from those of men. This difference is reflected to some extent in both the occupational distribution and in the income of women. Table 23 shows that the medians for occupation groups among women showed a wide range from $500 to $2,600. However, nearly half of all employed women were either operatives or clerical workers, groups that had median incomes of $1,800 to $2,200 respectively. The lowest median income ($500) was received by private household workers who comprised about one-tenth of the female labor force. Service work outside of private households and sales work were also among the low-income pursuits engaged in by women. The highest median income was received by salaried professional workers ($2,600).

The differences in median income among major occupation groups are also reflected in the distribution of aggregate income among occupational groups. Table 23 indicates that, among men, the professional and managerial groups, which together comprised about 20 percent of employed men, received nearly one-third of the income. Clerical workers, sales workers, and craftsmen and foremen received a share of the income proportionate to their number. Men employed as operatives, service workers, and laborers received less than a proportionate share. Farmers also received less than a proportionate share of the money income payments; however, their share of total income, including income in kind, would undoubtedly be somewhat greater than that shown in the table. Among women, those employed in the professional and managerial group and as clerical workers appeared to be in a relatively more favorable position than other workers.

Although there are important rigidities in the occupational stratification of the population, the implication that the lower groups in the occupational distribution constitute an hereditary caste undoubtedly exaggerates the situation. One aspect of the Occupational Mobility Survey referred to earlier (see p. 31) was the analysis of the work histories of a representative sample of about 2,600 skilled male workers in six large American cities to determine the factors that affected their occupational choice.[4] In this study it was found that the fathers of only about half of the skilled workers were themselves skilled workers or members of the professional or managerial group. In about one-third of the cases, the fathers of the skilled workers were themselves either unskilled or semiskilled workers, and in an additional 15 percent they were farmers.

In this same study it was found after studying the pattern of behavior of workers under 45 years of age during a whole 10-year period that there is substantial movement up the occupational scale from apprenticeship, unskilled, and semiskilled trades into the skilled occupations. For example, only 27 percent of the workers between 35 and 44 years of age worked at skilled occupations during the entire period between 1940 and 1950. An

---

[4] *Patterns of Mobility of Skilled Workers and Factors Affecting Their Occupational Choice, Six Cities, 1940–1951*, Industrial Relations Section, Massachusetts Institute of Technology, Cambridge, Mass. (Mimeograph).

additional 27 percent moved up from unskilled or semiskilled workers, and most of the remaining workers fluctuated irregularly between skilled and semiskilled or unskilled employment.

Admittedly, the decade of the 1940's was characterized by a shortage of skilled labor, which may have facilitated the movement of workers from unskilled jobs to the skilled and semiskilled trades.   At the same time, however, it is important to remember that many other periods in American history were faced with similar problems of labor shortages, so that the evidence is not as atypical as it may appear to be at first.

Differences in the level of income among major occupation groups partially reflect variations in the age composition and educational attainment among these groups.   Professional workers, for example, contain a larger proportion of college graduates than other pursuits, and craftsmen are typically older than other workers.   Since both education and age are associated with income, it is necessary to standardize the data for these factors in the analysis of income differentials among occupations.

Table 24 indicates that occupational differences in income persist even when the factor of age is eliminated.   Thus, for example, in each age group beyond 35, nonfarm occupation groups could be ranked by average income in the following order: professional workers; managerial workers; clerical and sales workers; craftsmen; operatives; service workers; and laborers.   There were some inversions of this order among younger men, attributable perhaps to the fact that they had not yet reached their peak earnings.

The relationship between income and age varies among occupation groups.   Occupations differ considerably in their requirements of physical ability, initial skill, and experience.   Some occupations pay a premium for physical ability, but little for experience.   Others require a high level of initial ability in addition to a long, expensive training period.   Pursuits that require such different degrees of skill and ability can hardly be expected to show the same earnings pattern by age, and, as may be noted from table 24, there are important differences among the various occupation groups.[5]

In some occupation groups such as laborers, service workers, and operatives, workers tend to reach their peak earnings at a fairly young age and then show little variation until they approach retirement.   For example, the median earnings of operatives was between $3,200 and $3,300 for workers in each 10-year age group between 25 and 54 years.   The median then dropped to $2,800 for those between 55 and 64 years old.   Service

---

[5] This table shows the median earnings in a given year (1951) for men classified by occupation and age during a given month (April 1952).   The picture it presents is undoubtedly different from that which would be obtained if men were classified by lifetime earnings or some other income concept, or by usual or longest occupation.   See p. 64 for a further discussion of the problems associated with the interpretation of differences related to time based on data obtained in "cross-section" studies.

workers and laborers showed essentially the same pattern of variation as operatives. In contrast, such highly skilled workers as the professional group show a different pattern of variation of earnings with age from that noted above. The median earnings of this group increased sharply from $3,700 for those 25 to 34 years old to $4,800 for those 35 to 44 years old. Workers in this occupation who were between 45 and 54 years old had median earnings of $5,100. It is not until the retirement age is approached that average earnings decline in this occupation group.

TABLE 24.—MEDIAN EARNINGS IN 1951 OF EMPLOYED MEN 25 TO 64 YEARS OLD, BY OCCUPATION GROUP AND AGE

Major occupation group in April 1952	25 to 34 years	35 to 44 years	45 to 54 years	55 to 64 years
Total employed civilians...........................	$3,299	$3,621	$3,299	$3,031
Professional, technical, and kindred workers...........	3,744	4,813	5,053	(1)
Farmers and farm managers............................	1,592	1,944	1,921	967
Managers, officials, and proprietors, except farm......	3,563	4,451	4,368	4,175
Clerical, sales, and kindred workers..................	3,388	3,993	3,719	3,680
Craftsmen, foremen, and kindred workers...............	3,592	3,913	3,731	3,646
Operatives and kindred workers.......................	3,253	3,344	3,181	2,821
Service workers, including private household..........	3,045	3,125	2,882	2,313
Laborers, except mine...............................	2,361	2,291	1,985	2,152

[1] Median not shown where there were fewer than 100 cases in the sample reporting with earnings.

Source: U. S. Bureau of the Census, *Current Population Reports—Consumer Income*, Series P–60, No. 11, table B. Data for 55-to-64-year age group derived from unpublished data of the Bureau of the Census.

TABLE 25.—MEDIAN EARNINGS IN 1946 OF EMPLOYED MEN 25 TO 44 YEARS OLD IN SELECTED OCCUPATION GROUPS, BY EDUCATIONAL ATTAINMENT AND AGE

Educational attainment and age	All earners	Farmers and farm managers	Clerical and sales workers	Craftsmen and foremen	Operatives	Service workers and laborers
25 to 34 years.................	$2,008	$863	$2,253	$2,202	$2,021	$1,389
Elementary: Under 8 years.........	1,279	413	(1)	1,743	1,679	1,084
8 years..............	1,895	1,375	1,795	2,184	2,109	1,395
High school: 1 to 3 years...........	1,997	900	2,185	2,176	2,024	1,545
4 years..............	2,161	1,675	2,282	2,256	2,088	1,642
College: 1 to 3 years...........	2,420	(1)	2,403	2,653	2,182	944
4 years or more.......	2,670	(1)	2,693	(1)	(1)	(1)
35 to 44 years.................	$2,391	$1,140	$2,668	$2,629	$2,333	$1,660
Elementary: Under 8 years.........	1,642	750	1,425	2,175	1,950	1,429
8 years..............	2,283	1,336	2,523	2,641	2,344	1,725
High school: 1 to 3 years...........	2,426	889	2,648	2,617	2,515	1,730
4 years..............	2,885	2,393	2,746	2,939	2,680	2,223
College: 1 to 3 years...........	3,192	(1)	2,830	3,073	(1)	(1)
4 years or more.......	3,486	(1)	3,217	(1)	(1)	(1)

[1] Number of cases in the sample reporting with earnings too small for the computation of medians.

Source: Unpublished tabulation from the April 1947 Current Population Survey.

Because of the relatively small size of the Current Population Survey sample, only the most tentative conclusions can be reached regarding oc-

cupational differentials in income when the effects of both age and education are eliminated.   One important conclusion suggested by the data in
table 25 is that income differences among occupations remain after both
of these factors have been eliminated.   The clerical and sales groups and
the craftsmen have considerably higher incomes than operatives who in
turn have higher incomes than service workers and laborers of the same
age and educational attainment.   The one striking reversal of these patterns exists among clerical and sales workers 35 to 44 years old who did
not complete grammar school.   The income of these men, on the average,
was as low as that received by laborers and service workers and reflects
perhaps their part-time employment as sales workers or their employment
in the least skilled clerical operations such as office boys, messengers, etc.

Level of income for detailed occupations

The data presented above for major occupation groups show the income
differentials that exist for broad categories of workers.   Perhaps the chief
utility of this information is that it permits the casual observer to obtain a
quick and ready view of the interrelation between occupation and income.
For purposes of technical analysis, however, it is important that more refined occupational groupings be considered, since the major groups may
conceal important differences.

The data in appendix tables C–1 and C–3 have been used to show
income differentials among detailed occupations.   These tables provide
information on the wage or salary income in 1939 and 1949 for wage or
salary workers in 118 occupations for men and 32 occupations for women.
The data on wage or salary income were used in preference to data on
total income that are available for 1949 because they permit the analysis
of the occupational structure for two markedly different periods.   For each
year, the occupations were first ranked from lowest to highest according to
median wage or salary income and they were then divided into deciles
based on the number of workers in each occupation.   First, the occupations containing the lowest paid tenth of the workers in each year were
identified.   This procedure was then applied to each succeeding tenth of
the workers.   The results of this analysis for men are shown in table 26.

This table clearly shows that there is a very high correlation between
the relative income position of a major occupation group and the detailed
occupations that comprise it.   The lowest paid among the nonfarm major
occupation groups were laborers and service workers.   The detailed occupations within these major groups dominated the lowest deciles.   Only
two groups of laborers (those employed in the chemicals and motor vehicles industries) reached the fifth decile in 1949, and two groups of service
workers (policemen and firemen) reached the eighth decile.   Operatives
ranked next among the major occupation groups, and it is apparent that
the component parts of this group were concentrated in the fourth and

TABLE **26.**—SELECTED OCCUPATIONS FOR MALE WAGE OR SALARY WORKERS RANKED BY MEDIAN
WAGE OR SALARY INCOME: 1949 AND 1939

Occupations ranked by median wage or salary income	Occupations included in each tenth	
	1949	1939

Lowest tenth.........	Messengers
	Newsboys
	Attendants
	Operatives--lumber
	Private household workers
	Service workers (n.e.c.)
	Fishermen
	Lumbermen
	Laborers--lumber; construction; trade
		Messengers
		Newsboys
		Apprentices
		Private household workers
		Service workers (n.e.c.)
		Fishermen
		Lumbermen
		Laborers--textiles; lumber;
		  construction; transportation
		  (except railroad); trade

Second tenth.........	Shoemakers Apprentices Operatives--textiles; footwear Barbers Charmen Cooks Elevators operators Waiters Laborers--food; textiles; transportation (except railroad); telecommunications	Shoemakers Attendants Sailors Operatives--textiles; lumber Charmen Cooks Waiters Laborers--stone; railroads

Third tenth..........	Clergymen
	Painters (construction)
	Mine operatives
	Sailors
	Operatives--leather
	Guards and watchmen
	Longshoremen
	Laborers--paper; stone; iron and steel;
	  nonferrous metals; machinery; transpor-
	  tation equipment; railroads
		Carpenters
		Painters (construction)
		Mine operatives
		Operatives--footwear
		Longshoremen
		Laborers--food; paper; chemicals;
		  transportation equipment

Fourth tenth.........	Carpenters Chauffeurs	Plasterers Chauffeurs Operatives--knitting mills; apparel Barbers Laborers--iron and steel; machinery

Fifth tenth..........	Musicians
	Shipping clerks
	Bakers
	Metal molders
	Plasterers
	Stationary firemen
	Painters (except construction)
	Operatives--food; knitting mills;
	  apparel; paper; stone; iron and steel;
	  nonferrous metals
	Laborers--chemicals; motor vehicles
		Musicians
		Shipping clerks
		Blacksmiths
		Masons
		Tailors
		Painters (except construction)
		Operatives--food; paper; leather; stone;
		  nonferrous metals; transportation
		  equipment
		Guards and watchmen
		Elevator operators
		Laborers--nonferrous metals; motor
		  vehicles; telecommunications

Sixth tenth..........	Masons Mechanics Operatives--machinery	Dancers Bakers Cabinet makers Mechanics Metal molders Roofers Stationary firemen Operatives--machinery; iron and steel

Seventh tenth........	Dancers
	Salaried managers--eating and drinking
	  places
	Salesmen
	Blacksmiths
	Cabinet makers
	Metal rollers
	Roofers
	Tailors
	Operatives--rubber; transportation
	  equipment
		Clergymen
		Salaried managers--eating and drinking
		  places
		Salesmen
		Structural metal workers
		Operatives--rubber; motor vehicles

TABLE **26.**—SELECTED OCCUPATIONS FOR MALE WAGE OR SALARY WORKERS RANKED BY MEDIAN
WAGE OR SALARY INCOME: 1949 AND 1939—Cont.

Occupations ranked by median wage or salary income	Occupations included in each tenth	
	1949	1939
Eighth tenth.........	Social workers Salaried managers--personal services Stenographers Real estate agents Linemen Machinists Stationary engineers Motormen (mine and railway) Welders Operatives--chemicals; motor vehicles Firemen Policemen	Teachers Stenographers Real estate agents Boilermakers Compositors Foremen--construction Machinists Plumbers Metal rollers Stationary engineers Motormen (mine and railway) Welders Operatives--chemicals

Ninth tenth..........	Artists
	Designers
	Teachers
	Postmasters
	Baggagemen
	Bookkeepers
	Mail carriers
	Telegraph operators
	Insurance agents
	Boilermakers
	Electricians
	Foremen--construction
	Inspectors
	Locomotive firemen
	Plumbers
	Structural metal workers
	Brakemen
		Artists
		Designers
		Pharmacists
		Social workers
		Salaried managers--retail trade;
		  business and repair services;
		  personal services
		Bookkeepers
		Telegraph operators
		Electricians
		Foremen--manufacturing
		Inspectors
		Linemen
		Locomotive firemen
		Printing craftsmen
		Brakemen

Highest tenth........	Authors
	Chemists
	College presidents and professors
	Engineers--civil; electrical; mechanical
	Pharmacists
	Railroad conductors
	Salaried managers--manufacturing;
	  transportation; wholesale trade;
	  retail trade; finance; business
	  and repair services
	Compositors
	Foremen--manufacturing; transportation
	Locomotive engineers
	Printing craftsmen
		Authors
		Chemists
		College presidents and professors
		Engineers--civil; electrical; mechanical
		Railroad conductors
		Postmasters
		Salaried managers--manufacturing;
		  transportation; wholesale trade;
		  finance
		Baggagemen
		Mail carriers
		Insurance agents
		Foremen--transportation
		Locomotive engineers
		Firemen
		Policemen

Source: Derived from appendix tables C–1 and C–3.

fifth deciles. However, some of the higher paid operatives (those employed in the chemicals and motor vehicles industries) reached the eighth decile. Craftsmen, clerical, and sales workers, whose median incomes did not differ significantly, ranked next among the major occupation groups. The detailed occupations within these groups dominated the eighth and ninth deciles. Professional and managerial workers, needless to say, were concentrated in the highest decile.

Despite the many changes in both labor market demands and practices that took place between 1939 and 1949, there were comparatively few changes in the relative position of occupations when ranked by income. With very few exceptions, occupations, when ranked by median income in 1949, remained either in the same decile or in an adjacent decile to the one they had in 1939. The comparatively fixed-income occupations like firemen, policemen, and clergymen experienced a marked drop in relative income position.   Many of the occupations like masons, plasterers, and other construction trades, which are among the highest paid on an hourly basis, are much nearer to the middle of the distribution when ranked by annual income.   Surprisingly, these occupations had about the same relative income position during the depressed conditions of the late 1930's as they had during the peak building boom of the late 1940's.   The stability of the occupational structure (in terms of income) during the past decade lends further support to the thesis that wage structures tend to change relatively little over time.   Data based on fragmentary evidence indicate that in the United States, there is "a striking similarity of wage structures, maintained over a third to a half century." [6]

Income dispersion within occupations

A general view of the distribution of income within selected major occupation groups has already been indicated (see figures 6 and 9).   It was demonstrated that, although the income distribution exhibits considerable skewness for some occupation groups, such as farmers, and bimodality for others, such as service workers, the income curve for the vast majority of workers who are in the blue-collar and white-collar fields is quite symmetrical.   Indeed, the general conclusion that was reached in the earlier discussion was that there are some very important elements of symmetry in income distribution that frequently tend to be overlooked.   The earlier data referred to major occupation groups for the country as a whole and therefore had the defect of possibly concealing important differences.   In the present section, 1950 Census income data for finer occupational groupings are presented in order to test the conclusions reached earlier on the basis of data for major occupation groups.

Appendix tables C–1 to C–4 contain data that provide several measures of dispersion for wage or salary workers in 118 occupations for men and 32 occupations for women.   These tables show, first, the arithmetic mean and the median for each occupation.   A comparison of these measures gives a quick rough clue regarding the symmetry of a distribution.   In a symmetrical distribution the mean and the median will be much the same figure; in a skewed distribution they will differ, and the greater the skewness the greater the difference.   In addition, the first and third quartiles are presented as well as the ratio of each of these quartiles to the median.   If the ratio of the first quartile to the median is the same as the ratio of the third quartile to the median, the distribution tends to be symmetrical throughout its central portion.   Finally, the relative quartile range, which

---

[6] Stanley Lebergott, "Wage Structures." *The Review of Economic Statistics*, Vol. 29, No. 4, November 1947, p. 274.

is the distance between the quartiles expressed as a ratio to the median, is presented for each occupation.

With the exception of some of the professional, managerial, and sales occupations, there is a very close correspondence between the mean and the median for most of the occupations. In addition, the quartiles are quite symmetrical about the median. These facts tend to substantiate the conclusion that the great majority of detailed occupations are characterized by symmetrical rather than skewed curves. The distributions for the professional, managerial, and sales workers also show considerable symmetry about the median; however, they exhibit a greater divergence between the mean and the median, reflecting a greater concentration of income in the upper ranges of the distribution.

A summary of the data in appendix table C–1, which is presented in table 27, indicates that occupations can be classified into several groups with respect to income dispersion. The occupations were first ranked by dispersion $\left(\dfrac{Q_3 - Q_1}{Q_2}\right)$ in 1949, then weighted by the number of workers, and finally grouped into class intervals. The measure of dispersion shown in table 27 can be given the following meaning. If persons within an occupation are ranked from lowest to highest according to income, the dispersion is the income gap between the person at the 25th percentile and the 75th percentile expressed as a ratio to the income received by the middlemost person. For example, if mail carriers were ranked by wage or salary income in 1949, the person at the 25 percent mark would have an income of $2,740 and the person at the 75 percent mark would have an income of $3,765. In other words, the income gap between these two persons is $1,025, which is about one-third (0.303) of the income received by the middlemost person ($3,381). It is apparent from this interpretation that the greater the dispersion, the greater the amount of spread between incomes within the distribution. For 1949, the occupations have been classified as follows with respect to dispersion: Those in which the income gap between the first and third quartile is less than 40 percent of the median; between 40 and 50 percent of the median; between 50 and 60 percent of the median; between 60 and 80 percent of the median; and 80 percent of the median or greater.

In 1949, occupations could be classified into at least three major groups with respect to income dispersion. The first group, which comprised about one-tenth of the male labor force represented occupations with relatively little dispersion (i.e., those with a relative quartile range of less than 40 percent). The second group comprised somewhat more than one-tenth of the male labor force and represented occupations with relatively great dispersion (i.e., those with a relative quartile range of 80 percent or more). The remaining occupations, which included about four-fifths of the male labor force, can be tentatively classified as having moderate dispersion;

TABLE **27.**—SELECTED OCCUPATIONS FOR MALE WAGE OR SALARY WORKERS RANKED BY
DISPERSION OF WAGE OR SALARY INCOME IN 1949

Dispersion of wage or salary income $\left(\dfrac{Q_3 - Q_1}{Q_2}\right)$	Percent of workers	Occupations included in each group	
Total..........	100.0		
Less than .40.......	9.4	Railroad conductors Baggagemen Mail carriers Telegraph operators Inspectors Locomotive engineers Machinists	Brakemen Motormen (mine and railway) Operatives--motor vehicles; transportation equipment Firemen Policemen

.40 to .49..........	26.1	Designers
		Shipping clerks
		Bakers
		Blacksmiths
		Boilermakers
		Electricians
		Foremen--manufacturing;
		  transportation
		Linemen
		Locomotive firemen
		Mechanics
			Metal molders
			Metal rollers
			Stationary engineers
			Stationary firemen
			Welders
			Operatives--paper; chemicals;
			  stone; iron and steel; nonferrous
			  metals; machinery
			Elevator operators
			Laborers--iron and steel; nonferrous
			  metals; motor vehicles

.50 to .59..........	20.2	Chemists
		Engineers--civil; electrical;
		  mechanical
		Pharmacists
		Teachers
		Postmasters
		Salaried managers--transportation
		Bookkeepers
		Cabinetmakers
		Compositors
		Foremen--construction
		Plumbers
			Printing craftsmen
			Roofers
			Structural metal workers
			Tailors
			Mine operatives
			Painters (except construction)
			Operatives--food; textiles;
			  footwear; leather
			Guards and watchmen
			Laborers--textile; paper; stone;
			  machinery; transportation
			  equipment; railroads

.60 to .79..........	30.8	Artists
		Authors
		College presidents and professors
		Social workers
		Salaried managers--wholesale trade;
		  eating and drinking places;
		  retail trade; finance; business and
		  repair services; personal services
		Stenographers
		Insurance agents
		Salemen
		Carpenters
		Masons
			Painters (construction)
			Plasterers
			Apprentices
			Chauffeurs
			Sailors
			Operatives--knitting mills; apparel
			Barbers
			Charmen
			Cooks
			Longshoremen
			Laborers--food; chemicals;
			  transportation (except railroad);
			  telecommunications

.80 or more.........	13.5	Clergymen Dancers Musicians Salaried managers--manufacturing Messengers Newsboys Real estate agents Shoemakers Attendants	Operatives--lumber Private household workers Waiters Service workers (n.e.c.) Fishermen Lumbermen Laborers--lumber; construction; wholesale trade

Source: Derived from appendix table C–1.

however, subsequent analysis will indicate that even these occupations can be further subdivided with respect to dispersion.

The occupations in the first group are typically those in which the employees work either for a fixed annual salary, generally within a rather narrow range, or in which they work for an hourly rate but are almost guaranteed a year's work by the nature of their employment. Thus, for example, the group includes mail carriers, firemen, policemen, and inspectors, who are government workers and who typically work for an annual wage or salary. The group also includes telegraph operators and various types of railroad workers such as locomotive engineers, conductors, brakemen, and baggagemen who generally have about the same security and regularity of employment as do government workers.

In the second group of occupations, those characterized by relatively great dispersion, incomes received during a given year tend to be most uncertain either because of irregularity of employment or the uncertainty of receipts. Some of the highest paid workers such as salaried managers and officials in manufacturing plants (usually presidents of corporations) and real estate brokers are included in this group; however, the group is heavily dominated by such low-paid occupations as messengers, private household workers, certain types of laborers, apprentices, attendants, etc.

A closer examination of the third group of workers (i.e., those in occupations classified as having moderate dispersion) indicates that several additional categories can be established largely on the basis of regularity of receipts rather than on level of income. The occupations classified as having a relative quartile range between 40 and 50 percent are comprised basically of two broad groups of workers: (a) salaried workers such as foremen, linemen, designers, shipping clerks, and elevator operators who typically work for an annual wage but who have a wider range of incomes than the salaried workers previously described; and (b) workers in the metal trades such as mechanical craftsmen (blacksmiths, boilermakers, metal molders, and mechanics) and both operatives and laborers in the heavy goods industries. Workers in the metal-trades and heavy goods industries had steady employment in 1949 and relatively narrow wage differentials.

Occupations classified as having a relative quartile range between 60 and 80 percent are also comprised of two basically different types of workers: (a) those who are seriously affected by irregularity of employment such as construction workers (carpenters, painters, plasterers, masons), longshoremen, sailors and deck hands, and cooks; and (b) those who are affected by uncertainty of receipts such as authors, artists, salesmen, insurance agents, and various types of salaried managers, many of whose incomes, as presidents of small corporations, depend heavily upon the success of the business during a given year.

The occupational structure shows somewhat less stability when ranked with respect to dispersion than when ranked with respect to level of income. However, an examination of the data in table 28 leaves little doubt that occupations do form a definite and reasonably stable pattern when ranked with respect to dispersion. Of the 118 occupations shown in table 28, 75 were in the same decile or in an adjacent decile when ranked by dispersion in 1939 and 1949. Only 17 occupations changed by as many as three deciles.

TABLE **28.**—SELECTED OCCUPATIONS FOR MALE WAGE OR SALARY WORKERS RANKED BY
DISPERSION OF WAGE OR SALARY INCOME: 1949 AND 1939

Occupations ranked by dispersion of wage or salary income $\left(\frac{Q_3 - Q_1}{Q_2}\right)$	Occupations included in each tenth	
	1949	1939
Lowest tenth.........	Railroad conductors Baggagemen Mail carriers Telegraph operators Boilermakers Foremen--transportation Inspectors Locomotive engineers Machinists Brakemen Motormen (mine and railway) Operatives--rubber; motor vehicles; transportation equipment Firemen Policemen	Pharmacists Railroad conductors Baggagemen Mail carriers Telegraph operators Foremen--manufacturing; transportation Inspectors Locomotive engineers Stationary engineers Motormen (mine and railway) Operatives--paper; chemicals; motor vehicles Firemen Policemen
Second tenth.........	Shipping clerks Foremen--manufacturing Locomotive firemen Metal molders Metal rollers Welders Operatives--chemicals; iron and steel; machinery Laborers--iron and steel; motor vehicles	Shipping clerks Bakers Boilermakers Linemen Machinists Brakemen Welders Operatives--textiles; rubber: nonferrous metals; iron and steel Elevator operators Laborers--nonferrous metals
Third tenth..........	Designers Electricians Linemen Mechanics Stationary engineers Operatives--paper; nonferrous metals Laborers--nonferrous metals	Designers Electricians Mechanics Metal molders Metal rollers Operatives--footwear; leather; stone; machinery Guards and watchmen Laborers--textiles; railroads
Fourth tenth.........	Engineers--civil; mechanical Pharmacists Salaried managers--transportation Bakers Blacksmiths Structural metal workers Stationary firemen Painters (except construction) Operatives--textiles; stone Elevator operators Laborers--transportation equipment; railroads; paper	Engineers--civil Social workers Postmasters Salaried managers--business and repair services Bookkeepers Cabinetmakers Foremen--construction Locomotive firemen Printing craftsmen Tailors Stationary firemen Painters (except construction) Operatives--food Barbers Laborers--paper; machinery; motor vehicles; iron and steel
Fifth tenth..........	Engineers--electrical Teachers Postmasters Bookkeepers Cabinetmakers Foremen--construction Plumbers Roofers Tailors Operatives--footwear; leather Guards and watchmen Laborers--textiles	Chemists Salaried managers--retail trade Stenographers Compositors Plumbers Roofers Structural metal workers Mine operatives Operatives--lumber; transportation equipment Laborers--stone; telecommunications

TABLE **28.**—SELECTED OCCUPATIONS FOR MALE WAGE OR SALARY WORKERS RANKED BY DISPERSION OF WAGE OR SALARY INCOME: 1949 AND 1939—Cont.

Occupations ranked by dispersion of wage or salary income $\left(\dfrac{Q_3 - Q_1}{Q_2}\right)$	Occupations included in each tenth	
	1949	1939
Sixth tenth..........	Chemists Social workers Salaried managers--eating and drinking places; retail trade Insurance agents Compositors Printing craftsmen Apprentices Mine operatives Operatives--food Barbers Laborers--chemicals; telecommunications	Clergymen College presidents and professors Engineers--electrical; mechanical Teachers Salaried managers--transportation; eating and drinking places Insurance agents Blacksmiths Shoemakers Sailors Operatives--knitting mills; apparel Cooks Service workers (n.e.c.) Laborers--lumber; transportation equipment
Seventh tenth.........	Salaried managers--finance Chauffeurs Operatives--apparel Charmen	Masons Attendants Chauffeurs Waiters
Eighth tenth..........	Artists College presidents and professors Salaried managers--business and repair services; personal services Stenographers Salesmen Masons Sailors Cooks Longshoremen Laborers--food	Messengers Salesmen Plasterers Charmen Laborers--food
Ninth tenth..........	Authors Clergymen Dancers Salaried managers--wholesale trade Carpenters Painters (construction) Plasterers Shoemakers Operatives--knitting mills; lumber Waiters Laborers--transportation (except railroad)	Salaried managers--personal services Carpenters Painters (construction) Apprentices Longshoremen Laborers--trade; chemicals
Highest tenth.........	Musicians Salaried managers--manufacturing Messengers Newsboys Real estate agents Attendants Private household workers Service workers (n.e.c.) Fishermen Lumbermen Laborers--lumber; construction; trade	Artists Authors Dancers Musicians Salaried managers--finance; manufacturing; wholesale trade Newsboys Real estate agents Private household workers Fishermen Lumbermen Laborers--construction; transportation (except railroad)

Source: Derived from appendix tables C–1 and C–3.

C H A P T E R 6

AGE AS A FACTOR IN INCOME DISTRIBUTION

Variation of income by age

The average male worker enters the labor market either on a full-time or a part-time basis when he is in his teens. For several years he goes through an apprenticeship or training phase during which he is paid relatively little. During this period he learns general rather than specific skills and he tends to change jobs and interests frequently. By the time he is in his midtwenties he has usually selected the general field in which he plans to work, and he spends the next period of his working life acquiring skill and experience. When he is in his forties or early fifties he has usually attained the peak of his earning power, and from that time until he is ready to retire from the labor market his annual earnings shrink until they are not any higher than those he received as a young man. In retirement, his earnings are frequently replaced by receipts from other sources such as pensions or public assistance; but his total income is, on the average, still far below what he received in his prime.

The general pattern described above shows up very clearly in the figures in table 29.[1] The median income of male income recipients increased steeply from about $400 for those 14 to 19 years old to $1,700 for men 20 to 24 years old and $2,700 for men 25 to 34 years old. In the age group 35 to 44, the median reached its peak of $3,100 and then declined moderately for men between 45 and 64 years of age. Beyond age 65, sharply lower incomes were typical, reflecting, as in the case of the youngest group, the increasing prevalence of part-time employment. Among men 65 years old and over, the median was $1,100. Approximately the same pattern of variation was noted for white and nonwhite men and for farm and nonfarm residents.

---

[1] The Bureau of the Census data on income and age show the variations in the payments that the economic system makes to persons in different age groups at a given time (specifically, a given calendar year). These variations may be different from those that would be revealed by life-cycle data (i.e., records that trace a man's income from the time he first starts to work until he retires). There is some theoretical justification for the use of annual income data rather than life-cycle data for the analysis of the variation of income with age. It has been argued in earlier works touching upon this subject that annual data may be more useful for this type of analysis because they are "free from the influence of variants such as periods of industrial depression or unusual activity with their changes in opportunities for employment, in wage rates, and in the cost of living." (See W. S. Woytinsky, "Income cycle in the Life of Families and Individuals," *Social Security Bulletin,* June 1943, p. 9.)

There was much less variation of income by age among women than among men. The median income of women in age groups between 20 and 54 years ranged between $1,300 and $1,400. The median declined to $1,000 for women between 55 and 64 years old. Women 65 years of age and over who were income recipients had a median of $600.

TABLE 29.—MEDIAN INCOME IN 1949 OF PERSONS, BY RESIDENCE, AGE, COLOR, AND SEX

Age and sex	United States			Nonfarm			Farm		
	Total	White	Non-white	Total	White	Non-white	Total	White	Non-white
MALE									
Total with income....	$2,434	$2,572	$1,341	$2,613	$2,741	$1,571	$1,339	$1,489	$577
14 to 19 years..........	435	442	389	462	464	435	356	365	319
20 to 24 years..........	1,669	1,750	1,130	1,772	1,842	1,280	1,090	1,212	582
25 to 34 years..........	2,737	2,878	1,627	2,850	2,962	1,790	1,719	1,880	788
35 to 44 years..........	3,073	3,208	1,697	3,207	3,332	1,882	1,850	2,034	758
45 to 54 years..........	2,979	3,123	1,601	3,140	3,269	1,821	1,697	1,884	680
55 to 64 years..........	2,551	2,670	1,260	2,766	2,871	1,529	1,354	1,463	585
65 years and over........	1,128	1,212	593	1,246	1,314	692	789	860	406
FEMALE									
Total with income....	$1,029	$1,137	$584	$1,104	$1,200	$672	$458	$533	$311
14 to 19 years..........	419	437	313	441	454	335	320	338	268
20 to 24 years..........	1,276	1,386	551	1,323	1,422	514	657	889	308
25 to 34 years..........	1,309	1,448	750	1,366	1,497	817	525	742	324
35 to 44 years..........	1,358	1,504	742	1,426	1,568	810	547	732	329
45 to 54 years..........	1,316	1,456	641	1,391	1,525	712	542	693	327
55 to 64 years..........	1,006	1,092	497	1,077	1,154	572	481	549	321
65 years and over........	602	630	390	631	654	415	399	421	308

Source: U. S. Bureau of the Census, *U. S. Census of Population: 1950*, Vol. II, *Characteristics of the Population*, Part 1, U. S. Summary, table 139.

While the data in table 29 are useful for portraying the over-all picture of the variation of income with age, they have some serious shortcomings. Income is highly correlated with educational attainment, and men in the older age groups have considerably less schooling than younger men. For example, in April 1950 the average (median) years of school completed decreased from 12 years for men under 30 years of age to 8 years for men over 55.[2] Variations of this magnitude in educational attainment could introduce important differences in the level of income among age groups. It is therefore important to analyze the variation of income with age separately for men with different educational backgrounds. The data required for this analysis are shown in tables 30 and 31 and in figure 10. These data clearly show that the variation of income with age is more striking when each of the education groups is examined separately than when they are merged. Thus, although the 1949 data indicate that the average income of all men over 25 years old (without respect to educational attainment) is at a plateau between the ages of 30 and 54, it is quite evident from the data for each of the education groups that the average income of

[2] U. S. Bureau of the Census, *U. S. Census of Population: 1950*, Series P-E, No. 5B, *Education*, table 12.

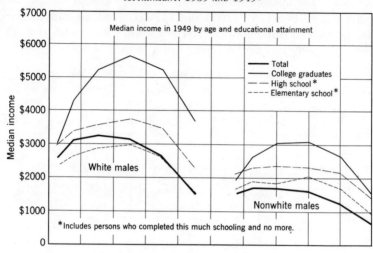

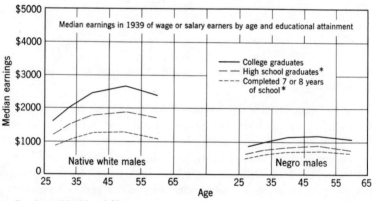

Note: Based on tables 30 and 31.

white men rises gradually between the ages of 25 and 45 years; it reaches a peak between the ages of 45 and 54 years and declines beyond that point. The pattern is substantially the same for nonwhite men except that their average income is at a plateau between the ages of 35 and 54. These patterns are quite stable inasmuch as they appeared in the figures for 1939 as well as 1949.

Another conclusion suggested by the data in tables 30 and 31 is that there are striking differences in the pattern of variation of income with age among men having varying amounts of schooling. In 1949, the median income of white men who completed grammar school, but went no further in their education, increased from about $2,300 for those who were in their late twenties to a peak of $3,000 for those who were either in or near

TABLE **30.**—MEDIAN INCOME IN 1949 OF MEN 25 YEARS OLD AND OVER, BY YEARS OF SCHOOL COMPLETED, AGE, AND COLOR

Years of school completed and color	Total, 25 years old and over	25 to 29 years	30 to 34 years	35 to 44 years	45 to 54 years	55 to 64 years	65 to 74 years	75 years and over
WHITE								
Total with income..........	$2,842	$2,648	$3,099	$3,241	$3,145	$2,671	$1,469	$785
No schooling...................	1,371	1,154	1,242	1,435	1,860	2,038	941	572
Elementary: 1 to 4 years.......	1,550	1,470	1,690	1,854	2,067	1,998	917	603
5 to 7 years.......	2,151	1,923	2,205	2,426	2,511	2,250	1,210	699
8 years............	2,582	2,318	2,623	2,870	2,965	2,629	1,527	803
High school: 1 to 3 years.......	2,994	2,652	3,000	3,251	3,269	2,984	1,816	963
4 years............	3,325	2,927	3,346	3,563	3,733	3,477	2,291	1,233
College: 1 to 3 years.......	3,573	2,810	3,638	4,026	4,183	3,650	2,395	1,353
4 years or more....	4,469	2,961	4,277	5,216	5,625	5,217	3,665	1,920
NONWHITE								
Total with income..........	$1,486	$1,542	$1,708	$1,703	$1,615	$1,255	$667	$440
No schooling...................	782	882	1,000	1,085	1,038	834	531	389
Elementary: 1 to 4 years.......	1,031	1,069	1,201	1,254	1,238	947	570	423
5 to 7 years.......	1,489	1,390	1,516	1,615	1,665	1,410	747	499
8 years............	1,851	1,678	1,885	1,983	2,048	1,803	916	614
High school: 1 to 3 years.......	1,982	1,816	2,034	2,127	2,111	1,911	968	563
4 years............	2,245	2,123	2,306	2,371	2,336	2,179	1,419	(1)
College: 1 to 3 years.......	2,255	1,845	2,453	2,490	2,417	2,116	1,405	(1)
4 years or more....	2,633	1,969	2,615	3,048	3,100	2,676	1,533	(1)

[1] Median not shown because there were fewer than 3,000 persons in the population.

Source: Derived from U. S. Bureau of the Census, *U. S. Census of Population: 1950*, Series P–E, No. 5B, *Education*, tables 12 and 13.

TABLE **31.**—MEDIAN EARNINGS IN 1939 OF MALE WAGE OR SALARY EARNERS 25 TO 64 YEARS OLD, BY YEARS OF SCHOOL COMPLETED, AGE, NATIVITY, AND COLOR

Nativity, color, and years of school completed	25 to 29 years	30 to 34 years	35 to 44 years	45 to 54 years	55 to 64 years
NATIVE WHITE					
Total........................	$1,017	$1,229	$1,370	$1,349	$1,090
No schooling........................	407	471	486	503	463
Elementary: 1 to 4 years............	406	497	620	694	598
5 and 6 years...........	565	730	893	952	825
7 and 8 years...........	820	1,019	1,228	1,280	1,095
High school: 1 to 3 years............	1,024	1,259	1,480	1,556	1,332
4 years.................	1,176	1,473	1,764	1,875	1,711
College: 1 to 3 years............	1,330	1,654	1,915	1,953	1,518
4 years or more........	1,567	1,998	2,465	2,679	2,395
NEGRO					
Total........................	$448	$527	$580	$541	$480
No schooling........................	316	348	387	373	364
Elementary: 1 to 4 years...........	345	390	446	424	402
5 and 6 years.........	410	507	570	600	559
7 and 8 years...........	522	633	711	732	682
High school: 1 to 3 years............	596	682	755	753	678
4 years.................	689	770	856	902	787
College: 1 to 3 years............	704	792	888	968	875
4 years or more........	882	1,000	1,157	1,201	1,103

Source: Derived from Sixteenth Decennial Census of Population, *Education: Educational Attainment by Economic Characteristics and Marital Status*, tables 29 and 31. The data in this table are restricted to persons reporting $1 or more of wage or salary income and no other income.

their fifties.   In other words, the difference in average income between men in this group who were beginning their working careers and those who were at their peak was only about $700 or 30 percent.   About the same relative difference was found for white high school graduates.   In the case of college graduates, however, the median incomes for white men in these age groups were $3,000 and $5,600 respectively.   Obviously, the income differential between young men and those who have reached the age of peak income is much greater for college graduates than that for other men.   The income of the 50-year-old college graduate is 90 percent greater than that of the college graduate who is in his late twenties as compared with the 30-percent differential that was noted for grammar school graduates and high school graduates.   The comparable proportions for nonwhite men were 20 percent for grammar school graduates, 10 percent for high school graduates, and 90 percent for college graduates.

Income of the aged

The past few years have witnessed a great expansion of both interest and information on problems of the aged.   This increase is perhaps directly attributable to general recognition of the fact that the aged are becoming of increasing importance in our population.   In 1900, only 4 in every 100 Americans were 65 years old and over.   In 1950, the proportion was 8 in 100, and it is estimated that in 1975 the proportion will be about 10 in 100.[3]   There are, of course, many different facets to the problems associated with an aging population.   In this study, attention is focused primarily on those aspects of the problem that relate to income distribution.

There were, at the time of the 1950 Census, about 12.3 million persons 65 years old and over in the United States.[4] Approximately 385,000 lived in institutions (218,000 in old-age homes, 141,000 in mental hospitals, and 27,000 in other places)[5] and the rest lived in households.   The 1950 Census data regarding the income of institutional inmates are not complete because a large proportion did not provide the information.   The data obtained from those who did report, however, indicate that this group was not at all well off financially.   As table 32 shows, about two-thirds of the inmates 65 years old and over who provided the income information had no income at all during 1949, and only half of those with income received as much as $700.

Because of their greater numbers and also because the institutional pop-

---

[3] Estimates for 1900 and 1950 derived from U. S. Bureau of the Census, *U. S. Census of Population: 1950*, Vol. II, *Characteristics of the Population*, Part 1, U. S. Summary, table 39.   Estimates for 1975 derived from U. S. Bureau of the Census, *Current Population Reports—Population Estimates*, Series P–25, No. 78, table 1.

[4] U. S. Bureau of the Census, *U. S. Census of Population: 1950*, Vol. II, *Characteristics of the Population*, Part 1, U. S. Summary, table 39.

[5] U. S. Bureau of the Census, *U. S. Census of Population: 1950*, Series P–E, No. 2C, *Institutional Population*, tables 3, 5, and 7.

ulation largely includes persons suffering from various types of disabilities that prevent normal participation in economic activity, there is more interest in the circumstances of the noninstitutional population than in those of institutional inmates. Although some data relating to the living arrangements of aged persons are available for this group from the 1950 Census, a more complete picture may be obtained from information collected in a special survey of persons 65 years old and over, conducted in April 1952 by the Bureau of the Census for the Institute of Industrial Relations of the University of California. In this survey it was found that the 12.0 million noninstitutional persons aged 65 or more formed 9.8 million economic units; i.e., 3.8 million married couples in which the husband was 65 or more, and 1.8 million men and 4.2 million women who either had no spouse or were living apart from their spouse at the time of the survey. A large proportion of the married couples tend to maintain their own households; however, male individuals and particularly female individuals are much more apt to move in with their children. As table 33 shows, two-thirds of the married couples live alone, whereas only one-half of the male individuals and two-fifths of the female individuals live apart from their relatives. Where elderly married couples lived with relatives, in 9 cases out of 10 the husband retained his status as family head; however, only one-third of the male and female individuals who lived with relatives were regarded as family heads. Particularly significant is the fact that where an elderly couple lived with one or more of their children, the husband was regarded as the family head, whereas male and female individuals who lived with their children were reported as dependents.

The data in table 33 suggest some of the complexities that are encountered in the interpretation of the income data for a segment of the population that, typically, depends upon others for support. Married couples or individuals who live alone tend to rely entirely upon their own resources.

TABLE 32.—INCOME IN 1949 OF PERSONS 65 YEARS OLD AND OVER IN THE INSTITUTIONAL POPULATION

Total money income in 1949	Number	Percent	Total money income in 1949	Number	Percent
Total..................	[1]378,150	100.0	Total with income......	53,520	100.0
Reporting on income........	165,360	43.7	Under $500..................	16,950	31.7
Not reporting on income....	212,790	56.3	$500 to $999................	23,970	44.8
			$1,000 to $1,499...........	7,920	14.8
			$1,500 to $1,999...........	2,280	4.3
Total reporting........	165,360	100.0	$2,000 to $2,999...........	1,200	2.2
			$3,000 to $3,999...........	510	1.0
Without income.............	111,840	67.6	$4,000 and over............	690	1.3
With income................	53,520	32.4			
			Median income..............	$705	...

[1] This total is based on 3⅓-percent sample tabulations and therefore differs slightly from the previously mentioned total of 385,000 which was derived from a 100-percent count.

Source: Derived from U. S. Bureau of the Census, *U. S. Census of Population: 1950*, Series P–E, No. 2C, *Institutional Population*, table 18.

Therefore, the income data for this group have a reasonably clear meaning.[6] However, the income figures for married couples or individuals living with relatives have a somewhat different meaning because of the possibility that these groups will pool their resources with those of their relatives. For example, table 33 shows that the receipts of women over 65 who lived alone were almost twice as great as those of women in the same age group who were living with relatives. It is also true, however, that the total receipts of the family group with which women 65 and over resided

TABLE **33.**—MEDIAN RECEIPTS IN 1951 OF ELDERLY COUPLES AND OTHER INDIVIDUALS, BY TYPE OF LIVING ARRANGEMENTS AND SEX

Living arrangements in April 1952[1]	Married couples	Male individuals	Female individuals	Married couples	Male individuals	Female individuals
Number................thousands..	3,763	1,810	4,230	...	...	...
	Percent distribution			Median receipts[2]		
Total..........................	100.0	100.0	100.0	$1,491	$732	$447
Living with relatives................	30.9	49.2	59.2	1,289	629	370
Not living with relatives............	69.1	50.8	40.8	1,599	801	664
Total living with relatives......	100.0	100.0	100.0	...	...	...
Family head.........................	87.7	36.3	34.2	$1,375	(3)	$444
Living with adult children.........	73.1	22.5	26.9	1,357	(3)	410
Not living with adult children.....	14.6	13.8	7.3	(3)	(3)	(3)
Parent of family head...............	10.6	40.1	49.7	(3)	(3)	330
Other relative of family head........	1.7	23.6	16.1	(3)	(3)	378

[1] Describes the living arrangements of the married couple or the individual. For example, the category "Family head" represents cases where the husband of the elderly couple or the individual was classified as the head of the family group in a given household. Similarly, the category "Parent of family head" represents cases in which the head of the elderly couple or the individual was classified as the parent of the person who was regarded as the head of the household by the respondent.

The units in this table are restricted to couples in which the husband was 65 years of age and over and to other individuals 65 years of age and over, who were not living in institutions.

[2] The term "receipts" as used here is defined more broadly than income. In addition to income as defined elsewhere in this study, it includes miscellaneous cash receipts as well as savings used to meet ·expenses.

[3] Median not shown where there were fewer than 100 cases in the sample reporting on receipts.

Source: Unpublished data prepared by the Bureau of the Census for the Institute of Industrial Relations of the University of California.

were considerably greater than $700. It is apparent therefore that, although the figures on income or receipts for older persons are quite meaningful for some subgroups of that population, they must be used with caution when considering other subgroups. One interesting fact that the figures on receipts in table 33 show is that the income differential between elderly women who were living with relatives and those who were not living with relatives was considerably greater than the corresponding differ-

[6] There is some ambiguity in the meaning of the income data for the members of this group who receive contributions from their children or other relatives not living with them.

ential for elderly men or married couples. Economic necessity is apparently a much more important factor in the explanation of the decision of elderly women to move in with their children than it is in the case of either elderly men or married couples.

Source of income by age

The source pattern of income varies considerably among persons in different age groups. Earnings represent the most important source of income among all men except those in the very oldest age group. As indicated in table 34, there is a steady decrease with advancing age in the importance of wages or salaries and an increase in the importance of self-employment as a source of income among men in each age group between 25 and 64 years. Wages and salaries were the only source of income for nearly three-fourths of the men between 25 and 34 years, whereas they constituted the sole source for only a little more than half of the men between 55 and 64 years. In contrast, the proportion of men in these same age groups who derived their entire income from the operation of a farm, business, or professional practice increased from 7 percent to 19 percent.

Some of the economic aspects of old age may be seen by comparing the income source pattern of men aged 65 and over with that of men about

TABLE **34.**—SOURCE OF INCOME IN 1951 OF PERSONS, BY AGE AND SEX

Source of income in 1951	Total, 65 years and over	14 to 24 years	25 to 34 years	35 to 44 years	45 to 54 years	55 to 64 years	65 years and over
MALE							
Total..........................	100.0	100.0	100.0	100.0	100.0	100.0	100.0
Percent with income..................	90.1	62.0	98.8	98.8	98.2	95.4	88.9
Percent without income..............	9.9	38.0	1.2	1.2	1.8	4.6	11.1
Total with income................	100.0	100.0	100.0	100.0	100.0	100.0	100.0
Earnings only........................	80.0	94.2	82.4	87.7	86.8	77.1	32.9
Wages or salary only..............	65.6	89.2	72.2	70.8	66.2	55.3	20.3
Self-employment income only........	11.2	3.7	6.8	12.5	16.5	18.5	10.8
Wages or salary and self-employment income..............................	3.2	1.3	3.4	4.4	4.2	3.3	1.8
Earnings and other income...........	13.1	4.3	16.5	11.7	11.4	15.2	19.9
Other income; no earnings...........	6.9	1.5	1.1	0.7	1.8	7.6	47.2
FEMALE							
Total..........................	100.0	100.0	100.0	100.0	100.0	100.0	100.0
Percent with income..................	43.7	43.7	41.6	42.6	44.4	38.0	55.1
Percent without income..............	56.3	56.3	58.4	57.4	55.6	62.0	44.9
Total with income................	100.0	100.0	100.0	100.0	100.0	100.0	100.0
Earnings only........................	72.4	91.3	86.8	86.4	77.8	55.4	11.9
Wages or salary only..............	68.2	90.5	83.8	80.3	70.0	48.0	9.1
Self-employment income only........	3.7	0.3	2.4	5.1	6.9	7.0	2.8
Wages or salary and self-employment income..............................	0.6	0.5	0.7	1.0	0.9	0.4	...
Earnings and other income...........	6.6	3.4	4.9	6.0	7.9	14.6	7.3
Other income; no earnings...........	20.9	5.3	8.3	7.6	14.3	29.9	80.8

Source: U. S. Bureau of the Census, *Current Population Reports—Consumer Income*, Series P–60, No. 11, table C.

10 years younger, on the average (i.e., those between 55 and 64 years of age). All but a small proportion of the men between 55 and 64 years old were income recipients, the great majority of whom derived their income entirely from earnings. Less than 10 percent of them depended entirely upon income other than earnings. In contrast, about one-tenth of the men aged 65 or more received no income during the year, and about one-half of those who were income recipients derived their income entirely from pensions, assistance, and other forms of income other than earnings. Only one-third of the men in this age group depended entirely upon earnings.

For women, as in the case of men, there was relatively little variation in the proportion between the ages of 25 and 64 who were income recipients. Unlike the pattern for men, however, the proportion of female income recipients increased in the oldest age group. Over half of the female income recipients in the 55-to-64-year age group depended entirely upon earnings, and less than one-third derived all their income from sources other than earnings. In contrast, only one-tenth of those in the oldest age group derived all their income from earnings, and four-fifths depended entirely upon sources other than earnings.

There is some evidence that the relative income position of older persons in the United States, particularly older men, has worsened during the post-World War II period. Between 1947 and 1951 the median income of men of all ages increased by about one-third, whereas there was no change in the median income of older men or women. Moreover, this period witnessed a substantial increase in prices, which undoubtedly reduced the purchasing power of older persons (table 35).

Despite evidence of a declining labor force rate for older men and a stable labor force rate for older women, the proportion of income recipients has increased for both groups. This change suggests that during the past few years an increasing proportion of older men have become eligible for social security or private pension plans, or have turned to public relief, and other forms of income other than earnings as a source of financial support. The increase in the proportion of income recipients among older women may be attributable to the gain in the number of social insurance beneficiaries, many of whom, in the absence of a benefit program, would have no current income of their own and would have been living either with relatives or by converting their assets into cash. These additional income recipients were very likely to be found at the lower end of the income scale, thereby reducing the averages for both men and women.

The discussion of income and labor force status of elderly persons brings to the fore the question of employment as a source of income maintenance in old age. This is a subject on which society has not taken a very consistent stand.

In the 1930's, when the labor supply problem was one of surplus, efforts were made to get older workers out of the labor market. A program de-

TABLE **35.**—MEDIAN INCOME, LABOR FORCE RATE, AND PROPORTION OF INCOME RECIPIENTS, BY AGE AND SEX: 1947 TO 1951

Year	Male						Female					
	14 years and over			65 years and over			14 years and over			65 years and over		
	Median income	Percent		Median income	Percent		Median income	Percent		Median income	Percent	
		In labor force	With income		In labor force	With income		In labor force	With income		In labor force	With income
1947.............	$2,230	84	89	$956	48	84	$1,017	31	39	$551	8	47
1948.............	2,396	85	90	998	47	89	1,009	32	41	589	9	49
1949.............	2,346	85	90	1,016	47	88	960	32	42	516	10	53
1950.............	2,570	84	90	986	46	90	953	33	43	531	10	54
1951.............	2,952	85	90	1,008	45	89	1,045	34	44	536	9	55

Source: U. S. Bureau of the Census, *Current Population Reports—Consumer Income*, Series P–60, No. 11, table E.

signed to promote retirement at 65 for the bulk of American workers was born in this period. Advanced thinking hailed it as the means for a happy, leisurely future for the tired laborer and as a relief to the crowded labor market. One eminent labor official proclaimed in 1933: "Older persons must be enabled to retire voluntarily from industry, at 60 in the case of men and 55 in the case of females. . . . Such a course would remove from the labor market the marginal older workers and reduce the competition among employable workers for the available jobs." [7] An authority on industrial pensions, who was one of the fathers of the Social Security Act, proclaimed in 1935 before a Congressional committee: "Older workers are a disrupting factor in the labor market when both unemployed and looking for work and frequently when employed." [8]

During World War II and the postwar period the labor supply situation was radically different. Instead of surplus, there was shortage. The problem of supporting the aged still existed, social security and private pension plans not yet having reached full maturity. But hope for the "double-play" solution was born anew. The same labor official who was so anxious in 1933 to get the workers out of the labor market at age 55 or 60, concluded in 1952 that ". . . the social and economic costs of retirement are so huge that we must consider means of extending employment opportunities. . . . The larger number of workers increases output and relieves the economy of the cost of maintaining unproductive persons." [9] The Federal Security Agency no longer regards the older worker as a "disrupting factor." On the contrary, its chief official announced in 1951: "We have been too much inclined to put these people (the aged) on the shelf. The

---

[7] Solomon Barkin, *The Older Worker in Industry*, J. B. Lyon Co., 1933, New York, p. 401.

[8] Testimony of Murray Latimer in *Hearings Before House Committee on Ways and Means on H.R. 4120*, 74th Congress, 1st Session, January–February 1935, p. 222.

[9] Solomon Barkin, "Should There Be a Fixed Retirement Age?—Organized Labor Says No," *Annals of the American Academy of Political and Social Science*, January 1952, p. 78.

present emergency calls for every short-cut we can devise to bring into the service of the country the skills and the wisdom of those who have been pushed out. This calls for their reemployment wherever possible. . . ." [10]

The reasoning during the prosperous 1950's is simple and appealing, just as was the contrary thinking of the depressed 1930's. But which is realistic? It may be instructive to examine a few facts about the employment situation and behavior of our aging population.

In March 1951, when an intensive survey of the labor reserve was made by the Bureau of the Census,[11] there were 11.6 million people 65 years of age or over in the noninstitutional population. About 6.2 million were women and 5.5 million were men. One-half of these people were 72 years old and over. Nearly 3 million of the total were employed, and an additional 1½ million classified themselves as physically unable to work.[12] This left a "labor reserve" of about 7 million people over 65 who were ostensibly able to work but who were not either working or seeking work. Why were these people out of the labor force? To what extent was their economic inactivity a function of discrimination, disinterest, or a mixture of both? Some of the answers to these questions may be obtained from an examination of their collective work histories during the decade between 1941 and 1951.

In the Bureau of the Census study referred to above, persons 65 years old or over were asked about their work experience during the preceding 10 years. Able-bodied people who were not working at the time of the survey were asked when and why they had stopped. Of the 7 million people in this group, 5.3 million (mainly women) reported that they had not been gainfully employed even a single day during the decade.[13] Their total absence from the labor market during this period indicates that not even the pressures of World War II could induce them to accept jobs or employers to provide jobs for them. Of the remaining 1.7 million with some work experience, 0.6 million worked during the war but did not have any paid employment during the postwar years.[14] Fewer than 50,000 said they stopped working involuntarily because they were laid off or could not find suitable work. About three-fourths of the group said they stopped working because they were too old, too ill, or because they voluntarily retired.[15]

On the basis of these figures, it could be said that in March 1951 there were about 1.1 million elderly people who were not working but who, by

---

[10] Press release of the Federal Security Agency, January 24, 1951.

[11] For a description of this survey as well as a summary of the results see, U. S. Bureau of the Census, *Current Population Reports—Labor Force*, Series P–50, No. 38.

[12] U. S. Bureau of the Census, *Current Population Reports—Labor Force*, Series P–57, No. 105, table 6.

[13] U. S. Bureau of the Census, *Current Population Reports—Labor Force*, Series P–50, No. 38, table 1.

[14] *Ibid.*, table 1.

[15] *Ibid.*, table 6.

their actions, exhibited some recent interest in work. The reasons given by these people in the survey for stopping work do not indicate any strong proclivity on their part to return to work.[16] Only about 100,000 indicated that they quit the labor market because they were laid off, could not find suitable work, or because working conditions or community facilities were poor. Once again the vast majority (80 percent) indicated that they felt too ill or too old to work or that they had voluntarily retired. There is undoubtedly some hidden unemployment among this group, and it is hazardous to estimate the proportion that could be induced to return to work. It is known, however, that about 200,000 gave up their own farms or businesses to go into retirement.[17] Many of the remaining 900,000 were retired on pensions or were well along in years, even for old people, and would probably resist efforts to get them back to work.

Recent evidence regarding the attitudes of older persons towards employment suggest even more strongly that disinterest or inability to hold down a job under prevailing conditions of employment rather than discrimination is probably the basic factor that keeps a large proportion of older persons out of the labor market. The unpublished data of the University of California referred to above show that only 14 percent of the aged persons with work experience withdrew from the labor market involuntarily and only half of these because of compulsory retirement systems. Further, the results of a national survey of Old-Age and Survivors Insurance beneficiaries, which was conducted in 1951, shows that only one-eighth of this group was able and willing to work but was not working.[18] Published results for the state of Rhode Island[19] and unpublished results of the national survey sponsored by the University of California indicate that the proportion for the total population over 65 is about the same as that for Old-Age and Survivors Insurance beneficiaries.

The above calculations are quite consistent with the observed past behavior of the Nation's labor force. In fact, in historical perspective, it can only be concluded that the attempts to solve the problems of the aged by putting them to work is like swimming upstream against a very strong current. One of the very striking trends in the employment picture for the United States has been the persistent decline in the proportion of workers among older people. Until recently, this decline has frequently been pointed to with pride as a reflection of our high standard of living. In 1890, about 68 percent of the men 65 and over were in the labor market. By 1920, this proportion had dropped to 56 percent, and in 1940 it had de-

---

[16] *Ibid.*, table 6.

[17] *Ibid.*, table 5.

[18] Preliminary findings from the national survey of Old-Age and Survivors Insurance beneficiaries, May 1952, Fact Sheet 6, "Ability to Work and Attitude Toward Employment."

[19] *Old Age in Rhode Island*, Report of the Governors Commission to Study Problems of the Aged, July 1953, table VII.

clined still more to about 42 percent.[20] The temporary increase in this proportion during the war has since leveled off, and in 1951 about the same proportion of the aged were in the labor force as in 1940. If the long-range trend established in the past continues to exert an influence, the proportions in the future will be still lower.

The facts indicated should dispel some of the illusions that still exist about the attitudes of older persons towards employment and about the importance of employment as a source of income maintenance for the aged. There may be little basis for challenging the view that older people should continue to work because they will be healthier and happier. However, there are excellent reasons for doubting that they *prefer* to work. The available evidence indicates that even when there is an abundance of job opportunities, only a relatively small proportion of the aged reenter the labor market. The evidence is by no means complete; nevertheless, it should induce some doubt as to whether the fundamental element in solving the problems of the aged really lies in "maximizing opportunities for them to support themselves, primarily through employment. . . ." as prescribed by the National Conference on Aging.[21] Perhaps there are other solutions to this problem more in accord with the desires of the aged themselves.

Age and veteran status

The period between 1947 and 1951 witnessed some rather important and striking changes in the income relationships within some of the younger age groups as well as the older age groups in the population. During this period, the median income of World War II veterans in the 25-to-34-year age group (which includes a majority of the veterans) increased by about 40 percent (from $2,400 to $3,400) whereas the income of nonveterans in this age group increased by only about 10 percent (from $2,600 to $2,900). In 1947, the median income of nonveterans was slightly higher than that of veterans, and in 1948 the income of both groups was about the same. By 1949, the fourth full year after the end of the war, the median income of veterans was higher than that of nonveterans; and, in 1950, as a result of relatively greater gains for veterans, the gap in the incomes of the two groups was widened still further. The relative difference between the incomes of veterans and nonveterans in 1951 was about the same as it was during the preceding year.

The relatively large increase in the income of veterans in this age group (25 to 34 years) is attributable in part to the fact that many of them were employed only part time in 1947 while they were attending school or seek-

---

[20]John D. Durand, *The Labor Force in the United States: 1890–1960*, Social Science Research Council, New York, 1948, p. 208.

[21] *Man and His Years: An Account of the First National Conference on Aging*, Health Publications Institute, North Carolina, p. 41.

ing suitable employment. For many veterans, 1948 was the first full year of civilian employment. In addition, for those veterans who did not go to school, the three full years of civilian working experience they had obtained by 1948 may have been required to bring them up to the level of nonveterans in skill and experience. The higher incomes of these veterans during the past three years may reflect the combined influence of the increase in work experience and the higher level of education that veterans have achieved as compared with nonveterans.

TABLE **36.**—MEDIAN INCOME OF MEN 25 TO 34 YEARS OLD, BY VETERAN STATUS: 1947 TO 1951

Year	Veterans	Nonveterans
1947..	$2,401	$2,585
1948..	2,734	2,692
1949..	2,828	2,562
1950..	3,058	2,626
1951..	3,359	2,875

Source: U. S. Bureau of the Census, *Current Population Reports—Consumer Income*, Series P–60, No. 11, table D.

FIGURE **11.**—MEDIAN INCOME OF MEN 25 TO 34 YEARS OLD, BY VETERAN STATUS: 1947 TO 1951

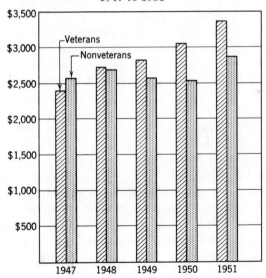

Source: U. S. Bureau of the Census, *Current Population Reports—Consumer Income*, Series P–60, No. 14, p. 3.

CHAPTER 7

INCOME AND FAMILY STATUS

Personal income and family income

The discussion up to this point has been in terms of the analysis of individual income rather than family income because in our society income generally accrues to the individual rather than to the family group. At the same time, however, family status is an important factor in determining whether or not an individual will be an income recipient. Therefore, no discussion of individual income would be complete without giving consideration to the role of family status.

A relatively small proportion of the civilian noninstitutional population (about 6 percent) live as unrelated individuals, which means that they are not members of family groups as defined by the Bureau of the Census. These unrelated individuals either provide entirely for their own support or else they are supported in part or in full by people who do not live with them. The remainder of the civilian noninstitutional population belong to family groups. Some members of these groups such as husbands and grown children tend to assume the role of providers. Others, such as housewives and small children, tend to be dependents. They frequently are also income recipients; however, their attachment to the economic world is basically different from that of individuals who are providers. The members of a family group generally attempt to maximize the welfare of the entire group rather than that of any individual in the group. This fact must be considered in the analysis of personal income, particularly with respect to individuals who do not have permanent attachments to the economic world. It is only by considering the family income of these individuals, rather than their personal income, that their economic activity can be understood. It is for this reason that the consideration of family status as a factor in income distribution brings to the fore the problems associated with the transition from personal income to family income. Family status is undoubtedly an important factor in explaining the income position of many individuals. However, as subsequent analysis will show, the reverse is also true; namely, that for many other individuals income is an important part of the explanation of family status.

Considering the personal income of individuals with respect to their family status, it is apparent from table 37 that, among men, the proportion who were income recipients ranged from 96 percent of the married men

living with their wives to between 85 and 90 percent of the men who were
unrelated individuals, adult relatives of family head (i.e., relatives between
20 and 64 years old), or family heads who were either not married or not
living with their wives. Among the men in the youngest and oldest age
groups, only about two-fifths of those between 14 and 19 years old and
three-fifths of those over 65 were income recipients.

In contrast to men, there were much larger variations in the proportions
of income recipients among women. The largest proportions of income
recipients (between 70 and 80 percent) were found among unrelated individuals and family heads; i.e., those primarily responsible for their own
support and the support of others. A relatively large proportion of the
adult relatives were also income recipients; and, as might be expected, a
comparatively small proportion (about one-third) of the wives or young
daughters of family heads were income recipients. To some extent, however, the use of proportions in this connection is somewhat misleading because the last two groups, the wives and daughters, comprise more than
half of the female labor force and also about half of the income recipients
among women.

TABLE 37.—INCOME IN 1949 OF PERSONS, BY FAMILY STATUS, AGE, AND SEX

Family status, age, and sex	Percent with income	Median income in 1949	Family status, age, and sex	Percent with income	Median income in 1949
MALE			FEMALE		
Families:			Families:		
Head......................	95.9	$2,849	Head......................	71.2	$1,199
Married, wife present.....	96.3	2,880	Wife of head..............	32.1	937
Other marital status......	88.2	2,017	Other relative of head......	48.0	1,074
Relative of head...........	65.9	1,304	14 to 19 years...........	29.0	410
14 to 19 years...........	40.8	402	20 to 64 years...........	64.2	1,602
20 to 64 years...........	86.2	1,892	65 years and over........	40.9	457
65 years and over........	61.2	686	Unrelated individuals........	79.0	1,138
Unrelated individuals........	89.1	1,447			

Source: U. S. Bureau of the Census, *U. S. Census of Population: 1950*, Vol. II, *Characteristics of
the Population*, Part 1, U. S. Summary, table 140.

The amount of income received, as well as the likelihood of receiving
any income at all, is related to family status. The highest incomes were
received by male heads of families living with their wives. This group
averaged about $2,900. The average income of family heads who were
not married or who were living apart from their wives ($2,000) was not
much higher than that received by men 20 to 64 years old who were relatives (mostly sons) of family heads. The average income of male unrelated individuals was about $1,400, and, of course, the lowest average
incomes were received by the youngest and the oldest men ($400 and $700
respectively).

Whereas there was a marked variation of income among the different
groups of men, female income recipients who were family heads had about

the same average income ($1,200) as unrelated individuals and only slightly higher incomes (in an absolute sense) than wives. The highest average incomes ($1,600) were received by relatives (largely daughters) in the 20-to-64-year age group.

Income as a factor in family formation

Family formation is a complex phenomenon that is a function of many different social, psychological, and economic factors. The income data obtained in the 1950 Census provide, at best, very limited insight into the process of family formation; however, the data do suggest that, among men, the tendency to marry and to assume family responsibility is very closely related to income. Moreover, there is considerable evidence that income differences among families can be explained largely, although by no means entirely, in terms of the characteristics of the family head.

At the time of the 1950 Census there were 54.6 million men over 14 years of age in the United States. Of these, about 35.0 million were married and living with their wives; 5.2 million had been married but were widowed, divorced, or living apart from their wives at the time of the census; and 14.4 million were never married.[1] About two-thirds of the last group were under 25 years old. A large proportion of them will undoubtedly marry at some time; however, about 5 million were past the age when most marriages occur. Table 38 compares the incomes of married men living with their wives with the incomes of single men in the same age groups. One of the striking facts shown in this table is that in each age group, married men have higher incomes, on the average, than single men. Moreover, the table also shows that men who marry and form their own households have higher average incomes than men who marry but become part of existing households. Thus, for example, 76 percent of the married men between 25 and 34 years old who were household heads had incomes over $2,000 in 1949, whereas only 56 percent of the married men who continued to live with their parents (or in-laws) and only 64 percent of the married men who joined other family groups had incomes this high. Among single men in this age group, those who were household heads (e.g., those who supported their parents or other relatives) had the highest incomes. About 62 percent of these men had incomes over $2,000 in 1949; however, less than one-half of the other single men in this age group had incomes this high.

In most of the age groups for which data are presented, marriage preceded the income period (1949) by at least several years, and in some of the age groups by many years. Therefore, there is no simple relation between these two variables. For example, it would be somewhat hazardous

---

[1] U. S. Bureau of the Census, *U. S. Census of Population: 1950*, Series P–E, No. 2D, *Marital Status*, table 6.

TABLE 38.—INCOME IN 1949 OF MEN IN SELECTED AGE AND FAMILY STATUS GROUPS, BY MARITAL STATUS

Family status and age	Total	No income	$1 to $999	$1,000 to $1,999	$2,000 to $2,999	$3,000 to $3,999	$4,000 and over
SINGLE							
Primary family head:							
20 to 24 years	100.0	6.1	24.7	25.6	28.6	12.6	2.4
25 to 34 years	100.0	3.9	14.2	20.0	28.5	21.1	12.3
35 to 44 years	100.0	4.2	18.0	18.1	23.9	19.4	16.4
45 to 54 years	100.0	6.9	20.7	17.8	21.3	16.5	16.8
Child of head:							
20 to 24 years	100.0	17.2	30.8	23.8		28.1	
25 to 34 years	100.0	12.2	20.8	21.4		45.5	
35 to 44 years	100.0	14.2	21.2	18.1		46.5	
45 years and over	100.0	18.7	25.7	16.9		38.6	
Other member of primary family:[1]							
18 to 24 years	100.0	19.3	34.4	24.2		22.2	
25 to 34 years	100.0	11.6	21.1	23.5		43.8	
35 to 44 years	100.0	14.6	22.1	20.4		42.9	
45 to 54 years	100.0	18.7	23.8	17.8		39.7	
Unrelated individual:							
25 to 34 years	100.0	7.3	20.4	27.2	22.4	22.7	
35 to 44 years	100.0	7.1	19.6	22.9	22.8	27.5	
45 to 54 years	100.0	8.1	23.5	21.4	22.1	24.9	
MARRIED, WIFE PRESENT							
Primary family head:							
20 to 24 years	100.0	2.0	12.1	27.7	34.2	18.4	5.6
25 to 34 years	100.0	1.5	6.8	15.8	27.6	28.0	20.3
35 to 44 years	100.0	1.9	7.4	13.1	22.2	25.5	30.0
45 to 54 years	100.0	3.1	9.7	13.8	21.1	22.6	29.6
Child of head:							
20 to 24 years	100.0	8.1	24.1	30.4		37.4	
25 to 34 years	100.0	6.0	14.8	23.6		55.6	
35 to 44 years	100.0	6.6	13.8	20.2		59.4	
45 years and over	100.0	11.4	16.2	18.8		53.6	
Other member of primary family:[1]							
18 to 24 years	100.0	8.7	19.7	29.6		42.1	
25 to 34 years	100.0	6.4	10.0	19.8		63.8	
35 to 44 years	100.0	9.5	9.6	15.1		65.8	
45 to 54 years	100.0	15.5	11.6	14.2		58.6	

[1]Excludes parents and grandchildren of family heads.

Source: Derived from U. S. Bureau of the Census, *U. S. Census of Population: 1950*, Series P—E, No. 2D, *Marital Status*, table 6.

to say on the basis of these figures that men who marry have higher incomes at the time of their marriage than those who do not marry. However, there is good reason to believe that men who marry have a higher income *potential*, on the average, than those who do not marry, and that the very same factors that produce this higher income potential may also make these men more desirable for marriage. Of course, there is no gainsaying the possibility that married men have higher incomes than single men simply because the needs and pressures of married life force them to work harder. Although there is probably much truth in this hypothesis, it cannot be tested with the available evidence. Perhaps all that the evidence permits one to say at the present time is that, for men, there is a correlation between marital status and income. The reason for this correlation must remain for the present, at least, a matter for speculation.

The family head and family income

The family head occupies a crucial position in determining the economic status of his dependents. Families headed by a person who cannot work or who lacks the training or ability to command a good wage tend to be concentrated at the low end of the income scale. Conversely, families headed by a person whose occupational skills are more highly developed comprise a large proportion of the higher income groups.

FIGURE 12.—MEDIAN INCOME OF FAMILIES, BY SEX OF HEAD: 1947, 1949, AND 1951

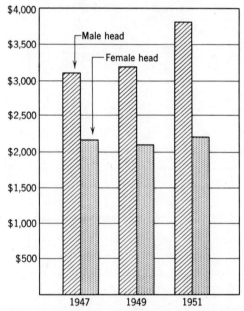

Source: U. S. Bureau of the Census, *Current Population Reports—Consumer Income*, Series P–60, No. 15, p. 3.

As table 39 shows, in April 1952 approximately 35 million families were husband-and-wife families, and about 5 million were "broken" families, 4 million of which were headed by women. Since most "broken" families have been affected by either death or divorce, it is not surprising to find that their incomes are lower, on the average, than those of normal families because in most instances the chief breadwinner has been separated from the family group. The median income of families headed by men was about $3,800 as compared with a median of only $2,200 for the families headed by women.

The relatively low incomes of the families headed by women can be explained in large measure by the fact that the chief breadwinner in these families tends to be a person who did not expect to assume the responsibility of providing for a family and may not have been well prepared for

TABLE **39.**—INCOME IN 1951 OF FAMILIES AND UNRELATED INDIVIDUALS, BY RESIDENCE AND TYPE OF FAMILY

Total money income in 1951	Families								Unrelated individuals		
	Total	Male head						Female head	Total	Male	Female
		Total male heads	Married, wife present				Other marital status				
			Total	Wife in paid labor force	Wife not in paid labor force						
UNITED STATES											
Number..thousands..	40,442	36,412	35,196	8,044	27,152	1,216	4,030		9,015	3,945	5,070
Percent..........	100.0	100.0	100.0	100.0	100.0	100.0	100.0		100.0	100.0	100.0
Under $500..........	4.4	3.3	3.2	2.0	3.5	5.4	15.4		25.6	19.0	30.3
$500 to $999........	4.7	4.0	3.8	1.8	4.5	9.7	11.2		21.0	17.3	23.6
$1,000 to $1,499.....	5.3	4.8	4.8	2.8	5.4	5.7	9.5		8.7	7.6	9.5
$1,500 to $1,999.....	6.1	5.6	5.5	4.0	6.0	8.2	10.6		9.1	7.5	10.3
$2,000 to $2,499.....	7.6	7.7	7.6	5.5	8.2	9.1	7.4		9.4	9.9	9.1
$2,500 to $2,999.....	7.8	7.8	7.9	5.5	8.6	4.8	7.4		6.8	8.5	5.7
$3,000 to $3,499.....	9.9	10.1	10.1	7.7	10.9	7.9	8.9		7.3	10.3	5.2
$3,500 to $3,999.....	9.8	10.3	10.4	8.6	10.9	7.3	5.3		4.7	6.6	3.3
$4,000 to $4,499.....	9.2	9.6	9.6	10.0	9.5	8.2	5.4		2.7	4.7	1.3
$4,500 to $4,999.....	6.4	6.6	6.7	8.3	6.2	5.7	4.5		1.4	2.5	0.7
$5,000 to $5,999.....	10.8	11.5	11.6	16.1	10.2	8.2	4.3		1.7	3.1	0.6
$6,000 to $6,999.....	6.8	7.0	7.0	10.7	5.9	6.6	5.1		0.9	1.8	0.2
$7,000 to $9,999.....	7.5	7.9	7.9	13.0	6.3	10.6	3.7		0.5	0.9	0.2
$10,000 to $14,999...	2.4	2.5	2.5	3.3	2.3	2.1	1.0		0.2	0.3	0.1
$15,000 and over.....	1.2	1.3	1.4	0.8	1.5	0.6	0.2		0.1	0.1	0.1
Median income........	$3,709	$3,829	$3,837	$4,631	$3,634	$3,452	$2,220		$1,195	$1,909	$917
URBAN											
Number..thousands..	26,918	23,808	23,090	6,088	17,002	718	3,110		6,877	2,775	4,102
Median income........	$4,071	$4,216	$4,217	$4,883	$4,028	$4,191	$2,493		$1,540	$2,328	$1,054
RURAL NONFARM											
Number..thousands..	7,844	7,218	6,998	1,496	5,502	220	626		1,444	696	748
Median income........	$3,365	$3,451	$3,462	$4,353	$3,306	(1)	$1,675		$740	$963	$586
RURAL FARM											
Number..thousands..	5,680	5,386	5,108	460	4,648	278	294		694	474	220
Median income........	$2,131	$2,184	$2,194	$3,000	$2,131	(1)	(1)		$733	$833	(1)

[1] Median not shown where there were fewer than 100 cases in the sample reporting on income.

Source: U. S. Bureau of the Census, *Current Population Reports—Consumer Income*, Series P–60, No. 12, table 3.

this task when faced with it. About 58 percent of these families were headed by widows, and an additional 32 percent were headed by women who were divorced or living apart from their husbands. Families headed by women tend to depend much more upon pensions, social security, alimony, or other types of relatively fixed incomes than do other families. Perhaps this fact provides a partial explanation for the relative stability in the incomes of these families during the period following World War II, when most other families were experiencing substantial increases in income (figure 12).

The income of husband-and-wife families in which the wife was a paid worker was considerably higher, on the average, than that of families in which the wife did not have a paid job or did only unpaid work on the family farm or in the family business. The importance of the working wife's contribution to family income is indicated in table 39, which shows that almost one-half of the families with working wives had incomes of $5,000 or more, whereas only one-fourth of the families in which the wives did not work had this much income. Viewed in another way, only about 15 percent of the families in the lower income groups had working wives (figure 13). This proportion rose to 37 percent for families with incomes between $6,000 and $10,000 and about 30 percent for families with incomes between $10,000 and $15,000. It dropped back to 14 percent, however, for families in the highest income bracket ($15,000 or more).

FIGURE 13.—PERCENT OF FAMILIES WITH WORKING WIVES, BY FAMILY INCOME IN 1951

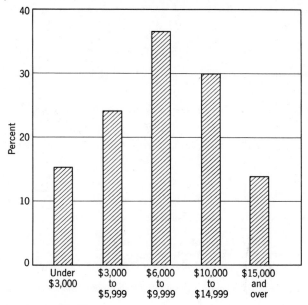

Note: Based on data in table 39.

Since most families derive their incomes entirely or largely from the employment of the head of the family, his labor force status is an important factor in determining family income. The data in table 40 indicate that families headed by a person who is employed have considerably higher average incomes than those headed by an unemployed person or by a person who is not in the labor market because of ill health, disability, retirement, or other reasons. The median income of families headed by an employed civilian ($3,900) was twice that of families in which the head was not employed in April 1952. Among the group in which the head was not employed, the median income was somewhat higher for families in which the head was seeking work than for those in which the head did not seek em-

TABLE **40.**—INCOME IN 1951 OF FAMILIES, BY RESIDENCE, LABOR FORCE STATUS, AND AGE OF HEAD

Total money income in 1951 and age of head	Total families	Families with head in labor force in April 1952				Families with head not in labor force in April 1952		
		Total	Head employed as civilian	Head unemployed	Head in Armed Forces[1]	Total	Head unable to work	Other
UNITED STATES								
Total								
Number........thousands..	40,442	35,002	33,606	504	892	5,440	1,022	4,418
Percent.................	100.0	100.0	100.0	100.0	100.0	100.0	100.0	100.0
Under $500..................	4.4	2.8	2.8	4.6	...	15.2	14.4	15.4
$500 to $999................	4.7	2.9	2.9	8.5	0.4	16.8	17.1	16.8
$1,000 to $1,499............	5.3	4.0	3.9	13.1	3.0	13.7	15.8	13.2
$1,500 to $1,999............	6.1	5.4	5.1	22.2	6.3	10.6	11.6	10.4
$2,000 to $2,499............	7.6	7.7	7.6	10.5	8.9	7.1	6.8	7.2
$2,500 to $2,999............	7.8	8.0	7.9	6.5	12.9	5.9	8.9	5.1
$3,000 to $3,499............	9.9	10.5	10.6	11.1	6.3	6.5	4.5	7.0
$3,500 to $3,999............	9.8	10.6	10.7	5.2	8.5	4.7	4.1	4.8
$4,000 to $4,499............	9.2	9.9	10.1	2.6	9.6	4.3	4.8	4.2
$4,500 to $4,999............	6.4	7.0	7.0	2.6	7.7	2.7	2.4	2.8
$5,000 to $5,999............	10.8	11.9	11.8	6.5	18.1	3.5	2.4	3.8
$6,000 to $6,999............	6.8	7.2	7.3	1.3	8.1	4.3	4.1	4.4
$7,000 to $9,999............	7.5	8.2	8.2	5.2	9.6	3.1	2.7	3.2
$10,000 to $14,999..........	2.4	2.6	2.7	...	0.7	1.1	...	1.3
$15,000 and over............	1.2	1.4	1.4	...	...	0.3	0.3	0.3
Median income...............	$3,709	$3,910	$3,927	$2,078	$4,202	$1,703	$1,618	$1,726
Head Under 25 Years Old								
Number........thousands..	1,914	1,812	1,498	10	304	102	...	102
Median income...............	$3,085	$3,134	$3,231	(²)	(²)	(²)	...	(²)
Head 25 to 64 Years Old								
Number........thousands..	33,350	31,044	30,024	432	588	2,306	376	1,930
Median income...............	$3,920	$4,017	$4,023	$2,100	$4,726	$1,959	$1,975	$1,953
Head 65 Years Old and Over								
Number........thousands..	5,178	2,146	2,084	62	...	3,032	646	2,386
Median income...............	$1,956	$2,773	$2,792	(²)	...	$1,479	$1,328	$1,543
URBAN								
Number........thousands..	26,918	23,338	22,314	380	644	3,580	644	2,936
Median income...............	$4,071	$4,253	$4,290	$2,214	$3,833	$1,951	$1,711	$2,014
RURAL NONFARM								
Number........thousands..	7,844	6,584	6,254	92	238	1,260	230	1,030
Median income...............	$3,365	$3,639	$3,609	(²)	(²)	$1,398	(²)	$1,417
RURAL FARM								
Number........thousands..	5,680	5,080	5,038	32	10	600	148	452
Median income...............	$2,131	$2,231	$2,233	(²)	(²)	$1,293	(²)	$1,111

[1] Includes only members of the Armed Forces living off post or with their families on military reservations.

[2] Median not shown where there were fewer than 100 cases in the sample reporting on income.

Source: U. S. Bureau of the Census, *Current Population Reports—Consumer Income*, Series P–60, No. 12, table 9.

ployment either because he felt he was physically unable to work or for other reasons. Over half of the family heads who were not in the labor force in April 1952 were 65 years old or over.

Family income is related not only to the employment status of the head

but also to the type of work he does.   Table 41 indicates that families
headed by persons in the more highly skilled occupations comprise a large
proportion of the higher income group.   Approximately one-half of the
families with incomes under $2,000 were headed by farmers or by labor-
ers, two of the lowest paid occupation groups, and only about one-tenth
were headed by professional or technical workers or by nonfarm managers,
officials, or proprietors, which are among the highest paid occupation
groups.   In contrast, almost one-half of the families with incomes of
$7,000 or more were headed by persons who were employed in these high-
paid occupation groups, whereas less than one-tenth were farmers or laborers.   As discussed earlier, farmers often have a considerable amount of nonmoney income that is not taken into account in the money income figures
presented here, and an allowance should be made for this factor in inter-
preting the differences.

TABLE **41.**—FAMILIES IN SELECTED INCOME LEVELS IN 1951, BY OCCUPATION GROUP OF HEAD

Major occupation group of head in April 1952	Under $2,000	$7,000 and over
Total families with heads employed as civilians....	100.0	100.0
Professional, technical, and kindred workers..........	2.3	16.5
Farmers and farm managers............................	34.7	5.8
Managers, officials, and proprietors, except farm......	6.7	28.0
Clerical, sales, and kindred workers..................	5.7	13.4
Craftsmen, foremen, and kindred workers...............	8.4	20.2
Operatives and kindred workers.......................	11.7	11.3
Service workers, including private household..........	12.3	2.9
Laborers, except mine................................	18.1	2.0

Source: U. S. Bureau of the Census, *Current Population Reports—Consumer Income*, Series P–60,
No. 12, table L.

According to the results of the April 1952 Current Population Survey,
families headed by self-employed professional workers (doctors, dentists,
lawyers, etc.) had a higher median income in 1951 ($7,400) than those
headed by salaried professional workers ($5,100).   Among families
headed by managerial workers, however, the median income of the salaried group ($5,600) was higher than that received by the self-employed
($4,300).   The lowest incomes were received by families headed by serv-
ice workers, farmers, and laborers.   Approximately one-third of all the
families were headed by persons who were engaged in one of four occupation groups (salesworkers; nonfarm proprietors; craftsmen, foremen, and
kindred workers; or clerical and kindred workers) in which the average
income ranged from about $4,200 to $4,600.   The nearly 7 million families headed by operatives (largely semiskilled workers in manufacturing
and related industries) had a median income of $3,800.

The working wife

The working wife has become such a characteristic feature of the American economy that no discussion of family income would be complete with-

out a consideration of the factors that influence the labor force participation of married women. It is important to emphasize, however, that the income figures represent money received before deductions for taxes and expenses incurred because of employment. For working mothers, the expenses for household help and child care are frequently substantial and should be considered when the incomes of their families are compared with the incomes of families in which the mother does not work.

Most married women who have some income get it from paid work. The labor force participation of married women depends upon several factors such as the attitude of the community toward their employment, the availability of jobs, the presence of small children in the home or other household responsibilities, the earning power of the husband, and the desire to perform certain types of work irrespective of income needs. Only some of these factors can be examined through the available figures.

There has been a considerable increase in labor force activity among married women since 1940. In 1952, 25 percent of the married women who were living with their husbands were in the labor force as compared with only 15 percent in 1940. The data indicate that this increase was not confined to any group or groups in the population; on the contrary, labor force participation appears to have increased among married women of all ages and at all income levels. For example, despite the high birth rate of the war and postwar years, the proportion of married women in their twenties and thirties who were working was higher in 1952 than in 1940. Table 42 indicates a very substantial increase in the labor force participation of married women at all income levels for which data are available. The dollar values shown in the table do not have the same meaning for both of the periods covered; but even after rough corrections for changes in the value of the dollar, the increases in labor force participation are substantial for comparable income classes. For example, about

TABLE 42.—PERCENT OF NONFARM WIVES IN THE LABOR FORCE, BY WAGE OR SALARY INCOME OF HUSBAND: 1951 AND 1939

(Data are restricted to nonfarm married couples in which the wife was between 18 and 64 years of age and the husband had $1 or more of wage or salary income but no other income. The wage or salary income covers the years 1951 and 1939, respectively. Data for 1939 are revisions of figures that appeared originally in table 23 of the 1940 Census report on Population, *The Labor Force (Sample Statisitcs): Employment and Family Characteristics of Women)*

Wage or salary income of husband	April 1952	March 1940	Wage or salary income of husband	April 1952	March 1940
$1 to $999................	40.2	22.4	$3,000 and over............	24.5	6.0
$1,000 to $1,499..........	37.8	19.2	$3,000 to $3,999..........	27.4	(1)
$1,500 to $1,999..........	34.6	14.4	$4,000 to $4,999..........	25.6	(1)
$2,000 to $2,999..........	32.0	9.4	$5,000 to $5,999..........	21.3	(1)
			$6,000 and over..........	13.3	(1)

[1] Comparable figures not available.

Source: U. S. Bureau of the Census, *Current Population Reports—Consumer Income*, Series P–60, No. 12, table D.

40 percent of the women whose husbands earned under $1,000 in wage or salary income in 1951 were in the labor force. In 1940, only 22 percent of the women whose husbands earned under $1,000 were in the labor force, and the proportion was not much higher for those whose husbands earned as little as $200. Perhaps because of greater job opportunities in 1952, women were in a much better position than they were in 1940 to enter the labor market and supplement the income of a husband with relatively low earning power. Table 42 also shows that the increased labor force participation among married women was by no means confined to the lowest income groups. Roughly 5 percent of the husbands had wage or salary incomes of $3,000 or more in 1939, and about the same proportion received $6,000 or more in 1951. In the earlier year, only about 6 percent of the women whose husbands earned $3,000 or more were in the labor force. Proportionately more than twice as many of the women whose husbands made $6,000 or more were in the labor force in 1951.

The above data showing the relationship between the income of the husband and the labor force participation of the wife are somewhat restricted because of the necessity to limit the comparison to wage or salary income, which was the only type of income reported in the 1940 Census. A more adequate picture of this relationship may be found in table 43. In all residence groups, there is an inverse correlation between the labor force activity of married women and the income of their husbands. In urban areas, the proportion of working wives declined from about one-third of those whose husbands had incomes under $3,000 to about one-seventh of those whose husbands had incomes of $10,000 or more. In rural areas a similar pattern may be observed, except that a lower proportion of the women were in the labor force. Many of the women in rural-farm families, however, who were not in the labor force in April 1952 probably assisted in the farm work during periods of peak activity.

There is some evidence that the labor force participation of married women may be related to the husband's occupation as well as to his income. For example, among men with incomes under $3,000, the wives of professional and managerial workers have higher labor force participation rates than the wives of men employed in most other occupations. Moreover, the data in table 44 suggest that the wives of the professional and managerial workers may be somewhat more inclined to drop out of the labor market as their husband's incomes increase than are the wives of workers in most other occupation groups. It is possible that these patterns are affected by age, presence of children, and other factors that cannot be analyzed on the basis of the available data.

There is a direct correlation between the income of the wife (if she is doing paid work) and that of her husband. The median income of women doing paid work in April 1951 was $900 for those whose husbands had incomes under $1,000 and about $2,000 for those whose husbands had incomes of $4,000 or more. Although the income of the wife tends to increase with that of the husband, it does not increase at the same rate. Thus, at the lowest income level, the labor force activity of the wife more than doubled the income of the couple, on the average; whereas, at the higher income levels, the working wife's contribution was proportionately much less.

TABLE 43.—PERCENT OF WIVES IN THE LABOR FORCE IN APRIL 1952, BY RESIDENCE AND INCOME OF HUSBAND

Income of husband in 1951	Total	Urban	Rural nonfarm	Rural farm
Total..................................	25	27	23	17
Under $1,000..............................	24	29	27	18
$1,000 to $1,999..........................	28	36	23	18
$2,000 to $2,999..........................	29	33	26	16
$3,000 to $3,999..........................	27	28	23	21
$4,000 to $4,999..........................	24	25	23	16
$5,000 to $5,999..........................	20	22	17	
$6,000 to $9,999.........................	15	16	10	12
$10,000 and over..........................	13	14		

Source: U. S. Bureau of the Census, *Current Population Reports—Consumer Income*, Series P–60, No. 12, table E.

TABLE 44.—PERCENT OF WIVES IN THE LABOR FORCE IN APRIL 1952, BY OCCUPATION GROUP AND INCOME OF HUSBAND

Major occupation group of husband in April 1952	Income of husband in 1951			
	Under $3,000	$3,000 to $3,999	$4,000 to $4,999	$5,000 and over
Professional, technical, and kindred workers...............	40	30	25	18
Farmers and farm managers........................	22	(1)	(1)	(1)
Managers, officials, and proprietors, except farm..........	41	24	28	21
Clerical, sales, and kindred workers......................	32	31	32	18
Craftsmen, foremen, and kindred workers..................	30	25	23	14
Operatives and kindred workers..........................	32	26	25	22
Service workers, including private household...............	34	30	(1)	(1)
Farm laborers and foremen.............................	18	(1)	(1)	(1)
Laborers, except farm and mine.........................	26	29	(1)	(1)

[1] Percent not shown where there were fewer than 100 cases in the sample reporting on income.

Source: U. S. Bureau of the Census, *Current Population Reports—Consumer Income*, Series P–60, No. 12, table F.

The presence or absence of small children and the income of their husbands together represent two of the most important factors that affect the labor force participation of married women. Some insight into the combined effect of these factors may be obtained from the data shown in table 46. As noted earlier, the labor force participation of wives is highest among couples in which the husband's income is most limited, declining steadily as the husband's income increases. A modification of this pattern appears to exist for couples with relatively high incomes, where the availability of financial resources to hire household workers may enable

TABLE **45.**—MEDIAN INCOME OF WIVES IN THE PAID LABOR FORCE IN APRIL 1951, BY INCOME
OF HUSBAND

Income of husband in 1950	Median income of wife in 1950
Under $1,000...	$908
$1,000 to $1,999...	1,094
$2,000 to $2,999...	1,548
$3,000 to $3,999...	1,718
$4,000 and over..	1,954

Source: U. S. Bureau of the Census, *Current Population Reports—Consumer Income*, Series P–60,
No. 12, table G.

TABLE **46.**—PERCENT OF WIVES IN THE LABOR FORCE IN APRIL 1951, BY NUMBER OF
CHILDREN AND INCOME OF HUSBAND

Income of husband in 1950	All wives	Wives 20 to 44 years				
		Total	No children under 18 years	With children under 18 years		
				Total	Some under 6 years	None under 6 years
Total......................	25.3	28.2	52.9	20.5	14.4	33.1
None......................	36.6	54.9	75.0	37.0	10.0	52.9
Under $500................	27.7	38.2	53.3	32.2	27.5	41.0
$500 to $999..............	26.4	34.4	53.4	23.9	16.2	42.4
$1,000 to $1,499..........	30.7	38.0	51.1	32.3	23.4	51.9
$1,500 to $1,999..........	28.0	33.2	59.1	23.8	19.0	35.0
$2,000 to $2,499..........	29.3	33.7	63.4	22.7	17.1	37.4
$2,500 to $2,999..........	27.3	30.7	54.5	23.2	14.0	44.4
$3,000 to $3,499..........	26.8	28.7	53.7	21.1	15.3	32.6
$3,500 to $3,999..........	26.1	28.4	51.7	22.6	14.7	39.4
$4,000 to $4,499..........	21.2	22.0	49.2	14.7	9.6	25.1
$4,500 to $4,999..........	20.3	22.2	56.1	15.4	7.4	30.5
$5,000 to $5,999..........	15.9	14.8	29.3	11.3	7.3	18.1
$6,000 to $6,999..........	15.2	14.8	31.0	12.0	9.4	16.1
$7,000 to $9,999..........	7.3	5.3	8.6	4.8	5.1	4.3
$10,000 and over..........	11.8	10.6	21.1	8.3	5.4	11.4

Source: U. S. Bureau of the Census, *Current Population Reports—Labor Force*, Series P–50, No.
39, table 6.

the wife to work outside the home if she so desires. Also, since there
appears to be a strong correlation between the earning capacity of the husband and that of the wife—probably because of a similarity in educational
backgrounds—greater personal incentive may exist for the wives in upper-
income families to accept employment than exists for wives whose earning potential is somewhat less. It is also possible that prestige considerations as to the wife's working may differ between middle- and upper-income
families. In middle-income families, greater prestige may attach to stay-
ing at home than in having a job, whereas in upper-income families there
may be more prestige in having a "career" than in being a housewife.

Generally, the relationship between labor force participation and husband's income described above was evident for all wives, whether or not
they had children and, if they had children, regardless of the age of their
children. As might be expected, however, labor force participation rates
were lowest for mothers of preschool-age children, somewhat greater for

those with school-age children only, and greatest for those with no children under 18 years old.

The adequacy of family income

The notion of a measurable boundary marking off the range on the lower part of the income scale that can be designated substandard has crept into our thinking about size distributions of income practically unchallenged. Theorists of all persuasions utilize such a concept implicitly while proponents of various types of social policy exploit the "poverty line" almost melodramatically. Yet, when faced directly with the problem of determining this measure for a given time and place, the theorist will deny the possibility of a unique answer and the propagandist will settle for any one of many solutions if the result suits his purposes. [Dorothy S. Brady, "Research on the Size Distribution of Income," *Studies in Income and Wealth*, Vol. 13, National Bureau of Economic Research, New York, 1951, p. 30.]

One of the most persistent and difficult questions that the income analyst is called upon to answer relates to the adequacy of family income. The question generally takes this form: What proportion of the families have incomes that are continuously too low to maintain an adequate level of living? Despite the fact that this question can be answered at best very imperfectly, there is much interest in the subject and no discussion of family income would be complete without some reference to it.

Several years ago, the American Federation of Labor reported that the income of about one-third of the city families in America was too low to maintain an "adequate living standard." [2] At about the same time, Congresswoman Helen Gahagan Douglas stated on a radio program that she believed about 60 percent of the American families do not have sufficiently large incomes to provide adequate living standards for their families. [3] Although these statements are not necessarily inconsistent, they do convey different impressions. Even the lower estimate may seem alarmingly high to some people, especially for a prosperous year like 1948. It may therefore be of some value to examine critically some of the data that underlie statements of this type.

In February 1948, the Bureau of Labor Statistics published a report showing the estimated cost of the budget required to maintain a family of four persons with an "adequate standard of living" in 34 cities in March 1946 and June 1947. [4] The general description of this budget indicates that it "is not a 'subsistence' budget, nor is it a 'luxury' budget; it is an attempt to describe and measure a modest but adequate standard of living." [5] A budget of this type is difficult to summarize in a few words without the possibility of misinterpretation. At the same time, however, the

[2] *Labor's Monthly Survey*, June-July 1948.

[3] Capitol Cloakroom program on radio station WTOP, Washington, D. C., August 4, 1948.

[4] U. S. Department of Labor, Bureau of Labor Statistics, *The City Worker's Family Budget*, Serial No. R1909, February 1948.

[5] *Ibid.*, p. 1.

phrase "modest but adequate" is too vague to provide even a rough idea of the level of living being described. Therefore, a brief description of some of the contents of the budget is provided to lend some precision to the concept.

The report that describes the budget indicates that the family dwelling is rented and contains five rooms, including a kitchen and a bathroom. The unit is supplied with hot and cold running water; it has at least one window in each room, and electric lighting equipment is installed in each room. The heating plant must be sufficient to maintain an average room temperature of 70°F. during the winter months. The home is also equipped with "the usual furnishings and the mechanical aids which are considered household necessities—a gas or electric cook stove, a mechanical refrigerator, and a washing machine." [6]

With respect to food, the report notes that "the food budget provides a diet that approximates the nutritional allowances recommended by the Food and Nutrition Board of the National Research Council." It is within the limits of the budget "to serve meat for dinner several times a week, if the cheaper cuts of beef, pork, lamb, and veal are served on weekdays; a chicken or a roast may be served on Sunday and a turkey on Thanksgiving."

The clothing budget may perhaps best be illustrated by the following examples. The husband is permitted one heavy wool suit every 2 years, one light-wool suit every 3 years, five shirts and two pairs of shoes each year. The wife may purchase a heavy wool coat every 4 years and four dresses and three pairs of shoes each year.

The family covered by the budget includes an employed father, a housewife not gainfully employed, and two children under 15 years of age. Data on the money income received by families of this general type during the calendar years 1946 and 1947 are available for groups of cities classified by size from the Current Population Surveys of the Bureau of the Census. By comparing the cost of the budget with the incomes actually received by these families, it is possible to obtain some measure of the proportion of families with incomes below the cost of the budget. Ignoring for the moment some of the many qualifications associated with the interpretation of these data, it is apparent from table 47 that about two-fifths of the families of the type specified, living in large cities, reported incomes to the Bureau of the Census that were below the cost of an "adequate standard of living." Since income surveys are known to have a downward bias,[7] some crude attempt to adjust the income data for the amount and the distribution of underreporting was attempted. The per-

---

[6] *Ibid.*, p. 3.

[7] There are, no doubt, measurement biases in the estimates of the cost of the budget as well as in the income figures. Just as the field surveys of income produce underreporting of income, so field surveys of prices may produce biases of one type or another. For purposes of this analysis, however, it is assumed that the biases in the cost of the budget estimates cannot be adjusted, whereas those in the income estimates can be adjusted.

cent of families with incomes less than the cost of the budget is shown in
table 47 assuming no underreporting of income (i.e., the unadjusted survey results), 10 percent, 15 percent, and 20 percent underreporting.
Where 10 percent underreporting of income was assumed, all income levels
were inflated by 10 percent and the percent of families with adjusted incomes
below the cost of the budget was computed. A similar computation was
made where 15 percent and 20 percent underreporting was assumed. It
is apparent that when 10 percent underreporting is assumed in the income
figure about one-third of the families have incomes below the cost of the
budget and when 20 percent underreporting is assumed about one-fourth
of the families have incomes below the cost of an "adequate standard of
living."

TABLE 47.—INCOME OF "CITY-WORKER" FAMILIES: 1947 AND 1946

(Excludes families in cities with less than 100,000 inhabitants)

Total money income	1947	1946
Total...	100.0	100.0
Under $500...................................	...	1.4
$500 to $999.................................	0.9	0.8
$1,000 to $1,499.............................	2.1	3.2
$1,500 to $1,999.............................	5.5	7.9
$2,000 to $2,499.............................	9.8	20.4
$2,500 to $2,999.............................	14.4	19.1
$3,000 to $3,499.............................	18.3	18.4
$3,500 to $3,999.............................	15.3	6.5
$4,000 to $4,499.............................	11.9	5.9
$4,500 to $4,999.............................	5.2	3.7
$5,000 to $5,999.............................	8.0	5.5
$6,000 to $9,999.............................	6.4	5.1
$10,000 and over.............................	2.1	2.3
Median income................................	$3,471	$2,929
Median cost of the budget....................	3,232	2,764
Percent below budget, assuming--		
No underreporting of income..................	41.3	43.7
10 percent underreporting of income..........	30.9	34.0
15 percent underreporting of income..........	27.2	29.6
20 percent underreporting of income..........	23.9	25.6

Source: Income data obtained from unpublished tabulations of the Bureau of the Census. The
median cost of the budget is derived from U. S. Department of Labor, Bureau of Labor Statistics, *The
City Worker's Family Budget*, Serial No. R1909, February 1948.

There is no scientific basis for adjusting the median of an income distribution for underreporting. Studies that have been made indicate that
the aggregate derived from the field survey of income conducted by the
Bureau of the Census in April 1947 was about 20 percent below the comparable estimate prepared independently by the National Income Division
of the Department of Commerce.[8] In the absence of other evidence, it
would therefore seem appropriate to assume that the median was also underreported by about 20 percent.

[8] S. F. Goldsmith, "Appraisal of Basic Data Available for Constructing Income Size Distributions,"
Studies in Income and Wealth, Vol. 13, National Bureau of Economic Research, New York, 1951,
p. 289.

In addition to the qualifications in the analysis that arise from biases inherent in the measurement technique, there are several other factors that must be considered. These factors relate to the definition of the family; coverage (i.e., specific cities versus city-size groups); and the time period. Some of the problems associated with each of these factors are indicated below.

Definition of the family. The family used by the Bureau of Labor Statistics in computing the "City Worker's Family Budget" is "an employed worker's family of four; husband, aged 38, who is the breadwinner; wife, aged 36, the homemaker; and two children, a boy 13 years of age in high school and a girl, aged 8, in grade school. The family lives in a separate house or apartment; there are no lodgers or cotenants, and the husband has no dependents other than his wife and children."

Income data for this identical type of family were, of course, not collected by the Bureau of the Census. However, by making special tabulations of the data that were collected it was possible to provide income information for families of the same general type. The family to which the income data apply is a four-person husband-and-wife family having two children under 18 years of age. In the case of the 1946 income data, the family is a primary family with one civilian earner and no unrelated persons in the household. The 1947 income data apply to primary and a few secondary families with one person in the labor force in April 1948. No control was kept on the presence of unrelated persons in the household in the 1947 tabulations; however, the number of families of this type with unrelated persons in the household is negligible.

Coverage. Estimates of the cost of the budget were prepared by the Bureau of Labor Statistics for 34 specific cities. For purposes of this analysis the 30 largest cities in the Bureau of Labor Statistics survey were classified into four city-size groups based on the population of each city in 1940. The median cost of the budget shown in table 49 is based on the costs of the budget for the cities covered by the Bureau of Labor Statistics within each city-size group. Since budget estimates were prepared for only four of the more than 3,000 cities having less than 100,000 inhabitants in 1940, these cities were excluded from the analysis.

The Bureau of the Census income data for 1946 are based on a sample that included all cities of 250,000 or more inhabitants and those for 1947 are based on a sample that included all cities of 500,000 inhabitants or more. Income estimates were prepared by the Bureau of the Census for city-size groups rather than for specific cities. Table 48 shows the total number of cities in each city-size group in 1940 and the number covered in the studies of the Bureau of Labor Statistics and the Bureau of the Census.

In view of the differences in the coverage of the various city-size groups in each survey, it is of some importance to compare the percent of families with incomes below the cost of the budget for each city-size group. Table

49 shows that about one-fourth of the families in cities of 500,000 or more, which were all included in each survey, and about the same proportion of families in cities between 100,000 and 250,000 had incomes below the cost of the budget in 1946. This proportion is based on the assumption of 20 percent underreporting of income. The proportion of families with incomes below the cost of the budget was somewhat smaller in cities between 250,000 and 500,000 than in other city-size groups.

TABLE **48.**—NUMBER OF CITIES IN EACH CITY-SIZE GROUP INCLUDED IN THE CURRENT POPULATION SURVEY AND IN THE *City Worker's Family Budget* REPORT

(Excludes cities with less than 100,000 inhabitants)

| City-size group | Total cities | Number of cities included in-- | | BLS report, The City Worker's Family Budget |
| | | Current Population Survey | | |
		1946	1947	
1,000,000 and over.........................	5	5	5	5
500,000 to 999,999.........................	9	9	9	9
250,000 to 499,999.........................	23	23	8	12
100,000 to 249,000.........................	55	21	11	4

TABLE **49.**—INCOME IN 1946 OF "CITY-WORKER" FAMILIES, BY COST OF FAMILY BUDGET AND SIZE OF PLACE

| Size of place of residence | Estimated cost of budget, March 1946[1] | | Median income in 1946[3] | Percent of families with incomes below median cost of budget, assuming-- | |
	Range	Median cost[2]		No under-reporting of income	20 percent under-reporting of income
All cities of 100,000 and over...	$2,985-$2,532	$2,764	$2,929	43.7	25.6
1,000,000 and over................	2,820- 2,681	2,793	2,842	48.0	29.3
500,000 to 999,999................	2,985- 2,615	2,811	2,852	48.1	25.2
250,000 to 499,999................	2,913- 2,532	2,701	3,112	32.3	18.1
100,000 to 249,999................	2,804- 2,623	2,727	2,888	46.2	27.8

[1] U. S. Department of Labor, Bureau of Labor Statistics, *The City Worker's Family Budget,* Serial No. R1909, February 1948.

[2] The median is the cost of the budget for the middle city when cities in each city-size group are arrayed by the amount of the cost of the budget.

[3] Unpublished data of the Bureau of the Census.

Time period. The quantities represented in the budget estimates were priced in March 1946 and June 1947. Therefore, the cost of the budget is typical for these months and not for the calendar years 1946 and 1947. In contrast, the income figures represent the total money income received during the calendar years 1946 and 1947.

If the items in the budget were valued at their average price during the year, the cost of the budget would have probably been greater and the percentage of families with incomes less than the cost of the budget would be larger than that shown in the above table. The Consumer's Price Index for March 1946 was 130.2, whereas the average for 1946 was 139.3; the index for June 1947 was 157.1, and the average for 1947 was 159.2.

Several years ago a member of the staff of the Bureau of Labor Statistics calculated the proportion of families and unrelated individuals with incomes below the cost of the budget in one city, Indianapolis, Indiana.[9] Since both the income data and the budget data utilized the same set of definitions, many of the technical problems of comparability referred to above were avoided. In addition, an attempt was made to work out the cost of the budget for families of different sizes, thereby extending the scope of the analysis. In this study it was found that 22 percent of the Indianapolis families of two or more with male head and 30 percent of the unrelated individuals had incomes below the cost of the budget.[10]

One final caution, which should be mentioned with respect to the interpretation of these data, relates to the use of an income distribution for a single year. There is considerable movement of groups in and out of the lower part of the income curve. At any given time, the lower income group includes many families and individuals temporarily affected by business reverses, sickness, or unemployment. In addition, this group includes young, newly created families that can confidently aspire to higher incomes in the future.[11]

---

[9] Abner Hurwitz, "Family Incomes and Cost of Family Budgets," U. S. Department of Labor, Bureau of Labor Statistics, *Workers Budgets in the United States*, Bull. 927.

[10] *Ibid.*, p. 47.

[11] See U. S. Department of Commerce, Office of Business Economics, *Income Distribution in the United States*, pp. 5, 6, for a more detailed discussion of this problem.

C H A P T E R   8

RECENT CHANGES IN INCOME DISTRIBUTION

The American economy for many decades has had a rising standard of per capita income, and no evidence exists that the distribution of income during the period was appreciably different from that which now exists. [Testimony of Margaret G. Reid, *Hearings Before the Subcommittee on Low-Income Families of the Joint Committee on the Economic Report*, 81st Congress, 1st Session, December, 1949, p. 347.]

The transformation in the distribution of our national income that has occurred within the past twenty years . . . may already be counted as one of the great social revolutions in history. [Arthur F. Burns, *Looking Forward*, 31st Annual Report of the National Bureau of Economic Research, 1951, p. 3.]

The current interest in the problem of changes in income distribution has been met by a wave of data and interpretations, much of which is of a confusing or contradictory nature. The quotations above merely illustrate the differences of opinion on this subject that exist among many "experts" as well as laymen.

Until quite recently the distribution of income was regarded as a highly stable economic phenomenon. Despite the fact that the income distribution curve is obtained by grouping together incomes from various sources, much evidence (a good deal of it of a questionable nature) had been brought to bear to show that the distribution of income does not change. Pareto was one of the first economists to make a statistical inquiry into the distribution of income and his findings, based for the most part on conclusions drawn from inadequate data, have seeped into economic literature. It was Pareto's belief that the distribution of income is a fixed datum in economics and that regardless of changes in economic conditions, short of a revolutionary change from a competitive to a collectivist society, the distribution of income is fixed in all places and at all times.[1]

Pareto's theory of income distribution has been subjected to widespread criticism. In 1922, for example, the National Bureau of Economic Research conducted an intensive investigation of Pareto's methods and findings. The conclusions of this study were not only that "Pareto's Law" was inadequate as a mathematical generalization, but that it was doubtful that any mathematical law describing income distribution could ever be

---

[1] "Pareto's Law" has been widely discussed in economic literature. Excellent summaries may be found in *Income in the United States—Its Amount and Distribution*, Vol. 2, National Bureau of Economic Research, New York, 1922; and A. C. Pigou, *Economics of Welfare*, third edition, Part 4, Chapter 2, Macmillan and Company, London, 1929.

developed.[2]   Despite these findings, the influence of Pareto's theory of income distribution is still widely felt in economic literature.

Economists are anything but unanimous in their opinions regarding the stability of the distribution of income.   There is, however, even greater difference of opinion regarding the economic importance that should be attached to changes in the distribution of income.   The labor unions and some economists have tended to stress the economic importance of redistribution measures as public policies.   For example, a recent report of the C.I.O. notes that "A more equitable distribution of income among the families of the nation is important to the national welfare.   It must go hand in hand with a general increase in the total level of real disposable income."[3]   In much the same vein, Leon Keyserling, as chairman of the Council of Economic Advisers, testified at a Congressional hearing that "income distribution is . . . better than before the war, which makes for improved economic stability."[4]   In contrast, David McCord Wright has sharply criticized the efficacy of the redistribution measures of the New Deal.[5]

In view of the longstanding controversy regarding the stability and the meaning of income distribution, it would be presumptuous to say that the facts and opinions set forth here will provide a definitive answer to the problem.   It will probably still take many more years of research before unqualified statements regarding changes in the distribution of income can be made.   In this section an attempt will be made to interpret the meaning of the changes in the size distribution of income as they are reflected in the available data, chiefly those obtained in the field surveys of income conducted by the Bureau of the Census.   Although census data are subject to many limitations, they are the only nationwide statistics on income distribution covering the period before and after World War II that were collected by a single agency using a single set of procedures and definitions.

Income of persons: 1939 to 1951

Changes in the level of wage or salary income.   The marked increase in income levels, indicated by the national income aggregates, is very vividly shown in the census figures on income distribution.   In 1939, the average wage or salary recipient earned about $800 during the year.[6] By 1947, this figure had more than doubled, and it has continued to rise

---

[2] *Income in the United States—Its Amount and Distribution*, Vol. 2, pp. 393, 394.

[3] Congress of Industrial Organizations, Committee on Economic Policy, *Maintaining Prosperity* (no publication date), p. 18.

[4] U. S. Congress, Joint Committee on the Economic Report.   *Hearings on the January 1949 Economic Report of the President*, 81st Congress, 1st Session, 1949.

[5] David McCord Wright, *The Creation of Purchasing Power*, Harvard University Press, Cambridge, Mass., 1942, p. 58.

[6] Since only the amount of wage or salary income was reported in the 1940 Census, income comparisons between 1939 and later years, based on census data, must be restricted to this source.

ever since. In 1939, only 1 percent of the wage or salary recipients had incomes of $5,000 or more and 60 percent had incomes below $1,000. By 1951, the proportions in the higher income brackets increased eight-fold and the proportion in the lowest bracket was cut by two-thirds. For men alone, who typically are the primary income recipients in their families, the changes are even more striking (table 50).

The increases in wage or salary incomes were by no means restricted to any group or groups in the population. On the contrary, these increases were widespread and affected most occupations and industries (table 51).

TABLE 50.—WAGE OR SALARY INCOME OF PERSONS, BY SEX: 1951, 1947, AND 1939

Wage or salary income	Both sexes			Male			Female		
	1951	1947	1939	1951	1947	1939	1951	1947	1939
Total with wage or salary income........	100.0	100.0	100.0	100.0	100.0	100.0	100.0	100.0	100.0
$1 to $999.................	23.6	27.7	60.0	14.1	19.3	52.8	41.9	45.5	79.0
$1,000 to $1,999..........	16.8	26.4	29.2	12.5	22.2	33.4	25.3	35.1	18.1
$2,000 to $2,499..........	11.3	14.9	5.3	10.2	16.4	6.8	13.5	11.6	1.6
$2,500 to $2,999..........	10.2	9.7	2.0	10.8	12.4	2.6	9.1	4.1	0.5
$3,000 to $4,999..........	29.7	17.9	2.4	39.9	25.0	3.1	9.7	3.1	0.6
$5,000 and over...........	8.4	3.4	1.0	12.4	4.8	1.4	0.5	0.5	0.1

Source: Data for 1939 and 1951 from U. S. Bureau of the Census, *Current Population Reports—Consumer Income*, Series P–60, No. 11, table 9, and data for 1947 from Series P–60, No. 5, table 21.

TABLE 51.—MEDIAN WAGE OR SALARY INCOME OF PERSONS, BY INDUSTRY GROUP, COLOR, AND SEX: 1951 AND 1939

(Restricted to persons who were wage and salary workers at the time of the survey)

Major industry group and color	Both sexes		Male		Female	
	1951	1939[1]	1951	1939[1]	1951	1939[1]
COLOR						
White.......................................	$2,875	$956	$3,345	$1,112	$1,855	$676
Nonwhite....................................	1,572	364	2,060	460	781	246
MAJOR INDUSTRY GROUP						
Agriculture, forestry, and fisheries.....	$1,187	$292	$1,205	$301	([2])	$154
Mining.....................................	3,667	957	3,683	956	([2])	1,077
Construction...............................	2,752	777	2,766	777	([2])	804
Manufacturing.............................	3,003	988	3,393	1,141	$1,923	646
Transportation, communication, and other public utilities........................	3,302	1,365	3,348	1,425	2,221	1,068
Wholesale trade...........................	3,278	1,215	3,500	1,326	([2])	828
Retail trade..............................	2,082	793	2,705	969	1,470	599
Finance, insurance, and real estate......	2,633	1,257	3,462	1,487	2,012	977
Business and repair services.............	2,727	971	2,903	995	([2])	838
Personal services........................	782	360	1,875	738	653	292
Entertainment and recreation services....	1,625	814	([2])	888	([2])	639
Professional and related services........	2,359	995	3,004	1,235	2,081	896
Public administration.....................	3,338	1,492	3,565	1,625	2,631	1,233

[1] Excludes public emergency workers.
[2] Median is not shown where there were fewer than 100 cases in the sample reporting with wage or salary income.

Source: U. S. Bureau of the Census, *Current Population Reports—Consumer Income*, Series P–60, No. 11, table 10.

Among men, the rate of increase was greater for nonwhite workers than for white workers. The median for white men increased from $1,100 to $3,300, whereas that for nonwhite men increased from $500 to $2,100. For women, the median for whites increased from $700 to $1,900 and that for nonwhites increased from $200 to $800.

Significant gains in money wages and salaries were recorded in all industry groups between 1939 and 1951. Among the wage workers showing the greatest relative gains were those in agriculture, mining, construction, and manufacturing. In general, the industries employing a large proportion of "white-collar" workers showed smaller relative increases than the ones cited above (table 51).

Changes in the level of total income.   Although the above data on wage or salary income are of considerable importance, particularly since they extend back to the pre-World War II period, greatest interest naturally centers in the changes in total money income. Unfortunately, distributions of persons by total money income are available only as far back as 1944; however, even the data for this relatively short period present some rather interesting trends.

During the postwar period, there was a general rise in the median income of men from about $1,800 in 1945 to about $3,000 in 1951 but only a slight rise in the median income of women (table 52 and figure 14). The stability in the average income of women may seem surprising inasmuch as about two-thirds of all female income recipients derive all their income from wages or salaries and there have been substantial increases in the wage rates of women workers since 1945. Moreover, the median

FIGURE 14.—MEDIAN INCOME OF MEN AND WOMEN: 1945 TO 1951

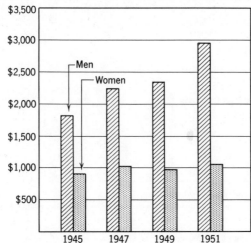

Source: U. S. Bureau of the Census, *Current Population Reports—Consumer Income*, Series P–60, No. 14, p. 2.

TABLE **52.**—INCOME OF PERSONS, BY RESIDENCE AND SEX: 1944 TO 1951

Total money income	1951	1950	1949	1948	1947	1946	1945	1944
UNITED STATES--MALE								
Total...................	100.0	100.0	100.0	100.0	100.0	100.0	100.0	100.0
Percent with income.................	90.1	90.1	89.9	89.9	88.9	(1)	89.5	88.9
Percent without income...............	9.9	9.9	10.1	10.1	11.1	(1)	10.5	11.1
Total with income................	100.0	100.0	100.0	100.0	100.0	100.0	100.0	100.0
Loss....................................	0.4	0.7	0.8	0.5	0.4	(1)	0.6	0.5
$1 to $499.............................	8.7	10.6	11.6	9.6	9.8	(1)	11.6	13.0
$500 to $999...........................	8.4	9.4	10.7	10.4	11.1	(1)	16.5	12.2
$1,000 to $1,499.......................	7.0	8.0	9.4	9.8	10.5	(1)	13.8	11.1
$1,500 to $1,999.......................	6.9	8.4	9.3	9.3	11.3	(1)	12.2	11.9
$2,000 to $2,499.......................	9.6	11.4	11.7	13.2	14.9	(1)	13.2	14.1
$2,500 to $2,999.......................	9.8	10.2	11.6	11.5	11.3	(1)	10.7	11.6
$3,000 to $3,499.......................	12.3	12.5	11.5	12.2	10.9	(1)	8.4	9.5
$3,500 to $3,999.......................	10.3	8.4	7.7	7.3	5.9	(1)	4.8	5.6
$4,000 to $4,499.......................	8.0	6.2	4.8	5.1	4.3	(1)	2.3	3.0
$4,500 to $4,999.......................	4.7	3.4	2.9	2.9	2.1	(1)	1.5	2.0
$5,000 to $5,999.......................	6.4	4.6	3.4	3.6	3.0	(1)	2.4	2.2
$6,000 to $9,999.......................	5.5	4.0	3.0	3.1	3.0	(1)	1.3	2.0
$10,000 and over......................	1.9	2.0	1.4	1.6	1.6	(1)	0.8	1.2
Median income for persons with income..	$2,952	$2,570	$2,346	$2,396	$2,230	(1)	$1,811	$2,046
UNITED STATES--FEMALE								
Total...............................	100.0	100.0	100.0	100.0	100.0	100.0	100.0	100.0
Percent with income.................	43.7	43.2	41.8	40.9	39.2	(1)	45.1	47.9
Percent without income...............	56.3	56.8	58.2	59.1	60.8	(1)	54.9	52.1
Total with income................	100.0	100.0	100.0	100.0	100.0	100.0	100.0	100.0
Loss....................................	0.2	0.3	0.3	0.1	0.2	(1)	0.1	0.1
$1 to $499.............................	29.2	31.7	31.3	28.9	29.8	(1)	30.3	30.5
$500 to $999...........................	19.6	19.8	20.0	20.6	19.5	(1)	24.3	23.7
$1,000 to $1,499.......................	10.9	11.4	13.5	14.5	16.0	(1)	19.4	19.3
$1,500 to $1,999.......................	12.3	12.2	12.7	13.9	15.6	(1)	13.8	12.9
$2,000 to $2,499.......................	11.0	11.6	11.2	11.6	10.4	(1)	7.0	7.3
$2,500 to $2,999.......................	7.2	6.5	5.2	5.2	3.8	(1)	2.7	2.9
$3,000 to $3,499.......................	4.9	3.3	3.1	2.4	2.1	(1)	1.1	1.2
$3,500 to $3,999.......................	2.2	1.2	1.0	1.0	0.9	(1)	0.3	0.6
$4,000 to $4,499.......................	1.0	0.8	0.9	0.5	0.6	(1)	0.2	0.4
$4,500 to $4,999.......................	0.5	0.4	0.3	0.2	0.3	(1)	0.2	0.3
$5,000 to $5,999.......................	0.5	0.3	0.2	0.3	0.3	(1)	0.1	0.3
$6,000 to $9,999.......................	0.4	0.3	0.3	0.3	0.3	(1)	0.1	0.3
$10,000 and over......................	0.1	0.2	0.1	0.2	0.3	(1)	0.1	0.3
Median income for persons with income..	$1,045	$953	$960	$1,009	$1,017	(1)	$901	$909
URBAN AND RURAL NONFARM--MALE								
Total...............................	100.0	100.0	100.0	100.0	100.0	100.0	100.0	100.0
Percent with income.................	90.7	90.8	90.5	90.7	89.6	91.5	90.5	90.0
Percent without income...............	9.3	9.2	9.5	9.3	10.4	8.5	9.5	10.0
Median income for persons with income..	$3,130	$2,784	$2,563	$2,585	$2,368	$2,116	$2,042	$2,265
URBAN AND RURAL NONFARM--FEMALE								
Total...............................	100.0	100.0	100.0	100.0	100.0	100.0	100.0	100.0
Percent with income.................	46.2	45.2	44.1	43.1	41.2	51.7	48.8	51.5
Percent without income...............	53.8	54.8	55.9	56.9	58.8	48.3	51.2	48.5
Median income for persons with income..	$1,147	$1,043	$1,049	$1,122	$1,103	$909	$962	$969
RURAL FARM--MALE								
Total...............................	100.0	100.0	100.0	100.0	100.0	100.0	100.0	100.0
Percent with income.................	86.4	86.7	87.0	85.5	85.8	(1)	85.3	84.7
Percent without income...............	13.6	13.3	13.0	14.5	14.2	(1)	14.7	15.3
Median income for persons with income..	$1,486	$1,328	$1,054	$1,385	$1,360	(1)	$904	$951
RURAL FARM--FEMALE								
Total...............................	100.0	100.0	100.0	100.0	100.0	100.0	100.0	100.0
Percent with income.................	27.7	31.0	28.0	29.7	28.6	(1)	27.6	29.4
Percent without income...............	72.3	69.0	72.0	70.3	71.4	(1)	72.4	70.6
Median income for persons with income..	$440	$417	$392	$467	$483	(1)	$431	$349

[1] Comparable figures not available.

Source: U. S. Bureau of the Census, *Current Population Reports—Consumer Income*, Series P–60, No. 11, table 8.

annual earnings of women employed in some occupation groups (professional and technical workers, clerical workers, and operatives) showed significant increases.   There is some evidence, however, that the effect of wage rate increases for women workers as a whole was offset by an increase in the proportion of intermittent workers, particularly married women, whose annual earnings tend to be low.

Changes in economic conditions are reflected somewhat differently in the income statistics for men and women.   Although the median money income of men varied considerably during the period 1944 to 1951, the proportion of income recipients remained fairly constant (about 90 percent).   The relative stability of the proportion of income recipients among men largely reflects the fact that at any given time the great majority of men who are not disabled or handicapped are in the labor force.

The median money income of women was almost unchanged between 1944 and 1951 (about $1,000), but there were considerable changes in the proportion of income recipients.   The largest proportion of income recipients among women was found during the war years 1944 and 1945, when nearly half of the women had income.   The proportion of female income recipients fell to 39 percent in 1947 but has increased since then.

Over-all changes in income dispersion.   The increase in the level of income as well as the effect of this increase on the distribution of persons by income levels was discussed above.   It now remains to be seen if these increases were accompanied by changes in income dispersion (or "inequality").   An income distribution in which most of the persons are clustered about some central value has by definition little dispersion and therefore shows little concentration of income.   For example, an examination of the income distribution for firemen in appendix tables C–1 and C–5 shows that this distribution has a narrow range of incomes (i.e., it has little dispersion of income) and, as a result, the aggregate income in this occupation is shared by the many rather than concentrated in the hands of the few.   The lowest paid fifth received 13 percent of the total wages paid to firemen in 1949, and the highest paid fifth received only 28 percent of the wages.   In contrast, the income distribution for salaried managers and officials of manufacturing plants exhibits a wider range of incomes, or great dispersion of income and, as a result, it contains a greater amount of income concentration.   The lowest paid fifth of the salaried managers and officials of manufacturing plants received only 7 percent of the aggregate wages paid in this occupation in 1949, whereas the highest paid fifth received half of the wages.

The data in table 53 show the relative distribution of total income between 1944 and 1951.   These data were obtained by ranking the income recipients from lowest to highest according to income and cumulating the percent of persons and the percent of income for each fifth of the distribution.   A given quintile, of course, does not contain the same individuals from year to year. Thus, for example, although the lowest fifth of the income recipients received about the same share of aggregate income payments in 1944 and 1951,[7] it would be erroneous to conclude that the same individuals were involved in each year. On the contrary, it is very likely that the composition of the lowest income group changed somewhat during this period, and there is considerable evidence that the composition of the lowest quintile has changed markedly since 1939.

TABLE 53.—PERCENT OF AGGREGATE INCOME RECEIVED BY EACH FIFTH OF INCOME RECIPIENTS RANKED BY INCOME, BY SEX: 1944 TO 1951

Income recipients	1951	1950	1949	1948	1947	1945	1944
Both sexes	100.0	100.0	100.0	100.0	100.0	100.0	100.0
Lowest fifth	2.5	2.3	2.4	2.9	3.0	3.1	2.6
Second fifth	8.4	7.9	8.4	8.7	8.9	9.0	8.5
Middle fifth	16.7	16.4	16.5	16.6	16.2	16.0	15.6
Fourth fifth	24.7	24.3	25.0	24.2	23.4	24.5	24.2
Highest fifth	47.7	49.1	47.7	47.6	48.5	47.4	49.1
Male	100.0	100.0	100.0	100.0	100.0	100.0	100.0
Lowest fifth	3.5	3.0	3.2	3.5	3.7	4.1	3.4
Second fifth	11.3	10.7	10.2	10.7	10.6	9.5	10.0
Middle fifth	17.9	17.2	17.8	17.4	16.7	17.0	17.2
Fourth fifth	23.4	23.4	24.1	23.1	22.7	24.1	23.8
Highest fifth	43.9	45.7	44.7	45.3	46.3	45.3	45.6
Female	100.0	100.0	100.0	100.0	100.0	100.0	100.0
Lowest fifth	3.5	3.7	3.8	3.9	3.8	4.7	4.3
Second fifth	7.3	6.9	7.4	8.2	7.9	9.1	8.4
Middle fifth	14.6	14.6	15.3	15.7	15.9	16.4	15.4
Fourth fifth	27.5	27.3	26.7	26.5	25.3	26.1	24.3
Highest fifth	47.1	47.5	46.8	45.7	47.1	43.7	47.6

Source: Data for both sexes from U. S. Bureau of the Census, *Current Population Reports—Consumer Income*, Series P–60, No. 11, table F. Figures for males and females derived from unpublished data of the Bureau of the Census.

Despite the substantial increase in the level of income during the period immediately following World War II, there was little change in the distribution of aggregate income. In 1944, the lowest 20 percent of the male income recipients received 3.4 percent of the aggregate income whereas the highest 20 percent received 45.6 percent. These proportions remained virtually unchanged during each of the years between 1944 and 1951. For women, there was also relatively little change in the share of income received by the highest fifth of income recipients; however, there is some evidence of a decrease in the share received by the lower income groups.

---

[7] The following is the income range for each fifth of the income recipients in 1944 and 1951:

Income recipients	Income range for both sexes	
	1951	1944
Lowest fifth	Under $648	Under $483
Second fifth	$648 to $1,662	$483 to $1,079
Middle fifth	$1,663 to $2,720	$1,080 to $1,816
Fourth fifth	$2,721 to $3,859	$1,817 to $2,763
Highest fifth	$3,860 and over	$2,764 and over

During the war years of 1944 and 1945 the lowest 40 percent of the female income recipients received between 13 and 14 percent of the aggregate income paid to women. By 1947, the proportion dropped to 12 percent; and in 1950 and 1951, it was only 11 percent. The drop in the share of the aggregate income received by the lowest 40 percent of the female income recipients during recent years probably reflects the increase in the proportion of part-time workers among women.

Although the distribution of aggregate income was apparently quite stable during the period 1944 to 1951, there is ample evidence of change if the time period is extended back to 1939. Unfortunately, the longer time period must be restricted to the analysis of wage or salary income rather than total income. The wage or salary data in table 54 present

TABLE **54.**—PERCENT OF AGGREGATE WAGE OR SALARY INCOME RECEIVED BY EACH FIFTH OF WAGE OR SALARY RECIPIENTS RANKED BY INCOME, BY SEX: 1939 TO 1951

Wage or salary recipients	1951	1950	1949	1948	1947	1945	1939
Both sexes..............	100.0	100.0	100.0	100.0	100.0	100.0	100.0
Lowest fifth..................	3.0	2.3	2.6	2.9	2.9	2.9	3.4
Second fifth..................	10.6	9.7	10.1	10.2	10.3	10.1	8.4
Middle fifth..................	18.9	18.3	18.7	18.6	17.8	17.4	15.0
Fourth fifth..................	25.9	25.7	26.2	25.5	24.7	25.7	23.9
Highest fifth.................	41.6	44.0	42.4	42.8	44.3	43.9	49.3
Male.....................	100.0	100.0	100.0	100.0	100.0	100.0	100.0
Lowest fifth.................	4.9	3.5	3.6	3.9	4.5	3.8	3.5
Second fifth.................	13.1	12.5	12.3	12.7	11.9	12.4	9.0
Middle fifth.................	19.3	18.7	19.2	19.0	17.9	18.5	15.5
Fourth fifth.................	24.4	24.3	24.8	24.7	26.4	25.4	23.3
Highest fifth................	38.3	41.0	40.1	39.7	39.3	39.9	48.7
Female....................	100.0	100.0	100.0	100.0	100.0	100.0	100.0
Lowest fifth.................	3.3	2.0	2.2	3.0	2.8	4.5	3.0
Second fifth.................	7.8	7.5	8.0	8.5	8.7	10.3	9.2
Middle fifth.................	18.3	17.6	18.3	18.4	18.0	18.5	16.8
Fourth fifth.................	27.7	29.5	28.6	28.6	26.7	27.0	24.5
Highest fifth................	42.9	43.4	42.9	41.5	43.8	39.7	46.5

Source: Data for both sexes from U. S. Bureau of the Census, *Current Population Reports—Consumer Income*, Series P–60, No. 11, table G. Figures for males and females derived from unpublished data of the Bureau of the Census.

essentially the same pattern of income distribution for the postwar period as that shown above for total income; however, these data indicate that substantial changes in the distribution of wage or salary income occurred between 1939 and 1945. During this period, the share of wage or salary income received by the highest 20 percent of wage or salary recipients decreased from 49 percent to 44 percent.[8] The conclusion suggested by

---

[8] The following is the income range for each fifth of the wage or salary income recipients in 1939 and 1951:

Wage or salary recipients	Wage or salary range for both sexes	
	1951	1939
Lowest fifth..................	$1 to $799.........	$1 to $303
Second fifth..................	$800 to $1,976.....	$304 to $622
Middle fifth..................	$1,977 to $2,903...	$623 to $999
Fourth fifth..................	$2,904 to $3,884...	$1,000 to $1,531
Highest fifth.................	$3,885 and over....	$1,532 and over

these data is that income concentration decreased with the expansion of economic activities engendered by World War II; however, during the post-war period, when employment levels were high, there was relatively little change in income concentration.

On the basis of this evidence, it can tentatively be concluded that changes in income distribution do take place over a period of time. Before accepting this conclusion, however, it is important that a closer study be made of the changes within occupation groups.

Income changes for major occupation groups. An examination of the changes in the level of wage or salary income among major occupation groups shows that the greatest relative advances were received by farm and nonfarm laborers, operatives, and craftsmen. Workers in such "white-collar"fields as the professional, sales, and clerical more than doubled their incomes since 1939, but they had smaller relative increases than the groups cited above. Private household workers were among those with the smallest relative gains, perhaps because this group is composed to an increasing extent of baby sitters and other part-time workers. Several occupation groups that contain a large proportion of self-employed workers (nonfarm managers, officials, and proprietors, and farmers and farm managers) also showed relatively small gains in wages or salary; but many of the workers in these occupations may have had considerably greater gains from the operation of their business (table 55).

TABLE 55.—MEDIAN WAGE OR SALARY INCOME OF EXPERIENCED CIVILIAN WORKERS, BY OCCUPATION GROUP AND SEX: 1951 AND 1939

Major occupation group	Both sexes		Male		Female	
	1951	1939[1]	1951	1939[1]	1951	1939[1]
Professional, technical, and kindred workers.....	$3,342	$1,373	$4,071	$1,809	$2,495	$1,023
Farmers and farm managers.......................	472	372	482	373	([2])	348
Managers, officials, and proprietors, exc. farm..	3,926	2,030	4,143	2,136	2,679	1,107
Clerical and kindred workers....................	2,494	1,152	3,366	1,421	2,147	966
Sales workers...................................	2,516	1,032	3,539	1,277	1,176	636
Craftsmen, foremen, and kindred workers.........	3,568	1,298	3,601	1,309	([2])	827
Operatives and kindred workers..................	2,646	850	3,064	1,007	1,739	582
Private household workers.......................	455	305	([2])	429	447	296
Service workers, except private household.......	1,679	693	2,426	833	996	493
Farm laborers and foremen.......................	934	305	982	309	([2])	176
Laborers, except farm and mine.................	2,142	667	2,170	673	([2])	538

[1] Excludes public emergency workers and persons having less than $100 of wage or salary income but includes members of the Armed Forces.

[2] Median not shown where there were fewer than 100 cases in the sample reporting with $1 or more of wage or salary income.

Source: U. S. Bureau of the Census, *Current Population Reports—Consumer Income*, Series P–60, No. 11, table 11.

Some changes have occurred since 1939 both in the occupational distribution of that part of the labor force that works for wage or salary income and in the relative shares of wage or salary income received by occupational groups. Among men, the proportion who were craftsmen increased by about one-third between 1940 and 1952, and the proportion who were nonfarm laborers decreased by about one-fifth. During this period, the share of the income received by craftsmen increased by about 40 percent, whereas the share of income received by nonfarm laborers decreased by about 10 percent.   Although there was relatively little change in the proportion of men who were clerical workers, the share of income received by this group dropped by about one-fifth.   The data in tables 56 and 57 suggest that changes in the occupational distribution of wage or salary workers as well as changes in the distribution of income within

TABLE **56.**—PERCENT OF AGGREGATE WAGE OR SALARY INCOME RECEIVED BY EXPERIENCED CIVILIAN WORKERS, BY OCCUPATION GROUP AND SEX: 1951 AND 1939

Major occupation group	Male				Female			
	1951		1939		1951		1939	
	Income recipients	Wage or salary income	Income recipients	Wage or salary income	Income recipients	Wage or salary income	Income recipients	Wage or salary income
Total experienced civilian labor force[1].............................	100.0	100.0	100.0	100.0	100.0	100.0	100.0	100.0
Professional, technical, and kindred wkrs.	([2])	([2])	([2])	([2])	11.9	17.3	13.6	21.7
Clerical and kindred workers..............	8.1	8.2	8.7	10.5	31.5	38.1	25.5	33.7
Sales workers..........................	5.5	6.5	7.3	9.1	7.5	5.6	6.9	6.0
Craftsmen, foremen, and kindred workers...	24.7	27.4	18.2	19.3	1.2	1.3	1.1	1.3
Operatives and kindred workers...........	24.9	22.8	24.3	20.0	21.8	21.8	21.9	17.2
Private household workers................	([2])	([2])	([2])	([2])	10.4	3.5	16.7	7.7
Service workers, exc. private household...	6.4	4.7	8.0	6.0	11.7	7.7	10.6	7.6
Laborers, except farm and mine...........	10.2	6.7	12.7	7.3	0.6	0.4	1.1	0.8
Other occupations[3]......................	20.2	23.7	20.8	27.8	3.3	4.2	2.6	3.9

[1] The base of the distribution of income recipients is 34.4 million men and 14.4 million women for 1951 and 27.0 million men and 9.2 million women for 1939.   The data for 1951 relate to persons having $1 or more of wage or salary income, whereas the data for 1939 relate to persons having $100 or more of wage or salary income.   Moreover, the data for 1939 exclude public emergency workers but include members of the Armed Forces.

[2] Included in the category "Other occupations."

[3] The occupation groups not shown separately generally include those in which a relatively large proportion of the workers are not primarily dependent upon money wage or salary income.   These occupations include male professional, technical, and kindred workers; farmers and farm managers; managers, officials, and proprietors, except farm; male private household workers; and farm laborers and foremen.

Source: U. S. Bureau of the Census, *Current Population Reports—Consumer Income*, Series P–60, No. 11, table I.

major occupation groups are related to the general narrowing of income differentials that has been observed since 1939.   There has been a relative decrease in the importance of occupations like service workers and laborers that are characterized by a relatively great amount of income dispersion and a relative increase in the importance of occupations like craftsmen that have considerably less income dispersion.   In other words, over-all income differentials narrowed since 1939 in part because relatively more workers are currently employed in occupations that have only moderate income dispersion.   Moreover, the observed change in the occupational distribution of wage or salary workers reflects a shift from the less to the more remunerative jobs. The earnings of craftsmen are considerably closer to the average for all workers than are the earnings of service workers or laborers. The effect of this change is both to raise the average and to narrow the dispersion of the distribution. Subsequent analysis will indicate, however, that these factors were only part, and perhaps a relatively minor part, of the explanation of the decrease in income dispersion since the depression of the 1930's.

TABLE 57.—PERCENT OF AGGREGATE WAGE OR SALARY INCOME RECEIVED BY EACH FIFTH OF EXPERIENCED CIVILIAN WORKERS IN SELECTED OCCUPATION GROUPS RANKED BY INCOME, BY SEX: 1951 AND 1939

Major occupation group and sex	Total	Lowest fifth	Second fifth	Middle fifth	Fourth fifth	Highest fifth
1951						
Male:						
Clerical and kindred workers...............	100.0	8.4	16.5	20.2	23.6	31.3
Sales workers..........................	100.0	5.7	13.9	17.8	22.4	40.2
Craftsmen, foremen, and kindred workers.....	100.0	8.8	15.7	19.6	23.6	32.3
Operatives and kindred workers.............	100.0	7.8	16.1	20.2	23.6	32.3
Service workers, except private household...	100.0	4.7	14.0	20.2	25.9	35.2
Laborers, except farm and mine.............	100.0	4.8	9.1	24.5	26.3	35.3
Female:						
Professional, technical, and kindred wkrs...	100.0	6.0	15.5	19.8	24.8	33.9
Clerical and kindred workers...............	100.0	6.5	15.3	20.7	24.7	32.8
Sales workers..........................	100.0	3.9	7.6	17.7	28.9	41.9
Operatives and kindred workers.............	100.0	5.8	14.6	20.2	25.2	34.2
Private household workers.................	100.0	8.5	8.5	12.0	25.4	45.6
Service workers, except private household...	100.0	4.4	10.9	17.5	26.5	40.7
1939						
Male:						
Clerical and kindred workers...............	100.0	6.7	13.6	17.7	24.0	38.0
Sales workers..........................	100.0	5.0	10.6	15.5	22.1	46.8
Craftsmen, foremen, and kindred workers.....	100.0	6.6	13.3	18.8	24.2	37.1
Operatives and kindred workers.............	100.0	6.5	13.0	18.4	24.7	37.4
Service workers, except private household...	100.0	5.5	11.5	16.5	24.1	42.4
Laborers, except farm and mine.............	100.0	6.3	11.6	17.4	25.8	38.9
Female:						
Professional, technical, and kindred wkrs...	100.0	5.9	12.2	16.5	23.8	41.6
Clerical and kindred workers...............	100.0	7.3	14.9	19.1	23.8	34.9
Sales workers..........................	100.0	6.6	13.1	19.4	23.6	37.3
Operatives and kindred workers.............	100.0	8.2	14.1	19.3	23.8	34.6
Private household workers.................	100.0	8.5	12.2	17.1	22.7	39.5
Service workers, except private household...	100.0	7.6	11.3	18.2	24.5	38.4

Source: U. S. Bureau of the Census, *Current Population Reports—Consumer Income*, Series P–60, No. 11, table K.

Among women, operatives were among those who had the greatest relative increase in their share of income. Although there was no evidence of an increase in the proportion of women in this occupation group, the share of income received by this group increased by about one-fourth. The proportion of women who were clerical workers increased by about one-fourth, and the proportion employed as private household workers decreased by about two-fifths. The relative share of the income received by the former group increased by only about 13 percent, and the share of the income received by the private household workers dropped by about 55 percent.

The available evidence indicates that important changes have taken place since 1939 in the distribution of wage or salary income within certain major occupation groups. Among men, there appears to have been a decrease in income concentration for all the occupation groups (except laborers) shown in table 57. For example, among male operatives and craftsmen, the share of the income received by the lowest fifth increased from 7 percent to about 8 or 9 percent, and the share received by the top fifth decreased from 37 percent to 32 percent. Changes of approximately the same magnitude were noted for male clerical workers. Although there was no change in the share of the income received by the lowest fifth of the salesmen, the share received by the highest fifth of the men in this group decreased from 47 percent to 40 percent. Among male service workers there was also a decrease in the share of income received by the highest fifth.

Only one of the important occupations among women (professional, technical, and kindred workers) showed evidence of a decrease in income concentration. The share of income received by the top fifth for this group decreased from 42 percent to 34 percent. Among sales workers and private household workers, there was an increase in income concentration attributable perhaps to the increase in the proportion of part-time workers. There was also an increase in income concentration among operatives and service workers.

Income changes for detailed occupations. The narrowing of income differentials that was noted within major occupation groups was even more apparent for detailed occupations. This conclusion is strongly supported by several different measures of dispersion that are shown for each occupation in the appendix tables. These tables show the relative quartile range $\left(\dfrac{Q_3 - Q_1}{Q_2}\right)$ for each occupation in 1939 and 1949 (appendix tables C–1 to C–4), the share of the aggregate income received by the highest paid fifth of the workers in each occupation in both years (appendix table C–5), and the percent change for each of these measures between 1939 and 1949 (appendix table C–6).

Considering the relative quartile range (and the same conclusions could be supported by the analysis of the share of the aggregate received by the highest paid fifth of the workers), it is evident from appendix table C–6 that only 12 of the 118 occupations shown for men exhibited an increase in income dispersion between 1939 and 1949. An additional 12 occupations showed a relatively small decrease in income dispersion of less than 10 percent. However, the remaining 94 occupations, which account for eight-tenths of the total, showed substantial decreases in income dispersion during this period. It is highly significant that the decrease in dispersion was as great for full-year workers as it was for all workers. This indicates that the narrowing of wage differentials was probably a more important factor than variations in extent of employment for explaining the diminution of inequality of income. These conclusions apply only to men. For women, there was an *increase* in income dispersion between 1939 and 1949 for about two-thirds of the occupations for all workers and for full-year workers.

Income of families: 1935 to 1950

The great increase in aggregate consumer income in the United States since the 1930's has been accompanied by a marked change in the level and distribution of income among American families as well as among individual income recipients. As table 58 shows, aggregate income received by families and unrelated individuals more than tripled between 1935 and 1950. The aggregate, unadjusted for price changes, increased from $63 billion to $217 billion. Some of this increase was absorbed in a rise in the cost of living. Even after allowance is made for the increase in prices, however, it appears that aggregate income almost doubled during this period.

TABLE **58.**—FAMILIES AND UNRELATED INDIVIDUALS, AGGREGATE INCOME, AND AVERAGE INCOME: 1935–36, 1941, 1944, 1946, 1947, AND 1950

Year	Families and unrelated individuals (thousands)	Aggregate family personal income[1] (billions)		Mean family personal income	
		Current dollars	1950 dollars	Current dollars	1950 dollars
1935–36.............................	38,410	$62.7	$112.8	$1,631	$2,937
1941.................................	41,370	91.4	151.6	2,209	3,664
1944.................................	40,880	147.7	190.1	3,614	4,650
1946.................................	43,330	170.7	199.0	3,940	4,592
1947.................................	44,740	184.6	195.9	4,126	4,379
1950.................................	48,590	216.8	216.8	4,461	4,461

[1] With minor exceptions, aggregate family personal income is the same as personal income as defined by the U. S. Department of Commerce. This concept also differs somewhat from family total money income as defined by the Bureau of the Census.

Source: Selma Goldsmith, *et al.*, "Size Distribution of Income Since the Mid-Thirties," *Review of Economics and Statistics*, Vol. 36, February 1954, table 1.

The increase in aggregate income was reflected in a rise in the income of the average family. Measured in current dollars, which are unadjusted for changes in prices, the average (mean) family income increased continuously from about $1,600 in 1935 to about $4,500 in 1950. When the actual dollar amounts are adjusted for price changes, however, there appears to have been no increase in the average family's real income since 1944. On the contrary, the figures indicate a slight decrease in the purchasing power of the average family during the period after World War II. This conclusion is supported by independently derived data from surveys conducted by the Bureau of the Census shown in figure 15.

As might be expected, the great rise in both the aggregate and the average family income since the 1930's resulted in a marked change in the

FIGURE **15.**—MEDIAN INCOME OF NONFARM FAMILIES: 1944 TO 1952

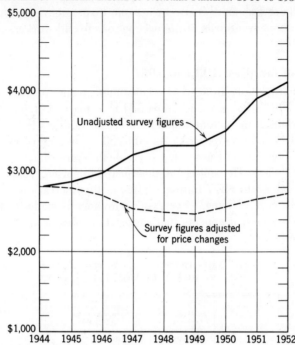

Source: U. S. Bureau of the Census, *Current Population Reports—Consumer Income*, Series P–60, No. 15, p. 2.

distribution of families and unrelated individuals by income levels.   In 1936, over two-fifths of the families and unrelated individuals had incomes under $1,000 and about three-fourths received less than $2,000 (or about $40 per week).   Less than 2 percent had incomes over $7,500 during this period (table 59).   In marked contrast, in 1950, less than one-tenth of the families and unrelated individuals had incomes under $1,000 and less than

TABLE **59.**—PERCENT DISTRIBUTION OF FAMILIES AND UNRELATED INDIVIDUALS BY FAMILY PERSONAL INCOME, FOR THE UNITED STATES: 1935–36, 1941, 1944, AND 1950

Family personal income	1935–36	1941	1944	1950
Number of families and unrelated individuals..............thousands..	38,410	41,370	40,880	48,590
Percent............................	100.0	100.0	100.0	100.0
Under $1,000.............................	43.5	29.0	10.7	7.6
$1,000 to $1,999.........................	34.2	29.9	19.8	15.1
$2,000 to $2,999.........................	13.1	22.3	21.4	16.5
$3,000 to $3,999.........................	4.4	9.8	18.9	17.4
$4,000 to $4,999.........................	1.7	4.0	11.1	14.4
$5,000 to $7,499..,......................	1.6	2.8	11.7	17.5
$7,500 to $9,999.........................	0.6	0.9	3.4	5.9
$10,000 and over.........................	0.9	1.3	3.0	5.6

Source: Selma Goldsmith, *et al.*, "Size Distribution of Income Since the Mid-Thirties," *Review of Economics and Statistics*, Vol. 36, February 1954, table 2.

one-fourth had incomes under $2,000. The proportion with incomes over $7,500 increased eightfold to about 12 percent during this 15-year interval.

The above data relate only to changes in the level of income and the distribution of families and unrelated individuals by income levels. Further insight into the nature of the change in income distribution since the depressed 1930's may be obtained by focusing attention on different segments of the income curve. Table 60 shows the change in the mean income (adjused for price changes) during the period 1935 to 1950 for each fifth of the families and unrelated individuals ranked from lowest to highest according to income. It is apparent from this table that during the entire 15-year period the lower income groups made substantially greater relative gains than the highest income groups. Whereas the mean income for the three lowest quintiles (the bottom 60 percent of the families and unrelated individuals) increased by about 75 to 80 percent, the mean for the highest quintile increased by only one-third. The mean for the top 5 percent of the families and unrelated individuals increased by only about one-sixth.

TABLE 60.—MEAN FAMILY PERSONAL INCOME IN 1950 DOLLARS OF QUINTILES AND TOP 5 PERCENT OF FAMILIES AND UNRELATED INDIVIDUALS RANKED BY SIZE OF FAMILY PERSONAL INCOME: 1935–36, 1941, 1944, AND 1950

Quintile	Mean family personal income in 1950 dollars				Percent increase in mean income		
	1935–36	1941	1944	1950	1935–36 to 1950	1935–36 to 1941	1941 to 1944
Lowest.....................	$607	$746	$1,135	$1,080	78	23	52
Second.....................	1,349	1,731	2,547	2,444	81	28	47
Third......................	2,063	2,809	3,758	3,612	75	36	34
Fourth.....................	3,075	4,085	5,165	4,971	62	33	26
Highest....................	7,591	8,949	10,645	10,197	34	18	19
Total...................	2,937	3,663	4,651	4,461	52	25	27
Top 5 percent..............	15,582	17,607	19,255	18,250	17	13	9

Source: Selma Goldsmith, et al., "Size Distribution of Income Since the Mid-Thirties," *Review of Economics and Statistics*, Vol. 36, February 1954, table 5.

The data in table 60 clearly suggest that there was a narrowing of the spread of incomes between 1935 and 1950, and reference to table 61 and figure 16 leaves no doubt about it. The share of the aggregate income received by the lowest fifth of the families and unrelated individuals increased by about one-sixth from 4.1 percent of the total to about 4.8 percent. Approximately the same relative increases were received by the next two-fifths of the families and unrelated individuals. In contrast, the share of the aggregate received by the highest fifth *decreased* by 12 percent, and the share received by the highest 5 percent decreased by 23 percent. These figures show beyond any doubt that families and unrelated individuals at the bottom and in the middle of the income distribution increased their share of

FIGURE 16.—LORENZ CURVES FOR THE DISTRIBUTION OF FAMILY PERSONAL INCOME FOR
SELECTED YEARS FROM 1935–36 TO 1950

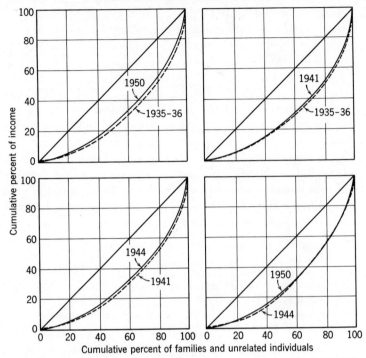

Source: Selma Goldsmith, *et al.*, "Size Distribution of Income Since the Mid-Thirties," *Review of Economics and Statistics*, Vol. 36, February 1954, p. 8.

income payments between 1935 and 1950. Virtually all the change in income distribution occurred prior to and during World War II. Income distribution in the United States has been practically unchanged during the postwar period.

TABLE 61.—DISTRIBUTION OF FAMILY PERSONAL INCOME AMONG QUINTILES AND TOP 5 PERCENT OF FAMILIES AND UNRELATED INDIVIDUALS RANKED BY SIZE OF FAMILY PERSONAL INCOME: 1935–36, 1941, 1944, AND 1950

Quintile	1935–36	1941	1944	1950	Percent change, 1935–36 to 1950
Lowest............................	4.1	4.1	4.9	4.8	+17
Second............................	9.2	9.5	10.9	11.0	+20
Third.............................	14.1	15.3	16.2	16.2	+15
Fourth............................	20.9	22.3	22.2	22.3	+7
Highest...........................	51.7	48.8	45.8	45.7	-12
Total.........................	100.0	100.0	100.0	100.0	...
Top 5 percent.....................	26.5	24.0	20.7	20.4	-23

Source: Selma Goldsmith, *et al.*, "Size Distribution of Income Since the Mid-Thirties," *Review of Economics and Statistics*, Vol. 36, February 1954, table 4.

CHAPTER 9

FACTORS RELATED TO RECENT CHANGES
IN INCOME DISTRIBUTION

The data that have been presented for both persons and for families support the thesis that income in the United States was more equally distributed after World War II than it was during the prewar period. The problem that now remains is the analysis of the factors that account for the observed changes in income distribution. In view of the complexity of the structure of income distribution, it would be almost impossible to make an exhaustive list of the many factors that may affect that distribution. Such a list would require an accounting of the changed relationships among the many economic and sociological factors that determine the size distribution of income. By way of compromise, the present discussion will be confined to the examination of several hypotheses regarding the change in income distribution that have been suggested by the Council of Economic Advisers. In the *Economic Report of the President,* January 1949, the Council suggests that "the decline in income concentration from the depression period to the immediate postwar period is most probably due to the virtual elimination of unemployment which raised the share of the lower and middle groups. The increase in the number of families with more than one earner and the relative increase in farm income are also significant factors." [1] These hypotheses are examined in some detail below.

Variations in employment

The thesis that changes in income distribution are related to variations in employment is not new. It appears in several places in economic literature and was cogently stated as follows by Horst Mendershausen in his book, *Changes in Income Distribution During the Great Depression:*

> The inverse correlation between changes in the income level and the degree of inequality within, roughly, the lower two-thirds of income recipients can be explained by variations in unemployment, and, to some extent, in wage rates. There are three contributing factors: (*a*) changes in the significance of the income gap between the

---

[1] *The Economic Report of the President,* January 1949, pp. 91, 92.

employed and the unemployed, (*b*) uneven incidence of unemployment among low- and high-pay employees, and (*c*) changes in wage differentials between low- and high-pay workers.[2]

Several hypotheses regarding the specific manner in which changes in income distribution are related to changes in employment suggested by the above paragraph can be tested, perhaps for the first time, by the data shown in appendix tables C–1 to C–6. These hypotheses may be summarized in the following manner. The over-all decrease in the inequality of income distribution among wage or salary workers between 1939 and 1949 may be explained by:

1. A change in the occupational structure which resulted in a larger proportion of workers in occupations having higher incomes and/or more equal distributions of income.

2. A general decrease of inequality within occupations because of an increase in the proportion of full-year workers.

3. A general decrease of inequality within occupations because of a narrowing of the income differentials among full-year workers.

4. A decrease in the income differential between high-paid and low-paid occupations.

The first hypothesis was validated to some extent by the data previously presented in table 56, which showed that between 1939 and 1951 there was a change in the occupational distribution of male wage or salary recipients which resulted in an increase in the proportion employed as craftsmen and a decrease in the proportion employed as service workers and laborers. This change suggested an increase in the importance of occupations characterized by both higher incomes and less dispersion. An examination of the data for more detailed occupations in Appendix C lends some support to this conclusion. These data, which are summarized in table 62, show that there has been a slight decrease in the numerical importance of the lower paid occupations and a correspondingly small increase in the importance of the higher paid occupations. For example, the occupations for the three lowest deciles of male workers ranked by median wage or salary income in 1949 accounted for 28 percent of all workers in 1949 and 32 percent of the workers in 1939. In contrast, the occupations in the three highest deciles accounted for 33 percent of the male workers in 1949 and 32 percent of the workers in 1939. Apparently, the lower paid occupations in 1949 accounted for a somewhat smaller proportion of the male workers than in 1939, and the better paid occupations accounted for a somewhat larger proportion. These changes undoubtedly had some impact on the distribution of wage or salary income; however, their importance should not be overemphasized inasmuch as they were

---

[2] H. Mendershausen, *Changes in Income Distribution During the Great Depression*, National Bureau of Economic Research, New York, 1946, p. 68.

quite small as compared with the changes in income distribution during this period.

Changes in the occupational distribution of male wage or salary workers between 1939 and 1949 appear to be somewhat more closely related to dispersion of income than to level of income.   As table 62 indicates, the occupations in the three lowest deciles accounted for 33 percent of the male workers ranked by dispersion of wage or salary income in 1949 and only 27 percent of the workers in 1939, whereas the occupations in the three highest deciles accounted for 30 percent of the workers in 1949 and 32 percent of the workers in 1939.   In other words, during the decade there was a significant increase in the relative importance of occupations characterized by comparatively little income dispersion, and this factor is undoubtedly related to the over-all narrowing of wage differentials during this period.   Most of the increase in the proportion of workers within the lowest third of the occupations (in terms of dispersion) occurred among mechanics, foremen in manufacturing industries, welders, and operatives in machinery manufacturing industries.   Most of the other occupations within this group had about the same relative number of workers in 1939 and 1949.   In general, the data support the hypothesis that changes in the occupational structure operated in the direction of reducing the spread of incomes among male wage or salary workers during the 10-year period following 1939; however, as subsequent analysis will indicate, there are other factors that appear to have played a more basic role in this process.

TABLE **62.**—PERCENT OF MALE WAGE OR SALARY WORKERS IN SELECTED OCCUPATIONS RANKED BY MEDIAN AND DISPERSION OF WAGE OR SALARY INCOME: 1949 AND 1939

Occupations ranked by median or by dispersion of wage or salary income in 1949	Ranked by median wage or salary income		Ranked by dispersion of wage or salary income $\left(\dfrac{Q_3 - Q_1}{Q_2}\right)$	
	1949[1]	1939	1949[1]	1939
Total.........................	100.0	100.0	100.0	100.0
Lowest tenth..........................	9.0	9.9	10.0	9.6
Second tenth..........................	9.6	10.7	10.4	8.6
Third tenth...........................	8.9	11.7	12.5	8.9
Fourth tenth..........................	10.5	10.0	7.7	8.0
Fifth tenth...........................	9.4	9.5	9.0	10.4
Sixth tenth...........................	9.2	5.7	9.4	11.2
Seventh tenth.........................	10.0	10.9	11.3	11.2
Eighth tenth..........................	11.1	10.0	10.9	12.2
Ninth tenth...........................	10.6	10.7	9.3	8.9
Highest tenth.........................	11.5	10.9	9.9	11.0

[1]All occupations were first ranked from lowest to highest by median wage or salary income in 1949 or by level of dispersion of wage or salary income in 1949.   They were then divided approximately into deciles based on the number of workers in each occupation.   The occupations included in each decile in 1949 were then identified.   The proportion of workers included in each decile for 1949 differs from 10 percent because of the necessity to attribute to all the workers in a given occupation the decile designation of that occupation.   The percentages for 1939 in the above table show the proportion of workers in 1939 in the occupations included in each decile in 1949.

Source: Appendix tables C–1, C–3, and C–6.

The second hypothesis attempts to relate the observed decrease in income differentials to the fuller employment patterns that prevailed in 1949 as compared with 1939. According to this hypothesis, the dispersion of income within occupations should have been reduced during this period because there was a marked decrease in unemployment, and, as a result, there should have been a reduction in income differences within occupations attributable to variations in extent of employment. To test this hypothesis adequately, it would be necessary to have data showing the distribution of persons by weeks worked for each occupation in 1939 and 1949. In the absence of such information, it may be of interest to see what clues can be developed, from the data in appendix table C–6 relating to the proportion of full-year workers in each occupation in 1939 and 1949.

TABLE 63.—SELECTED OCCUPATIONS FOR MEN BY PERCENT CHANGE BETWEEN 1939 AND 1949 IN THE PROPORTION OF FULL-YEAR WORKERS AND DISPERSION OF WAGE OR SALARY INCOME

Percent change in proportion of full-year workers between 1939 and 1949	Total	Percent change in dispersion of wage or salary income between 1939 and 1949 $\left(\dfrac{Q_3 - Q_1}{Q_2} \right)$				
		Decrease				Increase
		30.0 percent or more	20.0 to 29.9 percent	10.0 to 19.9 percent	Less than 10.0 percent	
Total......................	118	21	39	33	12	13
Decrease......................	46	6	13	12	7	8
Increase......................	72	15	26	21	5	5
0.1 to 4.9......................	14	1	5	6	1	1
5.0 to 9.9......................	12	2	6	3	1	...
10.0 to 14.9......................	9	3	3	1	...	2
15.0 to 19.9......................	7	...	3	3	...	1
20.0 or more......................	30	9	9	8	3	1

Source: Appendix table C–6.

One would have expected, on *a priori* grounds, that the great majority of occupations would have had a larger proportion of full-year workers in 1949 than in 1939. Yet, the data in table 63, which were derived from table C–6, show that there was a *decrease* in the proportion of full-year workers in 46 of the occupations examined for men. These occupations, which account for about two-fifths of the 118 occupations which were studied and for about one-third of the workers, were concentrated in the "white-collar" and service trades. Thus, for example, there was a decrease in the proportion of full-year workers in all the occupations within the salaried managers and officials and service workers groups, in four-fifths of the clerical and sales occupations, and in more than half of the occupations in the professional workers group. In total, 37 of the 46 occupations that showed a decrease in the proportion of full-year workers were in these occupation groups. Most of the occupations that showed a decrease in the proportion of full-year workers ranked high on the income scale in 1939 and 1949. They had a comparatively large proportion of full-year workers even during the earlier period and also had relatively smaller increases in median income than most other occupations. There was a decrease in income dispersion within four-fifths of these occupations, despite the drop in the proportion of full-year workers. As table 63 indicates, income dispersion decreased by 20 percent or more in about two-fifths of these occupations.

Among the remaining three-fifths of the occupations that did show a relative increase in the proportion of full-year workers, there was some correlation between the extent of this increase and the relative change in dispersion. Only one-tenth of the occupations in which the proportion of full-year workers increased by less than 10 percent had a decrease in dispersion of 30 percent or more. In contrast, nearly one-third of the occupations in which the proportion of full-year workers increased by 20 percent or more had this great a decrease in dispersion. In other words, there was a relatively greater reduction in the spread of incomes within occupations that had comparatively greater increases in the proportion of full-year workers, and thus the hypothesis appears to be supported by the data. As subsequent analysis will indicate, the increase in the proportion of full-year workers not only narrowed the income gap within occupations; it also narrowed the gap between high-paid and low-paid occupations.

TABLE **64.**—SELECTED OCCUPATIONS FOR MEN BY PERCENT CHANGE BETWEEN 1939 AND 1949 IN THE PROPORTION OF FULL-YEAR WORKERS AND IN MEDIAN WAGE OR SALARY INCOME

Percent change in proportion of full-year workers between 1939 and 1949	Percent increase in median wage or salary income between 1939 and 1949				
	Total	Less than 100.0	100.0 to 149.9	150.0 to 199.9	200.0 or more
Total............................	118	24	53	36	5
Decrease.........................	46	21	21	4	...
Increase.........................	72	3	32	32	5
0.1 to 4.9....................	14	2	10	2	...
5.0 to 9.9....................	12	1	9	2	...
10.0 to 14.9..................	9	...	5	2	2
15.0 to 19.9..................	7	...	1	6	...
20.0 or more.................	30	...	7	20	3

Source: Appendix table C–6.

There is a very strong correlation between the relative increase in full-year workers, the relative increase in median income, and the position of an occupation on the income scale. In general, the occupations that had the greatest relative increases in the proportion of full-year workers also had the greatest relative increases in median income. Table 64 shows that over two-thirds of the occupations in which the proportion of full-year workers increased by 20 percent or more also had an increase in median income of 150 percent or more. In contrast, only one-fifth of the occupations in which the proportion of full-year workers increased by less than

10 percent had gains in median income that were this high. Moreover, lower paid occupations had the greatest relative gains in both the proportion of full-year workers and in median income. About three-fifths of the occupations that had a decrease in the proportion of full-year workers were in the highest three deciles ranked by income in 1949, whereas only one-half of the occupations that had an increase of less than 10 percent in the proportion of full-year workers and only one-eighth of the occupations that had an increase of 20 percent or more ranked this high on the income scale. Thus, the fuller employment patterns that prevailed in 1949 as compared with 1939 had greater relative impact on the lower paid occupations than on the higher paid ones and thereby contributed to the narrowing of income differentials.

The third hypothesis relates changes in income distribution within occupations to changes in wage rates rather than to variations in extent of employment. According to this hypothesis, any decrease in the income spread between 1939 and 1949 among full-year workers within an occupation, reflects a narrowing of wage-rate differentials within the occupation since all the workers considered in the comparison were presumably fully employed throughout the year. This interpretation is valid for the data for 1939; however, the data for 1949 may include persons who did regular part-time work during the year but were employed for at least one day during every week. This difference in definition would tend to increase the dispersion in the 1949 data, and, therefore, the figures tend to understate the extent to which income dispersion decreased among full-year workers during this period.

One of the most striking facts indicated by the data for full-year workers in appendix table C–6 is the widespread nature of the decrease in wage-rate differentials within occupations. There was a decrease in relative income dispersion between 1939 and 1949 in all but nine of the occupations that were studied for men. The same conclusion is suggested by the data relating to the share of the aggregate income received by the highest paid fifth of the full-year workers in each occupation. The tendency for the spread of wages among production workers to narrow has, of course, been previously noted. For example, one recent writer has remarked that "wartime regulation of wages led to a narrowing of wage differentials between industries, between firms in the same industry, and between different classes of work in the same plant. Such effects have been more than temporary. Developments since V–J Day indicate that much of this wartime heritage has become an important ingredient of our economy." [3] The data presented here indicate that a narrowing of wage differentials has been

---

[3] David R. Roberts in *Insights into Labor Issues*, edited by R. A. Lester and J. Shister, Macmillan Company, New York, 1948. This quotation and additional evidence on the subject appear in Frederic Meyers, "Notes on Changes in the Distribution of Manufacturing Wage Earners by Straight-Time Hourly Earnings, 1941–48," *Review of Economics and Statistics*, Vol. 32, November 1950.

characteristic of virtually all occupations and has by no means been restricted to production workers.

Another important fact suggested by the data for full-year workers is that the decrease in income dispersion was relatively greater for the higher paid occupations than for those near the bottom or the middle of the income scale. Table 65 shows that income dispersion decreased by 20 percent or more in over half of the occupations in the three highest deciles ranked by income. In contrast, only one-fifth of the occupations in the three lowest deciles had this much of a decrease in income dispersion. All but one of the occupations in which income dispersion decreased by 30 percent or more were in the four highest deciles. Apparently there is greater stability in the income spread between high-paid and low-paid workers among occupations near the bottom of the income scale than among those near the top.

TABLE 65.—Selected Occupations for Male Full-Year Wage or Salary Workers Ranked by Median Wage or Salary Income in 1949, by Percent Change in Dispersion of Wage or Salary Income

Occupations ranked by median wage or salary income in 1949	Total	Percent change in dispersion of wage or salary income between 1939 and 1949 $\left(\dfrac{Q_3 - Q_1}{Q_2}\right)$				
		Decrease				Increase
		30.0 percent or more	20.0 to 29.9 percent	10.0 to 19.9 percent	Less than 10.0 percent	
Total......................	118	17	31	37	24	9
Lowest tenth.....................	11	1	...	4	2	4
Second tenth.....................	13	...	4	5	4	...
Third tenth......................	14	...	4	4	2	4
Fourth tenth.....................	2	...	1	1	...	...
Fifth tenth......................	16	...	2	8	6	...
Sixth tenth......................	3	...	1	2	...	...
Seventh tenth....................	10	3	6	1	...	...
Eighth tenth.....................	13	2	3	4	3	1
Ninth tenth......................	17	2	7	4	4	...
Highest tenth....................	19	9	3	4	3	...

Source: Appendix table C–6.

The fourth hypothesis relates the decrease in dispersion in the over-all income curve to a decrease in the income spread between high-paid and low-paid occupations. In other words, if the occupations near the bottom of the income scale had relatively greater income gains between 1939 and 1949 than those near the top of the scale, income dispersion would have been reduced in the over-all distribution. An examination of table 66 indicates that there is considerable validity to this hypothesis. Most of the occupations that had the greatest proportionate gains in median income were relatively-low paid. About one-half of the occupations in which the median income increased by 150 percent or more were in the three lowest deciles ranked by income. In contrast, all but two of the occupations

TABLE **66.**—SELECTED OCCUPATIONS FOR MALE WAGE OR SALARY WORKERS RANKED BY MEDIAN WAGE OR SALARY INCOME IN 1949, BY PERCENT INCREASE IN MEDIAN INCOME BETWEEN 1939 AND 1949

Occupations ranked by median wage or salary income in 1949	Total	Percent increase in median wage or salary income between 1939 and 1949				
		Less than 100.0	100.0 to 124.9	125.0 to 149.9	150.0 to 199.9	200.0 or more
Total.....................	118	24	18	35	36	5
Lowest tenth.................	11	1	1	3	4	2
Second tenth.................	13	...	2	3	5	3
Third tenth..................	14	1	...	3	10	...
Fourth tenth.................	2	...	...	...	2	...
Fifth tenth..................	16	...	...	9	7	...
Sixth tenth..................	3	...	...	2	1	...
Seventh tenth................	10	...	1	5	4	...
Eighth tenth.................	13	4	5	4	...	...
Ninth tenth..................	17	7	5	2	3	...
Highest tenth................	19	11	4	4	...	...

Source: Appendix table C–6.

TABLE **67.**—SELECTED OCCUPATIONS FOR MALE FULL-YEAR WAGE OR SALARY WORKERS RANKED BY MEDIAN WAGE OR SALARY INCOME IN 1949, BY PERCENT INCREASE IN MEDIAN INCOME BETWEEN 1939 AND 1949

Occupations ranked by median wage or salary income in 1949	Total	Percent increase in median wage or salary income between 1939 and 1949			
		Less than 100.0	100.0 to 124.9	125.0 to 149.9	150.0 or more
Total.........................	118	33	31	37	17
Lowest tenth.........................	11	1	...	2	8
Second tenth.........................	13	1	1	6	5
Third tenth..........................	14	1	3	8	2
Fourth tenth.........................	2	...	...	2	...
Fifth tenth..........................	16	1	6	7	2
Sixth tenth..........................	3	...	...	3	...
Seventh tenth........................	10	...	4	6	...
Eighth tenth.........................	13	7	6	...	...
Ninth tenth..........................	17	10	5	2	...
Highest tenth........................	19	12	6	1	...

Source: Appendix table C–6.

in which the median increased by less than 100 percent were in the highest three deciles. Thus, the greatest relative gains were experienced by the lower paid occupations, and the smallest relative gains were experienced by the higher paid occupations. There are several reasons for these differential income gains. As previously noted, the increase in employment between 1939 and 1949 had a greater impact on the lower paid occupations than on those that paid relatively well. There was a considerably greater increase in the proportion of full-year workers for occupations in the three lowest deciles ranked by income than in the three highest deciles. This factor undoubtedly helped to reduce the differences between the average incomes for these occupations. Moreover, even if variations in extent of employment are held constant and attention is focused on full-year workers, it is apparent from table 67 that the relative income gains

were highest among the lower paid occupations.   All but two of the occupations in which the median income for full-year workers increased by 150
percent or more were in the three lowest deciles, and, conversely, all but
four of the occupations in which the median increased by less than 100
percent were in the three highest deciles.   Thus, both the increase in employment and the decrease in wage-rate differentials operated to reduce the
income gap between high-paid and low-paid occupations.

Increase in earners per family

Despite the rapid increase in family formation between 1940 and 1951,
employment rose even more rapidly, and the result was an increase in the
average number of workers per family.   Census data indicate that the proportion of nonfarm families with more than one wage earner increased
from 28 percent in 1939 to 35 percent in 1951.[4]   The question that arises
is how the increase in the number of earners per family is related to the
diminution of inequality in the distribution of family income.

There is no necessary relationship between the increase in the number of earners per family and the decrease in income concentration.   If,
as a result of the increase in employment opportunities, earners were
added proportionately to families at all income levels, this factor in itself
would not necessarily have caused a change in income concentration.   The
point that must be demonstrated is that the increase in the number of
earners per family took place to a greater extent among the low- and
middle-income families than among the upper-income families.   The possibility that such a shift actually did take place may be deduced from the
figures shown in table 68.

TABLE **68.**—PERCENT OF FAMILIES WITH MORE THAN ONE EARNER, BY FAMILY INCOME IN 1951

Family income in 1951	Percent with more than one earner	Family income in 1951	Percent with more than one earner
Under $1,000	15	$5,000 to $5,999	56
$1,000 to $1,999	26	$6,000 to $6,999	66
$2,000 to $2,999	27	$7,000 to $9,999	68
$3,000 to $3,999	31	$10,000 to $14,999	58
$4,000 to $4,999	43	$15,000 and over	43

Source: U. S. Bureau of the Census, *Current Population Reports—Consumer Income*, Series P–60,
No. 12, table J.

The proportion of families with more than one earner increased with
each successive income level up to $10,000.   Only one-fourth of the fami-
lies with incomes under $3,000 were multiearner families, whereas about
one-half of the families with incomes between $4,000 and $6,000 and
about two-thirds of the families with incomes between $6,000 and $10,000
were multiearner families.   At the very highest income level less than

---

[4] U. S. Bureau of the Census, *Current Population Reports—Consumer Income*, Series P–60, No. 12,
p. 9.

one-half of the families had more than one earner. This pattern suggests that many of the middle-income families would probably be at lower income levels if they depended entirely upon the income of the family heads. It is very likely that during periods of great unemployment, when marginal workers find it difficult find jobs, many such families are pushed back into the lower income brackets because supplementary workers in these families are thrown out of work. On the other hand, the inability of many families to send more than one member into the labor market may explain to some extent the presence of a relatively large number of low-income families during a period of high employment.

Another way of viewing the relationship between family income and the number of earners per family is indicated in table 69, which shows the distribution of families and of family heads by total income level. These data do not cover the same time period or the same families as the data in table 68. They do provide, however, an indication of the extent to which families depend upon the supplementary income provided by persons other than the family head. Whereas nearly 4 million families had incomes between $6,000 and $10,000 in 1949, only 1.4 million family heads had this much income. These figures indicate that the number of families with incomes between $6,000 and $10,000 would be reduced by about two-thirds if they depended completely upon the income received by the family heads. In contrast, the number of families with incomes of $10,000 or more would be reduced by less than one-third if the supplementary earners were removed. These figures generally support the thesis that the increase in the number of earners per family probably occurred disproportionately among the middle-income families, thereby increasing the share of the income received by these families.

TABLE **69.**—INCOME OF FAMILIES AND FAMILY HEADS IN 1949

Total money income in 1949	Families	Family heads
Total..	39,200,000	39,200,000
Under $2,000...............................	10,600,000	14,900,000
$2,000 to $2,999...........................	8,100,000	9,200,000
$3,000 to $3,999...........................	7,800,000	8,100,000
$4,000 to $4,999...........................	4,700,000	3,400,000
$5,000 to $5,999...........................	3,100,000	1,500,000
$6,000 to $6,999...........................	1,900,000	700,000
$7,000 to $9,999...........................	2,000,000	700,000
$10,000 and over..........................	1,000,000	700,000

Source: Herman P. Miller, "Factors Related to Recent Changes in Income Distribution in the United States," *Review of Economics and Statistics*, Vol. 33, August 1951, table 3.

Increase in farm income

The average cash income of farm families is considerably lower than that of nonfarm families. Therefore, an increase in the income of farm families relative to that of nonfarm families may be regarded as a diminution of inequality for the income distribution as a whole.

Available statistics indicate that the mean income of farm families has increased relative to that of nonfarm families since the 1930's. The mean income of nonfarm families in 1936 was $2,020, and that of farm-operator families was $951. By 1947, the mean income of nonfarm families had increased to $4,775, and that of farm-operator families had increased to $3,511.[5] In other words, the mean income of nonfarm families in 1947 was only somewhat more than twice as high as it was in 1936, whereas the mean income of farm-operator families was nearly four times as high as it was in 1936.

Perhaps even more important than the relative increase in the average income of farm families is the change in the number and composition of the farm population which has taken place during recent years and which was referred to in an earlier section. As previously noted (page 35) there was a large migration of the farm population to nonfarm areas between 1940 and 1947. During this period, the number of farm households decreased from 7.1 million to 6.7 million (6 percent), whereas the number of nonfarm households increased from 28.0 million to 32.5 million (16 percent).[6] The most important aspect of the decrease in the farm population from the point of view of income distribution is that about four-fifths of it can be accounted for by the movement of nonwhite households (mostly southern Negro sharecroppers) from the farms to nonfarm areas.[7] This shift implies that many of the families that were at the very bottom of the income scale in 1939 are relatively much higher on the income scale today by virtue of the fact that they changed from farm to nonfarm occupations and also because they moved from areas in which the pay-and-price structure was low to those in which it was higher. During a period of full employment the movement of households from farms to the cities may be regarded as a factor tending to reduce income inequality because it means that many low-income families are being moved closer to the average income of all families.[8]

---

[5] Selma Goldsmith, et al., "Size Distribution of Income Since the Mid-Thirties," *Review of Economics and Statistics*, Vol. 36, February 1954, p. 12.

[6] U. S. Bureau of the Census, *Current Population Reports—Population Characteristics*, Series P–20, No. 11, table 2.

[7] In 1940 there were 7.1 million farm households of which 6.1 million were white and 1.0 million were nonwhite. In 1947 there were 6.7 million farm households of which 6.0 million were white and 0.7 million were nonwhite (U. S. Bureau of the Census, *Current Population Reports—Population Characteristics*, Series P–20, No. 11, table 2).

[8] A somewhat different view of the effect of population movements on income distribution appears in an article by M. A. Copeland, "The Social and Economic Determinants of the Distribution of Income in the United States," *American Economic Review*, Vol. 37, March 1947. In this article, Copeland states: "The movement of population into metropolitan areas has been a factor making for increased inequality of incomes, and . . . without this population movement the inequality of incomes would have been decreased during the past twenty-odd years" (p. 61).

BIBLIOGRAPHY

BOOKS

1. American Economic Association, *Readings in the Theory of Income Distribution*, Blakiston Company, Philadelphia, 1946.
2. Ascoli, M., and F. Lehmann, *Political and Economic Democracy*, W. W. Norton Company, New York, 1937.
3. Barkin, S., *The Older Worker in Industry*, J. B. Lyon Company, New York, 1933.
4. Blakey, R. G., and others, *Analyses of Minnesota Income, 1938–39*, University of Minnesota Press, 1944.
5. Brissenden, P. F., *Earnings of Factory Workers, 1899 to 1927*, Government Printing Office, Washington, D. C., 1929.
6. Burns, A. E., A. C. Neal, and D. S. Watson, *Modern Economics*, Harcourt, Brace and Company, New York, 1948.
7. Dalton, H., *Some Aspects of the Inequality of Incomes in Modern Communities*, George Routledge and Sons, London, 1920.
8. Davis, H. T., *The Analysis of Economic Time Series*, Principia Press, Bloomington, Indiana, 1941.
9. DeJouvenal, B., *The Ethics of Redistribution*, Cambridge University Press, London, 1951.
10. Durand, J. D., *The Labor Force in the United States: 1890–1960*, Social Science Research Council, New York, 1948.
11. Edwards, A. M., *Comparative Occupation Statistics for the United States, 1870 to 1940*, Government Printing Office, Washington, D. C., 1943.
12. Ellis, H. S., *A Survey of Contemporary Economics*, Blakiston Company, Philadelphia, 1949.
13. Friedman, M., and S. Kuznets, *Income From Independent Professional Practice*, National Bureau of Economic Research, New York, 1945.
14. Galton, F., *Hereditary Genius*, Macmillan and Company, London, 1869.
15. Hansen, A. H., *Fiscal Policy and Business Cycles*, W. W. Norton Company, New York, 1941.
16. *Income in the United States—Its Amount and Distribution, 1909–1919*, 2 vols., National Bureau of Economic Research, New York, 1922.
17. Keynes, J. M., *The General Theory of Employment, Interest, and Money*, Harcourt, Brace and Company, New York, 1935.
18. Kuznets, S., *National Income: A Summary of Findings*, National Bureau of Economic Research, New York, 1946.
    Shares of Upper Income Groups in Income and Savings, National Bureau of Economic Research, New York, 1953.
19. Kyrk, H., *The Family in the American Economy*, University of Chicago Press, Chicago, 1953.
20. Lerner, A. P., *The Economics of Control*, Macmillan Company, New York, 1946.
21. Lester, R. A., and J. Shister, *Insights into Labor Issues*, Macmillan Company, New York, 1948.
22. Leven, M., H. G. Moulton, and C. Warburton, *America's Capacity to Consume*, Brookings Institution, Washington, D. C., 1934.
23. Leven, M., *The Income Structure of the United States*, Brookings Institution, Washington, D. C., 1938.
24. Loria, A., *The Economic Synthesis: A Study of the Laws of Income*, George Allen and Company, London, 1914.
25. Meade, J. E., *An Introduction to Economic Analysis and Policy*, Oxford University Press, New York, 1937.
26. Moore, H. L., *Laws of Wages: An Essay in Statistical Economics*, Macmillan Company, New York, 1911.
27. Moulton, H. G., *Controlling Factors in Economic Development*, Brookings Institution, Washington, D. C., 1949.

28. Myrdal, G., *An American Dilemma*, Harper and Brothers, New York, 1944.
29. Palmer, G. L., *Labor Mobility in Six Cities*, Social Science Research Council, New York, 1954.
30. Parnes, H. S., *The Mobility of American Workers*. (Mimeograph of report prepared for the Labor · Market Research Committee of the Social Science Research Council.)
31. Pigou, A. C., *The Economics of Welfare*, third edition, Macmillan and Company, London, 1929.
    Income, An Introduction to Economics, Macmillan & Company, London, 1946.
32. Samuelson, P. A., *Economics: An Introductory Analysis*, McGraw-Hill, New York, 1948.
33. Shister, J., *Economics of the Labor Market*, J. B. Lippincott Company, Philadelphia, 1949.
34. Snyder, C., *Capitalism the Creator*, Macmillan Company, New York, 1940.
35. *Studies in Income and Wealth*, Conference on Research in Income and Wealth, Vols. 1–15, National Bureau of Economic Research, New York. The following volumes contain particularly valuable data on the size distribution of income:
    Vol. 5, *Income Size Distributions in the United States*, 1943.
    Vol. 6, Selected Papers on Income Measurement, 1943.
    Vol. 7, Mendershausen, H., *Changes in Income During the Great Depression*, 1946.
    Vol. 9, Hanna, F. A., J. A. Pechman, and S. M. Lerner, *Analysis of Wisconsin Income*, 1948.
    Vol. 13, Ten Papers on the Size Distribution of Income, 1951.
    Vol. 15, Eight Papers on the Size Distribution of Income, 1952.
36. Taussig, F. W., *Principles of Economics*, Macmillan Company, New York, 1920.
37. Toynbee, A. J., *Civilization on Trial*, Oxford University Press, New York, 1948.
38. Turgot, A., *Reflections on the Formation and the Distribution of Riches* (Ashley translation), Macmillan Company, New York, 1898.
39. Wright, D. McC., *The Creation of Purchasing Power*, Harvard University Press, Cambridge, Mass., 1942.
    Democracy and Progress, Macmillan Company, New York, 1948.

ARTICLES AND PAMPHLETS

40. Barkin, S., "Should There Be a Fixed Retirement Age? Organized Labor Says No," *Annals of the American Academy of Political and Social Science*, January 1952.
41. Bloch, J. W., "Regional Wage Differentials: 1907–46," *Monthly Labor Review*, Vol. 66, April 1948.
42. Board of Governors of the Federal Reserve System, Annual Surveys of Consumer Finances, 1945–1953, which appear in various issues of the *Federal Reserve Bulletin*.
43. Bogue, D. J., *A Methodological Study of Migration and Labor Mobility*, Scripps Foundation Studies in Population Distribution, June 1952.
44. Britton, V., "Sources of Earnings of Rural Farm Families," *Journal of Home Economics*, Vol. 45, May 1953.
45. Burns, A. F., *Looking Forward*, Thirty-First Annual Report of the National Bureau of Economic Research, 1951.
46. Cannan, E., "The Division of Income," *Quarterly Journal of Economics*, Vol. 19, May 1905.
47. Classon, C. C., "Some Social Applications of the Doctrine of Probability," *Journal of Political Economy*, Vol. 7, March 1899.
48. Congress of Industrial Organizations, Committee on Economic Policy, *Maintaining Prosperity*.
49. Copeland, M. A., "The Social and Economic Determinants of Distribution of Income in the United States," *American Economic Review*, Vol. 37, March 1947.
50. Crum, W. L., "Individual Shares in the National Income," *Review of Economic Statistics*, Vol. 17, November 1935.
51. Davis, H. T., "The Significance of the Curve of Income," *Cowles Commission for Research in Economics: Report of the Fourth Annual Research Conference on Economics and Statistics*, 1938.
52. Denison, E. F., "Income Types and the Size Distribution," *American Economic Review*, Vol. 44, May 1954.
53. Dewey, D., *Four Studies of Negro Employment in the Upper South*, Washington, D. C., National Planning Association, 1953.
54. Fréchet, M., "Nouveaux essais d'explication de la répartition des revenus," *Revue de l'institut international de statistique*, Vol. 13, 1945.
55. Friedman, M., "Choice, Chance, and the Personal Distribution of Income," *Journal of Political Economy*, Vol. 61, August 1953.
56. Friedman, M., and L. J. Savage, "The Utility Analysis of Choices Involving Risk," *Journal of Political Economy*, Vol. 56, August 1948.

57. Garvy, G., "Functional and Size Distributions of Income and Their Meaning," *American Economic Review*, Vol. 44, May 1954.
58. Glass, D. V., "Population Controversy in Eighteenth-Century England," *Population Studies*, Vol. 6, July 1952.
59. Goldfield, E. D., and H. P. Miller, "How Many Older Workers," *American Economic Security*, October–November 1952.
60. Goldsmith, S. F., "Statistical Information on the Distribution of Income by Size in the U. S.," *American Economic Review*, Vol. 40, May 1950.
      et al., "Size Distribution of Income Since the Mid-Thirties," *Review of Economics and Statistics*, Vol. 36, February 1954.
61. Grampp, W. D., "The Facts About 'Capitalistic Inequality,'" *Commentary*, June 1951.
62. Heilbroner, R., "Who Are the American Poor," *Harper's Magazine*, June 1950.
63. Industrial Relations Section, Massachusetts Institute of Technology, *Patterns of Mobility of Skilled Workers and Factors Affecting Their Occupational Choice, Six Cities, 1940–1951* (Mimeograph).
64. Johnson, N. O., "The Pareto Law," *Review of Economic Statistics*, Vol. 19, February 1937.
65. King, W. I., "Wealth Distribution in the Continental United States," *Journal of the American Statistical Association*, Vol. 22, June 1927.
66. Kingston, J., "A designaldade na distribuicão das rendas," *Revista Brasileira de economia*, Número 1, Março de 1952.
67. Kuznets, S., "National Income," *Encyclopedia of the Social Sciences*.
68. Kyrk, H., "The Income Distribution as a Measure of Economic Welfare," *American Economic Review*, Vol. 40, May 1950.
69. Lampman, R. J., "Recent Changes in Income Inequality," *American Economic Review*, Vol. 44, June 1954.
70. Lebergott, S., "Wage Structures," *Review of Economic Statistics*, Vol. 29, November 1947.
71. Lewis, L. E., "City Comparisons of Wage Levels and Skill Differentials," *Monthly Labor Review*, Vol. 74, June 1952.
72. Lydall, H. F., *National Survey of Personal Incomes and Savings*, Bulletin of the Oxford University Institute of Statistics, February and March 1953.
73. MacGregor, D. H., "Pareto's Law," *Economic Journal*, Vol. 46, 1936.
74. *Man and His Years: An Account of the First National Conference on Aging*, Health Publications Institute, North Carolina, 1951.
75. Mendershausen, H., "On Measurement of the Degree of Inequality of Income Distribution," *Cowles Commission for Research in Economics: Report of the Fifth Annual Research Commission*, 1939.
76. Meyers, F., "Notes on Changes in the Distribution of Manufacturing Wage-Earners by Straight-Time Hourly Earnings, 1941–48," *Review of Economics and Statistics*, Vol. 32, November 1950.
77. Miller, H. P., "Factors Related to Recent Changes in Income Distribution in the United States," *Review of Economics and Statistics*, Vol. 33, August 1951.
      "Changes in Income Distribution in the United States," *Journal of the American Statistical Association*, Vol. 46, December 1951.
      "An Appraisal of the 1950 Census Income Data," *Journal of the American Statistical Association*, Vol. 48, March 1953.
78. Moulton, H. G., *Income Distribution Under Capitalism*, University of Minnesota Press, 1936.
79. Ober, H., "Occupational Wage Differentials, 1907–1947," *Monthly Labor Review*, Vol. 67, August 1948.
80. Reder, M., "Age and Income," *American Economic Review*, Vol. 44, May 1954.
81. Shirras, G. F., "The Pareto Law and the Distribution of Income," *Economic Journal*, Vol. 45, 1935.
82. Slichter, S. H., "The High Cost of Low Incomes," *New York Times Magazine*, March 5, 1950.
83. Smelker, M., "Shifts in the Concentration of Income," *Review of Economics and Statistics*, Vol. 30, August 1948.
84. Snyder, C., "The Pareto Curve and Its Significance for Our Time," *Cowles Commission for Research in Economics: Report of Third Annual Research Conference on Economics and Statistics*, 1937.
85. Spengler, J. J., "Changes in Income Distribution and Social Stratification: A Note," *American Journal of Sociology*, Vol. 49, November 1953.
86. Staehle, H., "Short Period Variations in the Distribution of Income," *Review of Economic Statistics*, Vol. 19, August 1937.

87. Steiner, P. O., "The Size, Nature, and Adequacy of the Resources of the Aged," *American Economic Review*, Vol. 44, May 1954.

88. Stewart, M., *Income and Economic Progress*, Public Affairs Pamphlet, 1942.

89. Woytinsky, W. S., "Income Cycle in the Life of Families and Individuals," *Social Security Bulletin*, June 1943.

90. Yntema, D. B., "Measures of Inequality in the Personal Distribution of Wealth and Income," *Journal of the American Statistical Association*, Vol. 28, December 1933.

PUBLIC DOCUMENTS

91. Federal Security Agency, Social Security Administration, *National Survey of Old-Age and Survivors Insurance Beneficiaries*, 1951. (Preliminary findings released May 1952.)

92. National Resources Committee, *Consumer Incomes in the United States*, Government Printing Office, Washington, D. C., 1938.

93. *Old-Age in Rhode Island*, Report of the Governor's Commission to Study Problems of the Aged, July 1953.

94. Temporary National Economic Committee, *Concentration and Composition of Individual Incomes, 1918–1937*, Government Printing Office, Washington, D. C., 1940.

95. *The Economic Report of the President* (Annual reports for 1948–1953), Government Printing Office, Washington, D. C.

96. U. S. Congress, Joint Committee on the Economic Report, *Low-Income Families and Economic Stability: Report of the Subcommittee on Low-Income Families*, 81st Congress, 2nd Session, Government Printing Office, Washington, D. C., 1950.

    Low-Income Families and Economic Stability: Materials on the Problem of Low-Income Families, 81st Congress, 1st Session, Government Printing Office, Washington, D. C., 1949.

    Low-Income Families: Hearings Before the Subcommittee on Low-Income Families, 81st Congress, 1st Session, Government Printing Office, Washington, D. C., 1950.

    Hearings on the January 1949 Economic Report of the President, 81st Congress, 1st Session, Government Printing Office, Washington, D. C., 1949.

    Hearings before a Subcommittee of the Committee on Commerce on S. Res. 231 (A Resolution favoring the deletion from the Sixteenth Census Population Schedule of inquiries numbered 32 and 33, relating to compensation received), 76th Congress, 3rd Session, Government Printing Office, Washington, D. C., 1940.

97. U. S. Department of Agriculture, Bureau of Human Nutrition and Home Economics, *How Families Use Their Incomes*, Misc. Pub. 653, Government Printing Office, Washington, D. C.

98. U. S. Department of Commerce, Bureau of the Census. See Appendix A for a complete listing of the Bureau of the Census reports that contain data on the size distribution of income and related subjects.

    Office of Business Economics, *Income Distribution in the United States*, Government Printing Office, Washington, D. C., 1954.

99. U. S. Department of Labor, Bureau of Labor Statistics, *Family Spending and Saving in Wartime*, Bull. 822, Government Printing Office, Washington, D. C.

    Worker Budgets in the United States, Bull. 927, Government Printing Office, Washington, D. C.

    The City Worker's Family Budget, R1909, Government Printing Office, Washington, D. C., February 1948.

A P P E N D I X   A

DEFINITIONS AND EXPLANATIONS

Census income publications

Income data from various reports of the Bureau of the Census have been used in this monograph. The following is a complete list of census reports that contain income information.

1940 Census of Population. In the 1940 Census, income information was obtained for the first time in the history of the Population Census. All persons 14 years old and over (except inmates of specified institutions) were asked to report the amount of money wage or salary income received in 1939. Those who received over $5,000 were required only to report that they had received more than that amount. Persons 14 years old and over were also asked to report whether they had received $50 or more from sources other than money wages or salaries in 1939. This comparatively small amount was chosen in order to identify those persons whose incomes were, for all practical purposes, limited to receipts from wages or salaries. Data relating to wage or salary income in 1939 have been presented in the following Sixteenth Census Reports on Population: *Families: Family Wage or Salary Income in 1939; Families: Size of Family and Age of Head; Families: General Characteristics; Families: Characteristics of Rural-Farm Families; Families: Types of Families; Families: Tenure and Rent; Families: Income and Rent; The Labor Force (Sample Statistics): Wage or Salary Income in 1939; The Labor Force (Sample Statistics): Employment and Family Characteristics of Women; Vol. III, The Labor Force;* and *Education: Educational Attainment by Economic Characteristics and Marital Status.* In addition, a special report has been published: *Per Capita Income in Wage-Earner Families, by Size of Family: 1939,* Series P–44, No. 19.

1950 Census of Population. In the 1950 Census, information was requested of a 20-percent sample of persons 14 years of age and over on the following income categories: (*a*) the amount of money wages or salary received in 1949; (*b*) the amount of net money income received from self-employment in 1949; and (*c*) the amount of other money income received in 1949, e.g., interest, dividends, veterans' allowances, pensions, or rents. If the sample person was the head of a family, these three questions were repeated for the other family members as a group in order to obtain the income of the whole family. Persons who received more than $10,000 from any source were required only to report that they had received more than that amount.

129

The income concept used in the 1950 Census is much more inclusive than that used in 1940. Income, as defined in the 1950 Census, is the sum of the money received, less losses, from the following sources: wages or salary; net income (or loss) from the operation of a farm, ranch, business, or profession; net income (or loss) from rents, or receipts from roomers or boarders; royalties; interest, dividends, and periodic income from estates and trust funds; pensions; veterans' payments, Armed Forces allotments for dependents, and other governmental payments or assistance; and other income such as contributions for support from persons who are not members of the household, alimony, and periodic receipts from insurance policies or annuities. The figures represent the amount of income received before deductions for personal income taxes, social security, bond purchases, union dues, etc.

Receipts from the following sources were not included as income: money received from the sale of property, unless the recipient was engaged in the business of selling such property; the value of income "in kind," such as food produced and consumed in the home, free living quarters; withdrawals of bank deposits; money borrowed; tax refunds; gifts; and lump-sum inheritances or insurance payments.

The following reports of the 1950 Census of Population include income information: Volume II, *Characteristics of the Population* (the Series P–B and P–C bulletins constitute preprints of chapters of this volume); Series P–D, *Census Tract Statistics;* and Series P–E, *Special Reports: Occupational and Industrial Characteristics* (tabulated but not yet published); *Institutional Population; Marital Status; Nativity and Parentage* (tabulated but not yet published); *Nonwhite Population by Race; Persons of Spanish Surname; Puerto Ricans in Continental United States; Characteristics by Size of Place;* and *Education.* In addition, the following reports were prepared on the basis of income data for families and unrelated individuals obtained in the 1950 Census: *1950 Census of Population—Preliminary Reports,* "Estimated Distribution of Family Income in 1949, for the United States, Regions, and Selected States," Series PC–7, No. 5; and *Farms and Farm People—Population, Income, and Housing Characteristics by Economic Class of Farm.*

Income data may also be found in the following reports of the 1950 Census of Housing: Volume II, *Nonfarm Housing Characteristics* (Series H–B bulletins constitute preprints of a chapter of this volume); Volume III, *Farm Housing Characteristics;* and Volume IV, *Residential Financing.*

Current Population Survey.[1] Each year since 1944, the Bureau of the Census has published income data derived from the annual consumer income supplement to the Current Population Survey (CPS). This survey

---

[1] See U. S. Bureau of the Census, *Current Population Reports—Labor Force Memorandum* 5, "Concepts and Methods Used in the Current Labor Force Statistics Prepared by the Census Bureau."

is conducted each month by direct interview with a scientifically selected sample of 25,000 households representing the entire civilian population. It provides the current information on employment, unemployment, and related data presented each month by the Bureau of the Census in its "Monthly Report on the Labor Force." At various times during the year, the regular labor force survey is supplemented by additional inquiries that are designed to provide statistics on special problems. Once each year, generally in April, questions relating to income received during the preceding year are added to the survey. The income concept used in the Current Population Survey is identical with that used in the 1950 Census of Population, and the data collection methods are also very similar. However, the Current Population Survey tends to use more detailed questioning with respect to income. In addition, because of the relatively small size of the Current Population Survey sample, it has been possible to make various types of analytical tabulations from that survey which would have been too expensive to have prepared from the 1950 Census of Population. The Bureau of the Census publications, *Current Population Reports—Consumer Income*, Series P–60, Nos. 1–13, are entirely devoted to income. In addition, income information may be found in the following *Current Population Reports: Labor Force*, Series P–50, Nos. 39 and 44; and *Population Characteristics*, Series P–20, Nos. 23, 27, 32, and 38.

Definitions

Dwelling unit and household. A dwelling unit is defined, in general, as a house, apartment, or other group of rooms, or a single room, occupied or intended for occupancy as separate living quarters by a family or other group of persons living together or a person living alone. A household consists of the entire group of persons who occupy a dwelling unit. Living quarters that are not dwelling units, such as large rooming houses, dormitories, and YMCA buildings, are not regarded as households.

Family. The term "family" refers to a group of two or more persons related by blood, marriage, or adoption and residing together; all such persons are considered as members of the same family. Thus, if the son of the head of the household and the son's wife are in the household, they are treated as part of the head's family. On the other hand, a lodger and his wife not related to the head of the household or an unrelated servant and his wife are considered as additional families, and not as part of the household head's family.

Unrelated individual. The term "unrelated individuals" refers to persons who are not living with any relatives. An unrelated individual may constitute a one-person household by himself, or he may be part of a household including one or more other families or unrelated individuals, or he may reside in a quasi-household such as a hotel. Thus, a widow living by herself or with one or more other persons not related to her, a lodger not related to the head of the household or to anyone else in the household, and a servant living in an employer's household with no relatives are examples of unrelated individuals.

Primary families and individuals. The term "primary family" refers to the head of a household and all other persons in the household related to the head by blood, marriage, or adoption. If there is no person in the household related to the head, then the head himself constitutes a primary individual. A household can contain one and only one primary family or primary individual. The expression "primary families and individuals" is used here with the same meaning as the term "families" in the 1940 Census. It excludes families and individuals who are lodgers or servants, and families and individuals who do not reside as members of households in dwelling units. These other types of families and individuals are included in all family and individual tables that are not specifically restricted. The number of "primary families and individuals" is identical with the number of households.

Urban and rural residence. The same definition of urban and rural areas was used in the 1950 Census of Population and in the Current Population Surveys of April 1951 and April 1952. This definition differs slightly from that used in the March 1950 Current Population Survey, but it is markedly different from that used in earlier surveys and censuses. According to the new definition, the urban population comprises all persons living in (*a*) places of 2,500 inhabitants or more incorporated as cities, boroughs, towns, and villages; (*b*) incorporated towns of 2,500 inhabitants or more except in New England, New York, and Wisconsin, where "towns" are simply minor civil divisions of counties; (*c*) the densely settled urban fringe, including both incorporated and unincorporated areas, around cities of 50,000 or more; and (*d*) unincorporated places of 2,500 inhabitants or more outside of any urban fringe. The remaining population is classified as rural.

According to the definition used before March 1950, the urban population comprised all persons living in incorporated places of 2,500 inhabitants or more and in areas (usually minor civil divisions) classified as urban under special rules relating to population size and density.

Size of place. The urban population is classified as living in urbanized areas or in urban places outside urbanized areas. According to the definition used in the 1950 Census, the population in urbanized areas comprises all persons living in (*a*) cities of 50,000 inhabitants or more in 1940 or according to a special census taken between 1940 and 1950 and (*b*) the densely settled urban fringe, including both incorporated and unincorporated areas, surrounding these cities. Residents of urbanized areas were classified according to the size of the entire area rather than by the size of the place in which they lived. The remaining urban population is classified as living in the smaller urban places not in the urbanized areas.

Farm and nonfarm residence. The rural population is subdivided into the rural-farm population, which comprises all rural residents living on farms, and the rural-nonfarm population, which comprises the remaining rural population. The same method of determining farm and nonfarm residence was used in the 1950 Census of Population and in the Current Population Surveys of April 1951 and April 1952. This method differs from that used in earlier surveys and censuses in that persons on "farms" who are paying cash rent for their house and yard only are classified as nonfarm; furthermore, persons in institutions, summer camps, "motels," and tourist camps are classified as nonfarm.

Money wages or salary. Money wages or salary is defined as the total money earnings received for work performed as an employee during a calendar year. It includes wages, salary, Armed Forces pay, commissions, tips, piece-rate payments, and cash bonuses earned before deductions were made for taxes, bonds, pensions, union dues, etc.

Net income from nonfarm self-employment. This income is defined as net money income (gross receipts minus expenses) from a business or professional enterprise in which a person was engaged on his own account. Gross receipts include the value of all goods sold and services rendered. Expenses include costs of goods purchased, rent, heat, light, power, depreciation charges, wages and salaries paid, business taxes (not personal income taxes), etc. In general, inventory changes were not considered in determining net income; however, replies based on income tax returns or other official records may reflect inventory changes. The value of salable merchandise consumed by the proprietors of retail stores is not included as part of net income.

Net income from farm self-employment. This income is defined as net money income (gross receipts minus operating expenses) from the operation of a farm by a person on his own account, as an owner, renter, or sharecropper. Gross receipts include the value of all products sold, government crop loans, money received from the rental of farm equipment to others, and incidental receipts from the sale of wood, sand, gravel, etc. Operating expenses include costs of food, fertilizer, seed and other farming supplies, cash wages paid to farmhands, depreciation charges, cash rent, interest on farm mortgages, farm building repairs, farm taxes (not poll taxes or personal income taxes), etc. The value of fuel, food, or other farm products used for family living is not included as part of net income. In general, inventory changes were not considered in determining net income; however, replies based on income tax returns, or other official records, may reflect inventory changes.

Total money earnings. These earnings are defined as the algebraic sum of money wages and salaries and net income from self-employment.

Income other than earnings. This income includes net income from rents, royalties, or receipts from roomers or boarders; interest, dividends, and periodic income from estates and trust funds; pensions; veterans' payments, Armed Forces allotments for dependents, and other governmental payments or assistance; and other income such as contributions for support from persons who are not members of the household, alimony, and periodic receipts from insurance policies or annuities.

Receipts from the following sources were not included as income: money received from the sale of property, such as stocks, bonds, a house, or a car (unless the person was engaged in the business of selling such property, in which case the net proceeds would be counted as income from self-employment); withdrawals of bank deposits; money borrowed; tax refunds; gifts; and lump-sum inheritances or insurance payments.

Total money income.   This income is defined as the algebraic sum of money wages and salaries, net income from self-employment, and income other than earnings.

Aggregate income.   Aggregate income is the sum of the incomes received by all persons 14 years of age and over.

Color.   The term "color" refers to the division of the population into two groups, white and nonwhite.   The nonwhite group includes Negroes, Indians, Japanese, Chinese, and other nonwhite races.

Age.   The age classification is based on the age of the person at his last birthday.

Veteran of World War II.   A veteran of World War II is defined as a person who had been a member of the Armed Forces of the United States on active duty at any time between September 16, 1940, and July 25, 1947.

Employed.   Employed persons comprise those who, during the survey week, were either (*a*) "at work"—those who did any civilian work for pay or profit or worked without pay for 15 hours or more on a family farm or business or (*b*) "with a job but not at work"—those who did not work and were not looking for work but had a civilian job or business from which they were temporarily absent because of vacation, illness, industrial dispute, bad weather, or layoff with definite instructions to return to work within 30 days of layoff.   Also included are persons who had new jobs to which they were scheduled to report within 30 days.

Unemployed.   Unemployed persons include those who did not work at all during the survey week and who were looking for work.   Also included as unemployed are persons who would have been looking for work except that (*a*) they were temporarily ill, (*b*) they expected to return to a job from which they had been laid off for an indefinite period, or (*c*) they believed no work was available in their line of work or in the community.

Labor force.   Persons are classified as in the labor force if they were employed as civilians, unemployed, or in the Armed Forces during the survey week.   The "experienced civilian labor force" comprises employed workers and experienced unemployed workers.   The 1939 data shown in the tables on the experienced civilian labor force include the relatively small number of persons in the Armed Forces in 1940.

Not in labor force. All civilians 14 years of age and over who are not classified as employed or unemployed are defined as "not in the labor force." These persons are further classified as "keeping house," "in school," "unable to work" because of disability, and "other," the last group including for the most part retired persons, those too old to work, seasonal workers for whom the survey week fell in an "off" season, and the voluntarily idle. Persons doing only incidental unpaid family work (less than 15 hours) are also classified as not in the labor force.

Occupation and class of worker. The data on occupation and class of worker refer to the job held during the survey week. Persons employed at two or more jobs were reported in the job at which they worked the greatest number of hours during the week. Persons who were unemployed during the survey week are classified according to their last civilian job. The same major occupation groupings are used in the 1950 Census of Population and in the Current Population Surveys.

The class-of-worker classification comprises "wage and salary workers," "self-employed workers," and "unpaid family workers." Wage and salary workers are persons who worked as employees for wages or salaries. They include not only factory operatives, laborers, clerks, etc., who work for wages, but also other persons working for tips or for room or board, salesmen and other employees working for commissions, and salaried business managers, corporation executives, and government officials. Self-employed workers are persons working for profit or fees in their own business, profession, or trade, or operating a farm. Unpaid family workers are persons working without pay on a farm or in a business operated by a member of the household to whom they are related by blood or marriage.

The occupational classification system used in 1940 is basically the same as that used in 1950. There are a number of differences, however, in the specific content of particular groups, as well as several differences in title. The occupation data shown for 1940 have not been entirely adjusted for comparability with the 1950 classification system; however, available evidence indicates that the 1940–1950 relationships shown by the data are not significantly affected by these differences. The 1940 classification by class of worker is comparable with the 1950 classification.

Weeks worked. The data on weeks worked in 1949 pertain to the number of different weeks in which a person did any work for pay or profit (including paid vacations and sick leave), or worked without pay on a family farm or in a family business. Accordingly, persons such as salesgirls, newsboys, and others who worked part of every week during the year were counted as full-year workers. In contrast, the data on weeks worked in 1939 refer to equivalent full-time weeks. Although the respondents were asked to report the number of weeks in which they worked for pay or profit, the enumerators were instructed to convert periods of part-time work into equivalent full-time weeks. Thus, a full-year worker for 1939 is a person who worked full time during the entire year.

Medians. The median income is the amount that divides the distribution into two equal groups, one having incomes above the median and the other having incomes below the median. The medians for persons are based on the distributions of persons with income. The medians for wage or salary income, income from nonfarm self-employment, income from farm self-employment, total money earnings, and income other than earnings are based on the distributions of persons having these types of income. The medians for families and individuals are based on all families and individuals.

Percentages. Percentages are shown as calculated; therefore, they do not always add to exactly 100.0 percent. The totals, however, are always shown as 100.0 percent.

Method of estimating aggregate income from census data. An estimate of the number of persons at each income level was obtained by distributing the cases not reporting on income among all the income levels in the same proportion as those that did report. A mean income was then selected for each income level, and estimates of aggregate income were obtained by multiplying the number of persons at each income level by the mean for that level.

For income levels under $10,000, the midpoint of each level was assumed to be the mean; $250 was assumed as the mean for the "under $500" income level in the 1950 Census data. In the Current Population Survey data, $250 was selected as the mean for the "$1 to $499" level and "minus $250" was selected as the mean for the "loss" level. The procedure for estimating the mean for the open-end interval varied according to the data available for each year. In the April 1952 Current Population Survey, persons with incomes over $10,000 in 1951 were asked to report if their incomes were between $10,000 and $14,999 or $15,000 and over. On the basis of this information, a mean for each of these intervals was obtained from a Pareto curve fitted to the frequencies above $10,000. The actual means used for these intervals were $12,000 and $32,000 for total income and $11,000 and $27,000 for wage or salary income. These means were used in computing the aggregates for all distributions derived from the 1951 data. Because of the relatively small size of the sample, no attempt was made to fit Pareto curves to the open-end intervals for each major occupation group. The open-end intervals in the 1950 Census and in the Current Population Surveys covering the years 1944 to 1950 was $10,000 and over." An examination of the data for 1951 and information obtained from other sources indicate that $20,000 was a reasonable estimate of both the mean total income and the mean wage or salary income for this interval. The open-end interval in the wage or salary data for 1939 was "$5,000 and over." An examination of statistics on income tax returns for that year and an analysis of data obtained in the income surveys indicated that $9,000 was a reasonable estimate of the mean wage or salary income for this interval.

Reliability of the Current Population Survey (CPS) estimates. With the exception of the 1940 Census data on income by occupation all the income estimates presented in this study are based on sample data. Therefore, they are subject to sampling variability. The sampling variability of an estimated percentage depends upon both the size of the percentage and the size of the total on which it is based. Estimated percentages based on Current Population Survey (CPS) totals of selected sizes for the United States in April 1952 are subject to sampling variability that can be determined from the standard errors shown in table A–1. Estimated percentages based on urban and rural residence and nonwhite distributions are subject to somewhat greater sampling variability than that shown in this table.

TABLE **A–1.**—STANDARD ERROR OF ESTIMATED PERCENTAGE: APRIL 1952 CURRENT POPULATION SURVEY

(Range of 2 chances out of 3)

Estimated percentage	Base of percentage							
	500,000	1,000,000	2,000,000	3,000,000	5,000,000	10,000,000	20,000,000	40,000,000
2 or 98.............	1.6	1.1	0.8	0.7	0.5	0.4	0.3	0.2
5 or 95.............	2.4	1.7	1.2	1.0	0.8	0.6	0.4	0.3
10 or 90............	3.3	2.4	1.7	1.4	1.1	0.8	0.5	0.4
25 or 75............	4.8	3.4	2.4	2.0	1.5	1.1	0.8	0.6
50.................	5.5	3.9	2.8	2.3	1.8	1.3	0.9	0.6

The standard error is a measure of sampling variability. The chances are about 2 out of 3 that the difference due to sampling variability between an estimate and the figure that would have been obtained from a complete count of the population is less than the standard error. The amount by which the standard error must be multiplied to obtain other odds deemed more appropriate can be found in most statistical textbooks. For example, the chances are about 19 out of 20 that the difference is less than twice the standard error, and 99 out of 100 that it is less than two and one-half times the standard error.

The reliability of an estimated median depends upon both the form and the size of the distribution on which it is based. Table A–2 indicates the approximate sampling variability of selected estimated medians for the United States in 1951, based on the April 1952 Current Population Survey.

The sampling variability of a difference between two estimates depends upon the sampling variability of each of the estimates and the correlation between them.

TABLE **A-2.**—STANDARD ERROR OF SELECTED MEDIANS: APRIL 1952 CURRENT POPULATION SURVEY

(Range of 2 chances out of 3)

Distribution	Estimated median	Range of median
Male, total.....................................	$2,952	$2,923-$2,981
Female, total...................................	1,045	1,010- 1,080
Male, nonwhite..................................	1,708	1,635- 1,781
Male, 35 to 44 years old........................	3,617	3,574- 3,660
Female, 20 to 24 years old......................	1,397	1,329- 1,465
Male, unemployed................................	1,410	1,277- 1,542
Male:		
Professional workers, self-employed...........	6,167	5,105- 6,930
Craftsmen, foremen, and kindred workers.......	3,656	3,616- 3,696
Laborers, except farm and mine...............	2,281	2,123- 2,339
Female:		
Clerical and kindred workers..................	2,165	2,125- 2,205
Sales workers.................................	1,281	1,161- 1,401
Operatives and kindred workers...............	1,758	1,714- 1,802

For statements on the sampling variability of Current Population Survey estimates for other years, see the reports in the P–60 series.

The reliability of the estimated share of aggregate income received by a given quintile depends upon both the form of the distribution and the size of the total on which it is based. Table A–3 indicates the approximate sampling variability of the percent of aggregate income received in 1951 by the indicated quintiles for selected distributions.

TABLE **A-3.**—STANDARD ERROR OF PERCENT OF AGGREGATE INCOME FOR QUINTILES: APRIL 1952 CURRENT POPULATION SURVEY

(Range of 2 chances out of 3)

Distribution	Persons with income	Percent of aggregate income	Estimated range
Aggregate money income--both sexes.................	Lowest fifth	2.5	2.4-2.6
	Highest fifth	47.7	46.9-48.5
Aggregate wage or salary income--male craftsmen, foremen, and kindred workers......................	Highest fifth	32.3	30.6-34.0

In addition to sampling variation, the figures are subject to errors of response and nonreporting, but the possible effect of such errors is not included in the above measures of reliability. In most cases the schedule entries for income are based on memory rather than on records; and in the majority of households, on the memory or knowledge of some one person, usually the wife of the family head. The memory factor in data derived from field surveys of income probably produces underestimates, because the tendency is to forget minor or irregular sources of income. Other errors of reporting are due to misrepresentation or to misunderstanding as to the scope of the income concept. The figures on aggregate income are subject to errors of estimation in addition to those noted above.

Reliability of 1950 Census estimates. The 1950 Census data in this report derived from Volume II, *Characteristics of the Population,* are based on a 20-percent sample of the population, whereas the data derived from the Series P–E, *Special Reports,* are based on a 3⅓-percent sample of the population. The figures based on the 20-percent sample are subject to sampling variability that can be determined from the standard errors shown in tables A–4 and A–5, whereas the sampling variability for the figures based on the 3⅓-percent sample are shown in tables A–6 and A–7.

Some of the 1950 Census tables present estimates of medians as well as the corresponding distributions. The sampling variability of estimates of medians depends on the distribution upon which the medians are based.

TABLE **A–4.**—STANDARD ERROR OF ESTIMATED NUMBER FOR 20-PERCENT SAMPLE DATA: 1950 CENSUS

(Range of 2 chances out of 3)

Estimated number	Population of area[1]						
	50,000	100,000	500,000	1,000,000	5,000,000	25,000,000	150,000,000
100	20	20	20	20	20	20	20
500	50	50	50	50	50	50	50
1,000	60	70	70	70	70	70	70
2,500	100	100	100	100	100	100	100
5,000	140	140	150	150	150	150	150
10,000	190	200	200	210	210	210	210
25,000	240	290	320	320	330	330	330
50,000	130	340	440	450	460	460	460
75,000	...	310	530	550	560	560	560
100,000	...	180	590	620	650	650	650
250,000	...	...	760	910	1,010	1,030	1,030
500,000	...	...	410	1,070	1,390	1,450	1,460
1,000,000	...	...	...	570	1,870	2,030	2,060
2,500,000	...	...	...	...	2,400	3,110	3,240
5,000,000	...	...	...	...	1,280	4,170	4,550
10,000,000	...	...	...	...	...	5,190	6,330
15,000,000	...	...	...	...	...	5,370	7,630
25,000,000	...	...	...	...	...	2,830	9,510
50,000,000	...	...	...	...	...	...	12,170
150,000,000	...	...	...	...	...	...	7,070

[1] An area is the smallest complete geographic area to which the estimate under consideration pertains. Thus, the area may be the state, city, standard metropolitan area, or the urban or rural portion of the state. The rural-farm or rural-nonfarm population of the state, the nonwhite population, etc., do not represent a geographical area.

TABLE **A–5.**—STANDARD ERROR OF ESTIMATED PERCENTAGE FOR 20-PERCENT SAMPLE DATA: 1950 CENSUS

(Range of 2 chances out of 3)

Estimated percentage	Base of percentage							
	500	1,000	2,500	10,000	25,000	100,000	500,000	5,000,000
2 or 98	1.3	0.9	0.6	0.3	0.2	0.1	...	...
5 or 95	2.0	1.4	0.9	0.5	0.3	0.1	0.1	...
10 or 90	2.8	2.0	1.2	0.6	0.4	0.2	0.1	...
25 or 75	4.0	2.8	1.8	0.9	0.6	0.3	0.1	...
50	4.6	3.3	2.1	1.0	0.7	0.3	0.1	...

The standard error of a median based on sample data may be estimated as follows: If the estimated total number reporting the characteristic is N, compute the number $N/2 - \sqrt{N}$. Cumulate the frequencies in the table until the class interval that contains this number is located. By linear interpolation, obtain the value below which $N/2 - \sqrt{N}$ cases lie. In a similar manner, obtain the value below which $N/2 + \sqrt{N}$ cases lie. If information on the characteristics had been obtained from the total population, the chances are about 2 out of 3 that the median would lie between these two values. The chances will be about 19 out of 20 that the median will be in the interval computed similarly but using $\dfrac{N}{2} \pm 2\sqrt{N}$ and about 99 in 100 that it will be in the interval obtained by using $\dfrac{N}{2} \pm 2.5\sqrt{N}$.

TABLE **A–6.**—STANDARD ERROR OF ESTIMATED NUMBER FOR 3⅓-PERCENT SAMPLE DATA:
1950 CENSUS

(Range of 2 chances out of 3)

Estimated number	United States	Urban	Rural	Estimated number	United States	Urban	Rural
100...............	60	60	60	100,000...........	1,760	1,760	1,760
500...............	120	120	120	500,000..........	3,930	3,930	3,920
1,000............	180	180	180	1,000,000........	5,550	5,540	5,520
2,500............	280	280	280	5,000,000........	12,240	12,130	11,870
5,000............	390	390	390	10,000,000.......	17,020	16,680	15,920
10,000...........	560	560	560	25,000,000.......	25,460	24,010	20,530
25,000...........	880	880	880	50,000,000.......	32,290	27,490	11,650
50,000...........	1,240	1,240	1,240				

TABLE **A–7.**—STANDARD ERROR OF ESTIMATED PERCENTAGE FOR 3⅓-PERCENT SAMPLE DATA:
1950 CENSUS

(Range of 2 chances out of 3)

Estimated percentage	Base of percentage							
	3,000	5,000	10,000	25,000	50,000	100,000	500,000	5,000,000
2 or 98...................	1.4	1.1	1.0	0.5	0.3	0.2	0.1	0.0
5 or 95...................	2.2	1.7	1.2	0.8	0.5	0.4	0.2	0.1
10 or 90..................	3.0	2.4	1.7	1.1	0.7	0.5	0.2	0.1
25 or 75..................	4.4	3.4	2.4	1.5	1.1	0.8	0.3	0.1
50.......................	5.1	3.9	2.8	1.8	1.2	0.9	0.4	0.1

APPENDIX B

THE QUALITY OF CENSUS INCOME DATA

With the development of probability sampling, some of the statistical vacuum which has existed in many fields is at long last beginning to disappear. As a result, many scholars and technicians who only recently were looking for *a* number are now beginning to look for *the* number. The sophisticated user of statistical data is no longer satisfied to know that unemployment during a given month was 2 million or that median family income during a given year was $3,000. He also wants to know the answers to a host of questions regarding the nature of the sample on which the data are based, the skill and training of the interviewers, refusal rates, substitution procedures, and so on. Fundamentally, this attitude reflects the tendency of modern statisticians to regard a statistic as a commodity which, like other commodities, can vary considerably in quality. The purchaser of a statistical survey has about as wide a choice in the quality of the product he buys as does the purchaser of an automobile.

Various attempts have been made by the Bureau of the Census to appraise alternative methods of obtaining income information and to measure the quality of its product. This appendix summarizes some of the recent methodological experience of the Bureau in the collection of income data. It also presents findings of various attempts to measure the quality of census income data.

The one fact that seems to stand out in all quality checks of census income data of this work is that within the framework of the collection techniques currently employed by the Bureau of the Census (i.e., a household interview in which no attempt is made to balance income, expenditures, and savings) the differences that are obtained by alternative forms of questioning are not striking. Indeed, it appears that the same set of questions asked at different times in a given group of households, will produce variations in response that are of about the same magnitude as different sets of questions asked at the same time. The data suggest that if there is a substantial understatement in the amount of income reported in field surveys, there is no cheap and simple way of overcoming this difficulty. Moreover, there is no guarantee that expensive and complex methods can achieve this objective either. The fact that sworn income tax reports to the Bureau of Internal Revenue represent only about 85 percent of the aggregate income which should be reported to that Bureau, suggests that there may be a rather low limit beyond which the accuracy of data obtained in field surveys of income cannot be appreciably improved.[1]

Methodological inquiries

Variations in questionnaire wording.   Several different types of income questions were tested by the Bureau of the Census in the April 1948 Current Population Survey for the purpose of developing a simplified method of obtaining income data, suitable for the 1950 Census.   A total of 25,000 households were interviewed by trained enumerators, and the following alternative sets of income questions were asked of systematic' subsamples of the total sample, in addition to the usual labor force questions.   The type of question to be asked in each household was predetermined in the field office and indicated on each schedule.

Type 1.   On one-half of the schedules the enumerator was to ask the specific amount of (*a*) wages and salaries; (*b*) total money income for each person 14 years and over.

Type 2.   On one-fourth of the schedules the enumerator was to ask the specific amount of total money income for each primary family and for each person not a member of a primary family.

Type 3.   On one-fourth of the schedules the enumerator was to ask the respondent to indicate on a card the broad class interval into which the total money income fell for each primary family and for each person not a member of a primary family.

TABLE **B–1.**—MEDIAN INCOME IN 1947 OF FAMILIES AND UNRELATED INDIVIDUALS, BY RESIDENCE AND TYPE OF SCHEDULE: APRIL 1948 CURRENT POPULATION SURVEY

Area	Type 1	Type 2	Type 3
United States......................	$2,702	$2,741	$2,581
Urban.................................	2,961	2,985	2,741
Rural nonfarm.........................	2,607	2,620	2,544
Rural farm............................	1,760	1,896	1,923

Source: Herman P. Miller, "An Appraisal of the 1950 Census Income Data," *Journal of the American Statistical Association,* Vol. 48, March 1953, p. 30.

The findings of the field tests of each of the questions are presented in the above table.   One of the striking conclusions derived from these tests was that asking for an over-all figure on total income for the family *group* (type 2) and asking for information on wages or salary and total income for *each* family member (type 1) produced the same median income.

The median income of urban families and individuals reporting on types 1 and 2 ($2,961 and $2,985, respectively) was about $200 greater than

---

[1] Goldsmith, S. F., "Appraisal of Basic Data for Size Distributions," *Studies in Income and Wealth,* Vol. 13, National Bureau of Economic Research, New York, 1951, p. 302.

that of families and individuals reporting on type 3 ($2,741).   In contrast there was no significant difference in the median incomes of rural families and individuals reporting on each of the three types of questions.   This would seem to imply that in urban areas, where wages and salaries constitute a major portion of income, less underreporting of income occurred when a specific question on wages and salaries was asked.   However, in rural areas no gain in amount of income reported seemed to be derived from asking the additional question.

There is some evidence that reducing the number of income questions tends to reduce the number of persons who are classified as income recipients.   In the April 1947 income survey, when a battery of income questions was asked, 59.9 million nonfarm persons were classified as income recipients in 1946, as compared with 57.2 million for 1947, based on type 1 results.   The differences were concentrated in the lowest income brackets. Although this decrease may have been caused by several factors, a good part of it is probably explained by the fact that fewer income questions were used in the April 1948 survey.   Apparently, reducing the number of income questions means that many persons having only minor or irregular sources of income will not be classified as income recipients.

Variability of response to identical questions.   About one-fifth of the persons who reported on income in the March 1950 Current Population Survey (CPS) were also required to furnish income data in the 1950 Census.   Since essentially the same questions were asked in each interview, the differences between the two sets of reports provide an indication of the variability of response.   The data in the table below are based on an analysis of the income reported by 5,700 persons 14 years of age and over who were interviewed in both CPS and in the 1950 Census.

Of the 4,898 persons who reported on income in both surveys, 61 percent were in the same income interval in both surveys, 20 percent were in

TABLE **B-2.**—INCOME OF PERSONS IN 1949: 1950 CENSUS AND MARCH 1950 CURRENT POPULATION SURVEY

Comparison of Current Population Survey and census	All persons	Paid workers		
		Total	Wage or salary workers	Self-employed workers
Total in sample..............................	5,701	3,118	2,529	589
Total reporting on income in CPS and census........	4,898	2,607	2,165	442
Percent in same income interval in both[1].........	61	49	52	31
Percent in higher income interval in CPS.........	20	27	25	38
Percent in higher income interval in census......	18	25	23	31
Median income:				
Current Population Survey.......................	$1,914	$2,326	$2,389	$1,797
Census...	1,849	2,238	2,319	1,543

[1] Five-hundred-dollar income intervals were used below $5,000; $5,000 to $5,999 was treated as a single interval as was $6,000 to $9,999.

Source: Herman P. Miller, "An Appraisal of the 1950 Census Income Data," *Journal of the American Statistical Association*, Vol. 48, March 1953, table 4.

a higher income interval in CPS, and 18 percent were in a higher income interval in the census. (About 82 percent of the persons reporting on income in both surveys were either in the same interval or in one higher or lower adjacent interval.) Despite the fact that nearly two-fifths of the respondents reported different incomes in each survey, there was no significant difference between the medians or between the more detailed distributions by income levels. The similarity in the distributions largely reflects the fact that income was relatively overstated in each survey about as frequently as it was understated. These reporting and enumerative errors generally tended to cancel, leaving the income distributions relatively unchanged.

Over four-fifths of the persons reporting no income in the March 1950 CPS also reported no income for 1949 in the census, but only about one-half of the persons reporting some income in CPS were in the same income interval in the census. Some indication of the extent of variation in response among income recipients may be obtained from the figures for paid workers in table B–2. About one-half of the wage or salary workers were in different income intervals in each survey; however, the medians for these workers do not differ significantly. As might be expected, there was considerably greater variation of response for self-employed workers than there was for wage or salary workers. About 70 percent of these workers reported different incomes in the two surveys. Even here, however, incomes were underreported almost as frequently as they were overreported.

The table below indicates that about three-fourths of the women as com-

TABLE **B–3.**—CONSISTENCY OF INCOME REPORTING FOR PERSONS, BY AGE, SEX, AND VETERAN STATUS: 1950 CENSUS AND MARCH 1950 CURRENT POPULATION SURVEY

Age, sex, and veteran status	Percent in same income interval in CPS and census		Median income	
	Total reporting	Income recipients	CPS	Census
Total.............................	61	44	$1,914	$1,849
Male.............................	49	44	$2,432	$2,378
14 to 24 years:				
Total.............................	56	43	1,054	1,289
Veteran of World War II....................	48	48	2,185	2,231
Nonveteran of World War II.................	58	41	722	897
25 to 44 years:				
Total.............................	43	43	2,904	2,850
Veteran of World War II....................	43	43	2,955	2,918
Nonveteran of World War II.................	43	43	2,860	2,773
45 to 64 years.............................	46	46	2,644	2,646
65 years and over..........................	48	44	1,037	1,234
Female.............................	73	43	$910	$941
14 to 24 years.............................	72	47	838	992
25 to 44 years.............................	73	43	1,271	1,293
45 to 64 years.............................	72	41	888	915
65 years and over..........................	69	45	575	497

Source: Herman P. Miller, "An Appraisal of the 1950 Census Income Data," *Journal of the American Statistical Association*, Vol. 48, March 1953, table 5.

pared with only one-half of the men reported the same income in both surveys. However, nearly half of the women in the sample but only 6 percent of the men reported no income. Among income recipients, about the same proportion (one-half) were in the same income level for both sex groups. The medians and distributions by income level in CPS and the census differed by negligible amounts for both males and females.

Within each sex group, the proportion of income recipients who were in the same income level in both surveys did not vary by age or veteran status. The differences by age and veteran status in the median incomes derived from the two surveys were also insignificant.

Self-enumeration versus direct enumeration. In October 1948, various schedule forms and procedures were tested for use in the 1950 Census. One of the major purposes of the test was to evaluate statistics collected by two different types of procedures: direct enumeration and self-enumeration. The difficulty of obtaining accurate information on such items as work status, occupation, or income from the housewife has frequently suggested the use of self-enumeration. It has been argued that this procedure would allow the individual wage earners to give information about themselves and would improve the accuracy of the response without the expense of callbacks to interview the specific individual. One of the purposes of this experiment was to evaluate the quality of the economic statistics obtained by the use of each procedure. This experiment was conducted in two rural counties and in two census tracts in Minneapolis.

With respect to the extent and quality of actual self-enumeration, it is important to note that in about 60 percent of the "self-enumeration" cases, the enumerators rather than the respondents actually entered the income information. Even where the respondents entered the income information on the self-enumeration schedule, a large proportion of the entries were apparently rounded to hundreds of dollars. This indicates that the respondents did not take advantage of the advance distribution of schedules to refer to records.

On many of the schedules actually filled out by respondents, they reported hourly, weekly, or monthly income rather than annual income. Moreover, in many cases the respondents' entries were illegible or ambiguous. For example, some respondents reported their income in dollars and cents but failed to show the decimal point. Some of the errors were corrected by the enumerators or coders, others may have been missed.

Since field surveys of income generally produce underestimates of the amounts of income and of the numbers of income recipients, the comparison of the amounts and numbers obtained by alternative methods is an important criterion for evaluating these methods, on the assumption that the higher figures represent better reporting. In the October 1948 pretest, the direct-enumeration procedure produced a higher proportion of income recipients where both procedures were tested. Comparison of the medians obtained by self- and direct-enumeration procedures produces inconclusive results (table B–4).   In Union County, direct enumeration gave higher medians and in Minneapolis, lower medians.   In Carroll County, the differences were not significant.

TABLE **B–4.**—MEDIAN INCOME AND PROPORTION OF INCOME RECIPIENTS, BY AREA AND PROCEDURE: OCTOBER 1948 SELF-ENUMERATION PRETEST

Area and procedure	Median income		Percent with income
	Male	Female	
Union County, Indiana:			
Direct-enumeration procedure...........	$2,447	$697	57.6
Self-enumeration procedure.............	2,167	479	52.5
Carroll County, Kentucky:			
Direct-enumeration procedure...........	1,385	451	59.6
Self-enumeration procedure.............	1,394	478	55.6
Minneapolis, Minnesota:			
Direct-enumeration procedure...........	2,152	1,343	83.7
Self-enumeration procedure.............	2,500	1,402	78.4

Source: Unpublished data of the Bureau of the Census.

One of the facts that may account for the more complete reporting of income recipients in the direct-interview approach is the difference between the respondents' and the census definition of work and income.   It is generally known that respondents tend to forget short periods of employment and irregular sources of earnings and other income when reporting to census enumerators.   During the interview, respondents frequently recall these sporadic sources of employment and income; however, the recollection is often accompanied by a statement by the respondent that he did not think that the Bureau of the Census was interested in these sources. It is possible, when the respondent filled the schedule without the assistance of an enumerator, he tended to omit these sources and that when the respondent did have the benefit of consultation with an enumerator, these sources tended to be reported more completely.

Effect of improved interviewer training and respondent selection.   Under the sponsorship of the Public Housing Authority, the Bureau of the Census conducted a local housing survey in Watertown, New York, during August 1952.   Several experiments were attempted in this survey, which was limited to households living in substandard rented dwelling units.   In the field of income, an effort was made to determine whether the accuracy of the family income data resulting from the methods previously employed in the local housing surveys could be improved without substantially increasing the costs.

The experimental method selected was to employ two different procedures for collecting family income information.   The standard method, Procedure A, was used for one-half (about 400) of the households; and a more refined collection method, Procedure B, was used for the other half.

The schedules obtained by Procedure A contained three questions relating to the annual amount of income from wages or salary, self-employment, and other sources, received by each member of a primary family. The enumerators received four hours of training covering family composition, housing, income, and other items on the schedule. They were instructed to accept income estimates whenever the exact amount was not known to the respondent. As in the other local housing surveys, the enumerators were permitted to secure information about all household members from any responsible person found at home at the time of interview.

After completing the enumeration of the households covered by Procedure A, the same enumerators received four hours of special training for collecting income data under Procedure B. The schedules used in Procedure B contained a slight expansion in the number of income questions as well as a question relating to the number of weeks worked during the preceding 12 months. In the special training session, the enumerators were instructed to interview each person directly and to try as much as possible to get the respondents to refer to records and to show all calculations on the schedules. A member of the Washington staff was sent to Watertown to observe the enumeration and to make certain that the instructions were properly enforced.

The results of the income experiment in Watertown are shown in the table below. It is apparent that there was no significant difference in the results.

TABLE **B–5.**—INCOME IN 1952 OF PRIMARY FAMILIES IN SUBSTANDARD RENTED DWELLING UNITS IN WATERTOWN, NEW YORK

Total money income	Proce-dure A	Proce-dure B	Total money income	Proce-dure A	Proce-dure B
Number of families in sample..	480	446	$2,200 to $2,399...............	6.6	4.0
Number of families reporting			$2,400 to $2,599...............	5.3	4.7
on income....................	468	430	$2,600 to $2,799...............	6.6	5.3
			$2,800 to $2,999...............	6.8	11.4
Total reporting............	100.0	100.0	$3,000 to $3,499...............	12.2	14.7
			$3,500 to $3,999...............	12.2	11.4
Under $1,000.....................	12.2	9.3	$4,000 and over................	18.4	17.4
$1,000 to $1,499................	8.3	10.9			
$1,500 to $1,999................	7.3	8.4	Median income.................	$2,787	$2,886
$2,000 to $2,199................	4.1	2.6			

Source: Unpublished data of the Bureau of the Census.

Quality checks of census income data

Comparison of 1950 Census and Current Population Survey income distributions.

Distribution for persons. Essentially the same techniques were used to obtain personal income data in the March 1950 Current Population Survey and in the 1950 Census. Therefore, it is of some interest to compare the results. Table B–6 presents a summary of the numbers of income recipients and medians for each type of income. Although the data require adjustment to make them comparable with respect to population coverage, they provide a basis for comparing the PST and CPS [2] income distributions at the most crucial points.

With the exception of income other than earnings, PST and CPS appear to have reported about the same number of recipients of each type of income. The apparent similarity of these estimates is somewhat misleading inasmuch as the two surveys are not directly comparable with respect to population coverage. The PST included about 1.6 million institutional inmates,[3] and about 0.3 million members of the Armed Forces living on military posts who were excluded from CPS. Since these persons are in the population base from which the PST estimates of the numbers of income recipients are made, it is apparent that the PST estimates are somewhat overstated as compared with CPS.[4] If the institutional inmates and members of the Armed Forces living on post were excluded from the PST weighting of the data, the total number of income recipients in PST would have been estimated to be about 70.6 million rather than 72.1 million as shown in the table. Experience in the reconciliation of other estimates of this type indicates that the discrepancy of about 1 million between the CPS and the adjusted PST estimate of the number of income recipients is relatively small. For example, considerably greater differences in the estimates of the number of paid workers during a given year are usually obtained from the CPS surveys of work experience conducted in December and the income surveys conducted in April.

It is also apparent from table B–6 that, with the exception of income from self-employment, the medians obtained for each type of income in PST and CPS were about the same. However, a closer look at the full distributions by income levels in table B–7 indicates that PST consistently shows a larger proportion of income recipients in the upper-income brackets. The percentage differences do not appear great; however, since the upper-income groups possess a large share of the aggregate income, the small percentage differences shown in the table yield relatively large differences in the aggregates.

---

[2] The 1950 Census data discussed in tables B–6 to B–12 were obtained from a preliminary sample of census returns, which will be referred to as the Preliminary Sample Tabulations (PST). These data are compared with information obtained in the Current Population Survey (CPS) of the Bureau of the Census and with the income aggregates prepared by the National Income Division of the Department of Commerce (NID). In all cases where comparisons were possible, it has been found that the PST data do not differ significantly from the final 1950 Census tabulations. The PST data were used here in preference to the final 1950 Census data because many of the characteristics that are discussed are not available from the final tabulations.

[3] Income information was very poorly reported for institutional inmates in the 1950 Census. Of the 1.6 million inmates of institutions 14 years of age and over, an estimated 1.1 million did not report on income, 0.3 million reported no income, and 0.2 million reported $1 or more of income.

[4] No adjustment was made for the fact that the PST estimate of the civilian noninstitutional population is 0.4 million greater than the CPS estimate. The difference between these two figures arises from the fact that the population estimate used to inflate the CPS data is a projection of 1940 Census data, whereas the PST estimate represents an inflation of a sample of 1950 Census returns.

TABLE **B–6.**—NUMBER OF INCOME RECIPIENTS AND MEDIAN INCOME IN 1949, BY TYPE OF INCOME: 1950 CENSUS (PRELIMINARY SAMPLE TABULATIONS) AND MARCH 1950 CURRENT POPULATION SURVEY

Number of income recipients and median income, by type of income	PST (Total population, 14 years old and over)	CPS (Noninstitutional population, 14 years old and over, excl. members of Armed Forces on post)
Total population..........................	111,926,000	109,644,000
Total number of income recipients..........	72,054,000	71,768,000
Number of recipients of—		
Wage or salary income..................	54,974,000	54,912,000
Self-employment income.................	10,674,000	10,966,000
Income other than earnings.............	18,813,000	16,875,000
Median income:		
Total income..........................	$1,909	$1,814
Wage or salary income.................	2,032	2,016
Self-employment income.................	1,586	1,039
Income other than earnings.............	478	496

Source: Herman P. Miller, "An Appraisal of the 1950 Census Income Data," *Journal of the American Statistical Association,* Vol. 48, March 1953, table 1.

The discrepancy of approximately $600 between the PST and CPS estimates of median self-employment income is rather large. A full explanation for this difference is not available at present. Perhaps the census obtained more accurate income data than CPS in farm areas because of the use of the detailed farm schedule in the Census of Agriculture, which tended to improve the estimate of net income from farm self-employment on the population schedule. This improvement would have been reflected in less underreporting of income or in the higher median income of farm families. (See table B–8.) It is also possible that the census income data benefited from the self-enumeration procedure, which was tried in the Census of Agriculture in all farm areas except the South; however, in the absence of any firm data on the effects of self-enumeration or the extent to which it was actually used in the Census of Agriculture, this point can only be a matter of conjecture. The only available evidence on this point comes from the pretest of the census conducted in October 1948 in Union County, Indiana, and Carroll County, Kentucky, to determine the relative merits of self-enumeration and direct-enumeration techniques. As already indicated, this pretest showed that in about 60 percent of the cases where the self-enumeration procedure was to have been used, the census enumerators rather than the respondents actually completed the schedules. Even where the respondents entered the income information on the self-enumeration schedules, a large proportion of the entries were apparently rounded to hundreds of dollars, which indicates that the respondents probably did not take advantage of the advance distribution of schedules to refer to records. Moreover, there were no significant differences in the medians produced by each procedure.

TABLE **B-7.**—DISTRIBUTIONS OF PERSONS AND OF THEIR AGGREGATE INCOME IN 1949: 1950
CENSUS (PRELIMINARY SAMPLE TABULATIONS) AND MARCH 1950 CURRENT POPULATION SURVEY

Total money income in 1949	PST		CPS	
	Total population, 14 years old and over (thousands)	Aggregate income (billions)	Noninstitutional population, 14 years old and over (excl. members of Armed Forces on post) (thousands)	Aggregate income (billions)
Total................................	111,926	$171.4	109,644	$158.0
Total with income....................	72,054	...	71,768	...
Percent of those with income......	100.0	100.0	100.0	100.0
Loss or $1 to $499......................	17.3	1.8	18.9	2.1
$500 to $999............................	13.5	4.3	13.8	4.7
$1,000 to $1,499........................	10.9	5.7	10.8	6.1
$1,500 to $1,999........................	10.2	7.5	10.4	8.3
$2,000 to $2,499........................	11.2	10.6	11.6	11.9
$2,500 to $2,999........................	9.1	10.6	9.5	11.9
$3,000 to $3,499........................	9.0	12.3	8.7	12.8
$3,500 to $3,999........................	5.6	8.9	5.4	9.2
$4,000 to $4,499........................	4.0	7.1	3.5	6.8
$4,500 to $4,999........................	2.2	4.4	2.0	4.3
$5,000 to $5,999........................	2.9	6.8	2.3	5.7
$6,000 to $6,999........................	1.3	3.6	1.1	3.2
$7,000 to $9,999........................	1.4	5.0	1.0	3.9
$10,000 and over........................	1.4	11.5	1.0	9.1
Median income..........................	$1,909	...	$1,814	...

Source: Herman P. Miller, "An Appraisal of the 1950 Census Income Data," *Journal of the American Statistical Association*, Vol. 48, March 1953, table 2.

TABLE **B-8.**—MEDIAN INCOME IN 1949 OF FAMILIES BY RESIDENCE: 1950 CENSUS (PRELIMINARY SAMPLE TABULATIONS) AND MARCH 1950 CURRENT POPULATION SURVEY

Area	Total		White		Nonwhite	
	PST	CPS	PST	CPS	PST	CPS
United States..................	$3,068	$3,107	$3,216	$3,232	$1,425	$1,650
Urban..............................	3,429	3,486	3,581	3,619	1,850	2,084
Rural nonfarm......................	2,552	2,763	2,711	2,851	1,141	1,240
Rural farm.........................	1,734	1,587	1,936	1,757	733	691

Source: Herman P. Miller, "An Appraisal of the 1950 Census Income Data," *Journal of the American Statistical Association*, Vol. 48, March 1953, table 6.

Distributions for families. With respect to the income of families rather than persons, it is apparent from table B–8 that there is no significant difference between the PST and CPS median income for families within each color and residence group.[5] The more detailed distributions by income level and color in table B–9 indicate a similar correspondence between the results obtained in these surveys. The one marked difference between the two distributions is the larger proportion of "zero-income" families

[5] Unrelated individuals are excluded from this comparison because they are defined somewhat differently in CPS and in the census. For example, college students living away from home are treated as family members in CPS and as unrelated individuals in the census.

obtained in the PST results. This deficiency in the PST data resulted largely from the enumerative and editing procedures used in the 1950 Census and is discussed in some detail below.

Although the medians obtained in CPS and PST are substantially the same, patterns of small differences that appear in the data may be of some significance. Among both white and nonwhite families, the CPS medians in urban and rural-nonfarm areas are slightly (though not significantly) higher than the corresponding PST results; however, among rural-farm families PST showed somewhat higher medians than CPS. These differences may reflect differences in the procedures used in these areas. In nonfarm areas essentially the same procedures were used in CPS and census. Although a small part of the differences between CPS and PST are attributable to the fact that college students living away from home were included as family members in CPS but not in the census, it is likely that the higher CPS results in these areas reflect the superior schedule design and better enumeration.

Table B–9 indicates that there were perhaps four times as many families without income in PST as in CPS. In absolute terms these families numbered 1.6 million in PST as compared with 0.4 million in CPS. The relatively large number of families without income in PST is partly accounted for by the editing procedures used in the 1950 Census. About one-third,

TABLE **B–9.**—INCOME IN 1949 OF FAMILIES BY COLOR: 1950 CENSUS (PRELIMINARY SAMPLE TABULATIONS) AND MARCH 1950 CURRENT POPULATION SURVEY

Total money income in 1949	Total		White		Nonwhite	
	PST	CPS	PST	CPS	PST	CPS
Number.............thousands..	38,788	39,193	35,411	35,988	3,377	3,205
Total........................	100.0	100.0	100.0	100.0	100.0	100.0
Percent reporting on income........	93.9	(1)	93.8	(1)	95.9	(1)
Percent not reporting on income....	6.1	(1)	6.2	(1)	4.1	(1)
Total reporting..............	100.0	100.0	100.0	100.0	100.0	100.0
None..................................	4.1	0.9	3.9	0.9	6.3	0.9
Loss or $1 to $499..................	4.5	5.0	3.7	4.2	11.9	14.0
$500 to $999........................	6.8	6.2	5.7	5.3	18.4	16.0
$1,000 to $1,499....................	7.3	7.3	6.5	6.6	15.8	15.1
$1,500 to $1,999....................	7.5	7.6	7.0	7.1	12.6	13.5
$2,000 to $2,499....................	9.3	10.2	9.0	10.0	11.9	12.9
$2,500 to $2,999....................	9.0	10.4	9.2	10.5	7.0	9.2
$3,000 to $3,499....................	10.9	11.2	11.4	11.7	6.2	5.6
$3,500 to $3,999....................	8.7	8.8	9.3	9.3	3.0	3.7
$4,000 to $4,499....................	7.2	6.7	7.7	7.1	2.1	2.6
$4,500 to $4,999....................	4.9	5.3	5.3	5.6	1.0	1.9
$5,000 to $5,999....................	7.9	7.8	8.4	8.3	1.8	2.5
$6,000 to $6,999....................	4.3	4.8	4.6	5.1	1.0	1.3
$7,000 to $9,999....................	4.7	5.0	5.1	5.4	0.8	0.5
$10,000 and over...................	2.9	2.6	3.2	2.8	0.2	0.3
Median income......................	$3,068	$3,107	$3,216	$3,232	$1,425	$1,650

[1] Comparable figures not available.

Source: Herman P. Miller, "An Appraisal of the 1950 Census Income Data," *Journal of the American Statistical Association*, Vol. 48, March 1953, table 7.

or 0.5 million families without income in PST, were cases in which a family head had no income and income information for other relatives was not obtained. Although many of these families probably represented cases in which the head had no income but other family members did, they were all tabulated as having no income according to the income editing rules used in the 1950 Census (see discussion of effects of census editing procedures below). At present little is known about the remaining 1.1 million "zero-income" families. Nearly half of these families probably had no income as defined in the census, if the CPS figure of 0.4 million is taken to be accurate. They may have been living on savings, charity, or gifts, or else they were newly created families or families in which the sole breadwinner had only recently died or left the family. The remainder of these families appear at the "zero-income" level for a variety of reasons, such as errors in enumeration and coding.

Comparison of 1950 Census and Current Population Survey aggregates with national income estimates.

Aggregates for persons. Although the primary purpose of the income questions in the 1950 Census and in the March 1950 Current Population Survey was to provide a distribution of the population by income levels, estimates of the aggregates of each type of income can be derived from these data. The comparison of these estimates with those prepared by the National Income Division of the Department of Commerce provides further information regarding the reliability of the 1950 Census income data. Such a comparison is made in table B–10. The census aggregates shown

TABLE **B–10.**—ESTIMATES OF AGGREGATE INCOME IN 1949, BY TYPE: 1950 CENSUS (PRELIMINARY SAMPLE TABULATIONS), MARCH 1950 CURRENT POPULATION SURVEY, AND NATIONAL INCOME DIVISION

(In billions)

Type of income	PST (Total population, 14 years old and over)	CPS (Noninstitutional population, 14 years old and over (excl. members of Armed Forces on post)	NID (Total population)
Total income..................	[1]$171.4	[1]$158.0	$187.6
Wage or salary income............	124.3	120.0	127.5
Self-employment income...........	31.1	[2]26.5	[3]29.3
Income other than earnings.......	16.6	13.3	30.8

[1] The detail by type of income does not add to the total because each of the aggregates was estimated independently.

[2] Nonfarm self-employment estimate: $19.1 billion; farm self-employment estimate: $7.4 billion.

[3] Nonfarm self-employment estimate: $19.4 billion; farm self-employment estimate: $9.9 billion.

Source: Herman P. Miller, "An Appraisal of the 1950 Census Income Data," *Journal of the American Statistical Association*, Vol. 48, March 1953, table 3.

in this table largely represent estimates derived from the tabulated data and are subject to substantial errors of estimation.   Moreover, despite the fact that the NID aggregates are largely based on record data and may therefore be considered more reliable than the field survey data, they are also subject to errors of estimation.   For these reasons, small differences in the results must be interpreted with care.

As previously indicated (on page 136), the PST and CPS estimates of aggregate income shown in table B–10 were computed by multiplying the estimated number of persons in each income interval by the average income for that interval.   For intervals between $500 and $10,000, the midpoint of each interval was assumed to be the average; $250 was selected as the average for the "loss or $1 to $499" level, and $20,000 was selected as the average for the "$10,000 and over" level.[6]   The aggregates were obtained by multiplying the frequencies by the average income for each interval.   The NID aggregates with which the PST and CPS aggregates are compared were obtained by adjusting the Personal Income Series of the Department of Commerce to make it more comparable with the definition of income and the population coverage of the census income data.[7]

Perhaps the most striking fact shown in the above table is that the PST obtained about 90 percent of the comparable NID estimate of aggregate income.   This proportion is considerably greater than that obtained in any of the CPS income surveys that have been conducted to date.   The March 1950 CPS obtained only 84 percent of the NID aggregate.

Aggregates for families and unrelated individuals.   The PST tabulations for families and unrelated individuals yielded a considerably lower aggregate ($154.5 billion) [8] than the comparable tabulations for persons 14 years old and over ($168.0 billion).   Theoretically, the two estimates should have been about the same.   The lower estimates derived from the tabulations for families are largely attributable to the method used to collect family income data in the census.

As previously indicated, income information in the 1950 Census was

---

[6] The arithmetic mean for the "tail" of an income distribution having an open-end interval of $10,000 or more is generally estimated from a Pareto curve.   However, it was found after some investigation that although this method yields reasonable estimates for the distributions of families and unrelated individuals, it tends to overstate the mean for distributions of persons.   An examination of income tax returns for 1944 to 1949 showed that in each of these years the mean adjusted gross income for returns with $10,000 or more of adjusted gross income was between $21,000 and $22,000.   On the basis of this and other evidence it was assumed in deriving the data shown in tables B–7 and B–10 that $20,000 was a conservative approximation of the mean for the open-end interval.

[7] A detailed description of the method used to adjust the Personal Income Series for comparability with the census income data is described in a paper by S.F. Goldsmith, "Appraisal of Basic Data Available for Constructing Income Size Distributions," which appears in *Studies in Income and Wealth*, Vol. 13, National Bureau of Economic Research, New York, 1951.

[8] The average for the open-end interval was estimated from a Pareto curve in the tabulations for families and unrelated individuals, whereas $20,000 was assumed as the average for the open-end interval in the tabulations for persons.   If $20,000 had been used as the average in the family tabulations, the aggregate would have been $159.1 billion rather than $154.5 billion.

FOR PERSONS 14 YEARS OF AGE AND OVER

Income received by this person in 1949				If this person is a family head (see definition below) income received by his relatives in this household			
Last year (1949), how much money did he earn working as an employee for wages or salary? (Enter amount before deductions for taxes, etc.)	Last year, how much money did he earn working in his own business, professional practice, or farm? (Enter net income.)	Last year, how much money did he receive from interest, dividends, veteran's allowances, pensions, rents, or other income (aside from earnings)?	Leave blank	Last year (1949), how much money did his relatives in this household earn working for wages or salary? (Amount before deductions for taxes, etc.)	Last year, how much money did his relatives in this household earn in own business, professional practice, or farm? (Net income.)	Last year, how much money did his relatives in this household receive from interest, dividends, pensions, rents, or other income (aside from earnings)?	Leave blank
31a	31b	31c	F	32a	32b	32c	G
□ None $ _____	□ None $ _____	□ None $ _____		□ None $ _____	□ None $ _____	□ None $ _____	
□ None $ _____	□ None $ _____	□ None $ _____		□ None $ _____	□ None $ _____	□ None $ _____	

obtained from a 20-percent sample of the population. If a person came
into the sample, he was asked questions 31a–c indicated in the excerpt
from the 1950 Census schedule shown above. If the sample person was
not a family head, questions 32a–c were skipped; however, it he was a
family head, questions 32a–c were asked in order to obtain income information for the entire family group. Although this procedure provided an
unbiased sample of families and of persons, it increased the possibility of
introducing reporting errors.

As the collection procedure implies, the family income data are based
on replies to income questions asked separately for the head of the family
and for all relatives of the family head *as a group,* whereas the income
data for persons are based on replies to income questions asked for *each*
person in the sample. The failure, in the 1950 Census, to obtain income
information individually for relatives of family heads (as was done in the
March 1950 CPS) probably resulted in underreporting of income for this
group. Evidence supporting this view is shown in table B–11 in which it
may be noted that at each income level the CPS data have a larger proportion
of families in which the family income was greater than the head's income.
This is equivalent to saying that there were more families having income
recipients other than the head in CPS than in PST.

TABLE **B–11.**—PERCENT OF FAMILIES WITH FAMILY INCOME GREATER THAN INCOME OF HEAD,
BY FAMILY INCOME IN 1949: 1950 CENSUS (PRELIMINARY SAMPLE TABULATIONS) AND MARCH
1950 CURRENT POPULATION SURVEY

Family income in 1949	PST	CPS	Family income in 1949	PST	CPS
Under $1,000...............	19.3	27.1	$4,000 to $4,999..........	49.1	56.0
$1,000 to $1,999..........	30.7	40.6	$5,000 to $5,999..........	60.0	70.1
$2,000 to $2,999..........	29.6	38.0	$6,000 to $6,999..........	64.5	72.4
$3,000 to $3,999..........	33.9	41.3	$7,000 to $9,999..........	65.6	74.0

Note: Preliminary Sample Tabulations data showing the number of families with more than one
income recipient for the $10,000 and over interval not available.

Source: Herman P. Miller, "An Appraisal of the 1950 Census Income Data," *Journal of the American Statistical Association,* Vol. 48, March 1953, table 8.

There is also some evidence that the income editing procedures used in
the 1950 Census contributed to the downward bias of the family income
data. In the interest of economy, a relatively simple editing procedure was
used in processing the 1950 Census family income data. It was assumed
that if the income information was obtained for the family head, the total
family income was known even when the income information was not obtained for other family members. This procedure is different from the
CPS procedure in which any incompleteness in the returns for a family
would result in a not reported (NA) classification for the family. It was
adopted because it was one of the few editing procedures that would permit full utilization of the information obtained in the census. Some of the
pretests indicated that a relatively large proportion of the schedules sub-

mitted by the census enumerators would contain blanks in the items for relatives of the head that actually represented the absence of income rather than the failure to report the amount of income received. Another consideration that led to the adoption of this procedure is the fact that in about one-half of all families the head is the only income recipient and even where there are other recipients the head is generally the principal recipient. Although other editing procedures were considered, only the one finally adopted fitted in as part of the general coding and editing scheme used in the census.

In general, the editing scheme used in the 1950 Census produced the desired results of keeping the NA rate low without seriously distorting the income distribution (table B–12). The NA rate obtained using the 1950 Census editing procedures was half of what it would have been if the alternative procedure (classifying as NA families in which no report was made for family members other than the head) had been used. The median income based on the procedure which was used was about $70 lower than the median that would have been obtained from the alternative procedure. This procedure created a downward bias in the statistics inasmuch as all the missing entries were converted to zeros, although some of them must have actually represented amounts. The approximate magnitude of this bias is reflected in the fact that the aggregate computed from the distribution of families and individuals by income levels before editing was $4 billion higher than the aggregate derived from the data as tabulated (after

TABLE **B–12.**—EFFECT OF USING DIFFERENT NOT REPORTING (NA) CRITERIA ON THE DISTRIBUTION OF FAMILIES, BY INCOME IN 1949: 1950 CENSUS

Total money income in 1949	Distribution as tabulated	Distribution if families in which income information was not obtained for relatives of the head were tabulated as NA
Total..................................	100.0	100.0
Percent reporting on income...............	93.9	88.5
Percent not reporting on income...........	6.1	11.5
Total reporting......................	100.0	100.0
None....................................	4.0	2.8
Loss or $1 to $499......................	4.6	4.3
$500 to $999............................	6.8	6.7
$1,000 to $1,499........................	7.3	7.3
$1,500 to $1,999........................	7.5	7.4
$2,000 to $2,499........................	9.3	9.3
$2,500 to $2,999........................	9.1	9.2
$3,000 to $3,499........................	11.0	11.1
$3,500 to $3,999........................	8.7	8.9
$4,000 to $4,499........................	7.2	7.4
$4,500 to $4,999........................	4.9	5.0
$5,000 to $5,999........................	7.9	8.1
$6,000 to $6,999........................	4.3	4.4
$7,000 to $9,999........................	4.7	4.9
$10,000 and over........................	2.9	3.0
Median income..........................	$3,069	$3,135

Source: Herman P. Miller, "An Appraisal of the 1950 Census Income Data," *Journal of the American Statistical Association*, Vol. 48, March 1953, table 9.

editing). This result suggests that editing accounts for about one-fourth of the difference between the family aggregate and the aggregate for persons.

Post-enumeration surveys

Baltimore Housing Survey. In July 1949 the Bureau of the Census conducted a sample housing survey in Baltimore, Maryland, for the Public Housing Authority of that city. The purpose of this survey was to establish eligibility standards for low-rent public housing projects in the Baltimore area and to determine the amount of rent to be charged in these projects. For this reason, a low-income section of Baltimore known as the Hubbard area was selected for the survey. A representative sample of about 5,500 households in this area were interviewed by trained enumerators of the Bureau of the Census, and information on housing and population characteristics (including income) was obtained.

In order to determine the reliability of the response in the original enumeration, a quality check was conducted in September 1949 in which a subsample of the households originally enumerated were reinterviewed. This subsample consisted largely of households residing in tenant-occupied substandard dwelling units. In approximately 250 households a complete check of housing and population information was conducted.

In the original Baltimore Housing Survey each person in the sample 14 years of age and over was asked to report (*a*) the amount of money wages or salary earned in 1948; (*b*) the amount of income from self-employment earned in 1948; and (*c*) the amount of income, other than earnings, received in 1948. Since the procedures used in the income supplements to the Current Population Survey were employed here, it was not mandatory that each person report for himself. The information obtained from any responsible person was accepted.

Since only the most accurate results were aimed at in the quality check, the enumerators were required to interview each person directly. The only exception to this rule was that parents or guardians were considered acceptable respondents for persons between 14 and 18 years of age. An additional measure designed to improve the accuracy of the response was a detailed questionnaire for each person in which the work history for that person during the calendar year 1948, covering each period of employment or unemployment, was reconstructed. The schedule used to compute annual earnings included separate questions on taxes, social security, and other items that may have been originally deducted from pay, as well as on tips, bonuses, and commissions that may have been forgotten when the respondent originally reported his pay. In addition, detailed questions regarding income from roomers and boarders, unemployment compensation, social security or other old age benefits, other pensions or allowances, dependency allotments, relief, money for support from persons not living in the household, interest or dividends, and net rent from property were asked for each person.

The quality check of the Baltimore Housing Survey represents an intensive attempt by the Bureau of the Census to measure the enumerative and reporting errors present in field surveys of income. For this reason, although the results are based on a relatively small sample, they merit careful study. One important qualification that should be considered in analyzing the data is that the quality check of the Baltimore Housing Survey is representative only of a low-income group in one section of a particular city. Therefore, any extension of the findings of this study to field surveys of income in general would be unwarranted.

Perhaps the most important conclusion derived from this study is that the quality check failed to uncover any consistent bias in the income data obtained in the original enumeration. Although there were some substantial differences between the original and quality-check income distributions, the difference in the median income of families and unrelated individuals was less than $100 (table B–13). The small difference in the median income of families and individuals combined reflects an increase in the median income of families that was counterbalanced by a decrease in the median income of unrelated individuals. However, none of these differences was statistically significant.

TABLE **B–13.**—INCOME IN 1948 OF FAMILIES AND UNRELATED INDIVIDUALS IN A LOW-INCOME AREA: ORIGINAL BALTIMORE HOUSING SURVEY AND QUALITY CHECK

Total money income	Families and unrelated individuals		Families		Unrelated individuals	
	Original survey	Quality check	Original survey	Quality check	Original survey	Quality check
Number of sample cases..........	265	279	197	197	68	82
Number reporting on income......	261	250	194	180	67	70
Percent of those reporting....	100.0	100.0	100.0	100.0	100.0	100.0
Under $500..........................	6.1	8.0	2.1	1.1	17.9	25.7
$500 to $999.......................	12.3	16.0	6.2	6.7	29.9	40.0
$1,000 to $1,499...................	11.1	7.2	8.8	8.9	17.9	2.9
$1,500 to $1,999...................	12.3	12.8	12.9	13.3	10.4	11.4
$2,000 to $2,499...................	16.9	10.0	18.0	11.1	13.4	7.1
$2,500 to $2,999...................	14.6	16.0	17.5	18.9	6.0	8.6
$3,000 to $3,499...................	8.4	10.8	10.3	13.9	3.0	2.9
$3,500 to $3,999...................	6.1	8.4	7.7	11.1	1.5	1.4
$4,000 to $4,499...................	4.2	3.6	5.7	5.0	...	...
$4,500 to $4,999...................	1.9	2.0	2.6	2.8	...	...
$5,000 to $5,999...................	2.3	0.4	3.1	0.6	...	...
$6,000 to $9,999...................	3.4	4.4	4.6	6.1	...	...
$10,000 and over...................	0.4	0.4	0.5	0.6	...	...
Median income.....................	$2,244	$2,300	$2,559	$2,735	$1,063	$804

Source: Unpublished data of the Bureau of the Census.

· The similarity of the original and quality-check medians might give the impression that families and individuals generally reported the same income in both enumerations; however, this impression is incorrect. Of the 224 families and individuals who reported on income in both the original enumeration and in the quality check, only 113 (50 percent) were in the same $500 class interval before and after the quality check; 47

families and individuals (21 percent) were in a lower class interval after the quality check, and 64 families and individuals (29 percent) were in a higher class interval after the quality check (table B–14).

The similarity of the income distributions despite the relatively large proportion of families and individuals reporting differences in income is due largely to the fact that income was overstated almost as frequently as it was understated in the original enumeration. These reporting and enumerative errors generally tended to cancel themselves out, leaving the income distributions relatively unchanged.

1950 Census income data for persons. Upon the completion of the 1950 Census, an intensive Post-Enumeration Survey (PES) was conducted with a sample of about 25,000 households. In effect, this survey was a reenumeration of a representative sample of households employing a more detailed questionnaire and better trained interviewers than were used in the regular census. It was expected that these refinements would produce more accurate results than were obtained in the census and that the analysis of the differences in the answers received for identical families would provide a basis for appraising the quality of the census results.

With respect to the income data, the methods used in the Post-Enumeration Survey were basically the same as those previously used in the quality check of the Baltimore Housing Survey. Therefore, rather than describe the methodology,[9] attention is focused here directly upon the results. Some of the more important results based on the income data obtained in the Post-Enumeration Survey are shown in table B–15. Here it may be noted that the distribution of persons by income levels in the census is very similar to that obtained in the Post-Enumeration Survey. The median income of income recipients in the census ($1,917) is somewhat greater than in PES ($1,840); however, aggregate income estimated from the PES results ($180.8 billion) is somewhat greater than the aggregate based on census results ($173.6 billion). The higher aggregate income in PES is attributable in part to the fact that this survey had a larger proportion of income recipients than the census (68 percent of the PES respondents were reported as income recipients as compared with 65 percent of the census respondents). In addition, PES reported a slightly larger proportion of persons in the higher income levels.

As in the Baltimore Housing Survey, the PES results showed a considerable amount of variability of response. Nearly one-half of the persons were reported at different income levels in each survey; however, lower incomes were reported in PES almost as frequently as higher incomes so that the over-all income distributions for PES and census remained about the same.

---

[9] A description of the Post-Enumeration Survey of the 1950 Census appears in: Eli S. Marks, W. Parker Mauldin, and Harold Nisselson, "The Post-Enumeration Survey of the 1950 Census: A Case History in Survey Design," *Journal of the American Statistical Association*, Vol. 48, June 1953, pp. 220–243.

Table B–14.— Income in 1948 Reported for Families and Unrelated Individuals in Original Baltimore Housing Survey, by Income Reported in Quality Check

(The total shown in this table differs from that shown in table B–13 because it excludes a small number of persons who were missed or incorrectly classified in the original survey)

Total money income in original survey	Total families and unrelated individuals	Total money income in quality check													Not reported
		Under $500	$500 to $999	$1,000 to $1,499	$1,500 to $1,999	$2,000 to $2,499	$2,500 to $2,999	$3,000 to $3,499	$3,500 to $3,999	$4,000 to $4,499	$4,500 to $4,999	$5,000 to $5,999	$6,000 to $9,999	$10,000 and over	
Total.................	260	16	36	18	30	24	39	26	18	10	4	1	11	1	26
Under $500.................	16	11	2	1	1	1									
$500 to $999.................	30	4	17	3	1	2									3
$1,000 to $1,499.................	28	1	10	11	3	1									2
$1,500 to $1,999.................	31		2	1	18	3	2	1							4
$2,000 to $2,499.................	43		1	2	6	11	13	3	3	2					2
$2,500 to $2,999.................	38		3		1	4	20	7	1						2
$3,000 to $3,499.................	22						1	12	5	2					2
$3,500 to $3,999.................	16					1		3	6	2			1		3
$4,000 to $4,499.................	11						1		3	4	1		1		1
$4,500 to $4,999.................	5										2				3
$5,000 to $5,999.................	6						1				1	1	2		1
$6,000 to $9,999.................	9												7		2
$10,000 and over.................	1													1	
Not reported.................	4		1			1	1								1

Source: Unpublished data of the Bureau of the Census.

TABLE **B-15.**—DISTRIBUTIONS OF PERSONS AND OF THEIR AGGREGATE INCOME IN 1949: 1950
CENSUS AND POST-ENUMERATION SURVEY

Total money income in 1949	Post-Enumeration Survey		1950 Census	
	Persons	Aggregate income	Persons	Aggregate income
Number of persons..........thousands..	113,371	...	111,704	...
Total.................................	100.0	...	100.0	...
Percent reporting on income................	97.5	...	93.3	...
Percent not reporting on income............	2.5	...	6.7	...
Total reporting......................	100.0	100.0	100.0	100.0
None....................................	31.7	...	35.4	...
Loss or $1 to $499......................	12.6	2.0	11.2	1.8
$500 to $999............................	9.2	4.3	8.6	4.1
$1,000 to $1,499........................	7.3	5.7	7.0	5.6
$1,500 to $1,999........................	7.5	8.3	6.6	7.5
$2,000 to $2,499........................	7.1	10.0	7.4	10.7
$2,500 to $2,999........................	6.2	10.7	5.9	10.5
$3,000 to $3,499........................	5.7	11.6	5.8	12.1
$3,500 to $3,999........................	3.9	9.2	3.5	8.5
$4,000 to $4,499........................	3.0	7.9	2.5	6.9
$4,500 to $4,999........................	1.4	4.1	1.4	4.3
$5,000 to $5,999........................	1.7	5.7	1.9	6.7
$6,000 to $6,999........................	0.8	3.1	0.9	3.6
$7,000 to $9,999........................	1.1	6.0	0.9	5.1
$10,000 and over........................	0.9	11.3	1.0	12.7
Median income for persons with income......	$1,840	...	$1,917	...
Aggregate income......billions of dollars..	...	180.8	...	173.6

Source: Unpublished data of the Bureau of the Census.

Census-Survey Research Center matching study.

In the early
part of each year since 1945, the Survey Research Center of the University
of Michigan has conducted a Survey of Consumer Finances for the Federal
Reserve Board. These surveys, which have been generally based on interviews with approximately 3,000 households, provide, among other data,
information on the size distribution of income. Since the population coverage, the income concept, and the time reference in these surveys were
almost identical with those used by the Bureau of the Census, the income
distributions obtained in these surveys should have been the same. Nevertheless, each year substantial differences in the results were found. Therefore, upon the completion of the 1950 Census, a joint project was sponsored
by the Survey Research Center, the Federal Reserve Board, and the Bureau
of the Census designed to determine the reasons for the differences in the
personal income reports obtained in these surveys.

In August and September 1950, about seven months after the completion of the original enumeration in the Survey of Consumer Finances
(hereafter referred to as CFS), the Bureau of the Census, reinterviewed a
subsample of the identical households (hereafter the reinterview survey
will be referred to as CQC, Census Quality Check). Enumerators hired
and trained by the Bureau reinterviewed about one-half of the households
that had been interviewed earlier in the year in the CFS. The schedule
used in the regular Post-Enumeration Survey of the 1950 Census was also
used in the CQC. This schedule was less detailed than that used originally
in the CFS.

Since the CFS did not obtain the names of its respondents during the original interview, some problems of identification were encountered. The CQC enumerators were given exactly the same information to identify the sample dwelling units as the CFS enumerators had used. Where available, addresses of dwelling units were furnished; in open-country segments, highway maps and aerial photographs with clearly drawn segment boundaries were supplied. A carefully designed procedure was used to determine the match status of each household in the sample. Every household was classified as positively matched, probably matched, and not matched. The results showed that 62 percent of the families and individuals in the CQC were positively matched with units covered in the CFS; 10 percent were probably matched; and 28 percent were not matched. The nonmatched cases included families and individuals missed in the original enumeration as well as those that changed in composition, were living elsewhere at the time of the CFS enumeration, or could not be found for some other reason by the CQC enumerator.

Although the data derived from this survey have been tabulated, they were not available for inclusion in this monograph. However, an examination of the preliminary results tends to confirm the conclusions suggested by the post-enumeration surveys described above. The over-all differences in the income distribution for identical families and unrelated individuals interviewed in the CQC and in the CFS were small enough to be regarded as negligible by most analysts.

Comparisons of census reports with record data

Bureau of Internal Revenue tax returns. As part of the joint study described above, an attempt was made to locate the personal income tax return for each family and unrelated individual in that part of the CFS sample which was reinterviewed by enumerators of the Bureau of the Census. Using the names, addresses, family composition, and other identifying information obtained in each of the surveys, a search was made in the files of the Bureau of Internal Revenue to locate the tax returns for particular families and unrelated individuals. Of course, adequate safeguards were taken to maintain the confidentiality of both the tax returns and the reports to the census enumerators. Each family was then classified as a complete match, partial match, or nonmatch. About 55 percent of the families and unrelated individuals in CQC were completely matched, and 11 percent were partially matched. No tax return could be found for the remaining 34 percent. A large proportion of the nonmatched cases represents families and unrelated individuals whose incomes were below the tax-filing requirement. As table B–16 shows, the families and individuals in CQC that could not be matched with income tax returns had a relatively low median income of $1,700. It is also undoubtedly true that many of these families and individuals should have filed returns but did not and that many of the returns simply could not be identified.

TABLE **B–16.**—INCOME IN 1949 OF FAMILIES AND UNRELATED INDIVIDUALS: CENSUS QUALITY CHECK AND BUREAU OF INTERNAL REVENUE

Total money income in 1949	Income reported in CQC		Partially matched cases		Completely matched cases	
	All cases	Non-matched cases	Income in BIR	Income in CQC	Income in BIR	Income in CQC
Number of weighted sample cases..	7,360	2,705	786	786	3,869	3,869
Total.........................	100.0	100.0	100.0	100.0	100.0	100.0
Percent reporting on income..........	88.4	80.4	96.9	90.5	99.9	93.6
Percent not reporting on income......	11.6	19.6	3.1	9.5	0.1	6.4
Total reporting................	100.0	100.0	100.0	100.0	100.0	100.0
None or loss.........................	3.5	7.1	1.3	1.4	0.9	1.7
$1 to $449..........................	3.9	9.0	5.1	...	2.0	1.5
$450 to $949.........................	7.0	15.6	6.0	1.7	4.6	2.9
$950 to $1,949.......................	15.6	25.3	21.3	6.8	14.4	11.6
$1,950 to $2,949.....................	18.4	16.0	19.4	11.9	20.3	21.1
$2,950 to $3,949.....................	17.7	10.0	19.6	20.7	20.1	21.7
$3,950 to $4,949.....................	13.1	6.9	7.2	15.2	15.7	16.5
$4,950 to $7,449.....................	13.1	5.5	13.6	25.3	14.1	15.3
$7,450 to $9,949.....................	4.7	2.2	5.1	12.2	4.4	4.7
$9,950 or more.......................	3.0	2.5	1.3	4.8	3.5	2.9
Median income.......................	$3,040	$1,673	$2,790	$4,443	$3,338	$3,466

Source: Unpublished data of the Bureau of the Census.

The income differences for the partially matched group are difficult to interpret because the tax returns in these cases do not represent the entire family group. The point of primary interest in table B–16 is the striking similarity between the CQC and BIR income reports for families and individuals that were completely matched. The median income for CQC ($3,500) is slightly higher than the median for BIR ($3,300). Part of this difference may, of course, be due to the fact that certain types of receipts such as compensation, pensions, veterans' payments, and insurance payments are included in the census definition of income but are nontaxable and are therefore not shown on tax returns. Again it must be emphasized that although these results are not conclusive they suggest that the income data obtained in the census are sufficiently accurate for most analytical uses.

Bureau of Old-Age and Survivors' Insurance wage records. Another attempt that was made to check the accuracy of the income information obtained both in the 1950 Census and in the Post-Enumeration Survey (PES) was a matching study using the wage records of the Bureau of Old-Age and Survivors' Insurance (BOASI). In this study, an attempt was made to locate the wage records in the files of BOASI of persons who were included in the PES sample and in the census. Here again, each person was classified as having been matched, probably matched, and not matched with his wage record. The criteria for determining the match status were of course rigidly defined before the matching operation was started. The results of this study showed that 34 percent of all persons in the census sample were not matched, 62 percent were matched, and 4 percent were probably matched. The nonmatched cases undoubtedly included many people such as housewives and teen-agers who did not have wage records as well as workers who were employed in industries not covered by Social Security. In fact, if the matching comparison is restricted to males, it is found that only 23 percent could not be matched, 72 percent were matched, and 5 percent were probably matched.

This matching study provides information only for the wage or salary component of income. However, this type of income accounts for a large proportion of the total receipts of most people. Table B–17 presents some of the more important findings of this matching study. It shows that there was relatively little difference in the wage or salary income distributions in the census, PES, and BOASI for persons who were matched with the BOASI wage records. The reports to the Bureau of the Census appear to be somewhat higher than those made to BOASI; however, this difference may merely reflect the fact that the Bureau of the Census data include wages or salaries earned in employment not covered by Social Security. Although these comparisons are subject to several serious qualifications, they tend to confirm the conclusion that biases that may be inherent in the census income figures do not seriously jeopardize the validity of the census income estimates.

TABLE **B–17.**—WAGE OR SALARY INCOME IN 1949 OF POSITIVELY MATCHED PERSONS: 1950 CENSUS, POST-ENUMERATION SURVEY, AND BUREAU OF OLD-AGE AND SURVIVORS INSURANCE

Wage or salary income in 1949	Both sexes			Male			Female		
	PES	Census	BOASI	PES	Census	BOASI	PES	Census	BOASI
Number of persons..thousands..	68,595	67,958	68,595	39,102	38,849	39,102	29,493	29,109	29,493
Total......................	100.0	100.0	100.0	100.0	100.0	100.0	100.0	100.0	100.0
Percent reporting on wage or salary income...................	98.2	96.1	99.6	97.9	95.9	99.6	98.7	96.4	99.6
Percent not reporting on wage or salary income...................	1.8	3.9	0.4	2.1	4.1	0.4	1.3	3.6	0.4
Total reporting.............	100.0	100.0	100.0	100.0	100.0	100.0	100.0	100.0	100.0
Percent with income..........	64.4	62.0	52.3	76.9	75.7	62.9	47.9	43.8	38.2
Percent without income..........	35.6	38.0	47.7	23.1	24.3	37.1	52.1	56.2	61.8
Total with income..........	100.0	100.0	100.0	100.0	100.0	100.0	100.0	100.0	100.0
$1 to $499......................	16.3	14.9	20.7	11.0	10.4	15.3	27.3	25.2	32.5
$500 to $999....................	11.7	11.2	10.3	8.8	8.6	8.0	17.8	17.0	15.5
$1,000 to $1,499................	9.5	10.3	9.4	7.9	8.4	7.2	13.0	14.4	14.2
$1,500 to $1,999................	10.8	10.8	10.6	8.8	9.2	9.2	15.1	14.6	13.6
$2,000 to $2,499................	11.9	13.0	10.2	11.4	12.2	9.2	13.0	14.8	12.4
$2,500 to $2,999................	10.6	10.4	11.2	12.2	11.7	13.1	7.2	7.7	7.0
$3,000 or more..................	29.2	29.4	27.6	39.9	39.5	38.0	6.6	6.3	4.8
Median wage or salary income......	$2,072	$2,108	$1,953	$2,586	$2,552	$2,542	$1,188	$1,271	$1,071

Source: Unpublished data of the Bureau of the Census.

A P P E N D I X   C

STATISTICAL TABLES RELATING TO OCCUPATIONS

In order to simplify the text, several detailed tables showing changes in the extent of employment and income between 1939 and 1949 for selected occupations have been removed from the body of the report and are included as appendix materials for the use of those who are interested in pursuing the analysis more intensively. Tables C–1 to C–6 are for the country as a whole and show, for selected occupations, the level and distribution of wage or salary income in 1939 and 1949 for all workers and for full-year workers by sex. The data for 1949 in these tables are derived from unpublished tabulations of the Bureau of the Census; the data for 1939 are derived from the 1940 Census Report, Vol. III, *The Labor Force*, Part 1, United States Summary, table 72. There are several technical problems associated with the data in tables C–1 to C–6 that may affect the validity and interpretation of the results. Some of these problems are discussed below.

1. The data for 1949 in tables C–1 to C–6 are derived from the 3⅓-percent sample of 1950 Census returns and are for all wage or salary workers reporting $1 or more of wage or salary income. The data for 1939, however, are based on complete 1940 Census returns and are for persons in the experienced labor force reporting $100 or more of wage or salary income. These differences in coverage arise from differences in the tabulation procedures used in each year, and they probably do not have any serious effect on the statistics. With few exceptions, there is only a small difference between the number of persons in the experienced labor force and the number of wage or salary workers in each of the occupations studied. Similarly, there is only a negligible difference between the number of workers reporting $1 or more of wage or salary income and $100 or more of wage or salary income.

In tabulating the data from the 1940 Census, the lowest income used for each of these occupations was "0 to $99." If this level were used in the wage or salary distribution, some persons who were not wage or salary workers in 1939 and who did not have wage or salary income would have been included in the distribution. Accordingly, it was decided to omit this level from the 1939 data. In tabulating the data for 1949, the lowest level used was "$1 to $499," and, therefore, the lower limit for the distributions for this year was $1 and not $100. An analysis of the income data for major occupation groups in the Current Population Survey indicates that there is very little difference between distributions based on experienced workers with $1 or more of wage or salary income and those based on experienced workers with $100 or more of wage or salary income. It should also be noted that the effect of the exclusion of persons with $1 to $99 from the 1939 data is to increase the "equality" of the income distributions for these years. Therefore, the figures tend to understate the diminution of inequality of income distribution within most occupations between 1939 and 1949.

2. The occupation data for 1949 (with the exception of salaried managers and officials) were first tabulated by detailed occupation groups and were then merged to form the same intermediate occupation groups that were used in the 1940 Census. In the case of salaried managers and officials, it was assumed that managers and officials who had $100 or more of wage or salary income in 1939 were salaried, whereas in 1949 only the managers and officials who were classified as wage or salary workers at the time of interview were included in this category.

For various reasons, it was not feasible to include all occupations in this analysis. Some occupations contain a very small number of workers, and it was questionable that reliable statistics for these occupations could have been obtained from the 3⅓-percent sample of 1950 Census returns. Accordingly, the analysis was restricted to occupations having more than 25,000 workers with $100 or more of wage or salary income in 1940 in order to eliminate such occupations from the study. In addition, the fact that the data were tabulated by wage or salary income rather than by total income suggested that it would be desirable to eliminate certain occupations that contain a large proportion of self-employed workers or employees who receive a large part of their wages in the form of free meals, lodging, etc., rather than in cash. Accordingly, occupations such as physicians and surgeons, lawyers and judges, farmers and farm managers, and farm laborers were omitted from the study. Finally, certain occupation groups of a miscellaneous nature were omitted. These occupation groups were generally residuals of broader occupation groups. Frequently they could not be consistently identified in 1940 and 1950, or if they were identifiable they were so heterogeneous as to make the meaning of the data for them ambiguous. Some indication of the coverage of the data in tables C–1 to C–6 may be obtained from the fact that about 75 percent of the men and 80 percent of the women with $100 or more of wage or salary income in 1940 are represented by the occupations shown in these tables. In other words, the occupation groups that were deleted from the study for the reasons noted above account for somewhat less than one-fourth of all workers with $100 or more of wage or salary income in 1940. However, in terms of the total experienced labor force in 1940 rather than just workers with $100 or more of wage or salary income, slightly more than half of all workers in 1940 are accounted for in these tables.

3. Weeks worked, as defined in the 1950 Census of Population includes all weeks in 1949 during which any work was performed. Accordingly, full-year workers for 1949 are persons who did any work for pay or profit in 50 weeks or more. Persons who worked regularly on a part-time basis, such as newsboys, were thus counted as full-year workers. The definition of weeks worked in the 1940 Census was somewhat different from that used in the most recent census. In 1940, enumerators were instructed to convert part-time work to equivalent full-time weeks. Accordingly, a full-year worker for 1939 is a person who worked full-time during the entire year. The change in the definition of this concept therefore tended to increase the proportion of full-year workers in 1949.

4. Members of the Armed Forces are excluded from the data for 1949 shown in tables C–1 to C–6. The data for 1939 shown in these tables, however, include a relatively small number of servicemen. In the 1940 Census, most Armed Forces members were classified in the occupation, "soldiers, sailors, marines, coast guards," which has been excluded from these tables. However, servicemen who were commissioned officers, professional and clerical workers, or craftsmen were classified in the particular occupation in which they were engaged.

5. As indicated above, the income data for 1949 presented in tables C–1 to C–6 were first tabulated by detailed occupation groups and then merged to form the intermediate occupation groups as defined in the 1940 Census. The detailed occupations that comprise each of the intermediate groups shown for 1940 appear in the 1940 Census of Population Report, *The Labor Force (Sample Statistics): Occupational Characteristics*. The following list gives the detailed occupations included in each of the intermediate groups for 1949.

INTERMEDIATE OCCUPATIONAL CLASSIFICATION WITH COMPONENT DETAILED ITEMS
FOR TABLES C–1 TO C–6

(Detailed occupation is not shown where intermediate occupation consists of only one detailed occupation. "N.e.c." means not elsewhere classified)

Male

Professional, Technical, Kindred Workers
1. Artists and art teachers
2. Authors, editors, and reporters
   Authors
   Editors and reporters
3. Chemists
4. Clergymen
5. College presidents, professors, instructors (n.e.c.)
6. Designers and draftsmen
   Designers
   Draftsmen
7. Engineers, civil
8. Engineers, electrical
9. Engineers, mechanical
   Aeronautical engineers
   Mechanical engineers
   Technical engineers (n.e.c.)
10. Musicians and music teachers
11. Pharmacists
12. Social, welfare, and recreation workers
    Recreation and group workers
    Social and welfare workers, except group
13. Sports instructors, athletes, entertainers
    Athletes
    Dancers and dancing teachers
    Entertainers (n.e.c.)
    Sports instructors and officials

14. Teachers (n.e.c.)
    Farm and home management advisors
    Teachers (n.e.c.)

Salaried Managers and Officials

15. Conductors, railroad
16. Postmasters, and miscellaneous government
    officials
    Inspectors, public administration
        Federal public administration and
        postal service
        State public administration
        Local public administration
    Officials and administrators (n.e.c.), pub-
        lic administration
        Federal public administration and
        postal service (n.e.c.)
        State public administration (n.e.c.)
        Local public administration (n.e.c.)
    Postmasters
    Managers and officials
17.   Manufacturing
18.   Transportation, communication, and other
        public utilities
        Transportation
        Telecommunications, and utilities and
        sanitary services
19.   Wholesale trade
20.   Eating and drinking places
21.   Retail trade, except eating and drinking
        Food and dairy products stores, and
        milk retailing
        General merchandise and five and ten
        cent stores
        Apparel and accessories stores
        Furniture, home furnishings, and equip-
        ment stores
        Motor vehicles and accessories retailing
        Gasoline service stations
        Hardware, farm implement, and build-
        ing material retailing
        Other retail trade
22.   Finance, insurance, and real estate
        Banking and other finance
        Insurance and real estate
23.   Business and repair services
        Business services
        Automobile repair services and garages
        Miscellaneous repair services
24.   Personal services

Clerical, Sales, and Kindred Workers

25. Baggagemen, express messengers, railway
    mail clerks
    Baggagemen, transportation
    Express messengers and railway mail
    clerks

26. Bookkeepers, accountants, cashiers, ticket
    agents
    Accountants
    Bookkeepers
    Cashiers
    Ticket, station, and express agents
27. Mail carriers
28. Messengers, except express
    Messengers and office boys
    Telegraph messengers
29. Shipping and receiving clerks
30. Stenographers, typists, and secretaries
31. Telegraph operators
32. Newsboys
33. Insurance agents and brokers
34. Real estate agents and brokers
35. Salesmen and sales clerks (n.e.c.)
    Manufacturing
    Wholesale trade
    Retail trade
    Other industries (including "not re-
    ported")

Craftsmen, Foremen, and Kindred Workers

36. Bakers
37. Blacksmiths, forgemen, and hammermen
    Blacksmiths
    Forgemen and hammermen
38. Boilermakers
39. Cabinetmakers and patternmakers
    Cabinetmakers
    Pattern and model makers, except paper
40. Carpenters
41. Compositors and typesetters
42. Electricians
    Foremen (n.e.c.)
43.   Construction
44.   Manufacturing
        Metal industries
        Machinery, including electrical
        Transportation equipment
        Other durable goods
        Textiles, textile products, and apparel
        Other nondurable goods (including not
        specified manufacturing)
45.   Transportation, communication, and other
        public utilities
        Railroads and railway express service
        Transportation, except railroad
        Telecommunications, and utilities and
        sanitary services
46. Inspectors (n.e.c.)
    Construction
    Railroads and railway express service
    Transportation except railroad, communi-
    cation, and other public utilities
    Other industries (including "not re-
    ported")

47. Linemen and servicemen, telegraphers, etc.
48. Locomotive engineers
49. Locomotive firemen
50. Machinists, millwrights, and toolmakers
    Job setters, metal
    Machinists
    Millwrights
    Toolmakers, and die makers and setters
51. Masons, tile setters, and stone cutters
    Brickmasons, stonemasons, and tile setters
    Stone cutters and stone carvers
52. Mechanics and repairmen, and loom fixers
    Loom fixers
    Mechanics and repairmen
        Airplane
        Automobile
        Office Machine
        Radio and television
        Railroad and car shop
        Not elsewhere classified
53. Molders, metal
54. Painters (construction), paperhangers, glaziers
    Glaziers
    Painters, construction and maintenance
    Paperhangers
55. Plasterers and cement finishers
    Cement and concrete finishers
    Plasterers
56. Plumbers and pipe fitters
57. Printing craftsmen, except compositors and typesetters
    Electrotypers and stereotypers
    Photoengravers and lithographers
    Pressmen and plate printers, printing
58. Rollers and roll hands, metal
59. Roofers and sheet metal workers
    Roofers and slaters
    Tinsmiths, coppersmiths, and sheet metal workers
60. Shoemakers and repairers, except factory
61. Stationary engineers, cranemen, hoistmen
    Cranemen, derrickmen, and hoistmen
    Excavating, grading, and road machinery operators
    Stationary engineers
62. Structural metal workers
63. Tailors and furriers
    Furriers
    Tailors

Operatives and Kindred Workers

64. Apprentices
    Auto mechanics
    Bricklayers and masons
    Carpenters
    Electricians
    Machinists and toolmakers

    Mechanics, except auto
    Plumbers and pipe fitters
    Building trades (n.e.c.)
    Metal working trades (n.e.c.)
    Printing trades
    Other specified trades
    Trade not specified
65. Attendants, auto service and parking
66. Brakemen and switchmen, railroad
    Brakemen, railroad
    Switchmen, railroad
67. Drivers, bus, taxi, and truck, and deliverymen
    Bus drivers
    Deliverymen and routemen
    Taxicab drivers and chauffeurs
    Truck and tractor drivers
68. Stationary firemen
69. Mine operatives and laborers (n.e.c.)
    Coal mining
    Crude petroleum and natural gas extraction
    Mining and quarrying, except fuel
70. Motormen, railway, mine, factory, etc.
    Motormen, mine, factory, logging camp, etc.
    Motormen, street, subway, and elevated railway
71. Painters, except construction and maintenance
72. Sailors and deck hands
73. Welders and flame-cutters
    Operatives and kindred workers (n.e.c.)
74. Food and kindred products
    Meat products
    Dairy products
    Canning and preserving fruits, vegetables, and sea foods
    Grain-mill products
    Bakery products
    Confectionery and related products
    Beverage industries
    Miscellaneous food preparations and kindred products
    Not-specified food industries
75. Knitting mills
76. Textile mill products, except knitting mills
    Spinners, textile
    Weavers, textile
    Dyeing and finishing textiles, except knit goods
    Carpets, rugs, and other floor coverings
    Yarn, thread, and fabric mills
    Miscellaneous textile mill products
77. Apparel and other fabric textile products
    Apparel and accessories
    Miscellaneous fabricated textile products

78. Furniture, and lumber and wood products
    Sawmills, planing mills, and mill work
    Miscellaneous wood products
    Furniture and fixtures
79. Paper, paper products, and printing
    Bookbinders
    Pulp, paper, and paperboard mills
    Paperboard containers and boxes
    Miscellaneous paper and pulp products
    Printing, publishing, and allied industries
80. Chemicals and petroleum, and coal products
    Synthetic fibers
    Drugs and medicines
    Paints, varnishes, and related products
    Miscellaneous chemicals and allied products
    Petroleum refining
    Miscellaneous petroleum and coal products
81. Rubber products
82. Footwear industries, except rubber
83. Leather and leather products, except footwear
    Leather: tanned, curried, and finished
    Leather products, except footwear
84. Stone, clay, and glass products
    Glass and glass products
    Cement, and concrete, gypsum, and plaster products
    Structural clay products
    Pottery and related products
    Miscellaneous nonmetallic mineral and stone products
85. Iron and steel, and not-specified metal industries
    Blast furnaces, steel works, and rolling mills
    Other primary iron and steel industries
    Fabricated steel products
    Not-specified metal industries
86. Nonferrous metals and their products
    Primary nonferrous industries
    Fabricated nonferrous metal products
87. Machinery
    Agricultural machinery and tractors
    Office and store machines and devices
    Miscellaneous machinery
    Electrical machinery, equipment, and supplies
88. Motor vehicles and motor vehicle equipment
89. Transportation equipment, except motor vehicle
    Aircraft and parts
    Ship and boat building and repairing
    Railroad and miscellaneous transportation equipment

Service Workers

90. Private household workers
    Housekeepers, private household
        Living in
        Living out
    Launderers private household
        Living in
        Living out
    Private household workers (n.e.c.)
        Living in
        Living out
91. Firemen, fire protection
92. Guards and watchmen
    Guards, watchmen, and doorkeepers
    Watchmen (crossing) and bridge tenders
93. Policemen, sheriffs, and marshals
    Marshals and constables
    Government
    Private
    Sheriffs and bailiffs
94. Barbers, beauticians, and manicurists
95. Charmen, janitors, and porters
    Charmen and cleaners
    Janitors and sextons
    Porters
96. Cooks, except private household
97. Elevator operators
98. Waiters, bartenders, and counter workers
    Bartenders
    Counter and fountain workers
    Waiters
99. Service workers, except private household (n.e.c.)

Laborers, Except Farm and Mine

100. Fishermen and oystermen
101. Longshoremen and stevedores
102. Lumbermen, raftsmen, and woodchoppers
    Laborers (n.e.c.):
        Manufacturing industries:
103.   Food and kindred products
        Meat products
        Dairy products
        Canning and preserving fruits, vegetables, and sea foods
        Grain-mill products
        Bakery products
        Confectionery and related products
        Beverage industries
        Miscellaneous food preparations and kindred products
        Not-specified food industries
104.   Textiles, textile products, and apparel
        Knitting mills
        Dyeing and finishing textiles, except knit goods
        Carpets, rugs, and other floor coverings
        Yarn, thread, and fabric mills

Miscellaneous textile mill products
Apparel and accessories
Miscellaneous fabricated textile products

105. Furniture, and lumber and wood products
Sawmills, planing mills, and mill work
Miscellaneous wood products
Furniture and fixtures

106. Paper, paper products, and printing
Pulp, paper, and paperboard mills
Paperboard containers and boxes
Miscellaneous paper and pulp products
Printing, publishing, and allied industries

107. Chemicals and petroleum, and coal products
Synthetic fibers
Drugs and medicines
Paints, varnishes, and related products
Miscellaneous chemicals and allied products
Petroleum refining
Miscellaneous petroleum and coal products

108. Stone, clay, and glass products
Glass and glass products
Cement, and concrete, gypsum, and plaster products
Structural clay products
Pottery and related products
Miscellaneous nonmetallic mineral and stone products

109. Iron and steel and not-specified metal industries
Blast furnaces, steel works and rolling mills
Other primary iron and steel industries
Fabricated steel products
Not-specified metal industries

110. Nonferrous metals and their products
Primary nonferrous industries
Fabricated nonferrous metal products

111. Machinery
Agricultural machinery and tractors
Office and store machines and devices
Miscellaneous machinery
Electrical machinery, equipment, and supplies

112. Motor vehicles and motor vehicle equipment

113. Transportation equipment, except motor vehicle
Aircraft and parts
Ship and boat building and repairing
Railroad and miscellaneous transportation equipment

Nonmanufacturing industries

114. Construction
115. Railroads and railway express service
116. Transportation, except railroad
117. Telecommunications and utilities and sanitary services
118. Wholesale and retail trade

Female

Professional, Technical, Kindred Workers

1. Librarians
2. Musicians and music teachers
3. Social, welfare, and recreation workers
Recreation and group workers
Social and welfare workers, except group
4. Teachers (n.e.c.)
Farm and home management advisors
Teachers (n.e.c.)
5. Nurses, professional and student professional
Nurses, professional
Nurses, student professional

Clerical, Sales, and Kindred Workers

6. Bookkeepers, accountants, cashiers, ticket agents
Accountants
Bookkeepers
Cashiers
Ticket, station, and express agents
7. Office machine operators
8. Stenographers, typists, and secretaries
9. Telephone operators
10. Saleswomen and sales clerks (n.e.c.)
Manufacuring
Wholesale trade
Retail trade
Other industries (including "not reported")

Operatives and Kindred Workers

11. Dressmakers and seamstresses, except factory
Operatives and kindred workers (n.e.c.):
12. Food and kindred products
Meat products
Dairy products
Canning and preserving fruits, vegetables, and sea foods
Grain-mill products
Bakery products

Confectionery and related products
Beverage industries
Miscellaneous food preparations and kindred products
Not-specified food industries
13. Tobacco manufactures
14. Knitting mills
15. Textile mill products, except knitting mills
Spinners, textile
Weavers, textile
Dyeing and finishing textiles, except knit goods
Carpets, rugs, and other floor coverings
Yarn, thread, and fabric mills
Miscellaneous textile mill products
16. Apparel and other fabric textile products
Apparel and accessories
Miscellaneous fabricated textile products
17. Furniture, and lumber and wood products
Sawmills, planing mills, and mill work
Miscellaneous wood products
Furniture and fixtures
18. Paper, paper products, and printing
Bookbinders
Pulp, paper, and paperboard mills
Paperboard containers and boxes
Miscellaneous paper and pulp products
Printing, publishing, and allied industries
19. Chemicals and petroleum, and coal products
Synthetic fibers
Drugs and medicines
Paints, varnishes, and related products
Miscellaneous chemicals and allied products
Petroleum refining
Miscellaneous petroleum and coal products
20. Footwear industries, except rubber
21. Leather and leather products, except footwear
Leather: tanned, curried, and finished
Leather products, except footwear
22. Stone, clay, and glass products
Glass and glass products
Cement, and concrete, gypsum, and plaster products
Structural clay products
Pottery and related products

Miscellaneous nonmetallic mineral and stone products
23. Metal industries and machinery
Blast furnaces, steel works, and rolling mills
Other primary iron and steel industries
Primary nonferrous industries
Fabricated steel products
Fabricated nonferrous metal products
Not specified metal industries
Agricultural machinery and tractors
Office and store machines and devices
Miscellaneous machinery
Electrical machinery, equipment, and supplies
24. Transportation equipment
Motor vehicles and motor vehicle equipment
Aircraft and parts
Ship and boat building and repairing
Railroad and miscellaneous transportation equipment

Service Workers

25. Private household workers
Housekeepers, private household
Living in
Living out
Laundresses, private household
Living in
Living out
Private household workers (n.e.c.)
Living in
Living out
26. Barbers, beauticians, and manicurists
27. Charwomen, janitresses, and porters
Charwomen and cleaners
Janitresses and sextons
Porters
28. Cooks except private household
29. Housekeepers, stewardesses, except private household
30. Practical nurses and midwives
Midwives
Practical nurses
31. Waitresses, bartenders, counter workers
Bartenders
Counter and fountain workers
Waitresses
32. Service workers, except private household (n.e.c.)

TABLE C–1.—PERCENT DISTRIBUTION OF WAGE OR SALARY WORKERS IN SELECTED OCCUPATIONS, BY WAGE OR SALARY INCOME IN 1949, BY SEX, FOR THE UNITED STATES

Occupation and sex	Number reporting $1 or more (thousands)	Total	$1 to $499	$500 to $999	$1000 to $1499	$1500 to $1999	$2000 to $2499	$2500 to $2999	$3000 to $3499	$3500 to $3999	$4000 to $4499	$4500 to $4999	$5000 to $5999	$6000 to $6999	$7000 to $9999	$10,000 and over	Q1 (dollars)	Q2 (median, dollars)	Q3 (dollars)	Arithmetic mean (dollars)	$1-\dfrac{Q_1}{Q_2}$	$\dfrac{Q_3}{Q_2}-1$	$\dfrac{Q_3-Q_1}{Q_2}$
MALE, EXPERIENCED CIVILIAN LABOR FORCE																							
Prof'l, Techn'l, Kindred Wkrs.																							
Artists and art teachers	33	100.0	4.8	5.4	5.3	4.3	7.4	9.4	13.4	8.5	9.6	7.4	10.6	4.1	5.5	4.5	2,351	3,500	4,966	4,350	.329	.418	.747
Authors, editors, and reporters	54	100.0	3.8	4.2	3.8	4.9	4.9	6.5	8.3	7.1	9.2	6.9	14.8	8.7	10.5	8.0	2,885	4,440	6,253	5,562	.351	.408	.759
Chemists	63	100.0	1.8	2.6	2.8	5.6	5.6	8.2	12.2	12.1	11.3	8.7	8.6	7.3	10.5	2.7	3,019	4,004	5,405	4,593	.247	.349	.596
Clergymen	108	100.0	5.0	11.8	12.8	10.9	14.9	12.0	13.4	7.2	4.5	2.4	2.6	1.3	0.9	0.3	1,320	2,319	3,284	2,492	.431	.416	.847
Coll. pres., prof'rs, instr's (n.e.c.)	84	100.0	3.5	4.7	6.0	4.8	4.8	4.6	16.3	8.8	10.7	8.5	15.5	8.1	7.9	2.9	2,630	4,168	5,606	4,556	.369	.345	.714
Designers and draftsmen	127	100.0	2.1	3.1	2.7	4.1	8.5	12.1	16.3	15.8	13.6	7.4	9.0	2.9	1.8	0.6	2,686	3,535	4,379	3,666	.241	.238	.479
Engineers, civil	106	100.0	1.3	2.2	3.3	3.3	4.7	5.1	9.5	11.3	11.8	11.9	18.4	8.7	7.2	2.8	3,342	4,453	5,652	4,896	.250	.269	.519
Engineers, electrical	94	100.0	1.3	2.1	2.1	3.0	3.0	5.3	10.2	10.8	11.6	11.9	18.2	10.4	6.9	3.2	3,471	4,598	5,923	5,147	.246	.288	.534
Engineers, mechanical	173	100.0	1.1	1.4	2.0	3.2	4.4	4.4	9.3	11.5	12.5	10.2	17.6	10.3	9.8	3.0	3,552	4,608	5,966	5,333	.230	.294	.524
Musicians and music teachers	54	100.0	9.5	9.7	9.2	9.2	8.0	7.5	10.3	8.8	4.0	6.0	5.0	3.6	1.7	1.0	1,315	2,631	4,063	3,346	.501	.544	1.045
Pharmacists	38	100.0	2.6	3.3	3.8	4.0	7.5	13.0	14.9	11.7	8.5	4.4	12.0	4.7	3.0	2.1	2,713	3,713	4,659	3,807	.270	.254	.524
Social, welfare, and recreation wkrs.	30	100.0	6.2	4.7	6.8	6.3	13.0	13.5	13.5	11.7	7.4	4.6	7.3	3.3	3.0	0.3	2,043	3,052	4,081	3,337	.331	.337	.668
Sports instr's, athletes, entertainers	48	100.0	7.5	8.3	8.8	9.2	9.5	13.5	12.9	9.8	8.7	4.6	6.0	2.5	1.7	2.1	1,522	2,916	4,040	3,232	.479	.385	.864
Teachers (n.e.c.)	259	100.0	2.5	4.5	5.5	6.0	11.3	13.5	16.0	13.6	11.6	7.5	8.1	2.7	1.5	0.3	2,365	3,353	4,289	3,413	.295	.279	.574
Salaried Managers and Officials																							
Conductors, railroad	52	100.0	0.4	0.3	1.1	1.0	2.8	4.8	12.2	15.8	21.8	15.2	20.1	4.1	0.3		3,576	4,266	4,987	4,265	.162	.168	.330
Postmasters, and misc. govt. officials	187	100.0	2.5	2.8	3.6	4.7	9.8	9.8	14.8	13.8	12.2	7.9	8.9	4.2	4.3	2.2	2,658	3,627	4,658	4,071	.268	.284	.552
Managers and officials:																							
Manufacturing	335	100.0	0.6	1.0	1.2	1.5	3.5	4.1	7.8	8.7	9.6	6.9	14.2	9.2	13.6	17.9	3,805	5,359	8,478	7,672	.291	.581	.872
Trans., commun., & other pub. util.	132	100.0	0.5	0.7	1.6	2.9	4.4	5.6	9.6	11.9	11.9	11.9	18.2	9.4	7.3	5.7	3,555	4,605	5,857	5,507	.229	.271	.500
Wholesale trade	122	100.0	1.1	1.6	1.6	2.9	5.6	7.3	13.2	10.8	9.5	6.6	11.7	7.0	8.6	12.0	3,174	4,295	6,400	6,200	.261	.490	.751
Eating and drinking places	35	100.0	1.1	1.6	5.9	5.9	7.3	12.5	14.9	10.2	7.4	4.6	6.3	3.1	1.7	1.4	1,958	2,984	3,975	3,271	.344	.332	.676
Retail trade, exc. eating & drinking	305	100.0	4.9	5.7	7.1	7.9	9.4	12.5	15.0	12.3	10.0	5.9	5.0	2.9	5.2	5.7	2,701	3,659	5,071	4,730	.262	.386	.648
Finance, insur., and real estate	137	100.0	1.7	2.3	2.9	4.7	5.0	5.1	9.3	9.9	9.2	8.0	15.3	8.7	11.1	13.2	3,556	4,894	6,920	6,768	.274	.413	.687
Business and repair services	41	100.0	0.8	1.0	1.0	2.0	4.7	9.0	11.1	11.1	9.2	5.4	10.8	5.9	7.4	8.7	2,872	3,878	5,713	5,429	.260	.473	.733
Personal services	32	100.0	4.6	3.4	4.6	8.7	12.1	9.8	15.2	10.2	7.6	5.0	7.8	3.2	4.0	3.9	2,153	3,224	4,421	3,983	.333	.371	.704
Clerical, Sales, and Kindred Workers																							
Baggagemen, exp., mess., rwy., mail clk.	25	100.0	1.3	1.1	2.1	2.3	7.6	11.3	21.1	22.9	20.6	7.2	1.9	0.2	0.2	0.1	2,969	3,570	4,129	3,476	.169	.156	.325
Bookk'prs, accts., cashs., ticket agts.	505	100.0	2.5	3.7	2.8	5.3	9.8	12.2	17.1	13.7	8.4	6.3	7.8	3.6	3.0	1.2	2,493	3,370	4,347	3,679	.262	.290	.552
Mail carriers	156	100.0	2.3	1.7	2.8	3.2	6.3	17.3	21.0	37.7	4.6	1.7	1.0	0.1	0.1		2,740	3,381	3,765	3,162	.190	.113	.303
Messengers, except express	46	100.0	23.5	16.8	14.8	16.2	12.7	5.6	4.1	2.3	1.1	0.5	0.5		0.2		545	1,328	2,150	1,484	.590	.619	1.209
Shipping and receiving clerks	260	100.0	5.2	5.3	7.4	7.4	20.7	22.5	18.8	8.8	3.2	0.5	0.2	0.1	0.1		1,995	2,593	3,178	2,564	.231	.225	.456
Stenographers, typists, and secys.	77	100.0	3.8	5.3	4.8	7.4	12.9	13.8	13.8	8.8	6.0	4.4	6.2	4.1	5.0	3.7	2,143	3,072	4,367	3,924	.303	.421	.724

TABLE C-1.—PERCENT DISTRIBUTION OF WAGE OR SALARY WORKERS IN SELECTED OCCUPATIONS, BY WAGE OR SALARY INCOME IN 1949, BY SEX, FOR THE UNITED STATES—Cont.

Occupation and sex	Number reporting $1 or more (thousands)	Total	Percent distribution														Quartiles			Arithmetic mean (dollars)	$1-\frac{Q_1}{Q_2}$	$\frac{Q_3}{Q_2}-1$	$\frac{Q_3-Q_1}{Q_2}$
			$1 to $499	$500 to $999	$1000 to $1499	$1500 to $1999	$2000 to $2499	$2500 to $2999	$3000 to $3499	$3500 to $3999	$4000 to $4499	$4500 to $4999	$5000 to $5999	$6000 to $6699	$7000 to $9999	$10,000 and over	Q_1 (dollars)	Q_2 (median; dollars)	Q_3 (dollars)				
MALE—Con.																							
Clerical, Sales, & Kind. Wkrs.—Con.																							
Telegraph operators	25	100.0	2.6	2.1	2.7	3.3	6.6	11.6	33.8	23.7	7.1	2.4	2.4	0.9	0.7	0.1	2,832	3,312	3,759	3,254	.145	.135	.280
Newsboys	71	100.0	81.2	8.0	3.1	1.5	1.5	1.4	0.7	0.7	0.6	0.6	0.6	...	0.1	...	154	308	462	539	.500	.499	.999
Insurance agents and brokers	205	100.0	2.5	3.1	4.2	5.3	8.7	9.7	15.1	12.1	11.2	7.1	10.3	4.8	3.7	2.2	2,572	3,566	4,732	4,025	.279	.327	.606
Real estate agents and brokers	45	100.0	5.4	6.6	7.7	6.6	10.1	9.2	11.1	8.5	7.0	4.5	8.7	5.8	5.2	3.8	1,902	3,198	4,811	4,003	.406	.504	.910
Salesmen and sales clerks (n.e.c.)	1,643	100.0	6.2	6.4	6.6	8.2	13.1	12.0	13.1	9.1	6.9	3.9	6.5	2.8	3.1	2.1	1,854	2,896	4,022	3,383	.360	.388	.748
Craftsmen, Foremen, & Kindred Wkrs.																							
Bakers	88	100.0	2.7	4.5	6.1	9.0	15.7	16.8	20.9	11.5	7.5	2.4	2.2	0.4	0.2	...	2,086	2,857	3,483	2,797	.270	.219	.489
Blacksmiths, forgemen, and hammermen	40	100.0	3.6	4.1	5.9	7.9	14.1	17.9	20.3	12.4	6.9	2.8	2.9	0.7	0.2	0.1	2,124	2,902	3,548	2,854	.269	.222	.491
Boilermakers	36	100.0	1.5	2.3	3.1	5.3	8.7	13.7	21.9	17.6	14.5	5.1	4.6	1.3	0.3	0.2	2,650	3,352	4,031	3,330	.210	.202	.412
Cabinetmakers and patternmakers	85	100.0	3.0	4.6	6.5	9.4	13.6	15.3	18.2	12.3	8.5	3.9	3.7	0.3	0.3	0.2	2,055	2,922	3,679	2,915	.297	.259	.556
Carpenters	721	100.0	6.2	8.4	10.0	11.0	14.9	12.8	15.5	9.0	6.5	2.8	3.4	0.4	0.3	0.3	1,518	2,483	3,377	2,512	.389	.360	.749
Compositors and typesetters	143	100.0	2.0	2.6	3.1	5.3	9.6	9.9	13.9	10.8	13.1	10.1	14.4	3.4	1.6	0.3	2,621	3,667	4,733	3,747	.286	.290	.576
Electricians	269	100.0	1.8	2.4	3.4	4.1	9.1	11.1	20.0	16.2	12.7	7.7	8.8	1.9	0.7	0.2	2,689	3,453	4,272	3,497	.222	.237	.459
Foremen (n.e.c.):																							
Construction	56	100.0	1.6	1.8	3.3	5.5	11.6	11.6	14.7	13.4	11.0	8.9	10.9	3.6	1.6	0.5	2,552	3,497	4,528	3,675	.271	.294	.565
Manufacturing	438	100.0	0.5	0.7	1.0	1.2	5.4	8.6	14.6	14.6	11.0	15.3	15.3	5.6	2.9	0.6	3,214	3,879	4,763	4,246	.207	.228	.435
Trans., commun., & other pub. util.	112	100.0	0.4	0.3	0.8	1.3	5.0	9.4	15.7	15.7	13.4	10.6	12.9	3.7	0.7	0.2	3,157	3,752	4,679	3,970	.159	.247	.406
Inspectors (n.e.c.)	83	100.0	1.0	1.3	2.6	3.7	9.1	15.0	23.5	19.8	14.5	4.7	3.5	0.8	0.6	0.2	2,757	3,377	3,985	3,403	.184	.180	.364
Linemen & servicemen, t'graph, etc.	197	100.0	1.1	2.1	2.6	4.4	12.6	16.3	18.9	13.8	13.5	5.7	5.7	1.0	0.2	0.1	2,567	3,288	4,119	3,351	.220	.252	.472
Locomotive engineers	68	100.0	0.4	0.3	0.5	0.9	2.1	3.8	9.5	11.6	17.5	17.4	24.3	9.4	1.9	0.3	3,823	4,598	5,453	4,640	.169	.185	.354
Locomotive firemen	52	100.0	1.2	1.7	3.6	4.1	8.1	14.8	16.5	18.7	15.6	10.1	3.7	1.5	0.2	0.1	2,830	3,644	4,375	3,568	.224	.200	.424
Machinists, millwrights, & toolmakers	706	100.0	1.3	1.7	2.7	4.2	9.9	14.8	25.7	18.4	11.4	4.9	3.7	0.8	0.3	0.1	2,676	3,303	3,899	3,297	.190	.181	.371
Masons, tile setters, & stone cutters	141	100.0	4.3	6.6	8.4	9.5	11.9	17.3	13.4	9.6	9.2	6.0	2.9	1.4	0.4	0.1	1,800	2,884	3,958	2,943	.376	.372	.748
Mechanics & repairmen, & loom fixers	1,502	100.0	2.9	4.3	5.7	8.5	15.7	17.1	20.6	12.3	6.7	2.9	2.6	0.6	0.2	0.1	2,121	2,879	3,508	2,843	.264	.218	.482
Molders, metal	56	100.0	1.5	2.3	5.6	7.5	17.7	22.0	22.8	9.9	5.1	1.7	2.6	0.6	0.1	0.1	2,164	2,798	3,353	2,742	.227	.198	.425
Painters (const.), paperhgrs., glazrs.	281	100.0	6.9	8.9	10.3	12.1	17.7	15.3	9.9	5.1	2.3	1.5	1.7	0.4	0.1	0.1	1,447	2,399	3,258	2,417	.397	.358	.755
Plasterers and cement finishers	74	100.0	4.0	7.1	8.7	9.6	13.0	11.2	12.9	9.0	6.0	2.8	6.9	2.2	0.6	0.2	1,771	2,839	3,972	2,946	.377	.399	.776
Plumbers and pipe fitters	228	100.0	2.1	3.6	4.7	6.8	10.2	11.0	16.1	13.2	12.4	8.1	9.4	1.7	0.6	0.1	2,382	3,360	4,294	3,371	.292	.277	.569
Print. craft., exc. compos. & typeset.	82	100.0	2.0	2.0	2.6	4.5	7.6	6.9	10.2	10.2	11.1	5.7	16.9	9.1	6.3	0.8	3,046	4,180	5,491	4,383	.272	.313	.585
Rollers and roll hands, metal	30	100.0	1.5	2.2	3.5	5.0	14.6	22.8	21.0	11.0	6.7	3.0	3.9	2.2	1.2	1.1	2,425	3,000	3,682	3,316	.192	.227	.419
Roofers and sheet metal workers	145	100.0	3.2	4.9	6.3	8.0	13.2	14.4	19.4	12.6	9.1	4.6	3.6	0.4	0.2	0.1	2,098	3,000	3,722	2,926	.301	.240	.541
Shoemakers & repairers, exc. factory	17	100.0	9.2	12.4	14.7	15.4	17.1	14.5	9.4	3.1	1.6	1.0	1.0	0.3	...	...	1,116	1,945	2,714	1,989	.427	.395	.822
Stat. engineers, cranemen, hoistmen	404	100.0	1.2	2.2	3.6	5.8	10.9	20.1	20.1	15.0	10.8	5.7	6.4	2.2	1.3	0.6	2,559	3,303	4,097	3,476	.226	.240	.466
Structural metal workers	50	100.0	2.1	2.2	3.6	5.8	9.0	13.7	19.4	12.3	11.6	8.4	9.2	1.8	0.8	0.1	2,584	3,351	4,297	3,442	.229	.282	.511
Tailors and furriers	52	100.0	2.5	4.7	6.0	9.7	14.8	15.1	19.1	10.2	7.7	2.8	4.3	1.5	0.8	0.2	2,071	2,907	3,652	3,013	.288	.256	.544

TABLE C-1.—PERCENT DISTRIBUTION OF WAGE OR SALARY WORKERS IN SELECTED OCCUPATIONS, BY WAGE OR SALARY INCOME IN 1949, BY SEX, FOR THE UNITED STATES—Cont.

Occupation and sex	Number reporting $1 or more (thousands)	Total	$1 to $499	$500 to $999	$1000 to $1499	$1500 to $1999	$2000 to $2499	$2500 to $2999	$3000 to $3499	$3500 to $3999	$4000 to $4499	$4500 to $4999	$5000 to $5999	$6000 to $6999	$7000 to $9999	$10,000 and over	Q1 (dollars)	Q2 (median; dollars)	Q3 (dollars)	Arithmetic mean (dollars)	$1-\tfrac{Q_1}{Q_2}$	$\tfrac{Q_3}{Q_2}-1$	$\tfrac{Q_3-Q_1}{Q_2}$
MALE--Con.																						
Operatives and Kindred Workers																						
Apprentices.....	103	100.0	7.6	9.8	10.7	14.9	21.6	15.9	11.2	4.1	2.0	0.9	0.9	0.1	...	...	1,355	2,162	2,827	2,120	.374	.307	.681
Attendants, auto service and parking.	201	100.0	13.3	13.4	14.3	15.7	18.3	11.7	8.1	3.0	1.3	0.5	0.3	0.1	0.1	...	937	1,787	2,500	1,827	.476	.399	.875
Brakemen and switchmen, railroad....	132	100.0	1.1	1.7	3.0	3.9	7.6	10.8	19.1	19.9	17.9	8.8	5.4	0.7	0.1	0.1	2,856	3,570	4,221	3,486	.200	.182	.382
Drivers, bus, taxi, & truck, & delimen	1,653	100.0	2.4	7.4	9.3	10.7	16.5	14.6	19.6	8.4	5.3	2.4	2.0	0.5	0.3	0.1	1,618	2,482	3,314	2,524	.349	.335	.684
Stationary firemen...	118	100.0	2.4	3.8	6.7	10.7	17.1	17.5	19.6	7.0	5.8	2.9	1.3	0.7	0.3	0.3	2,041	2,741	3,383	2,710	.256	.234	.490
Mine operatives & laborers (n.e.c.).	536	100.0	4.6	6.6	8.9	12.4	22.3	19.2	13.0	5.6	1.9	1.2	1.2	0.7	...	0.3	1,698	2,392	3,111	2,468	.291	.300	.591
Motormen, rwy., mine, factory, etc.	51	100.0	0.6	3.0	3.0	3.0	15.6	17.9	21.0	14.0	5.6	2.2	1.3	0.8	0.8	...	2,462	3,079	3,511	3,037	.201	.140	.341
Painters, exc. constr. & maintenance.	96	100.0	3.2	5.6	6.6	6.6	16.0	12.5	21.0	6.4	4.1	1.9	1.7	0.8	...	0.1	1,980	2,740	3,374	2,680	.278	.231	.509
Sailors and deck hands...	43	100.0	3.2	2.9	5.2	13.6	18.6	12.5	14.2	4.1	1.5	1.5	3.0	0.8	0.4	0.8	1,471	2,379	3,165	2,379	.382	.358	.740
Welders and flame-cutters...	235	100.0	1.9	3.0	4.4	6.5	11.8	16.5	25.0	14.3	8.5	3.9	3.0	0.6	0.4	...	2,390	3,118	3,706	3,069	.234	.188	.422
Operatives & kindred workers (n.e.c.):																						
Food and kindred products...	290	100.0	4.9	7.1	8.3	11.0	18.2	17.7	13.0	8.3	4.0	1.3	1.0	0.3	0.2	0.1	1,714	2,514	3,219	2,491	.319	.280	.599
Knitting mills...	40	100.0	4.3	5.2	10.1	14.5	14.5	11.5	12.1	7.1	7.2	4.8	6.5	1.5	0.6	0.1	1,686	2,561	3,697	2,792	.342	.443	.785
Text. mill prod., exc. knit. mills	339	100.0	3.8	5.7	9.5	18.1	27.6	18.3	10.8	3.4	1.3	0.6	0.5	0.1	0.1	0.1	1,666	2,234	2,781	2,243	.255	.245	.500
Apparel & other fabric text. prod.	154	100.0	3.5	6.0	9.3	13.0	16.9	12.7	13.7	8.1	6.3	2.9	4.8	1.5	0.9	0.3	1,738	2,551	3,496	2,780	.319	.370	.689
Furniture, and lumber and wood prod.	243	100.0	9.2	13.4	17.0	16.1	15.5	11.9	9.7	4.2	1.8	0.6	0.5	0.1	...	...	1,071	1,823	2,660	1,906	.413	.458	.871
Paper, paper prod., and printing...	197	100.0	3.6	4.2	4.4	8.8	16.8	19.4	19.6	9.8	6.9	2.5	2.5	0.5	0.2	0.2	2,095	2,794	3,434	2,775	.251	.229	.480
Chemicals & petrol., & coal prod...	185	100.0	2.2	3.6	4.6	5.5	11.6	21.8	21.8	14.5	10.6	5.3	2.5	0.5	0.1	...	2,366	3,124	3,797	3,053	.243	.215	.458
Rubber products...	83	100.0	1.9	2.6	3.7	6.2	13.8	21.1	25.5	14.2	7.3	2.4	1.1	0.1	...	0.1	2,384	3,014	3,507	2,942	.209	.163	.372
Footwear industries, exc. rubber...	94	100.0	4.3	7.3	11.3	18.7	23.4	16.8	11.1	4.3	1.5	0.6	0.6	0.1	0.1	...	1,556	2,179	2,798	2,185	.287	.283	.570
Leather & leath. prod.,exc. footwear	42	100.0	3.8	5.6	14.3	19.1	19.1	17.1	5.6	5.6	2.9	1.1	1.4	...	...	...	1,713	2,440	3,099	2,399	.298	.270	.568
Stone, clay, and glass products...	125	100.0	2.9	4.7	5.5	11.5	19.6	21.0	16.5	8.8	5.0	2.1	1.7	0.6	0.3	0.3	2,018	2,645	3,306	2,684	.238	.249	.487
Iron & steel, & not spec. metal ind.	350	100.0	2.4	4.1	5.2	8.8	18.8	22.3	21.0	8.7	4.3	1.7	1.3	0.3	0.2	0.2	2,109	2,731	3,310	2,711	.228	.211	.439
Nonferrous metals & their products..	72	100.0	3.2	4.9	7.1	8.8	19.0	22.1	19.6	8.7	4.0	1.2	0.9	0.3	...	...	2,026	2,658	3,253	2,602	.238	.223	.461
Machinery...	419	100.0	2.7	4.2	5.6	7.3	11.8	20.7	20.5	13.1	5.9	1.8	1.5	0.3	0.1	0.1	2,172	2,865	3,408	2,797	.242	.189	.431
Motor vehicles & mtr. vehicle equip.	281	100.0	2.1	3.6	4.4	5.6	11.8	20.5	30.5	12.1	5.1	1.7	1.5	0.3	0.1	0.1	2,373	3,025	3,434	2,876	.226	.135	.351
Trans. equip., exc. motor vehicle...	80	100.0	2.1	3.8	4.5	6.7	12.6	20.9	25.0	13.0	6.4	2.8	1.5	0.3	0.2	0.2	2,313	2,986	3,488	2,910	.226	.168	.394
Service Workers																						
Private household workers...	63	100.0	22.9	21.7	20.2	15.9	10.6	4.2	2.1	1.1	0.5	0.2	...	0.1	0.2	0.1	548	1,134	1,821	1,289	.517	.606	1.123
Firemen, fire protection...	102	100.0	0.5	0.7	1.6	2.3	10.5	18.9	32.1	16.4	11.3	2.4	2.3	0.6	0.4	0.2	2,749	3,241	3,756	3,295	.153	.158	.311
Guards and watchmen...	236	100.0	4.0	4.9	8.7	12.5	20.9	17.0	16.3	7.2	3.3	1.2	0.6	0.2	0.1	0.4	1,796	2,476	3,120	2,462	.275	.259	.534
Policemen, sheriffs, and marshalls..	197	100.0	1.4	2.2	2.5	5.0	12.6	17.0	28.3	15.7	9.4	2.4	2.4	0.9	0.4	0.1	2,538	3,164	3,691	3,145	.198	.166	.364
Barbers, beauticians, & manicurists..	79	100.0	6.0	8.7	13.0	15.1	20.9	15.2	12.2	5.2	2.4	1.3	1.3	0.2	0.4	0.4	1,396	2,172	2,872	2,244	.358	.321	.679
Charmen, janitors, and porters...	573	100.0	8.7	11.8	15.7	20.1	22.2	10.2	6.1	1.7	0.7	0.3	0.3	0.1	...	0.3	1,143	1,843	2,421	1,842	.380	.313	.693
Cooks, exc. private household...	178	100.0	5.5	9.6	12.8	13.9	19.0	14.0	11.7	6.1	3.6	1.3	1.5	0.7	0.3	0.3	1,387	2,216	3,009	2,299	.375	.357	.732

TABLE C-1.—PERCENT DISTRIBUTION OF WAGE OR SALARY WORKERS IN SELECTED OCCUPATIONS, BY WAGE OR SALARY INCOME IN 1949, BY SEX, FOR THE UNITED STATES—Cont.

Occupation and sex	Number reporting $1 or more (thousands)	Total	\$1 to \$499	\$500 to \$999	\$1000 to \$1499	\$1500 to \$1999	\$2000 to \$2499	\$2500 to \$2999	\$3000 to \$3499	\$3500 to \$3999	\$4000 to \$4499	\$4500 to \$4999	\$5000 to \$5999	\$6000 to \$6699	\$7000 to \$9999	\$10,000 and over	Q_1 (dollars)	Q_2 (median; dollars)	Q_3 (dollars)	Arithmetic mean (dollars)	$1-\frac{Q_1}{Q_2}$	$\frac{Q_3}{Q_2}-1$	$\frac{Q_3-Q_1}{Q_2}$
MALE—Con.																							
Service Workers—Con.																							
Elevator operators	61	100.0	3.9	7.0	11.3	17.0	29.7	20.7	6.6	2.3	1.0	0.4	0.2	...	...	...	1,582	2,182	2,647	2,112	.275	.213	.488
Waiters, bartenders, & counter wkrs.	292	100.0	10.0	11.7	12.3	14.2	18.5	14.0	11.3	4.4	1.7	0.7	0.8	...	...	0.1	1,134	2,049	2,796	2,040	.447	.364	.811
Service wkrs., exc. pr. hshld.(n.e.c.)	178	100.0	18.9	20.4	19.2	17.9	14.0	5.2	2.4	0.9	0.5	0.2	0.3	0.1	0.1	0.1	650	1,279	1,961	1,406	.493	.533	1.026
Laborers, Except Farm and Mine																							
Fishermen and oystermen	31	100.0	10.4	15.3	15.1	13.7	11.3	7.2	8.1	4.8	5.0	2.0	3.1	1.4	1.9	0.5	977	1,836	3,123	2,295	.468	.701	1.169
Longshoremen and stevedores	60	100.0	4.3	7.3	11.5	11.7	15.9	14.1	16.8	7.2	5.5	2.8	2.3	0.3	...	...	1,581	2,478	3,304	2,488	.362	.333	.695
Lumbermen, raftsmen, & woodchoppers	141	100.0	19.9	24.7	19.3	12.4	7.6	5.0	4.5	2.8	1.6	0.7	1.0	0.3	0.1	0.1	603	1,140	1,948	1,457	.471	.708	1.179
Laborers (n.e.c.):																							
Manufacturing industries:																							
Food and kindred products	132	100.0	6.6	10.2	11.7	13.9	19.9	17.2	12.7	4.9	1.8	0.3	0.4	0.1	...	...	1,350	2,191	2,869	2,128	.384	.309	.693
Textiles, text. prod., & apparel.	57	100.0	6.5	8.6	14.6	26.1	25.2	9.4	6.0	1.8	0.8	0.4	0.1	0.1	...	...	1,339	1,889	2,381	1,913	.292	.260	.552
Furniture, and lumber & wood prod.	160	100.0	13.0	19.4	20.8	12.1	12.5	7.4	1.7	1.7	1.1	0.4	0.1	...	...	0.1	809	1,423	2,156	1,585	.432	.515	.947
Paper, paper prod., & printing	50	100.0	5.1	6.1	9.3	12.1	25.7	16.5	13.1	5.0	1.6	0.6	0.3	0.3	...	...	1,686	2,339	2,911	2,325	.280	.244	.524
Chemicals & petrol., & coal prod.	86	100.0	4.7	7.1	8.5	12.0	17.7	20.3	19.5	9.1	3.6	0.6	0.5	0.1	...	...	1,696	2,500	3,218	2,444	.322	.287	.609
Stone, clay, and glass products	72	100.0	4.4	7.9	10.9	14.7	24.3	17.8	12.0	3.6	1.8	0.4	0.1	0.1	0.2	...	1,561	2,249	2,832	2,213	.306	.259	.565
Iron & steel & not spec.metal ind.	223	100.0	3.4	5.4	8.0	13.3	27.8	19.3	12.0	3.9	1.8	0.8	0.3	0.1	...	...	1,806	2,356	2,881	2,325	.234	.222	.456
Nonferrous metals and their prod.	29	100.0	4.7	4.5	7.7	14.1	24.6	24.0	14.7	3.6	1.0	0.7	0.1	0.1	...	...	1,787	2,386	2,904	2,307	.252	.217	.469
Machinery	70	100.0	4.0	7.5	8.7	14.1	24.0	20.9	14.2	2.2	2.2	0.7	0.6	...	0.1	...	1,698	2,369	2,947	2,318	.284	.244	.528
Motor vehicles & mtr. veh. equip.	44	100.0	2.8	4.6	6.2	10.0	16.6	23.4	23.0	8.5	2.6	1.2	1.0	0.2	0.1	...	2,042	2,709	3,248	2,621	.247	.198	.445
Trans. equipment, exc. motor veh.	22	100.0	4.3	7.6	8.9	12.6	25.4	23.6	11.7	2.8	1.0	0.4	1.1	0.4	0.1	0.1	1,667	2,327	2,843	2,262	.284	.221	.505
Nonmanufacturing industries:																							
Construction	640	100.0	11.2	15.0	16.3	16.6	16.8	10.3	7.6	2.9	1.7	0.6	0.8	0.2	0.1	0.1	960	1,726	2,473	1,838	.444	.432	.876
Railroads & rvy. express service	259	100.0	4.5	7.2	10.3	14.4	27.5	21.8	2.4	2.4	0.9	0.3	0.3	0.2	...	...	1,604	2,247	2,755	2,160	.287	.225	.512
Transportation, exc. railroad	97	100.0	9.0	10.8	12.1	12.1	17.9	15.5	13.9	4.7	2.3	0.9	0.4	...	0.1	0.1	1,215	2,168	2,923	2,128	.440	.348	.788
Telecom. & util. & sanitary serv.	116	100.0	5.9	8.8	12.3	15.7	21.8	17.7	13.0	2.9	1.0	0.3	0.1	0.2	0.2	...	1,419	2,167	2,797	2,115	.346	.290	.636
Wholesale and retail trade	268	100.0	15.6	13.5	13.7	15.6	16.6	11.1	9.1	2.8	1.1	0.3	0.4	0.1	0.1	...	848	1,731	2,500	1,762	.510	.444	.954
FEMALE, EXPERIENCED CIVILIAN LABOR FORCE																							
Profes'l, Techn'l, Kindred Wkrs.																							
Librarians	45	100.0	14.1	10.9	9.1	11.8	13.8	12.8	13.3	6.3	4.0	1.9	1.5	0.3	0.1	0.1	1,000	2,149	3,094	2,159	.535	.439	.974
Musicians and music teachers	38	100.0	25.3	16.8	11.1	7.3	12.6	9.9	6.7	4.3	2.8	1.3	1.1	0.1	0.3	0.4	494	1,356	2,596	1,744	.636	.914	1.550
Social, welfare, and recreation wkrs.	53	100.0	6.6	6.6	10.6	10.6	21.2	18.1	14.1	7.5	4.3	1.5	0.4	0.4	0.2	0.2	1,722	2,474	3,170	2,474	.293	.298	.591
Teachers (n.e.c.)	713	100.0	7.2	8.4	8.5	12.6	18.2	16.1	12.6	7.3	4.7	2.5	1.6	0.2	0.1	...	1,536	2,365	3,159	2,371	.351	.335	.686
Nurses, professional & student prof.	332	100.0	12.2	11.5	10.7	13.3	22.1	15.1	9.3	3.2	1.5	0.6	0.4	0.1	0.1	...	1,061	2,052	2,672	1,947	.484	.302	.786

TABLE C-1.—PERCENT DISTRIBUTION OF WAGE OR SALARY WORKERS IN SELECTED OCCUPATIONS, BY WAGE OR SALARY INCOME IN 1949, BY SEX, FOR THE UNITED STATES—Cont.

Occupation and sex	Number reporting $1 or more (thousands)	Total	$1 to $499	$500 to $999	$1000 to $1499	$1500 to $1999	$2000 to $2499	$2500 to $2999	$3000 to $3499	$3500 to $3999	$4000 to $4499	$4500 to $4999	$5000 to $5999	$6000 to $6999	$7000 to $9999	$10,000 and over	Q1 (dollars)	Q2 (median; dollars)	Q3 (dollars)	Arithmetic mean (dollars)	1 − Q1/Q2	Q3/Q2 − 1	Q3−Q1/Q2
FEMALE.—Con.																							
Clerical, Sales, and Kindred Workers																							
Bookk'prs, accts, cashrs, ticket agts.	702	100.0	7.7	9.5	13.5	21.8	23.5	12.4	6.9	2.4	1.1	0.5	0.4	0.2	0.1	0.1	1,289	1,942	2,478	1,959	.336	.276	.612
Office machine operators	110	100.0	4.5	6.6	8.7	21.7	32.3	17.8	6.4	1.0	0.3	0.2	0.3	0.1	0.1	0.1	1,620	2,132	2,534	2,085	.241	.188	.429
Stenographers, typists, and secys.	1,370	100.0	5.9	7.8	9.8	20.1	26.3	17.1	8.5	2.4	1.0	0.4	0.4	0.1	0.1	0.1	1,537	2,122	2,649	2,094	.276	.248	.524
Telephone operators	319	100.0	6.3	7.8	10.9	20.9	29.5	14.4	7.3	1.8	0.9	0.4	0.4	0.1	…	0.1	1,500	2,083	2,514	2,021	.280	.206	.486
Saleswomen and sales clerks (n.e.c.)	951	100.0	22.8	18.2	22.8	18.9	10.4	3.6	1.7	0.6	0.4	0.2	0.2	0.1	…	0.1	560	1,197	1,796	1,293	.532	.500	1.032
Operatives and Kindred Workers																							
Dressmakers & seamstr., exc. factory	79	100.0	15.1	14.7	23.7	24.6	14.7	4.7	1.9	0.2	0.1		0.1		…	0.1	837	1,426	1,937	1,443	.414	.358	.772
Operatives & kindred wkrs. (n.e.c.):																							
Food and kindred products	182	100.0	17.9	19.3	19.0	17.4	17.4	5.7	1.9	0.3	0.1	0.1	0.1	0.1	…	0.1	684	1,354	2,020	1,384	.495	.492	.987
Tobacco manufactures	43	100.0	10.8	15.9	24.1	27.7	16.3	4.4	0.3	0.1		0.1	0.1			0.1	947	1,483	1,937	1,470	.362	.305	.667
Knitting mills	100	100.0	10.4	16.5	26.4	24.4	14.2	5.5	1.6	0.3	0.1		0.1		0.1	…	942	1,438	1,945	1,491	.345	.352	.697
Textile mill prod., exc. knit. mills	328	100.0	7.5	11.6	19.3	28.3	23.6	7.1	1.9	0.5	0.1	0.1	0.1	0.1		…	1,153	1,705	2,176	1,665	.324	.276	.600
Apparel & other fabric text. prod.	610	100.0	10.0	16.2	27.6	23.7	14.3	4.9	2.2	0.6	0.2	0.1	0.2	0.1	0.1	…	963	1,431	1,947	1,484	.328	.360	.688
Furniture, and lumber and wood prod.	39	100.0	15.5	16.0	22.0	20.9	15.4	6.7	2.4	0.7	0.3	0.2	0.2			…	797	1,420	2,019	1,462	.439	.421	.860
Paper, paper prod., and printing	113	100.0	9.3	10.1	18.0	27.6	23.4	8.1	1.7	0.7	0.3	0.1	0.1	0.1	0.1	0.1	1,156	1,728	2,214	1,711	.332	.280	.612
Chemicals & petrol., & coal prod.	42	100.0	7.3	9.6	22.5	22.5	26.4	6.7	2.7	0.7	0.2	0.1	0.1	0.2	0.1	0.1	1,300	1,944	2,426	1,886	.327	.247	.574
Footwear industries, exc. rubber.	104	100.0	9.2	10.8	28.6	29.0	14.0	3.6	0.8	0.4	0.1		0.1		0.1	0.1	1,038	1,476	1,907	1,495	.297	.292	.589
Leather & leath. prod.,exc. footwear	28	100.0	11.0	18.8	25.7	23.0	14.0	5.4	1.1	0.7	0.2	0.2	0.2	0.1		…	872	1,393	1,924	1,434	.374	.381	.755
Stone, clay, and glass products	41	100.0	9.3	12.6	18.3	26.8	22.1	6.9	2.3	0.7	0.2	0.2	0.2			0.1	1,085	1,683	2,181	1,661	.356	.296	.652
Metal industries and machinery	304	100.0	9.1	11.1	13.5	19.8	27.9	12.7	4.6	0.9	0.2	0.1	0.1	0.1		…	1,178	1,912	2,385	1,800	.384	.247	.631
Transportation equipment	64	100.0	5.2	6.5	8.6	12.8	25.2	27.2	11.7	1.7	0.8		0.1		0.2	…	1,684	2,335	2,807	2,201	.280	.201	.481
Service Workers																							
Private household workers	1,113	100.0	47.7	30.2	12.9	6.2	1.9	0.4	0.2	0.1	0.1		0.1	0.1	0.1	…	262	538	952	704	.513	.769	1.282
Barbers, beauticians, & manicurists	85	100.0	14.5	17.7	18.9	21.2	14.6	6.6	3.1	1.5	0.9	0.3	0.4	0.3	…	…	797	1,471	2,092	1,546	.459	.422	.881
Charwomen, janitors, and porters	116	100.0	20.4	21.4	24.2	17.5	11.8	2.8	1.0	0.3		0.1	0.2	0.1	…	…	607	1,169	1,757	1,269	.481	.502	.983
Cooks, exc. private household	204	100.0	23.5	29.4	21.9	13.1	7.4	2.8	1.0	0.4	0.2	0.1	…	…	…	0.1	526	951	1,511	1,123	.448	.589	1.037
Housek'prs, stewards, exc. pr. hshld.	73	100.0	11.2	20.9	24.0	20.0	14.7	5.2	2.6	0.7	0.5		0.2	0.1	…	0.2	830	1,373	1,973	1,455	.396	.436	.832
Practical nurses and midwives	98	100.0	25.3	24.3	20.2	14.5	9.9	3.3	1.4	0.5	0.2	0.1	0.1	0.2	…	…	494	1,010	1,679	1,212	.511	.662	1.173
Waitresses, bartenders, counter wkrs.	493	100.0	28.1	29.4	22.1	12.1	5.4	1.6	0.8	0.2	0.1		0.1	0.1	…	…	445	872	1,396	1,001	.491	.599	1.090
Service wkrs., exc. pr. hshld.(n.e.c.)	266	100.0	24.3	30.5	21.1	13.4	5.2	1.4	0.5	0.1	0.1	0.1	0.1		…	…	511	921	1,412	1,010	.445	.532	.977

Source: Unpublished data of the Bureau of the Census. See Appendix A for description of method used to estimate arithmetic mean.

TABLE C-2.—PERCENT DISTRIBUTION OF WAGE OR SALARY WORKERS IN SELECTED OCCUPATIONS WHO WORKED 50 WEEKS OR MORE IN 1949, BY WAGE OR SALARY INCOME IN 1949, BY SEX, FOR THE UNITED STATES

Occupation and sex	Number reporting $1 or more (thousands)	Total	$1 to $499	$500 to $999	$1000 to $1499	$1500 to $1999	$2000 to $2499	$2500 to $2999	$3000 to $3499	$3500 to $3999	$4000 to $4499	$4500 to $4999	$5000 to $5999	$6000 to $6999	$7000 to $9999	$10,000 and over	Q_1 (dollars)	Q_2 (median; dollars)	Q_3 (dollars)	Arithmetic mean (dollars)	$1-\frac{Q_1}{Q_2}$	$\frac{Q_3}{Q_2}-1$	$\frac{Q_3-Q_1}{Q_2}$
MALE, EXPERIENCED CIVILIAN LABOR FORCE																							
Profess'l, Techn'l, Kindred Wkrs.																							
Artists and art teachers	23	100.0	0.9	0.9	3.2	2.0	6.1	8.9	15.3	10.6	11.0	9.0	13.8	5.2	6.8	6.1	3,098	4,095	5,514	5,151	.244	.346	.590
Authors, editors, and reporters	42	100.0	1.0	1.1	2.4	1.9	4.6	6.3	8.7	7.9	10.2	8.0	17.4	9.6	12.1	8.8	3,443	4,869	6,573	6,113	.293	.350	.643
Chemists	51	100.0	0.2	0.3	1.4	1.2	3.8	7.5	13.7	13.0	13.0	9.6	14.8	8.4	8.5	3.1	3,368	4,288	5,669	5,026	.215	.321	.536
Clergymen	91	100.0	2.9	10.5	12.1	11.0	15.7	12.7	14.4	7.8	4.8	2.5	2.7	1.5	0.3	...	1,479	2,430	3,351	2,607	.392	.378	.770
Coll. pres., prof'rs, instr's (n.e.c.)	47	100.0	0.9	1.9	3.5	3.5	3.6	4.1	9.6	9.6	9.6	9.2	18.2	10.2	10.7	3.9	3,429	4,620	5,989	5,264	.258	.296	.554
Designers and draftsmen	101	100.0	0.3	0.6	0.7	1.8	8.0	12.5	17.6	17.9	15.5	8.5	10.5	3.3	2.0	0.7	3,031	3,737	4,506	3,977	.189	.205	.394
Engineers, civil	85	100.0	0.3	0.7	0.5	1.1	3.7	4.2	9.3	12.2	11.0	12.7	21.1	9.6	8.2	3.1	3,713	4,697	5,820	5,247	.210	.239	.449
Engineers, electrical	79	100.0	0.3	0.4	0.7	1.0	2.2	3.1	10.1	11.7	12.8	10.9	20.3	11.5	10.8	3.4	3,782	4,826	6,078	5,472	.217	.259	.476
Engineers, mechanical	142	100.0	0.2	0.3	0.4	0.8	2.0	3.2	9.0	11.9	13.2	11.3	19.8	11.8	11.3	4.7	3,882	4,898	6,246	5,748	.208	.275	.483
Musicians and music teachers	23	100.0	3.7	6.6	6.2	7.3	9.8	3.2	9.0	10.5	7.0	7.0	9.6	4.6	11.3	5.0	2,061	3,295	4,872	4,238	.375	.478	.853
Pharmacists	29	100.0	0.6	1.2	1.9	2.3	6.6	8.0	15.7	14.5	16.5	9.9	14.1	5.3	2.6	0.7	3,140	3,972	4,889	4,150	.210	.230	.440
Social, welfare, and recreation wkrs.	22	100.0	0.9	0.7	3.4	5.4	11.7	15.0	16.3	14.5	9.1	6.3	8.7	4.2	3.7	1.1	2,597	3,396	4,390	3,823	.236	.292	.528
Sports instr's, athletes, entertainers	22	100.0	1.5	3.0	5.1	7.3	8.2	10.6	14.0	12.4	13.2	7.0	9.2	3.1	2.4	3.0	2,494	3,512	4,489	4,019	.290	.278	.568
Teachers (n.e.c.)	126	100.0	0.7	1.6	2.3	3.9	7.6	9.8	17.4	15.5	13.5	9.5	11.4	3.8	2.4	0.5	2,954	3,716	4,642	3,901	.206	.249	.455
Salaried Managers and Officials																							
Conductors, railroad	36	100.0	0.2	...	0.4	0.2	1.6	3.0	10.9	14.8	23.8	16.6	23.0	5.1	0.4	...	3,794	4,397	5,152	4,467	.138	.171	.309
Postmasters, and misc. govt. officials	159	100.0	1.0	1.3	2.3	3.6	8.2	10.1	15.6	14.9	13.2	8.7	9.5	4.5	4.7	2.3	2,926	3,765	4,776	4,281	.223	.268	.491
Managers and officials:																							
Manufacturing	294	100.0	0.2	0.5	0.6	0.9	2.9	3.7	7.9	9.0	10.2	7.2	15.0	9.7	14.2	18.1	3,961	5,460	8,521	7,847	.275	.560	.835
Trans., commun., & other pub. util.	118	100.0	0.3	0.4	0.7	1.4	3.9	5.5	9.7	12.5	11.9	12.3	18.7	9.6	7.4	5.7	3,624	4,650	5,877	5,572	.221	.263	.484
Wholesale trade	108	100.0	0.4	0.4	1.1	2.2	5.3	7.0	14.1	11.2	10.1	6.7	12.7	7.3	9.2	12.2	3,305	4,411	6,521	6,389	.251	.478	.729
Eating and drinking places	27	100.0	1.0	2.1	4.1	6.3	12.0	13.8	17.9	12.7	9.0	5.7	7.7	3.9	2.2	1.5	2,479	3,299	4,283	3,705	.249	.298	.547
Retail trade, exc. eating & drinking	264	100.0	0.8	1.1	1.9	3.7	9.0	10.5	15.5	13.1	10.8	5.7	10.6	5.5	5.4	5.9	2,905	3,786	5,217	4,923	.232	.377	.610
Finance, insur., and real estate	122	100.0	0.4	0.4	0.8	1.7	4.5	5.1	9.6	10.5	10.2	8.3	15.3	9.0	11.5	12.6	3,619	4,910	6,911	6,743	.263	.407	.670
Business and repair services	35	100.0	0.4	0.8	1.4	2.8	7.5	5.1	15.0	10.5	9.7	6.6	12.0	6.6	7.5	3.1	3,087	4,026	5,842	5,644	.234	.451	.685
Personal services	25	100.0	1.8	1.1	2.8	6.2	12.0	10.3	17.0	11.7	9.1	5.7	9.3	4.0	4.7	4.3	2,553	3,465	4,763	4,389	.264	.374	.638
Clerical, Sales, and Kindred Workers																							
Baggagemen, exp. mess., rwy. mail clk.	20	100.0	...	0.3	0.7	1.0	6.6	10.0	21.8	26.0	22.4	8.3	2.1	0.3	...	0.1	3,147	3,685	4,192	3,662	.146	.137	.283
Book'prs, accts., cashs., ticket agts.	408	100.0	0.5	1.0	1.7	3.7	9.1	13.0	19.1	15.5	11.3	7.3	9.0	4.1	3.3	1.4	2,847	3,563	4,511	4,008	.201	.266	.467
Mail carriers	132	100.0	0.8	1.3	1.7	2.0	5.7	17.9	22.3	40.6	4.9	1.7	0.9	0.1	...	...	2,877	3,462	3,787	3,281	.169	.093	.262
Messengers, except express	26	100.0	6.6	9.7	16.1	22.7	18.9	8.7	3.7	1.6	0.3	...	0.1	...	...	...	1,270	1,888	2,543	1,979	.328	.347	.675
Shipping and receiving clerks	188	100.0	0.5	0.9	2.7	8.5	22.3	26.4	22.9	8.7	4.0	1.4	0.7	0.2	0.1	...	2,278	2,786	3,299	2,844	.183	.184	.367
Stenographers, typists, and secys.	61	100.0	0.6	1.5	2.7	5.8	14.0	15.1	16.3	10.4	6.9	5.3	7.0	4.8	5.4	4.3	2,513	3,316	4,660	4,359	.243	.405	.648

TABLE C-2.—PERCENT DISTRIBUTION OF WAGE OR SALARY WORKERS IN SELECTED OCCUPATIONS WHO WORKED 50 WEEKS OR MORE IN 1949, BY WAGE OR SALARY INCOME IN 1949, BY SEX, FOR THE UNITED STATES—Cont.

Occupation and sex	Number reporting $1 or more (thousands)	Total	$1 to $499	$500 to $999	$1000 to $1499	$1500 to $1999	$2000 to $2499	$2500 to $2999	$3000 to $3499	$3500 to $3999	$4000 to $4499	$4500 to $4999	$5000 to $5999	$6000 to $6999	$7000 to $9999	$10,000 and over	Q_1 (dollars)	Q_2 (median; dollars)	Q_3 (dollars)	Arithmetic mean (dollars)	$1-Q_1/Q_2$	Q_3/Q_2-1	$(Q_3-Q_1)/Q_2$
MALE—Con.																							
Clerical, Sales, & Kind. Wkrs.—Con.																							
Telegraph operators	20	100.0	0.3	0.5	0.8	1.4	4.8	11.1	38.4	27.8	8.3	2.3	2.8	1.2	0.5	...	3,079	3,405	3,818	3,479	.096	.121	.217
Newsboys	40	100.0	76.1	9.7	3.2	2.1	2.0	1.9	1.1	1.1	1.0	0.6	0.9		0.2		164	329	493	652	.500	.499	.999
Insurance agents and brokers	165	100.0	0.7	1.2	2.5	3.5	8.1	9.9	16.3	13.5	12.6	8.2	11.6	5.5	4.2	2.3	2,955	3,789	4,909	4,331	.221	.295	.516
Real estate agents and brokers	32	100.0	1.4	3.2	6.0	5.0	9.4	13.0	16.3	11.3	8.4	5.6	10.7	7.2	6.4	4.9	2,516	3,646	5,402	4,638	.311	.481	.792
Salesmen and sales clerks (n.e.c.)	1,205	100.0	1.6	2.7	4.1	7.1	13.6	15.4	15.4	11.0	8.4	4.8	8.0	3.5	3.7	2.5	2,349	3,237	4,351	3,860	.275	.344	.619
Craftsmen, Foremen, & Kindred Wkrs.																							
Bakers	64	100.0	0.6	1.1	3.7	7.4	15.5	17.8	24.5	14.2	9.1	2.8	2.4	0.6	0.2	...	2,394	3,080	3,655	3,060	.223	.186	.409
Blacksmiths, forgemen, and hammermen	24	100.0	1.1	1.5	3.3	6.1	12.4	17.2	23.8	16.5	9.4	3.2	4.1	1.0	0.3	...	2,517	3,176	3,791	3,194	.208	.193	.401
Boilermakers	20	100.0	0.9	1.0	0.9	1.5	5.1	12.9	25.4	22.4	17.2	5.8	5.5	1.8	0.4	0.1	3,073	3,574	4,172	3,655	.141	.167	.308
Cabinetmakers and patternmakers	53	100.0	0.6	1.0	3.4	7.1	12.1	16.8	21.9	10.0	10.3	5.3	4.8	0.7	0.3	0.2	2,524	3,205	3,888	3,267	.213	.212	.425
Carpenters	288	100.0	1.9	2.5	5.2	7.1	14.2	21.9	20.7	11.5	5.0	2.1	4.2	0.8	0.3	0.1	2,292	3,099	3,826	3,105	.261	.234	.495
Compositors and typesetters	114	100.0	0.6	0.5	1.5	4.1	7.6	15.0	14.5	12.9	14.1	11.0	6.1	1.5	0.5	0.2	2,917	3,883	4,873	3,970	.249	.255	.504
Electricians (n.e.c.)	181	100.0	0.6	0.5	1.5	2.7	7.6	10.8	20.9	18.2	14.1	8.9	10.6	2.5	0.9	0.1	3,031	3,648	4,430	3,769	.170	.214	.384
Foremen (n.e.c.):																							
Construction	38	100.0	0.5	0.6	1.7	4.4	9.8	15.3	14.2	14.2	9.8	6.0	13.0	4.3	2.0	0.6	2,817	3,680	4,740	3,927	.235	.288	.523
Manufacturing	375	100.0	0.2	0.1	0.4	1.2	4.5	8.1	15.3	15.3	16.3	12.3	16.2	6.0	3.1	0.7	3,335	4,141	5,062	4,391	.195	.222	.417
Trans., commun., & other pub. util.	97	100.0	0.2	0.1	0.3	0.7	4.1	8.8	16.0	16.0	14.0	11.1	13.4	3.9	1.2	1.2	3,208	3,809	4,721	4,048	.158	.239	.397
Inspectors (n.e.c.)	59	100.0	0.2	0.1	0.8	2.2	7.3	12.5	23.3	14.8	18.0	6.0	3.9	1.1	0.7	0.2	3,034	3,567	4,133	3,633	.150	.158	.308
Linemen & servicemen, t'graph, etc.	168	100.0	0.3	0.1	0.3	3.3	12.7	17.1	20.1	14.8	8.1	8.1	8.1	1.1	0.6	0.1	2,702	3,368	4,171	3,479	.198	.238	.436
Locomotive engineers	46	100.0	0.1	0.1	0.1	0.3	2.3	6.9	14.2	17.5	19.4	8.1	27.1	3.1	0.6	0.1	4,100	4,784	5,599	4,904	.143	.171	.313
Locomotive firemen	30	100.0	0.5	0.2	1.3	1.8	4.6	5.2	27.8	21.2	13.9	4.6	14.2	0.9	0.3	...	3,390	4,010	4,696	4,034	.155	.171	.326
Machinists, millwrights, & toolmakers	497	100.0	0.3	0.2	0.7	1.0	5.2	14.3	21.2	16.5	13.9	8.0	4.6	2.4	1.4	0.1	3,000	3,450	4,032	3,553	.131	.168	.299
Masons, tile setters, & stone cutters	53	100.0	1.2	2.2	5.0	6.9	13.6	19.0	15.6	14.7	8.0	3.5	11.3	2.4	0.7	0.1	2,445	3,327	4,421	3,478	.266	.328	.594
Mechanics & repairmen, & loom fixers	1,085	100.0	0.4	0.8	3.1	6.9	15.3	23.9	14.7	13.7	8.1	2.9	2.9	0.7	0.4	0.1	2,435	3,084	3,673	3,120	.211	.191	.402
Molders, metal	32	100.0	0.4	0.3	1.7	4.0	14.4	28.0	21.9	12.5	3.5	2.1	2.5	0.2	0.1	0.2	2,565	3,064	3,522	3,087	.163	.149	.312
Painters (const.), paperhgrs., glazrs.	115	100.0	1.0	1.3	4.3	4.4	15.0	21.9	14.7	13.7	7.1	4.5	2.6	0.2	0.1	0.2	2,337	3,057	3,706	3,084	.236	.212	.448
Plasterers and cement finishers	27	100.0	0.7	1.2	5.1	7.8	11.9	14.4	14.4	11.6	8.6	7.7	11.2	4.5	1.5	0.2	2,429	3,434	4,496	3,574	.293	.309	.602
Plumbers and pipe fitters	140	100.0	0.4	1.1	2.2	5.0	9.7	17.7	14.9	14.9	13.8	8.6	12.1	2.2	0.8	0.1	2,789	3,584	4,457	3,682	.222	.243	.465
Print. craft., exc. compos. & typeset.	66	100.0	0.4	1.0	1.2	2.9	7.2	7.2	10.3	10.3	11.4	10.5	18.5	6.8	1.4	0.9	3,238	4,364	5,616	4,620	.259	.286	.545
Rollers and roll hands, metal	10	100.0	0.9	1.2	2.3	2.9	8.4	24.9	15.0	15.0	9.2	2.0	4.6	3.2	1.4	0.1	2,738	3,253	3,923	3,809	.159	.206	.365
Roofers and sheet metal workers	83	100.0	0.5	0.9	2.3	2.0	15.4	23.9	15.0	16.3	11.6	6.3	5.4	0.5	0.3	0.1	2,662	3,305	3,982	3,370	.195	.204	.399
Shoemakers & repairers, exc. factory	11	100.0	5.5	4.5	11.9	16.9	20.1	12.9	12.9	4.2	2.1	1.1	1.1	...	1.7	0.9	1,592	2,279	2,924	2,309	.302	.283	.585
Stat. engineers, cranemen, hoistmen	273	100.0	0.5	0.1	0.5	3.7	9.3	13.5	17.5	17.5	12.7	6.6	7.6	2.7	1.7	0.9	2,841	3,493	4,283	3,782	.187	.226	.413
Structural metal workers	21	100.0	0.4	0.4	0.7	2.8	12.6	23.6	15.5	15.5	12.5	10.2	12.6	2.3	1.3	0.3	3,059	3,635	4,559	3,845	.159	.253	.412
Tailors and furriers	30	100.0	0.5	1.4	3.6	6.7	14.4	22.1	12.5	12.5	9.3	3.3	5.5	1.7	2.2	0.3	2,444	3,156	3,892	3,351	.226	.233	.459

TABLE C–2.—PERCENT DISTRIBUTION OF WAGE OR SALARY WORKERS IN SELECTED OCCUPATIONS WHO WORKED 50 WEEKS OR MORE IN 1949, BY WAGE OR SALARY INCOME IN 1949, BY SEX, FOR THE UNITED STATES—Cont.

Occupation and sex	Number reporting $1 or more (thousands)	Total	$1 to $499	$500 to $999	$1000 to $1499	$1500 to $1999	$2000 to $2499	$2500 to $2999	$3000 to $3499	$3500 to $3999	$4000 to $4499	$4500 to $4999	$5000 to $5999	$6000 to $6999	$7000 to $9999	$10,000 and over	Q1 (dollars)	Q2 (median; dollars)	Q3 (dollars)	Arithmetic mean (dollars)	$1-\frac{Q_1}{Q_2}$	$\frac{Q_3}{Q_2}-1$	$\frac{Q_3-Q_1}{Q_2}$
MALE—Con.																							
Operatives and Kindred Workers																							
Apprentices	58	100.0	1.7	3.2	7.0	14.2	26.5	20.6	15.2	5.8	2.9	1.2	1.2	0.2	0.2	0.1	1,961	2,451	3,059	2,535	.200	.248	.448
Attendants, auto service and parking	118	100.0	4.1	6.3	10.9	17.5	24.4	16.7	12.3	4.4	1.8	0.7	0.5	0.1	...	0.1	1,606	2,230	2,853	2,245	.280	.279	.559
Brakemen and switchmen, railroad	81	100.0	0.3	0.4	0.9	1.4	4.7	7.5	18.5	22.6	23.6	11.6	7.1	1.1	0.2	0.1	3,265	3,861	4,396	3,833	.155	.138	.293
Drivers, bus, taxi, & truck, & delmen	1,087	100.0	1.4	0.8	6.4	10.7	17.5	16.9	19.5	12.7	7.5	3.2	2.7	1.1	0.2	...	2,106	2,831	3,495	2,881	.257	.234	.491
Stationary firemen	84	100.0	0.4	1.3	4.2	9.0	15.1	21.0	17.7	15.7	7.5	2.3	1.5	2.0	0.7	...	2,299	2,933	3,485	2,931	.217	.187	.404
Mine operatives & laborers (n.e.c.)	141	100.0	1.4	2.2	4.3	8.0	16.9	17.7	17.2	9.3	7.5	4.5	4.1	0.5	0.3	0.1	2,301	3,127	3,876	3,202	.265	.239	.504
Motormen, rwy., mine, factory, etc.	27	100.0	0.1	0.1	0.8	1.6	5.6	17.7	39.5	12.9	12.9	3.4	1.7	0.3	0.3	...	3,057	3,373	3,844	3,427	.094	.139	.233
Painters, exc. constr. & maintenance	60	100.0	0.7	1.3	3.1	7.4	16.4	20.1	22.1	14.8	7.6	2.5	1.8	0.7	0.3	...	2,414	3,045	3,562	3,062	.208	.168	.376
Sailors and deck hands	14	100.0	1.3	3.4	4.2	8.4	16.6	15.1	22.1	7.4	7.4	2.5	3.6	1.9	...	...	2,235	2,991	3,619	3,063	.253	.210	.463
Welders and flame-cutters	136	100.0	0.3	0.6	1.5	2.8	8.7	15.7	29.0	19.1	11.4	5.4	4.1	0.5	...	...	2,854	3,352	3,929	3,454	.149	.172	.321
Operatives & kindred workers (n.e.c.):																							
Food and kindred products	191	100.0	1.0	2.1	4.6	9.1	19.6	21.2	22.8	10.8	5.2	1.7	0.3	0.3	0.1	...	2,209	2,821	3,382	2,834	.217	.198	.415
Knitting mills	23	100.0	0.0	0.8	5.3	4.8	16.0	15.7	15.7	14.8	9.4	6.8	9.4	2.1	1.8	...	2,225	3,105	4,202	3,337	.284	.353	.637
Text. mill prod., exc. knit. mills	210	100.0	0.6	1.0	4.3	14.8	32.3	23.7	14.7	4.8	1.8	0.7	0.6	0.3	0.3	...	2,067	2,454	2,964	2,577	.158	.208	.366
Apparel & other fabric text. prod.	66	100.0	0.7	1.9	5.4	16.8	18.2	15.0	15.9	9.3	3.0	3.3	6.7	0.2	...	...	2,140	2,897	3,823	3,191	.262	.319	.581
Furniture, and lumber and wood prod.	127	100.0	3.4	5.9	13.4	19.0	16.1	16.1	14.3	6.4	2.8	1.0	0.7	0.1	...	...	1,568	2,276	3,014	2,301	.311	.324	.635
Paper, paper prod., and printing	140	100.0	0.8	1.0	2.3	5.7	16.6	22.2	23.5	12.2	8.6	3.0	3.1	0.4	0.4	...	2,458	3,030	3,619	3,098	.189	.194	.383
Chemicals & petrol., & coal prod.	141	100.0	0.5	0.9	0.9	4.0	13.0	17.3	25.2	14.8	13.0	6.3	3.1	0.4	0.2	...	2,725	3,308	3,945	3,353	.176	.192	.368
Rubber products	55	100.0	0.3	0.5	1.1	2.7	12.5	21.6	29.3	18.0	9.2	3.2	1.3	0.2	0.1	...	2,683	3,193	3,694	3,224	.160	.157	.317
Footwear industries, exc. rubber	50	100.0	0.5	1.1	5.8	17.4	26.6	21.9	15.6	6.7	1.0	1.0	1.0	0.1	0.1	...	2,004	2,474	3,054	2,581	.190	.234	.424
Leather & leath. prod., exc. footwear	24	100.0	0.5	0.6	3.0	10.5	21.2	22.2	24.2	8.1	2.0	2.0	2.0	0.3	...	...	2,245	2,793	3,318	2,831	.197	.187	.384
Stone, clay, and glass products	79	100.0	0.5	1.0	3.6	8.0	19.4	22.0	20.8	12.0	6.4	2.6	1.8	0.8	...	...	2,307	2,894	3,488	2,986	.203	.205	.408
Iron & steel, & not spec. metal ind.	175	100.0	0.4	0.9	1.8	5.7	17.2	26.3	26.4	13.1	6.4	2.2	2.3	0.5	0.2	...	2,471	2,990	3,449	3,016	.174	.156	.330
Nonferrous metals & their products	41	100.0	0.5	0.6	2.1	4.4	16.3	23.1	30.6	14.8	6.0	1.6	1.8	0.5	0.2	...	2,500	2,975	3,449	3,180	.160	.159	.319
Machinery	265	100.0	0.5	0.6	1.3	3.0	13.0	18.1	30.6	14.8	5.6	2.5	2.5	0.5	0.4	...	2,641	3,137	3,595	3,311	.159	.145	.304
Motor vehicles & mtr. vehicle equip.	129	100.0	0.4	0.6	1.1	1.9	7.3	18.1	37.9	18.2	5.6	2.9	2.5	0.5	...	...	2,878	3,272	3,712	3,311	.121	.134	.255
Trans. equip., exc. motor vehicle	52	100.0	0.1	0.5	0.9	2.1	9.9	22.8	31.2	17.3	8.9	3.7	1.9	0.3	...	...	2,752	3,220	3,717	3,301	.146	.154	.300
Service Workers																							
Private household workers	36	100.0	9.9	18.5	23.0	21.1	15.1	6.4	2.7	1.5	0.8	0.4	0.2	...	...	0.2	908	1,470	2,083	1,603	.383	.417	.800
Firemen, fire protection	93	100.0	0.2	0.1	0.6	2.0	9.8	19.5	33.5	17.0	11.4	2.5	2.3	0.5	0.4	...	2,815	3,266	3,774	3,343	.138	.155	.293
Guards and watchmen	174	100.0	0.7	1.5	5.3	11.5	23.9	23.9	19.6	8.9	3.9	1.4	1.4	0.5	0.5	...	2,136	2,688	3,258	2,709	.206	.211	.417
Policemen, sheriffs, and marshals	170	100.0	0.3	0.6	1.6	3.8	12.4	17.8	30.5	17.1	9.9	2.5	2.3	0.5	...	...	2,685	3,226	3,743	3,283	.168	.160	.328
Barbers, beauticians, & manicurists	54	100.0	1.4	4.1	9.8	14.5	17.8	18.7	13.1	6.9	3.1	1.6	1.7	0.3	...	...	1,834	2,412	3,076	2,542	.240	.275	.515
Charmen, janitors, and porters	389	100.0	3.3	7.0	14.1	22.4	21.8	18.2	7.6	2.2	0.9	0.3	0.3	0.1	0.1	...	1,513	2,060	2,550	2,072	.266	.237	.503
Cooks, exc. private household	105	100.0	1.0	2.9	8.6	13.3	18.2	18.2	15.8	8.4	4.9	1.6	2.0	0.9	0.4	...	1,970	2,566	3,291	2,691	.233	.282	.515

Table C-2.— Percent Distribution of Wage or Salary Workers in Selected Occupations Who Worked 50 Weeks or More in 1949, by Wage or Salary Income in 1949, by Sex, for the United States—Cont.

Occupation and sex	Number reporting $1 or more (thousands)	Total	$1 to $499	$500 to $999	$1000 to $1499	$1500 to $1999	$2000 to $2499	$2500 to $2999	$3000 to $3499	$3500 to $3999	$4000 to $4499	$4500 to $4999	$5000 to $5999	$6000 to $6999	$7000 to $9999	$10,000 and over	Q1 (dollars)	Q2 (median; dollars)	Q3 (dollars)	Arithmetic mean (dollars)	1-Q1/Q2	Q3/Q2-1	Q3-Q1/Q2
MALE—Con.																							
Service Workers—Con.																							
Elevator operators	44	100.0	0.5	1.9	8.5	17.8	33.1	25.2	8.3	2.8	1.3	0.5	0.2	...	...	...	1,896	2,322	2,762	2,336	.184	.189	.373
Waiters, bartenders, & counter wkrs.	166	100.0	2.3	5.7	9.1	13.6	22.2	19.3	16.5	6.4	2.6	0.9	1.1	...	...	0.1	1,790	2,435	3,085	2,462	.265	.267	.532
Service wkrs., exc. pr. hshld.(n.e.c.)	85	100.0	4.7	11.4	20.4	24.5	23.0	8.5	4.1	1.5	0.9	0.3	0.3	0.2	...	0.1	1,218	1,776	2,304	1,824	.314	.297	.611
Laborers, Except Farm and Mine																							
Fishermen and oystermen	9	100.0	3.9	10.8	14.4	14.1	13.4	8.2	9.8	8.5	6.2	3.9	3.6	0.3	...	0.7	1,358	2,254	3,524	2,658	.398	.563	.961
Longshoremen and stevedores	23	100.0	0.8	2.9	6.8	7.7	15.6	17.9	20.9	10.3	7.5	4.8	4.1	0.5	0.1	...	2,218	2,953	3,617	2,966	.249	.224	.473
Lumbermen, raftsmen, & woodchoppers	42	100.0	12.5	18.9	25.4	16.0	9.4	5.8	4.4	3.2	2.0	0.6	1.1	0.5	0.1	0.1	831	1,366	2,117	1,640	.392	.549	.941
Laborers (n.e.c.):																							
Manufacturing industries:																							
Food and kindred products	77	100.0	1.1	3.0	7.1	13.0	23.1	22.8	18.5	7.2	3.0	0.4	0.5	0.1	0.1	0.1	2,017	2,559	3,132	2,549	.212	.223	.435
Textiles, text. prod., & apparel	34	100.0	1.2	2.0	9.6	28.3	32.2	12.8	9.0	2.4	1.2	0.7	0.3	0.2	...	...	1,716	2,138	2,566	2,235	.198	.200	.398
Furniture, and lumber & wood prod.	74	100.0	5.0	10.0	21.2	24.4	16.3	10.0	7.9	2.4	1.7	0.6	0.4	0.4	...	...	1,236	1,783	2,442	1,902	.307	.369	.676
Paper, paper prod., & printing	32	100.0	1.2	1.7	4.7	11.1	30.4	24.8	17.1	6.6	2.4	0.8	0.7	0.1	0.1	...	2,137	2,558	3,091	2,616	.165	.207	.372
Chemicals & petrol., & coal prod.	58	100.0	1.0	2.1	4.3	10.5	18.3	19.9	25.4	12.2	4.7	0.7	0.5	0.4	0.1	0.1	2,194	2,847	3,372	2,793	.230	.184	.414
Stone, clay, and glass products	41	100.0	0.7	2.4	5.6	11.1	27.2	26.8	17.0	5.3	2.4	0.5	0.9	0.1	0.1	...	2,096	2,556	3,035	2,575	.181	.187	.368
Iron & steel & not spec.metal ind.	84	100.0	0.8	1.0	2.9	9.9	29.8	33.3	18.4	5.8	2.7	1.0	0.4	0.1	0.1	0.1	2,175	2,603	3,092	2,652	.165	.188	.353
Nonferrous metals and their prod.	15	100.0	0.4	1.0	1.8	9.9	29.0	22.3	20.2	5.2	1.6	1.4	0.6	0.1	0.1	0.1	2,275	2,713	3,133	2,727	.162	.154	.316
Machinery	38	100.0	0.4	1.8	2.4	7.6	25.7	28.5	20.4	7.6	3.4	1.4	0.7	0.2	0.2	0.1	2,247	2,711	3,208	2,768	.171	.183	.354
Motor vehicles & mtr. veh. equip.	20	100.0	0.1	1.0	0.9	4.8	13.6	23.5	30.5	12.6	4.3	2.4	0.4	0.4	0.1	...	2,598	2,711	3,451	3,063	.159	.117	.276
Trans. equipment, exc. motor veh.	13	100.0	0.5	1.0	2.6	9.6	28.6	32.8	15.9	4.0	1.4	0.7	1.9	0.5	0.2	0.1	2,191	2,611	2,992	2,671	.162	.145	.307
Nonmanufacturing industries:																							
Construction	236	100.0	2.7	5.5	11.6	17.4	23.3	15.9	12.6	5.0	2.9	1.0	1.5	0.4	...	0.1	1,649	2,275	2,956	2,372	.275	.299	.574
Railroads & rwy. express service	153	100.0	0.8	1.6	4.7	10.2	32.3	30.2	14.4	3.5	1.3	0.5	0.4	...	...	0.1	2,119	2,507	2,921	2,509	.155	.165	.320
Transportation, exc. railroad	53	100.0	1.7	3.5	6.4	11.1	20.9	21.9	7.4	7.5	3.5	1.3	0.5	0.3	...	0.1	2,055	2,650	3,231	2,636	.225	.218	.443
Telecomm. & util. & sanitary serv.	78	100.0	1.4	2.9	9.1	15.8	25.3	22.4	17.2	3.5	1.1	0.4	0.4	0.2	0.2	...	1,867	2,411	2,958	2,409	.226	.226	.452
Wholesale and retail trade	147	100.0	4.4	6.2	11.6	17.7	22.5	16.1	14.1	4.4	1.7	0.5	0.6	0.2	0.1	...	1,579	2,224	2,891	2,235	.291	.299	.590
FEMALE, EXPERIENCED CIVILIAN LABOR FORCE																							
Profess'l, Techn'l, Kindred Wkrs.																							
Librarians	28	100.0	6.9	8.4	6.9	12.7	17.1	15.2	16.4	8.0	4.3	1.8	1.7	0.3	...	...	1,610	2,442	3,238	2,414	.341	.326	.667
Musicians and music teachers	11	100.0	18.4	16.0	10.9	9.1	13.1	11.5	7.2	4.8	1.9	1.6	0.3	0.3	...	0.3	706	1,758	2,826	1,995	.599	.607	1.206
Social, welfare, and recreation wkrs.	37	100.0	1.8	2.3	3.9	9.1	24.2	21.9	17.2	9.9	5.7	1.8	1.8	0.5	0.2	0.2	2,163	2,699	3,343	2,804	.199	.238	.437
Teachers (n.e.c.)	155	100.0	5.0	2.9	4.1	8.8	15.8	17.1	17.2	10.6	6.8	4.8	3.7	0.4	0.2	0.2	2,060	2,826	3,580	2,826	.271	.267	.538
Nurses, professional & student prof.	178	100.0	4.1	3.3	6.2	11.7	28.6	22.4	14.5	5.1	2.3	1.0	0.6	0.2	0.1	0.1	1,987	2,432	2,971	2,459	.183	.221	.404

TABLE C-2.—PERCENT DISTRIBUTION OF WAGE OR SALARY WORKERS IN SELECTED OCCUPATIONS WHO WORKED 50 WEEKS OR MORE IN 1949, BY WAGE OR SALARY INCOME IN 1949, BY SEX, FOR THE UNITED STATES—Cont.

Occupation and sex	Number reporting $1 or more (thousands)	Total	$1 to $499	$500 to $999	$1000 to $1499	$1500 to $1999	$2000 to $2499	$2500 to $2999	$3000 to $3499	$3500 to $3999	$4000 to $4499	$4500 to $4999	$5000 to $5999	$6000 to $6999	$7000 to $9999	$10,000 and over	Q_1 (dollars)	Q_2 (median; dollars)	Q_3 (dollars)	Arithmetic mean (dollars)	$1 - \frac{Q_1}{Q_2}$	$\frac{Q_3}{Q_2} - 1$	$\frac{Q_3 - Q_1}{Q_2}$
FEMALE—Con.																							
Clerical, Sales, and Kindred Workers																							
Bookk'prs, accs., cashs., ticket agts.	501	100.0	1.3	3.3	10.9	24.8	29.0	15.9	8.8	3.1	1.4	0.6	0.5	0.2	...	0.1	1,691	2,167	2,678	2,247	.220	.236	.456
Office machine operators	79	100.0	0.4	0.7	3.9	22.7	39.6	22.5	8.1	1.1	1.2	0.3	0.3	0.1	0.1	...	1,941	2,282	2,671	2,329	.150	.170	.320
Stenographers, typists, and secys	985	100.0	0.6	1.5	6.3	21.7	31.9	21.6	11.0	3.1	1.2	0.5	0.4	0.1	0.1	...	1,884	2,313	2,803	2,387	.186	.211	.397
Telephone operators	231	100.0	1.2	2.4	7.7	21.7	36.0	17.7	9.0	2.2	1.0	0.4	0.4	0.1	...	0.1	1,816	2,236	2,669	2,259	.189	.193	.382
Saleswomen and sales clerks (n.e.c.)	496	100.0	4.3	10.2	29.0	28.8	16.7	5.9	2.7	0.9	0.5	0.2	0.2	...	0.2	...	1,181	1,613	2,081	1,699	.268	.290	.558
Operatives and Kindred Workers																							
Dressmakers & seamstr., exc. factory	40	100.0	3.4	6.3	25.9	32.2	20.8	7.1	3.3	0.3	0.2	0.1	0.1	0.1	...	0.1	1,295	1,724	2,173	1,770	.249	.260	.509
Operatives & kindred wkrs. (n.e.c.):																							
Food and kindred products	75	100.0	1.8	5.1	15.2	28.8	32.5	11.5	3.8	0.6	0.2	0.2	0.1	0.1	...	0.1	1,550	1,984	2,371	1,974	.219	.194	.413
Tobacco manufactures	21	100.0	1.0	4.5	22.6	36.3	26.6	7.5	0.7	0.3	...	0.1	0.1	...	...	...	1,431	1,802	2,199	1,810	.206	.220	.426
Knitting mills	44	100.0	0.4	3.7	24.7	33.9	23.8	9.8	2.5	0.9	0.1	0.1	0.1	...	...	...	1,423	1,813	2,258	1,881	.215	.245	.460
Textile mill prod., exc. knit. mills	156	100.0	0.6	1.7	26.3	33.7	36.4	11.6	3.0	0.5	0.2	0.1	0.1	...	...	...	1,660	2,029	2,372	2,032	.182	.169	.351
Apparel & other fabric text. prod.	228	100.0	0.7	4.5	26.3	33.6	22.3	7.8	3.4	0.8	0.2	0.1	0.1	...	0.1	...	1,376	1,775	2,222	1,856	.225	.251	.476
Furniture, and lumber and wood prod	17	100.0	1.4	5.0	22.0	29.1	24.3	12.4	3.9	0.5	0.2	0.5	0.1	...	...	...	1,423	1,871	2,360	1,916	.240	.261	.501
Paper, paper prod., and printing	64	100.0	0.7	1.4	13.7	33.9	33.7	12.4	3.9	0.4	0.2	0.1	...	0.2	...	...	1,640	2,019	2,388	2,059	.188	.182	.370
Chemicals & petrol., & coal prod	25	100.0	0.5	1.0	8.2	24.6	35.7	21.8	7.1	1.0	0.4	...	0.1	...	...	...	1,819	2,225	2,624	2,254	.183	.178	.361
Footwear industries, exc. rubber	46	100.0	0.5	3.1	26.6	38.1	24.6	6.4	1.4	0.4	0.4	0.1	0.1	...	...	...	1,402	1,760	2,145	1,816	.204	.218	.422
Leather & leath. prod., exc. footwear	10	100.0	0.3	3.6	23.2	36.9	24.4	10.4	0.9	0.3	0.3	0.2	...	...	...	...	1,455	1,810	2,225	1,841	.197	.229	.426
Stone, clay, and glass products	20	100.0	0.3	2.2	23.0	32.8	36.5	11.7	4.5	1.1	0.6	0.2	0.3	0.1	...	...	1,691	2,064	2,407	2,098	.182	.165	.347
Metal industries and machinery	146	100.0	0.5	1.3	5.9	20.5	41.5	20.2	8.0	1.6	0.3	0.2	0.1	...	...	0.1	1,922	2,263	2,631	2,271	.151	.162	.313
Transportation equipment	27	100.0	0.4	0.7	3.3	9.9	26.7	36.9	18.1	2.4	1.2	0.2	...	...	0.1	...	2,200	2,622	2,961	2,589	.161	.129	.290
Service Workers																							
Private household workers	527	100.0	28.3	37.8	19.0	10.3	3.1	0.7	0.3	0.1	0.1	0.1	0.1	...	...	0.1	442	787	1,234	911	.439	.568	1.007
Barbers, beauticians, & manicurists	47	100.0	2.8	9.6	19.0	28.4	20.3	9.6	4.8	2.1	1.3	0.4	1.2	0.3	0.1	...	1,332	1,827	2,374	1,957	.272	.299	.571
Charwomen, janitors, and porters	73	100.0	10.0	18.9	27.8	21.6	15.5	4.0	1.5	0.4	0.1	0.1	...	...	...	...	897	1,380	1,924	1,440	.350	.394	.744
Cooks, exc. private household	88	100.0	5.7	22.7	27.8	24.5	14.9	5.0	1.8	0.8	0.6	0.6	0.2	...	...	0.3	925	1,376	1,911	1,489	.328	.388	.716
Housek'prs, stewards, exc. pr. hshld.	46	100.0	3.4	14.9	26.1	24.5	19.3	7.0	3.6	0.8	0.1	0.1	0.2	0.1	...	0.1	1,128	1,614	2,158	1,693	.302	.336	.638
Practical nurses and midwives	42	100.0	6.7	15.7	27.5	21.7	18.3	5.9	2.7	0.8	0.4	...	...	...	...	...	1,047	1,502	2,093	1,647	.303	.393	.696
Waitresses, bartenders, counter wkrs.	194	100.0	5.3	24.6	32.4	21.7	10.6	3.2	1.4	0.3	0.1	0.1	0.1	...	...	...	900	1,310	1,793	1,386	.313	.368	.681
Service wkrs., exc. pr. hshld.(n.e.c.)	135	100.0	6.5	27.9	32.5	21.2	8.6	2.2	0.7	0.1	0.1	...	...	...	...	...	832	1,240	1,691	1,288	.330	.363	.693

Source: Unpublished data of the Bureau of the Census.   See Appendix A for description of method used to estimate arithmetic means.

TABLE C–3.—PERCENT DISTRIBUTION OF EXPERIENCED PERSONS IN THE LABOR FORCE (EXCEPT PERSONS ON EMERGENCY WORK) IN SELECTED OCCUPATIONS, BY WAGE OR SALARY INCOME IN 1939, BY SEX, FOR THE UNITED STATES

Occupation and sex	Number reporting $100 or more (thousands)	Percent distribution														Quartiles			Arithmetic mean (dollars)	$1-\frac{Q_1}{Q_2}$	$\frac{Q_3}{Q_2}-1$	$\frac{Q_3-Q_1}{Q_2}$
		Total	$100 to $199	$200 to $399	$400 to $599	$600 to $799	$800 to $999	$1000 to $1199	$1200 to $1399	$1400 to $1599	$1600 to $1999	$2000 to $2499	$2500 to $2999	$3000 to $4999	$5000 and over	Q_1 (dollars)	Q_2 (median; dollars)	Q_3 (dollars)				
MALE, EXPERIENCED CIVILIAN LABOR FORCE																						
Prof'l, Techn'l, Kindred Wkrs.																						
Artists and art teachers	25	100.0	2.0	4.6	5.2	6.8	7.1	8.5	8.0	7.8	10.5	12.9	8.0	12.6	5.8	980	1,600	2,600	2,194	.388	.625	1.013
Authors, editors, and reporters	42	100.0	1.1	3.0	3.2	4.2	4.6	5.7	7.1	7.0	9.9	14.4	10.0	18.3	11.6	1,290	2,146	3,525	2,911	.399	.642	1.041
Chemists	53	100.0	0.7	2.4	2.4	3.6	3.6	5.2	7.1	9.5	17.4	16.3	16.5	6.1		1,404	1,976	2,859	2,517	.290	.446	.736
Clergymen	107	100.0	1.8	5.7	7.3	11.4	9.6	9.7	14.0	9.7	16.7	17.4	3.4	5.6	1.4	779	1,264	1,804	1,512	.384	.426	.810
Coll. pres., prof'rs, instr's (n.e.c.)	51	100.0	0.4	1.4	2.2	2.8	2.5	2.6	3.1	3.5	8.5	14.9	12.6	32.5	12.8	1,906	2,821	4,262	3,466	.325	.510	.835
Designers and draftsmen	90	100.0	1.0	2.5	2.8	3.9	2.5	6.7	3.6	10.1	18.2	20.8	10.1	8.9		1,267	1,802	2,385	1,971	.297	.323	.620
Engineers, civil	77	100.0	0.2	0.8	1.1	1.4	1.8	2.1	3.5	4.8	13.4	23.4	14.5	26.5	6.3	1,878	2,447	3,604	2,968	.233	.472	.705
Engineers, electrical	51	100.0	0.3	0.9	1.2	1.4	1.5	2.1	3.0	4.9	12.1	19.3	13.1	30.6	10.3	1,904	2,649	4,033	3,313	.282	.522	.804
Engineers, mechanical	76	100.0	0.3	1.0	1.3	1.7	1.7	1.9	3.0	4.6	10.9	19.3	13.2	29.0	12.1	1,949	2,663	4,110	3,409	.269	.543	.812
Musicians and music teachers	59	100.0	4.1	10.4	11.1	11.5	10.4	9.8	8.8	6.9	7.3	7.1	3.5	5.8	3.2	589	1,051	1,710	1,500	.440	.626	1.066
Pharmacists	45	100.0	0.8	2.3	3.1	5.0	5.9	7.3	12.4	14.1	22.7	16.2	5.0	3.9	1.2	1,210	1,587	2,043	1,739	.238	.287	.525
Social, welfare, and recreation wkrs.	25	100.0	1.1	2.9	3.4	4.7	5.7	8.2	11.8	12.4	18.1	14.4	5.4	9.2	2.7	1,176	1,597	2,233	1,950	.264	.398	.662
Sports instr's, athletes, entertainers	28	100.0	2.9	8.2	9.3	10.3	9.1	8.9	9.6	7.3	9.7	9.6	5.0	6.8	3.1	689	1,227	1,988	1,641	.439	.619	1.058
Teachers (n.e.c.)	246	100.0	0.7	3.0	5.6	6.9	10.5	9.0	9.5	8.5	14.4	13.0	7.3	10.0	1.5	968	1,513	2,265	1,818	.361	.497	.858
Salaried Managers and Officials																						
Conductors, railroad	46	100.0	0.1	0.4	0.5	0.7	1.1	1.8	2.8	4.2	13.3	32.8	25.0	17.2	0.1	2,002	2,383	2,846	2,500	.160	.194	.354
Postmasters, and misc. govt. officials	192	100.0	0.9	2.3	2.4	3.5	3.9	3.9	6.4	7.2	15.7	19.7	10.8	17.3	6.2	1,447	2,096	2,921	2,587	.310	.393	.703
Managers and officials:																						
Manufacturing	268	100.0	0.2	0.8	1.0	1.4	1.6	2.5	4.1	5.0	8.7	14.1	9.5	23.4	27.7	1,986	3,094	5,780	4,352	.359	.868	1.227
Trans., commun., & other pub. util.	108	100.0	0.2	0.6	0.7	1.2	1.2	2.2	3.0	5.0	11.6	18.1	12.1	29.3	12.7	1,903	2,669	4,160	3,432	.287	.558	.845
Wholesale trade	104	100.0	0.9	2.0	2.4	3.1	3.6	4.8	7.2	6.9	10.9	14.5	8.0	17.7	18.0	1,429	2,283	4,209	3,394	.375	.843	1.218
Eating and drinking places	45	100.0	1.8	5.8	7.3	9.0	8.6	11.5	13.1	10.3	9.8	9.8	4.5	5.9	3.2	826	1,292	1,910	1,669	.361	.478	.839
Retail trade, exc. eating & drinking	372	100.0	0.2	3.0	4.0	5.5	5.8	8.2	11.8	10.9	14.6	13.8	6.3	8.9	6.1	1,139	1,596	2,370	2,180	.287	.484	.771
Finance, insur., and real estate	136	100.0	0.2	0.6	0.6	1.5	1.5	2.1	4.0	4.6	9.8	13.2	9.2	25.1	25.2	1,984	3,016	5,032	4,227	.343	.668	1.011
Business and repair services	27	100.0	0.8	2.0	3.0	4.6	5.0	7.6	11.5	11.0	14.6	15.4	6.8	10.0	7.8	1,235	1,723	2,484	2,396	.284	.441	.725
Personal services	32	100.0	1.1	3.6	4.8	6.6	6.2	7.7	10.6	9.0	11.8	13.1	6.9	10.5	8.1	1,070	1,614	2,536	2,342	.337	.571	.908
Clerical, Sales, and Kindred Workers																						
Baggagemen, exp. mess., rwy. mail clk.	28	100.0	0.4	1.1	1.1	1.6	2.1	2.8	5.5	6.7	12.4	40.9	23.0	2.5	0.1	1,719	2,199	2,509	2,127	.219	.140	.359
Bookk'prs, accts., cashs., ticket agts.	432	100.0	1.1	2.9	3.2	5.0	6.7	7.8	11.1	10.9	17.3	15.7	6.9	9.0	2.4	1,154	1,628	2,283	1,946	.292	.402	.694
Mail carriers	117	100.0	1.1	3.4	2.8	3.0	2.8	3.0	4.6	4.4	15.8	52.6	4.3	0.2	0.1	1,595	2,087	2,324	1,918	.236	.113	.349
Messengers, except express	57	100.0	13.1	20.9	19.3	20.9	9.4	5.5	4.6	2.5	1.6	0.7	0.2	0.1	...	314	566	817	636	.446	.443	.889
Shipping and receiving clerks	206	100.0	2.2	5.6	6.4	11.3	13.9	17.3	16.7	12.3	9.8	3.4	0.6	0.3		791	1,123	1,426	1,130	.296	.270	.566
Stenographers, typists, and secys.	67	100.0	2.4	5.3	4.9	7.6	9.4	9.7	12.5	10.8	13.5	9.7	4.0	6.9	3.3	902	1,371	1,967	1,757	.343	.434	.777

TABLE C-3.—PERCENT DISTRIBUTION OF EXPERIENCED PERSONS IN THE LABOR FORCE (EXCEPT PERSONS ON EMERGENCY WORK) IN SELECTED OCCUPATIONS, BY WAGE OR SALARY INCOME IN 1939, BY SEX, FOR THE UNITED STATES—Cont.

Occupation and sex	Number reporting $100 or more (thousands)	Total	Percent distribution													Quartiles				$1-\frac{Q_1}{Q_2}$	$\frac{Q_3}{Q_2}-1$	$\frac{Q_3-Q_1}{Q_2}$
			$100 to $199	$200 to $399	$400 to $599	$600 to $799	$800 to $999	$1000 to $1199	$1200 to $1399	$1400 to $1599	$1600 to $1999	$2000 to $2499	$2500 to $2999	$3000 to $4999	$5000 and over	Q_1 (dollars)	Q_2 (median; dollars)	Q_3 (dollars)	Arithmetic mean (dollars)			
MALE.--Con.																						
Clerical, Sales, & Kind. Wkrs.--Con.																						
Telegraph operators	32	100.0	0.7	1.9	2.1	3.0	4.0	4.6	6.8	10.0	35.9	24.0	4.9	2.1	0.1	1,438	1,788	2,125	1,777	.196	.188	.384
Newsboys	27	100.0	42.7	28.6	9.2	6.4	3.9	2.5	2.1	1.4	1.4	1.0	0.4	0.3	0.1	159	251	480	431	.369	.913	1.282
Insurance agents and brokers	174	100.0	1.0	2.8	3.7	4.8	5.1	6.5	8.4	8.6	11.9	17.2	11.1	14.0	4.7	1,226	1,906	2,725	2,307	.357	.429	.786
Real estate agents and brokers	42	100.0	1.7	4.9	6.3	6.8	8.9	8.9	9.6	8.6	9.5	12.3	6.1	10.5	7.7	949	1,509	2,472	2,240	.372	.637	1.009
Salesmen and sales clerks (n.e.c.)	1,580	100.0	2.9	6.5	7.3	10.2	9.8	10.6	11.5	8.6	10.0	9.5	4.4	6.1	2.3	763	1,247	1,888	1,587	.389	.514	.903
Craftsmen, Foremen, & Kindred Wkrs.																						
Bakers	104	100.0	1.9	5.2	6.7	10.0	11.1	14.4	15.3	14.2	12.4	6.6	1.4	0.7	0.2	822	1,209	1,546	1,248	.321	.278	.599
Blacksmiths, forgemen, and hammermen	51	100.0	3.6	9.9	9.6	10.2	9.7	11.0	12.4	11.3	13.8	6.2	1.5	0.8		637	1,127	1,552	1,164	.435	.376	.811
Boilermakers	29	100.0	1.3	3.9	5.2	6.5	7.4	9.1	11.9	13.7	23.2	13.9	2.6	1.2	0.1	1,015	1,469	1,876	1,471	.309	.277	.586
Cabinetmakers and patternmakers	74	100.0	1.8	5.1	6.8	14.0	11.0	12.1	12.7	11.5	14.3	6.1	2.7	0.9	0.1	816	1,244	1,701	1,310	.344	.367	.711
Carpenters	526	100.0	3.9	11.8	13.2	14.0	12.4	10.6	9.7	8.3	9.0	5.1	1.3	0.7	0.1	541	915	1,388	1,034	.409	.517	.926
Compositors and typesetters	138	100.0	1.4	3.6	4.5	6.7	7.5	9.5	10.5	10.0	14.0	18.3	9.1	4.5	0.5	1,027	1,526	2,199	1,680	.327	.441	.768
Electricians	182	100.0	1.3	3.9	4.8	6.1	6.9	8.4	10.1	11.9	19.6	16.4	5.7	3.8	0.2	1,048	1,529	2,037	1,604	.316	.331	.647
Foremen (n.e.c.):																						
Construction	51	100.0	1.1	4.0	6.1	8.2	9.4	10.0	13.1	11.8	16.3	12.0	4.6	3.3	0.2	919	1,371	1,877	1,483	.330	.369	.699
Manufacturing	262	100.0	0.2	0.9	1.5	2.7	4.0	6.3	9.3	12.0	20.3	22.5	10.9	8.7	0.6	1,402	1,858	2,396	2,009	.246	.289	.535
Trans., commun., & other pub. util.	92	100.0	0.2	0.5	0.7	2.3	2.3	3.6	6.8	14.2	25.7	20.4	11.1	12.6	0.3	1,532	1,914	2,478	2,135	.200	.294	.494
Inspectors (n.e.c.)	67	100.0	0.5	1.5	1.9	2.8	3.7	4.6	7.9	11.8	31.6	23.3	6.2	3.8	0.3	1,436	1,794	2,187	1,841	.200	.219	.419
Linemen & servicemen, t'graph, etc.	104	100.0	0.8	2.4	2.7	3.3	4.2	5.4	8.8	9.9	17.8	23.2	14.1	7.3	0.1	1,341	1,881	2,425	1,936	.288	.289	.577
Locomotive engineers	69	100.0	0.2	0.7	0.9	1.7	1.7	2.5	3.4	8.9	11.1	23.3	22.7	27.3	0.3	1,960	2,509	3,198	2,639	.219	.274	.493
Locomotive firemen	46	100.0	0.9	3.4	4.7	6.0	6.5	7.7	8.9	8.7	19.1	22.2	9.6	2.5		1,091	1,667	2,205	1,674	.346	.322	.668
Machinists, millwrights, & toolmakers	602	100.0	1.1	3.3	4.2	6.2	7.8	10.8	13.6	14.8	20.9	13.2	2.5	1.1	0.1	1,044	1,441	1,853	1,470	.275	.286	.561
Masons, tile setters, & stone cutters	107	100.0	2.8	9.0	11.1	12.5	10.8	10.9	10.1	9.2	10.5	2.9	0.1			634	1,050	1,546	1,170	.397	.472	.869
Mechanics & repairmen, & loom fixers	786	100.0	2.1	6.2	7.4	11.4	10.9	15.2	15.2	12.4	11.6	4.6	1.0	0.9	0.1	784	1,215	1,578	1,244	.355	.298	.653
Molders, metal	78	100.0	1.7	5.8	7.9	10.7	11.4	13.0	14.4	13.0	11.2	3.2	0.4	0.3		768	1,134	1,477	1,151	.323	.302	.625
Painters (const.), paperhgrs., glaziers	279	100.0	4.1	12.5	14.4	15.3	13.1	11.1	9.5	7.6	8.5	3.9	0.4	0.8		518	860	1,298	1,073	.397	.509	.906
Plasterers and cement finishers	52	100.0	2.9	10.5	14.3	14.3	12.6	10.9	10.1	8.5	9.5	3.9				581	951	1,421	1,073	.389	.494	.883
Plumbers and pipe fitters	146	100.0	1.7	5.5	6.9	8.9	8.9	10.0	11.8	12.3	16.7	11.5	3.8	2.1	0.2	845	1,337	1,816	1,410	.357	.369	.726
Print. craft, exc. compos. & typeset.	61	100.0	0.8	2.2	2.9	4.0	5.3	7.4	8.8	8.8	13.5	19.1	13.0	13.0	1.0	1,242	1,879	2,570	2,062	.339	.368	.707
Rollers and roll hands, metal	28	100.0	0.4	4.6	4.9	4.0	7.6	11.7	15.1	13.0	18.1	9.1	5.4	1.0		979	1,372	1,865	1,558	.359	.287	.646
Roofers and sheet metal workers	96	100.0	2.1	6.7	10.7	7.6	8.4	11.7	14.4	13.0	15.1	9.1	2.5	0.4	0.1	742	1,180	1,625	1,249	.372	.376	.748
Shoemakers & repairers, exc. factory	21	100.0	4.9	13.4	15.8	17.7	13.0	13.9	5.9	3.2	1.6	0.4	0.2	0.2		485	780	1,147	875	.379	.470	.849
Stat. engineers, cranemen, hoistmen	296	100.0	0.9	3.0	4.1	6.2	7.5	9.4	13.3	14.0	22.4	11.2	3.2	2.9	0.3	1,070	1,480	1,896	1,556	.277	.281	.558
Structural metal workers	31	100.0	1.9	5.8	4.1	6.2	9.9	10.7	11.4	11.2	13.9	11.0	3.9	2.7	0.1	796	1,274	1,790	1,369	.376	.405	.781
Tailors and furriers	74	100.0	1.8	6.5	9.6	13.1	12.3	13.4	12.9	10.4	9.7	6.1	2.2	1.6	0.3	708	1,100	1,504	1,207	.356	.367	.723

TABLE C-3.—PERCENT DISTRIBUTION OF EXPERIENCED PERSONS IN THE LABOR FORCE (EXCEPT PERSONS ON EMERGENCY WORK) IN SELECTED OCCUPATIONS, BY WAGE OR SALARY INCOME IN 1939, BY SEX, FOR THE UNITED STATES—Cont.

Occupation and sex	Number reporting $100 or more (thousands)	Total	$100 to $199	$200 to $399	$400 to $599	$600 to $799	$800 to $999	$1000 to $1199	$1200 to $1399	$1400 to $1599	$1600 to $1999	$2000 to $2499	$2500 to $2999	$3000 to $4999	$5000 and over	Q_1 (dollars)	Q_2 (median; dollars)	Q_3 (dollars)	Arithmetic mean (dollars)	$1-\frac{Q_1}{Q_2}$	$\frac{Q_3}{Q_2}-1$	$\frac{Q_3-Q_1}{Q_2}$
MALE--Con.																						
Operatives and Kindred Workers																						
Apprentices..........	73	100.0	9.0	17.6	15.4	17.9	14.3	11.5	7.4	3.8	2.3	0.5	0.1	0.1	...	382	689	1,014	736	.447	.470	.917
Attendants, auto service and parking..	199	100.0	7.0	15.6	15.6	18.8	14.4	11.8	9.2	4.2	2.3	0.7	0.2	0.1	...	431	726	1,061	776	.407	.462	.869
Brakemen and switchmen, railroad...	110	100.0	0.8	2.6	3.8	4.9	5.7	6.6	8.1	9.2	22.0	27.0	8.0	1.2	0.1	1,215	1,751	2,209	1,710	.307	.261	.568
Drivers, bus, taxi, & del men	1,392	100.0	4.0	10.8	11.5	12.2	11.4	11.3	11.3	9.2	9.9	5.3	1.2	0.2	0.1	577	975	1,422	1,059	.409	.457	.866
Stationary firemen........	117	100.0	2.0	6.5	8.9	12.2	11.3	12.9	15.4	9.2	13.2	4.2	0.8	0.3	...	725	1,141	1,494	1,147	.366	.309	.675
Mine operatives & laborers (n.e.c.)...	679	100.0	3.8	12.0	13.7	16.3	16.3	13.2	13.1	6.1	6.1	0.4	0.1	0.1	...	534	859	1,206	921	.378	.404	.782
Motormen, rwy., mine, factory, etc...	54	100.0	0.5	1.7	2.9	5.1	7.7	10.4	13.1	16.2	29.7	11.2	0.5	0.3	0.1	1,137	1,506	1,834	1,494	.246	.217	.463
Painters, exc. constr. & maintenance..	83	100.0	2.3	7.1	9.6	14.2	13.7	14.7	14.7	11.2	9.4	2.8	0.2	0.2	...	685	1,042	1,386	1,066	.344	.330	.674
Sailors and deck hands........	40	100.0	3.8	12.0	16.4	19.5	16.3	10.4	7.5	4.7	5.7	2.1	0.7	0.2	...	512	783	1,135	904	.346	.449	.795
Welders and flame-cutters....	122	100.0	1.4	4.4	5.7	7.9	9.3	11.9	14.0	14.4	18.6	9.7	1.8	0.7	0.1	920	1,334	1,729	1,351	.311	.295	.606
Operatives & kindred workers (n.e.c.):																						
Food and kindred products........	205	100.0	3.0	7.9	8.9	11.4	11.9	14.9	15.6	11.0	10.1	4.1	0.7	0.3	0.2	691	1,093	1,425	1,119	.368	.304	.672
Knitting mills.........	59	100.0	2.4	8.1	12.1	18.3	13.9	11.6	13.9	8.1	9.6	5.2	1.2	0.3	0.4	626	931	1,385	1,046	.328	.487	.815
Text. mill prod., exc. knit. mills	359	100.0	2.8	9.9	17.3	30.2	18.2	10.8	5.2	2.8	1.7	0.6	0.2	0.2	...	542	732	963	782	.260	.314	.574
Apparel & other fabric text. prod..	139	100.0	2.7	8.7	12.5	16.4	13.3	12.6	10.3	8.0	7.6	5.2	1.8	0.9	0.1	613	946	1,371	1,068	.352	.449	.801
Furniture, and lumber and wood prod	151	100.0	3.8	12.1	15.3	19.8	15.4	13.1	9.8	5.6	3.7	1.1	0.2	0.1	...	519	790	1,131	852	.344	.432	.776
Paper, paper prod., and printing....	137	100.0	2.2	5.5	6.9	10.6	14.3	18.7	16.0	10.4	8.8	4.6	1.4	0.6	0.1	796	1,112	1,415	1,160	.285	.272	.557
Chemicals & petrol., & coal prod....	118	100.0	1.6	4.7	5.1	6.6	8.4	12.3	15.6	15.6	19.3	9.0	1.2	0.6	0.1	967	1,344	1,704	1,345	.281	.267	.548
Rubber products........	58	100.0	1.4	4.5	6.0	8.5	11.1	13.9	14.7	13.0	17.5	8.6	0.7	0.2	0.1	883	1,263	1,643	1,289	.301	.301	.602
Footwear industries, exc. rubber....	112	100.0	2.9	9.9	14.8	21.0	19.5	14.9	8.9	4.7	2.6	0.7	0.5	0.3	0.2	565	814	1,093	847	.307	.341	.648
Leather & leath. prod.,exc. footwear	47	100.0	2.5	7.6	10.3	14.5	14.5	17.9	15.1	8.9	5.5	1.7	0.5	0.3	...	664	999	1,293	1,015	.336	.294	.630
Stone, clay, and glass products....	90	100.0	2.0	6.3	8.7	12.1	14.2	16.8	15.0	10.0	9.1	4.0	1.1	0.6	0.1	732	1,080	1,399	1,114	.325	.295	.617
Iron & steel,& not spec. metal ind.	272	100.0	2.0	6.6	7.8	10.4	12.6	15.9	16.1	12.2	10.5	4.2	1.1	0.6	0.1	765	1,133	1,459	1,162	.325	.287	.612
Nonferrous metals & their products..	54	100.0	2.5	6.9	7.9	10.5	12.9	16.9	17.3	12.7	8.2	3.0	0.7	0.4	0.1	747	1,110	1,402	1,110	.328	.262	.590
Machinery........	200	100.0	2.5	6.7	7.4	9.7	14.3	14.9	15.3	13.4	12.3	4.6	1.0	0.4	0.1	768	1,157	1,497	1,177	.337	.293	.630
Motor vehicles & mtr. vehicle equip.	179	100.0	1.4	4.6	5.8	8.0	10.0	14.2	14.2	18.9	14.9	2.8	0.5	0.2	...	904	1,264	1,530	1,227	.285	.210	.495
Trans. equip., exc. motor vehicle...	57	100.0	3.2	8.6	10.1	11.5	11.6	12.8	13.5	11.9	10.1	4.9	1.1	0.5	0.1	654	1,078	1,462	1,112	.394	.356	.750
Service Workers																						
Private household workers........	126	100.0	18.0	29.2	18.9	14.9	8.0	4.0	3.6	1.6	1.2	0.4	0.1	0.1	...	248	430	719	538	.423	.674	1.097
Firemen, fire protection........	77	100.0	0.2	0.5	0.7	0.7	1.3	2.0	4.9	7.7	27.1	34.3	10.1	10.0	0.4	1,700	2,069	2,433	2,198	.178	.176	.354
Guards and watchmen........	214	100.0	2.5	7.0	8.5	13.7	15.6	15.6	15.9	9.6	6.5	3.1	0.5	0.2	...	702	1,042	1,360	1,065	.327	.304	.631
Policemen, sheriffs, and marshalls..	167	100.0	0.6	1.7	2.7	3.0	3.4	4.0	7.6	8.3	20.9	27.9	9.4	10.9	0.4	1,465	1,971	2,421	2,069	.257	.228	.485
Barbers, beauticians, & manicurists.	93	100.0	2.7	7.7	11.4	17.6	15.3	16.8	13.3	7.0	4.6	2.2	0.7	0.5	0.2	636	939	1,253	997	.322	.334	.656
Charmen, janitors, and porters......	486	100.0	5.1	13.5	15.5	18.2	13.2	11.7	11.9	5.6	3.6	1.2	0.7	0.2	...	483	775	1,162	847	.378	.500	.878
Cooks, exc. private household.......	170	100.0	4.0	12.7	15.8	17.6	14.0	11.8	9.9	6.1	4.9	2.2	0.5	0.4	0.1	505	799	1,185	899	.368	.482	.850

TABLE C–3.—PERCENT DISTRIBUTION OF EXPERIENCED PERSONS IN THE LABOR FORCE (EXCEPT PERSONS ON EMERGENCY WORK) IN SELECTED OCCUPATIONS, BY WAGE OR SALARY INCOME IN 1939, BY SEX, FOR THE UNITED STATES—Cont.

Occupation and sex	Number reporting $100 or more (thousands)	Total	$100 to $199	$200 to $399	$400 to $599	$600 to $799	$800 to $999	$1000 to $1199	$1200 to $1399	$1400 to $1599	$1600 to $1999	$2000 to $2499	$2500 to $2999	$3000 to $4999	$5000 and over	Q_1 (dollars)	Q_2 (median; dollars)	Q_3 (dollars)	Arithmetic mean (dollars)	$1-\frac{Q_1}{Q_2}$	$\frac{Q_3-Q_2}{Q_2}$	$\frac{Q_3-Q_1}{Q_2}$
MALE—Con.																						
Service Workers—Con.																						
Elevator operators	65	100.0	2.3	6.3	8.5	15.8	15.9	19.6	18.0	8.3	4.3	0.8	0.1	0.1	...	700	1,012	1,273	995	.309	.257	.566
Waiters, bartenders, & counter wkrs.	272	100.0	5.1	13.9	15.6	17.8	13.8	12.3	10.1	6.1	3.6	1.2	0.3	0.2	0.1	477	773	1,143	851	.384	.478	.862
Service wkrs., exc. pr. hshld.(n.e.c.)	138	100.0	9.2	22.0	21.4	21.6	12.8	7.2	3.4	1.3	0.7	0.2	0.1	...	...	344	576	813	616	.404	.411	.815
Laborers, Except Farm and Mine																						
Fishermen and oystermen	26	100.0	10.1	26.8	19.4	12.9	9.3	6.5	4.9	3.9	2.8	2.1	0.7	0.6	0.1	311	535	925	710	.419	.728	1.147
Longshoremen and stevedores	68	100.0	3.4	12.2	13.8	14.9	12.3	11.2	9.7	7.3	8.4	5.2	0.9	0.5	0.1	536	893	1,348	1,006	.400	.510	.910
Lumbermen, raftsmen, & woodchoppers	126	100.0	13.7	32.5	21.6	13.2	7.2	4.4	3.2	2.0	1.6	0.5	0.1	...	...	270	435	709	550	.381	.629	1.010
Laborers (n.e.c.):																						
Manufacturing industries:																						
Food and kindred products	146	100.0	5.6	14.9	14.3	14.3	12.5	14.3	13.2	6.1	3.9	0.8	0.1	0.1	...	463	814	1,187	853	.432	.458	.890
Textiles, text. prod., & apparel	76	100.0	5.2	15.1	22.5	28.2	13.9	8.4	4.0	1.7	0.7	0.2	...	...	...	442	651	858	675	.322	.317	.639
Furniture, and lumber & wood prod.	254	100.0	8.9	27.2	26.0	18.9	7.9	5.1	3.6	1.4	0.8	0.3	...	...	...	318	507	737	573	.372	.452	.824
Paper, paper prod., & printing.	56	100.0	4.0	10.5	12.3	16.2	18.1	19.1	11.8	4.8	2.3	0.6	0.2	0.1	...	571	877	1,146	871	.350	.305	.655
Chemicals & petrol., & coal prod.	108	100.0	4.9	12.5	16.0	12.6	11.4	15.7	13.3	9.8	6.3	1.5	0.1	0.1	...	481	882	1,287	912	.456	.458	.914
Stone, clay, and glass products	93	100.0	3.8	12.5	16.0	19.0	17.1	15.4	9.6	3.8	2.0	0.5	0.2	0.1	...	509	786	1,084	815	.353	.378	.731
Iron & steel & not spec.metal ind.	277	100.0	3.3	8.9	12.0	14.2	15.1	16.9	14.8	6.9	4.2	1.0	0.2	0.2	...	573	922	1,230	924	.379	.333	.712
Nonferrous metals and their prod.	40	100.0	3.2	8.3	11.3	11.1	19.3	19.7	9.6	3.8	3.8	0.8	0.2	0.2	...	659	1,035	1,292	990	.363	.248	.611
Machinery	66	100.0	3.8	10.2	13.6	13.6	15.5	17.0	13.9	8.2	4.9	1.2	0.2	0.3	...	595	943	1,252	943	.370	.327	.697
Motor vehicles & mtr. veh. equip.	57	100.0	2.4	8.9	9.3	11.2	12.1	16.1	16.1	14.5	10.1	1.5	0.3	0.1	...	691	1,095	1,419	1,074	.369	.296	.665
Trans. equipment, exc. motor veh.	29	100.0	4.5	13.5	14.1	15.5	14.0	13.8	13.6	6.8	3.1	0.9	0.3	0.1	...	499	834	1,194	866	.402	.431	.833
Nonmanufacturing industries:																						
Construction	617	100.0	9.5	25.3	21.7	16.6	10.1	6.8	4.8	2.7	1.6	0.6	0.2	0.1	...	323	540	838	635	.403	.550	.953
Railroads & rwy. express service	228	100.0	3.5	10.7	14.4	20.6	21.2	14.5	8.6	3.7	2.0	0.6	0.1	0.1	...	550	808	1,063	827	.319	.316	.635
Transportation, exc. railroad	87	100.0	7.5	18.5	15.4	14.4	10.6	10.0	9.9	6.8	5.6	0.9	0.1	0.1	...	389	719	1,172	811	.460	.629	1.089
Telecomm. & util. & sanitary serv.	88	100.0	3.5	9.8	11.1	12.8	11.1	12.2	14.3	11.3	11.5	1.9	0.4	0.2	...	609	1,028	1,404	1,038	.408	.365	.773
Wholesale and retail trade	199	100.0	8.3	19.0	17.8	17.8	12.2	9.7	7.3	4.4	2.7	0.6	0.1	0.2	0.1	376	655	998	729	.427	.523	.950
FEMALE, EXPERIENCED CIVILIAN LABOR FORCE																						
Profess'l, Techn'l, Kindred Wkrs.																						
Librarians	31	100.0	4.1	7.8	7.4	9.3	9.7	9.7	13.4	10.8	14.4	8.3	3.1	2.0	0.1	723	1,230	1,678	1,282	.413	.364	.777
Musicians and music teachers	30	100.0	10.0	19.9	15.5	12.3	10.9	8.5	6.5	4.5	4.7	3.6	1.6	1.4	0.5	351	675	1,151	893	.481	.704	1.185
Social, welfare, and recreation wkrs.	43	100.0	1.6	4.4	5.1	6.3	8.3	11.3	16.4	14.0	18.4	9.0	2.4	2.6	0.3	983	1,359	1,765	1,438	.277	.299	.576
Teachers (n.e.c.)	716	100.0	1.7	10.2	15.3	12.2	9.8	9.0	16.4	7.4	14.0	8.6	3.3	4.0	0.1	679	1,047	1,644	1,271	.352	.570	.922
Nurses, professional & student prof.	237	100.0	5.1	9.4	9.9	14.9	18.8	12.5	11.5	6.6	8.0	2.5	0.5	0.3	0.1	608	914	1,277	980	.335	.396	.731

TABLE C-3.—PERCENT DISTRIBUTION OF EXPERIENCED PERSONS IN THE LABOR FORCE (EXCEPT PERSONS ON EMERGENCY WORK) IN SELECTED OCCUPATIONS, BY WAGE OR SALARY INCOME IN 1939, BY SEX, FOR THE UNITED STATES—Cont.

Occupation and sex	Number reporting $100 or more (thousands)	Total	$100 to $199	$200 to $399	$400 to $599	$600 to $799	$800 to $999	$1000 to $1199	$1200 to $1399	$1400 to $1599	$1600 to $1999	$2000 to $2499	$2500 to $2999	$3000 to $4999	$5000 and over	Q_1 (dollars)	Q_2 (median) (dollars)	Q_3 (dollars)	Arithmetic mean (dollars)	$1-\frac{Q_1}{Q_2}$	$\frac{Q_3}{Q_2}-1$	$\frac{Q_3-Q_1}{Q_2}$
FEMALE—Con.																						
Clerical, Sales, and Kindred Workers																						
Book'prs, accts., cashs., ticket agts.	415	100.0	3.6	7.8	9.6	18.5	18.3	15.6	12.3	6.6	4.9	1.9	0.5	0.3	0.1	643	915	1,226	967	.297	.340	.637
Office machine operators	51	100.0	2.8	5.8	6.8	10.7	20.8	22.3	18.0	9.0	4.1	0.5	0.1	0.4	...	798	1,037	1,276	1,015	.231	.230	.461
Stenographers, typists, and secys.	954	100.0	3.3	5.9	5.8	13.6	18.0	16.5	14.9	9.2	7.4	2.5	0.6	0.4	0.1	719	1,018	1,334	1,061	.294	.310	.604
Telephone operators	181	100.0	3.6	8.0	9.3	16.2	18.0	18.0	14.1	7.2	4.0	1.1	0.2	0.1	0.1	651	943	1,227	947	.311	.300	.611
Saleswomen and sales clerks (n.e.c.)	602	100.0	10.3	17.0	18.2	27.2	14.7	6.7	3.0	1.2	0.9	0.4	0.1	0.2	0.1	373	633	831	656	.411	.312	.723
Operatives and Kindred Workers																						
Dressmakers & seamstr., exc. factory	68	100.0	11.5	21.5	19.3	21.8	12.6	6.9	3.4	1.4	0.8	0.4	0.1	0.1	0.1	326	576	814	625	.435	.413	.848
Operatives & kindred wkrs. (n.e.c.):																						
Food and kindred products	112	100.0	11.7	24.3	19.9	22.0	13.9	6.1	1.3	0.4	0.2	0.1	...	...	...	309	541	774	565	.428	.430	.858
Tobacco manufactures	54	100.0	5.3	20.4	30.8	26.0	11.5	3.9	1.7	0.3	0.2	0.1	...	...	...	393	558	742	580	.296	.330	.626
Knitting mills	113	100.0	5.0	17.9	26.0	30.2	13.5	5.4	1.4	0.4	0.2	...	...	...	...	416	607	773	611	.315	.272	.587
Textile mill prod., exc. knit. mills	303	100.0	6.2	19.1	26.9	33.1	10.6	3.0	0.7	0.3	0.1	...	...	...	...	397	584	738	577	.321	.263	.584
Apparel & other fabric text. prod.	445	100.0	7.1	23.7	28.9	23.9	9.0	4.3	1.7	0.8	0.4	0.1	...	...	...	351	533	728	565	.342	.366	.708
Furniture, and lumber and wood prod.	23	100.0	7.3	19.4	22.8	26.5	14.4	4.2	2.2	0.6	0.6	0.1	...	...	...	382	604	792	612	.367	.312	.679
Paper, paper prod., and printing	76	100.0	6.1	15.1	19.2	26.5	19.2	7.1	2.6	0.9	0.6	0.1	...	...	...	440	665	851	659	.339	.280	.619
Chemicals & petrol., & coal prod.	32	100.0	5.7	12.6	13.2	24.4	25.9	12.3	3.5	1.5	0.8	0.6	...	...	...	502	752	947	736	.333	.260	.593
Footwear industries, exc. rubber	89	100.0	6.3	13.1	30.5	26.5	9.8	4.0	3.4	0.9	0.1	...	...	...	...	369	542	722	557	.319	.332	.651
Leather & leath. prod.,exc. footwear	25	100.0	8.4	24.1	27.0	24.4	10.3	4.0	1.1	0.3	0.1	0.1	...	...	...	338	530	727	551	.363	.371	.734
Stone, clay, and glass products	24	100.0	6.1	17.6	14.2	29.9	19.9	9.0	2.1	0.7	0.5	...	...	...	...	455	674	873	674	.334	.281	.615
Metal industries and machinery	146	100.0	6.0	13.9	15.8	24.9	20.2	13.4	3.9	1.3	0.8	0.1	...	0.1	...	465	715	943	715	.351	.318	.669
Transportation equipment	28	100.0	4.2	12.5	14.2	18.3	22.1	18.6	7.1	2.0	0.8	0.2	...	...	...	517	807	1,040	788	.360	.287	.647
Service Workers																						
Private household workers	1,480	100.0	31.8	37.8	17.3	8.7	3.0	0.8	0.3	0.1	0.1	...	...	...	...	179	296	462	352	.398	.560	.958
Barbers, beauticians, & manicurists	116	100.0	7.0	15.6	18.9	23.3	17.5	9.2	4.4	1.8	1.1	0.6	0.2	0.2	0.1	425	673	917	714	.368	.361	.729
Charwomen, janitors, and porters	68	100.0	9.1	19.6	24.3	26.6	11.6	4.7	2.9	0.7	0.4	0.1	...	...	...	362	575	765	594	.371	.330	.701
Cooks, exc. private household	97	100.0	13.1	28.9	24.7	18.2	8.0	4.7	1.9	0.8	0.4	0.1	...	...	...	282	465	691	517	.393	.487	.880
Housek'prs, stewards, exc. pr. hshld	54	100.0	6.1	17.6	19.9	23.1	14.2	8.3	5.8	2.4	1.6	0.6	0.2	0.2	...	413	655	917	718	.370	.398	.768
Practical nurses and midwives	70	100.0	14.4	29.7	20.1	15.3	8.5	4.1	2.4	1.0	0.6	0.3	...	0.2	...	248	425	697	516	.416	.639	1.055
Waitresses, bartenders, counter wkrs.	310	100.0	14.8	32.5	26.7	16.2	6.2	2.5	0.9	0.3	0.1	...	...	...	...	265	423	617	470	.374	.458	.832
Service wkrs., exc. pr. hshld.(n.e.c.)	145	100.0	13.5	33.2	27.4	18.5	5.1	1.5	0.5	...	0.6	0.3	...	0.1	...	269	424	610	459	.366	.437	.803

Source: Derived from Sixteenth Decennial Census of the United States: 1940, Vol. III, The Labor Force, Part 1, table 72.   See Appendix A for description of method used to estimate arithmetic mean.

TABLE C-4.—PERCENT DISTRIBUTION OF EXPERIENCED PERSONS IN THE LABOR FORCE WHO WORKED 12 MONTHS IN 1939 (EXCEPT PERSONS ON EMERGENCY WORK) IN SELECTED OCCUPATIONS, BY WAGE OR SALARY INCOME IN 1939, BY SEX, FOR THE UNITED STATES

Occupation and sex	Number reporting $100 or more (thousands)	Total	Percent distribution													Quartiles			Arithmetic mean (dollars)	$1-\frac{Q_1}{Q_2}$	$\frac{Q_3}{Q_2}-1$	$\frac{Q_3-Q_1}{Q_2}$
			$100 to $199	$200 to $399	$400 to $599	$600 to $799	$800 to $999	$1000 to $1199	$1200 to $1399	$1400 to $1599	$1600 to $1999	$2000 to $2499	$2500 to $2999	$3000 to $4999	$5000 and over	Q_1 (dollars)	Q_2 (median; dollars)	Q_3 (dollars)				
MALE, EXPERIENCED CIVILIAN LABOR FORCE																						
Prof'l, Techn'l, Kindred Wkrs.																						
Artists and art teachers	17	100.0	0.2	0.9	1.6	3.8	5.2	8.3	8.7	8.9	12.2	15.6	10.0	16.5	8.1	1,315	2,006	2,980	2,657	.345	.485	.830
Authors, editors, and reporters	35	100.0	0.2	0.8	1.2	2.4	3.4	5.2	7.3	7.4	10.9	16.1	11.5	20.8	12.9	1,522	2,348	3,827	3,187	.352	.629	.981
Chemists	44	100.0	…	0.2	…	1.2	1.9	4.3	7.3	10.2	18.7	19.8	10.5	18.9	7.1	1,602	2,162	3,116	2,785	.259	.441	.700
Clergymen	97	100.0	1.1	4.3	6.7	11.2	9.7	10.1	14.6	10.1	11.9	9.6	3.5	5.8	1.4	835	1,295	1,842	1,551	.355	.422	.777
Coll. pres., prof'rs, instr's (n.e.c.)	26	100.0	0.1	0.4	0.6	1.1	1.3	1.7	2.5	3.0	7.5	14.4	12.7	37.6	17.2	2,236	3,250	4,580	3,980	.312	.409	.721
Designers and draftsmen	71	100.0	0.1	0.2	0.4	1.7	3.4	6.0	8.7	10.9	20.5	24.2	11.9	10.6	1.4	1,483	1,963	2,477	2,079	.245	.261	.506
Engineers, civil	66	100.0	0.1	0.1	0.1	0.2	0.5	1.1	2.7	4.4	13.5	25.0	15.8	29.5	7.1	2,048	2,576	3,786	3,179	.205	.469	.674
Engineers, electrical	46	100.0	…	0.1	0.1	0.2	0.5	1.4	2.7	4.7	15.6	19.3	14.0	33.1	13.5	2,062	2,789	4,158	3,496	.261	.490	.751
Engineers, mechanical	67	100.0	…	0.1	0.1	0.2	0.4	1.0	2.4	4.2	11.0	20.6	14.3	32.1	13.5	2,136	2,850	4,290	3,665	.251	.505	.756
Musicians and music teachers	23	100.0	0.7	3.5	5.3	8.9	9.1	11.6	12.4	9.5	9.8	9.8	4.9	8.7	1.3	945	1,376	2,214	2,024	.314	.609	.923
Pharmacists	37	100.0	0.1	0.4	1.0	2.9	4.1	6.5	12.9	15.6	25.8	18.9	5.9	4.5	1.3	1,355	1,701	2,151	1,886	.204	.264	.468
Social, welfare, and recreation wkrs.	20	100.0	0.2	0.7	4.7	2.6	4.0	8.0	12.9	14.0	20.4	5.9	6.1	10.5	3.2	1,329	1,725	2,333	2,143	.230	.352	.582
Sports instr's, athletes, entertainers	11	100.0	0.7	2.6	4.7	8.2	7.9	9.8	13.1	9.0	11.2	11.9	5.9	9.5	4.6	1,184	1,467	2,290	2,016	.306	.561	.867
Teachers (n.e.c.)	73	100.0	0.2	0.9	1.8	3.4	4.8	5.5	7.9	8.1	17.1	18.8	10.7	17.6	3.4	1,412	2,008	2,804	2,399	.297	.396	.693
Salaried Managers and Officials																						
Conductors, railroad	34	100.0	0.1	0.1	…	0.1	0.3	0.8	1.5	3.1	11.7	34.9	27.8	19.6	0.1	2,106	2,464	2,905	2,632	.146	.178	.324
Postmasters, and misc. govt. officials	170	100.0	0.4	1.2	1.3	2.3	2.9	3.3	6.3	7.3	16.7	21.3	11.7	18.8	6.7	1,600	2,195	3,032	2,737	.272	.381	.653
Managers and officials:																						
Manufacturing	249	100.0	0.1	0.3	0.4	0.8	1.1	2.1	3.8	4.9	8.8	14.5	9.9	24.5	28.8	2,093	3,269	6,056	4,493	.360	.852	1.212
Trans., commun., & other pub. util.	102	100.0	0.1	0.2	0.2	0.8	1.3	2.0	4.3	5.1	11.4	12.3	18.5	30.2	13.1	1,966	2,736	4,211	3,528	.279	.544	.823
Wholesale trade	95	100.0	0.3	0.9	1.3	2.4	3.0	4.5	7.3	7.1	11.4	11.5	8.5	18.9	19.0	1,549	2,386	4,376	3,554	.351	.834	1.185
Eating and drinking places	35	100.0	0.6	2.8	4.8	7.3	7.5	12.2	14.7	11.8	11.3	6.8	6.3	6.3	3.8	1,033	1,402	2,087	1,859	.264	.488	.752
Retail trade, exc. eating & drinking	332	100.0	0.4	1.6	2.7	4.5	5.2	8.1	12.3	11.6	15.6	14.9	6.8	9.7	6.5	1,241	1,692	2,436	2,296	.267	.439	.706
Finance, insur., and real estate	128	100.0	0.1	0.2	0.3	0.3	1.2	2.1	4.3	5.1	14.9	9.5	9.5	25.8	25.4	2,039	3,093	5,126	4,279	.341	.657	.998
Business and repair services	24	100.0	0.2	0.8	1.6	3.5	4.1	7.3	11.7	11.7	16.7	9.5	7.3	10.9	8.5	1,328	1,833	2,623	2,538	.276	.430	.706
Personal services	27	100.0	0.4	1.7	3.1	5.2	5.1	7.4	11.3	9.7	14.6	7.7	7.7	11.8	9.1	1,237	1,789	2,734	2,541	.309	.527	.836
Clerical, Sales, and Kindred Workers																						
Baggagemen, exp. mess., rwy. mail clk.	24	100.0	0.1	0.3	0.3	0.8	1.2	2.1	5.2	6.6	43.7	24.8	7.9	2.7	0.1	1,875	2,243	2,550	2,211	.164	.137	.301
Bookk'prs, accts., cashs., ticket agts.	366	100.0	0.1	0.4	1.8	3.3	5.6	7.7	11.9	12.0	17.8	7.9	7.9	10.3	2.8	1,318	1,767	2,385	2,130	.255	.349	.604
Mail carriers	104	100.0	0.6	2.1	2.1	2.1	2.1	2.4	16.5	16.5	56.8	4.6	2.4	2.4	0.1	1,731	2,122	2,342	2,002	.185	.103	.288
Messengers, except express	33	100.0	1.9	7.2	19.6	30.6	14.8	8.9	9.4	4.2	2.6	1.2	0.8	0.1	…	562	739	1,034	833	.240	.398	.638
Shipping and receiving clerks	148	100.0	0.1	1.5	1.5	8.9	13.8	20.3	20.7	15.7	12.7	2.6	0.8	0.4	0.1	1,003	1,248	1,518	1,300	.197	.216	.413
Stenographers, typists, and secys.	53	100.0	0.2	1.0	1.6	5.5	5.1	10.6	14.4	12.8	16.2	11.7	4.9	8.2	4.0	1,145	1,520	2,158	2,004	.247	.419	.666

TABLE C–4.—PERCENT DISTRIBUTION OF EXPERIENCED PERSONS IN THE LABOR FORCE WHO WORKED 12 MONTHS IN 1939 (EXCEPT PERSONS ON EMERGENCY WORK) IN SELECTED OCCUPATIONS, BY WAGE OR SALARY INCOME IN 1939, BY SEX, FOR THE UNITED STATES—Cont.

Occupation and sex	Number reporting $100 or more (thousands)	Total	$100 to $199	$200 to $399	$400 to $599	$600 to $799	$800 to $999	$1000 to $1199	$1200 to $1399	$1400 to $1599	$1600 to $1999	$2000 to $2499	$2500 to $2999	$3000 to $4999	$5000 and over	Q_1 (dollars)	Q_2 (median; dollars)	Q_3 (dollars)	Arith‑metic mean (dollars)	$1-\frac{Q_1}{Q_2}$	$\frac{Q_3}{Q_2}-1$	$\frac{Q_3-Q_1}{Q_2}$
MALE—Con.																					
Clerical, Sales, & Kind. Wkrs.—Con.																					
Telegraph operators	25	100.0	0.1	0.3	0.4	1.3	2.4	3.4	5.9	9.7	39.9	28.1	5.9	2.4	0.2	1,615	1,866	2,206	1,920	.135	.182	.317
Newsboys	16	100.0	32.6	28.2	11.0	8.4	5.5	3.8	3.3	2.2	2.1	1.7	0.6	0.4	0.1	177	323	676	532	.454	1.090	1.544
Insurance agents and brokers	150	100.0	0.3	1.1	2.0	3.3	4.0	6.1	8.7	9.1	12.9	19.1	12.5	15.6	5.2	1,389	2,065	2,836	2,487	.328	.373	.701
Real estate agents and brokers	34	100.0	0.7	2.5	4.2	5.2	6.0	10.4	10.4	9.4	14.2	14.2	7.0	12.2	8.9	1,145	1,706	2,714	2,485	.329	.591	.920
Salesmen and sales clerks (n.e.c.)	1,208	100.0	0.4	1.9	4.0	8.9	9.3	11.6	13.4	10.7	12.2	11.8	5.4	7.6	2.9	1,009	1,409	2,110	1,833	.285	.497	.782
Craftsmen, Foremen, & Kindred Wkrs.																					
Bakers	77	100.0	0.2	1.1	3.1	7.7	10.0	15.9	18.1	17.4	15.3	8.5	1.8	0.9	0.2	1,036	1,333	1,639	1,404	.223	.230	.453
Blacksmiths, forgemen, and hammermen	27	100.0	1.4	5.2	5.8	7.5	7.1	10.6	14.8	15.2	19.9	9.3	2.0	1.3	0.1	944	1,368	1,749	1,384	.310	.278	.588
Boilermakers	16	100.0	0.1	0.3	0.6	1.6	2.7	6.3	12.3	16.3	32.5	21.5	3.8	2.0	0.2	1,414	1,721	2,053	1,776	.179	.193	.372
Cabinetmakers and patternmakers	42	100.0	0.3	0.9	2.1	6.9	8.1	13.4	14.8	14.6	18.6	15.5	4.1	1.5	0.2	1,107	1,460	1,918	1,558	.242	.313	.555
Carpenters	149	100.0	0.7	2.9	5.2	8.7	8.9	11.9	14.3	14.5	16.6	11.1	3.1	1.9	0.3	969	1,364	1,790	1,448	.290	.312	.602
Compositors and typesetters	97	100.0	0.1	0.7	1.8	4.8	6.1	9.4	11.0	10.9	15.1	21.8	11.6	6.0	0.6	1,238	1,738	2,346	1,885	.288	.350	.638
Electricians	117	100.0	0.1	0.5	1.1	2.8	4.2	7.2	11.5	13.9	24.4	21.5	7.3	5.2	0.3	1,358	1,743	2,216	1,860	.221	.271	.492
Foremen (n.e.c.):																					
Construction	30	100.0	0.1	0.7	1.5	3.9	6.2	9.0	15.4	14.5	21.0	16.3	6.3	4.8	0.3	1,247	1,582	2,083	1,747	.212	.316	.528
Manufacturing	221	100.0	...	0.1	0.3	1.3	2.5	5.3	8.9	16.3	25.0	16.3	12.4	9.9	0.7	1,508	1,964	2,462	2,136	.233	.253	.486
Trans., commun., & other pub. util.	83	100.0	0.1	0.1	0.2	0.8	1.6	3.0	6.4	14.3	26.8	21.3	11.7	13.4	0.3	1,579	1,951	2,517	2,199	.191	.290	.481
Inspectors (n.e.c.)	53	100.0	0.1	0.2	0.3	0.9	1.6	3.0	6.8	11.7	35.6	27.5	7.4	4.6	0.4	1,604	1,885	2,269	2,003	.149	.203	.352
Linemen & servicemen, t'graph, etc.	89	100.0	0.1	0.3	0.6	1.5	2.7	4.9	9.1	10.7	20.5	24.8	16.0	8.3	0.4	1,508	2,008	2,487	2,094	.249	.238	.487
Locomotive engineers	50	100.0	...	0.2	0.4	0.4	0.7	1.4	3.3	3.3	10.1	26.1	24.8	28.8	0.5	2,129	2,633	3,432	2,824	.191	.303	.495
Locomotive firemen	24	100.0	...	0.4	0.7	1.7	2.4	4.7	6.9	8.2	22.8	33.1	14.9	4.0	0.1	1,602	2,035	2,412	2,027	.213	.185	.398
Machinists, millwrights, & toolmakers	378	100.0	0.1	0.3	0.7	2.7	4.7	9.7	14.2	17.3	26.3	18.4	4.1	1.6	0.1	1,296	1,605	1,985	1,690	.192	.236	.429
Masons, tile setters, & stone cutters	22	100.0	0.5	2.2	4.4	7.5	8.0	11.0	12.3	16.1	14.8	12.4	6.3	4.2	0.3	1,044	1,464	2,045	1,616	.287	.396	.683
Mechanics & repairmen, & loom fixers	535	100.0	0.1	1.6	3.3	5.5	9.0	13.6	17.4	18.4	18.2	9.0	2.1	1.2	0.1	1,046	1,367	1,732	1,426	.235	.267	.502
Molders, metal	33	100.0	0.1	0.5	1.5	3.3	8.0	16.5	20.1	18.2	18.0	10.0	1.5	0.6	0.1	1,114	1,378	1,697	1,443	.192	.231	.423
Painters (const.), paperhgrs., glaziers	73	100.0	0.5	2.4	4.6	4.6	9.7	15.6	15.7	14.9	18.4	9.5	2.7	1.2	0.2	979	1,326	1,712	1,403	.262	.291	.553
Plasterers and cement finishers	10	100.0	0.5	2.3	6.6	10.8	10.1	13.0	13.0	12.3	12.6	11.6	4.1	2.7	0.2	895	1,303	1,803	1,430	.314	.383	.697
Plumbers and pipe fitters	76	100.0	0.2	0.8	2.1	4.8	5.6	9.4	13.7	15.8	22.7	15.9	5.3	3.4	0.3	1,231	1,570	1,998	1,691	.216	.273	.489
Print. craft, exc. compos. & typeset.	43	100.0	0.1	0.3	0.8	2.6	3.7	6.5	8.3	8.8	20.5	23.9	15.5	6.7	1.3	1,461	2,123	2,771	1,948	.312	.305	.617
Rollers and roll hands, metal	11	100.0	0.1	0.2	0.5	3.7	3.7	9.7	16.7	17.2	19.1	13.9	5.9	8.7	1.4	1,310	1,606	2,173	1,583	.185	.352	.537
Roofers and sheet metal workers	44	100.0	...	0.9	5.4	5.4	7.4	13.1	15.5	15.0	15.2	10.0	4.2	1.9	0.2	1,139	1,473	1,925	1,525	.227	.306	.533
Shoemakers & repairmen, exc. factory	15	100.0	1.7	7.8	13.3	18.2	14.1	17.3	12.4	7.6	4.2	2.1	0.6	0.6	0.2	624	928	1,242	994	.328	.338	.666
Stat. engineers, cranemen, hoistmen	200	100.0	0.1	0.5	0.9	2.8	4.5	10.2	13.8	16.3	28.5	15.8	5.0	3.8	0.4	1,325	1,649	2,000	1,768	.197	.212	.409
Structural metal workers	10	100.0	0.1	0.5	1.3	4.6	5.5	14.4	16.5	16.5	20.1	9.9	6.1	5.4	0.7	1,257	1,579	2,098	1,759	.204	.328	.532
Tailors and furriers	33	100.0	0.3	1.5	4.5	8.2	8.5	14.4	16.3	14.7	13.9	10.0	4.0	3.0	0.7	1,028	1,355	1,790	1,518	.242	.321	.563

TABLE C-4.—PERCENT DISTRIBUTION OF EXPERIENCED PERSONS IN THE LABOR FORCE WHO WORKED 12 MONTHS IN 1939 (EXCEPT PERSONS ON EMERGENCY WORK) IN SELECTED OCCUPATIONS, BY WAGE OR SALARY INCOME IN 1939, BY SEX, FOR THE UNITED STATES—Cont.

Occupation and sex	Number reporting $100 or more (thousands)	Percent distribution														Quartiles				$1-\frac{Q_1}{Q_2}$	$\frac{Q_3}{Q_2}-1$	$\frac{Q_3-Q_1}{Q_2}$
		Total	$100 to $199	$200 to $399	$400 to $599	$600 to $799	$800 to $999	$1000 to $1199	$1200 to $1399	$1400 to $1599	$1600 to $1999	$2000 to $2499	$2500 to $2999	$3000 to $4999	$5000 and over	Q_1 (dollars)	Q_2 (median; dollars)	Q_3 (dollars)	Arithmetic mean (dollars)			
MALE—Con.																						
Operatives and Kindred Workers																						
Apprentices	34	100.0	1.2	4.6	9.9	21.6	19.5	18.5	12.8	6.7	3.9	0.9	0.2	0.1	...	686	930	1,197	962	.263	.286	.549
Attendants, auto service and parking	128	100.0	1.0	6.5	12.3	21.3	17.8	15.5	13.4	6.2	3.4	1.0	0.3	0.2	...	649	900	1,195	940	.280	.327	.607
Brakemen and switchmen, railroad	63	100.0	0.1	0.1	0.4	1.3	2.1	3.8	6.1	8.6	25.7	37.8	11.9	1.8	...	1,636	2,021	2,352	2,003	.191	.163	.354
Drivers, bus, taxi, & truck, & delivmen	884	100.0	0.8	4.2	6.9	12.3	11.1	13.4	14.7	12.5	14.0	7.8	1.0	0.6	0.1	814	1,218	1,586	1,268	.332	.302	.634
Stationary firemen	78	100.0	0.2	1.3	3.8	9.9	9.8	14.2	15.0	16.3	17.8	8.1	1.7	1.5	0.1	998	1,310	1,600	1,338	.239	.221	.460
Mine operatives & laborers (n.e.c.)	127	100.0	0.7	3.2	5.8	9.1	9.7	14.0	19.4	14.8	17.8	4.1	1.0	0.4	...	928	1,310	1,695	1,360	.302	.275	.577
Motormen, rwy., mine, factory, etc.	33	100.0	...	0.8	2.7	0.8	1.5	4.0	10.3	20.1	43.0	12.5	1.8	0.3	0.1	1,480	1,720	1,953	1,743	.140	.135	.275
Painters, exc. constr. & maintenance	41	100.0	0.2	0.8	2.7	11.3	12.3	10.3	19.3	15.5	17.4	5.0	0.8	0.3	...	966	1,247	1,532	1,283	.228	.228	.456
Sailors and deck hands	14	100.0	0.5	2.7	5.0	15.0	16.7	16.3	14.4	9.5	12.3	4.4	1.3	1.5	0.3	822	1,124	1,493	1,241	.270	.328	.598
Welders and flame-cutters	62	100.0	0.1	0.5	1.4	3.1	5.1	10.3	15.0	17.4	26.7	16.5	2.9	1.2	0.1	1,264	1,570	1,936	1,633	.195	.232	.427
Operatives & kindred workers (n.e.c.):																						
Food and kindred products	133	100.0	0.3	1.6	3.6	8.6	11.0	18.0	20.6	14.9	13.7	5.9	1.1	0.6	0.2	998	1,267	1,552	1,323	.213	.224	.437
Knitting mills	22	100.0	0.2	1.9	4.2	19.9	14.8	14.0	10.9	10.6	9.3	2.5	0.6	...	0.2	798	1,143	1,591	1,278	.302	.391	.693
Text. mill prod., exc. knit. mills	158	100.0	0.2	1.1	5.5	36.4	23.6	16.4	7.9	4.5	2.8	1.0	0.4	0.4	...	701	858	1,101	949	.184	.282	.466
Apparel & other fabric text. prod.	41	100.0	0.2	2.9	4.8	15.4	17.1	18.1	15.2	11.3	10.2	4.2	0.4	0.2	0.2	858	1,214	1,651	1,377	.294	.360	.654
Furniture, and lumber and wood prod.	71	100.0	0.5	0.7	7.2	21.1	12.0	20.9	15.2	9.2	6.1	2.0	0.4	0.2	...	736	1,013	1,307	1,056	.274	.289	.563
Paper, paper prod., and printing	83	100.0	0.2	0.6	1.2	6.8	5.8	22.2	20.9	14.8	11.8	6.4	2.0	0.9	0.5	1,031	1,259	1,547	1,350	.182	.228	.410
Chemicals & petrol., & coal prod.	85	100.0	0.1	0.6	0.7	3.5	5.8	17.7	20.9	15.5	25.5	12.0	1.6	0.5	0.1	1,221	1,494	1,831	1,540	.183	.224	.407
Rubber products	32	100.0	0.1	0.9	0.7	3.7	5.8	15.4	18.3	23.0	23.0	12.5	1.1	0.3	...	1,168	1,449	1,807	1,509	.195	.247	.442
Footwear industries, exc. rubber	35	100.0	0.2	0.6	4.3	17.7	20.0	23.5	16.0	9.3	5.7	1.8	0.4	0.2	0.2	819	1,059	1,305	1,106	.227	.232	.459
Leather & leath. prod., exc. footwear	22	100.0	0.1	0.7	2.4	9.2	13.3	23.7	22.4	14.2	9.1	3.2	0.9	0.5	0.2	991	1,206	1,446	1,262	.179	.199	.378
Stone, clay, and glass products	41	100.0	0.1	0.5	1.4	7.1	11.2	20.3	21.3	13.3	13.2	6.2	1.8	0.8	0.8	1,036	1,279	1,564	1,355	.190	.222	.412
Iron & steel, & not spec. metal ind.	127	100.0	0.1	0.4	1.3	5.2	8.4	18.4	21.8	17.9	15.7	6.8	1.7	0.9	0.1	1,091	1,355	1,608	1,411	.185	.201	.386
Nonferrous metals & their products	29	100.0	0.1	0.4	1.3	5.6	9.9	19.9	24.2	19.2	12.5	4.9	1.2	0.6	0.1	1,075	1,304	1,540	1,359	.176	.180	.356
Machinery	105	100.0	0.2	0.4	1.0	4.6	8.4	16.8	20.1	19.3	18.7	7.8	1.7	0.7	0.9	1,123	1,384	1,688	1,447	.189	.219	.408
Motor vehicles & mtr. vehicle equip.	38	100.0	0.1	0.4	1.0	3.5	5.4	10.1	15.7	22.9	29.0	8.9	1.8	0.9	...	1,257	1,521	1,819	1,555	.174	.196	.370
Trans. equip., exc. motor vehicle	28	100.0	0.2	0.8	1.4	4.3	7.6	15.3	20.3	20.0	17.9	9.2	2.1	1.0	0.1	1,140	1,401	1,714	1,476	.187	.223	.410
Service Workers																						
Private household workers	81	100.0	10.0	24.6	20.7	18.9	10.4	5.5	5.1	2.3	1.7	0.5	0.1	0.1	...	322	549	815	628	.414	.485	.899
Firemen, fire protection	73	100.0	0.1	0.1	0.2	0.4	1.7	1.7	4.8	7.7	27.9	35.3	10.3	10.1	0.3	1,730	2,088	2,442	2,220	.172	.169	.341
Guards and watchmen	161	100.0	0.5	2.1	4.4	12.3	15.6	19.6	18.2	11.9	10.7	3.9	0.6	0.3	...	873	1,166	1,439	1,198	.252	.233	.485
Policemen, sheriffs, and marshalls	151	100.0	0.1	0.2	0.9	1.9	3.5	7.6	7.6	8.6	22.3	30.0	9.9	11.5	0.4	1,579	2,030	2,447	2,154	.223	.205	.428
Barbers, beauticians, & manicurists	74	100.0	0.6	3.3	8.8	17.8	16.1	19.6	15.7	8.3	8.3	2.7	0.4	0.6	0.2	738	1,035	1,312	1,092	.287	.268	.555
Charmen, janitors, and porters	361	100.0	1.9	8.1	13.3	19.5	14.6	14.1	14.8	7.0	4.6	1.5	0.4	0.2	...	617	899	1,247	950	.313	.388	.701
Cooks, exc. private household	103	100.0	0.7	5.6	11.9	17.6	14.9	15.4	13.7	8.7	7.0	3.3	0.8	0.5	0.1	677	991	1,330	1,064	.317	.342	.659

TABLE C-4.—PERCENT DISTRIBUTION OF EXPERIENCED PERSONS IN THE LABOR FORCE WHO WORKED 12 MONTHS IN 1939 (EXCEPT PERSONS ON EMERGENCY WORK) IN SELECTED OCCUPATIONS, BY WAGE OR SALARY INCOME IN 1939, BY SEX, FOR THE UNITED STATES—Cont.

Occupation and sex	Number reporting $100 or more (thousands)	Total	$100 to $199	$200 to $399	$400 to $599	$600 to $799	$800 to $999	$1000 to $1199	$1200 to $1399	$1400 to $1599	$1600 to $1999	$2000 to $2499	$2500 to $2999	$3000 to $4999	$5000 and over	Q_1 (dollars)	Q_2 (median; dollars)	Q_3 (dollars)	Arith. mean (dollars)	$1-\dfrac{Q_1}{Q_2}$	$\dfrac{Q_3}{Q_2}-1$	$\dfrac{Q_3-Q_1}{Q_2}$
MALE—Con.																						
Service Workers—Con.																						
Elevator operators	51	100.0	0.2	1.5	4.9	15.2	16.7	23.0	21.9	10.1	5.2	0.9	0.1	0.1	...	838	1,100	1,323	1,096	.238	.202	.440
Waiters, bartenders, & counter wkrs.	164	100.0	0.8	6.0	11.7	18.2	15.2	16.7	14.6	8.9	5.4	1.8	0.4	0.2	0.1	671	975	1,288	1,015	.312	.320	.632
Service wkrs., exc. pr. hshld.(n.e.c.)	83	100.0	2.3	12.7	20.4	27.6	17.6	10.7	5.1	2.0	1.0	0.3	0.1	0.1	...	498	706	936	741	.295	.326	.621
Laborers, Except Farm and Mine																						
Fishermen and oystermen	7	100.0	5.5	19.6	17.7	13.7	9.1	9.0	7.8	5.9	4.4	4.2	1.4	1.5	0.3	400	705	1,210	921	.435	.716	1.151
Longshoremen and stevedores	19	100.0	0.4	2.6	6.8	11.2	9.2	14.1	14.9	12.8	13.7	10.5	2.3	1.3	0.2	887	1,277	1,688	1,361	.306	.321	.627
Lumbermen, raftsmen, & woodchoppers	27	100.0	6.0	26.7	24.6	19.5	7.3	4.9	4.3	2.7	2.5	1.1	0.2	0.2	0.1	342	541	782	657	.367	.445	.812
Laborers (n.e.c.):																						
Manufacturing industries:																						
Food and kindred products	76	100.0	0.7	3.6	7.1	12.9	13.6	21.3	22.0	10.3	6.6	1.5	0.2	0.1	...	810	1,114	1,344	1,097	.273	.206	.479
Textiles, text. prod., & apparel	34	100.0	0.4	2.5	13.3	38.1	18.4	14.6	7.4	3.4	1.3	0.4	0.1	0.1	...	646	777	1,032	852	.169	.326	.495
Furniture, and lumber & wood prod.	99	100.0	2.2	12.0	23.8	31.8	11.1	7.8	6.5	2.7	1.8	0.4	...	0.1	...	491	675	894	736	.274	.322	.596
Paper, paper prod., & printing	31	100.0	0.5	1.9	5.0	13.3	19.5	28.0	18.8	7.8	3.8	1.0	0.3	0.1	...	844	1,070	1,272	1,073	.212	.189	.401
Chemicals & petrol., & coal prod.	60	100.0	0.7	3.6	6.0	11.2	11.6	17.0	20.6	16.3	10.6	2.0	0.2	0.1	...	860	1,199	1,453	1,169	.283	.211	.494
Stone, clay, and glass products	37	100.0	0.3	2.5	8.1	18.1	17.3	24.2	17.0	7.2	3.7	1.0	0.3	0.2	...	756	1,031	1,252	1,030	.267	.215	.482
Iron & steel & not spec. metal ind.	104	100.0	0.2	0.9	2.0	9.0	17.3	23.8	16.4	12.8	10.6	3.4	0.5	0.1	...	978	1,197	1,388	1,209	.184	.158	.342
Nonferrous metals and their prod.	20	100.0	0.2	0.7	2.0	6.3	11.1	24.3	30.8	16.4	6.6	1.3	0.3	...	...	1,039	1,235	1,397	1,202	.160	.131	.291
Machinery	31	100.0	0.2	1.1	2.2	8.6	14.9	22.9	22.9	13.2	8.3	2.3	0.9	0.5	...	965	1,183	1,397	1,230	.185	.183	.368
Motor vehicles & mtr. veh. equip.	13	100.0	0.2	1.0	2.8	6.4	8.0	16.5	17.5	16.6	22.5	4.3	0.8	0.4	...	1,109	1,413	1,657	1,393	.216	.172	.388
Trans. equipment, exc. motor veh.	13	100.0	0.3	1.6	3.6	10.7	14.1	22.4	25.9	13.3	5.9	1.8	0.2	0.1	...	925	1,176	1,372	1,164	.214	.166	.380
Nonmanufacturing industries:																						
Construction	153	100.0	1.2	7.7	15.0	22.2	14.1	14.1	11.9	7.3	4.0	1.6	0.4	0.2	0.2	610	855	1,212	929	.287	.416	.703
Railroads & rwy. express service	126	100.0	0.3	1.8	5.7	20.0	26.9	21.7	13.5	5.9	3.1	0.6	0.3	0.1	...	772	965	1,187	1,005	.201	.230	.431
Transportation, exc. railroad	42	100.0	1.3	5.9	9.4	14.9	12.0	15.1	16.9	12.2	10.2	1.6	0.3	0.1	...	713	1,086	1,394	1,080	.344	.283	.627
Telecomm. & util. & sanitary serv.	57	100.0	0.5	2.4	5.5	10.6	10.4	14.9	19.6	16.0	16.6	2.7	0.5	0.2	...	915	1,258	1,539	1,243	.273	.222	.495
Wholesale and retail trade	105	100.0	1.7	8.1	13.8	21.0	15.5	14.8	11.7	7.4	4.6	1.1	0.2	0.1	...	613	870	1,202	925	.295	.381	.676
FEMALE, EXPERIENCED CIVILIAN LABOR FORCE																						
Profess'l, Techn'l, Kindred Wrkrs.																						
Librarians	21	100.0	1.6	3.9	5.0	8.8	10.1	15.7	12.6	16.5	9.4	9.4	3.4	2.3	0.2	913	1,327	1,762	1,413	.313	.327	.640
Musicians and music teachers	10	100.0	6.3	16.7	15.3	14.4	11.3	9.7	7.5	5.2	4.8	4.0	1.9	3.0	1.0	426	763	1,235	1,019	.442	.619	1.061
Social, welfare, and recreation wkrs.	34	100.0	0.5	1.2	2.2	4.7	7.1	12.0	17.0	16.4	21.5	10.5	2.7	2.7	0.4	1,168	1,454	1,842	1,582	.197	.267	.464
Teachers (n.e.c.)	115	100.0	0.5	5.9	4.6	8.2	4.8	9.6	9.6	12.0	9.6	13.8	6.3	11.6	0.4	1,003	1,531	2,254	1,776	.346	.471	.817
Nurses, professional & student prof.	131	100.0	2.3	4.2	5.6	13.6	18.8	15.5	14.4	9.0	11.7	3.7	0.7	0.5	0.1	790	1,076	1,413	1,145	.267	.312	.579

TABLE C-4.—PERCENT DISTRIBUTION OF EXPERIENCED PERSONS IN THE LABOR FORCE WHO WORKED 12 MONTHS IN 1939 (EXCEPT PERSONS ON EMERGENCY WORK) IN SELECTED OCCUPATIONS, BY WAGE OR SALARY INCOME IN 1939, BY SEX, FOR THE UNITED STATES—Cont.

Occupation and sex	Number reporting $100 or more (thousands)	Total	$100 to $199	$200 to $399	$400 to $599	$600 to $799	$800 to $999	$1000 to $1199	$1200 to $1399	$1400 to $1599	$1600 to $1999	$2000 to $2499	$2500 to $2999	$3000 to $4999	$5000 and over	Q_1 (dollars)	Q_2 (median; dollars)	Q_3 (dollars)	Arithmetic mean (dollars)	$1-\frac{Q_1}{Q_2}$	$\frac{Q_3-Q_1}{Q_2}$	$\frac{Q_3}{Q_2}$
FEMALE—Con.																						
Clerical, Sales, and Kindred Workers																						
Bookk'prs, accts., cashs., ticket agts.	328	100.0	0.4	2.3	6.4	19.3	20.7	18.6	14.9	8.0	6.0	2.4	0.6	0.4	0.1	765	1,010	1,298	1,083	.243	.285	.528
Office machine operators	39	100.0	0.1	0.2	0.8	8.2	23.1	27.3	22.7	11.5	5.3	0.6	0.7	0.5	...	936	1,129	1,335	1,150	.171	.182	.353
Stenographers, typists, and secys.	746	100.0	0.2	1.1	3.2	13.1	20.1	19.6	18.2	11.3	9.1	3.0	...	0.1	0.1	874	1,126	1,395	1,193	.224	.238	.462
Telephone operators	144	100.0	0.7	3.4	6.5	16.6	20.1	21.0	16.6	8.6	4.8	1.3	0.3	0.1	...	773	1,026	1,281	1,045	.246	.248	.494
Saleswomen and sales clerks (n.e.c.)	368	100.0	1.2	5.9	16.9	36.8	20.8	9.8	4.5	1.8	1.2	0.6	0.2	0.2	0.1	605	741	937	800	.184	.263	.447
Operatives and Kindred Workers																						
Dressmakers & seamstr., exc. factory	31	100.0	4.4	10.9	15.4	29.2	18.1	11.4	5.9	2.3	1.3	0.6	0.2	0.1	0.1	526	732	967	776	.282	.320	.602
Operatives & kindred wkrs. (n.e.c.):																						
Food and kindred products	44	100.0	1.0	4.7	13.5	35.4	27.4	13.7	2.9	0.8	0.5	0.1	...	...	...	633	774	949	789	.183	.225	.408
Tobacco manufactures	21	100.0	0.3	3.0	23.4	39.3	22.2	7.5	3.4	0.6	0.1	0.1	...	...	...	585	719	881	741	.186	.226	.412
Knitting mills	38	100.0	0.3	2.0	14.4	46.1	22.2	10.7	3.0	0.9	0.3	0.1	...	...	...	636	744	910	779	.146	.222	.368
Textile mill prod., exc. knit. mills	103	100.0	0.5	1.7	12.3	56.2	20.4	6.6	1.6	0.6	0.3	0.1	...	...	...	638	727	844	754	.123	.160	.283
Apparel & other fabric text. prod.	129	100.0	0.5	3.8	21.2	42.9	15.8	9.2	3.5	1.8	0.8	0.3	0.1	...	...	595	714	884	758	.167	.237	.404
Furniture, and lumber and wood prod.	9	100.0	0.4	3.8	13.1	40.7	24.5	11.9	4.0	1.3	0.4	0.2	...	...	...	638	761	939	795	.162	.234	.396
Paper, paper prod., and printing	36	100.0	0.3	1.5	5.3	39.5	30.3	12.8	4.6	1.8	1.1	0.2	0.2	...	...	671	797	962	835	.159	.205	.364
Chemicals & petrol., & coal prod.	17	100.0	0.2	1.5	5.3	29.2	33.9	20.2	5.9	2.6	1.3	0.2	0.2	...	0.1	726	884	1,052	911	.179	.190	.369
Footwear industries, exc. rubber	24	100.0	0.3	2.6	19.9	46.0	18.7	8.8	2.4	0.8	0.3	0.1	...	...	...	610	746	866	746	.152	.206	.358
Leather & leath. prod., exc. footwear	7	100.0	0.2	2.5	15.2	44.0	23.5	10.3	2.8	0.9	0.4	0.1	...	...	...	632	746	911	776	.153	.221	.374
Stone, clay, and glass products	10	100.0	0.2	1.8	8.2	36.3	30.6	16.8	3.8	1.2	0.7	0.2	0.1	...	...	681	822	986	848	.172	.198	.370
Metal industries and machinery	66	100.0	0.2	1.1	5.3	29.6	30.3	23.0	7.0	2.4	0.9	0.2	...	...	...	724	891	1,074	911	.188	.205	.393
Transportation equipment	6	100.0	0.2	0.8	4.2	18.2	21.7	29.4	16.9	5.7	2.1	0.6	...	...	...	815	1,033	1,206	1,033	.212	.167	.379
Service Workers																						
Private household workers	984	100.0	23.5	38.2	20.9	11.5	4.1	1.1	0.4	0.1	0.1	...	...	...	...	208	339	527	392	.387	.556	.943
Barbers, beauticians, & manicurists	75	100.0	1.0	6.4	17.2	27.9	23.1	12.9	6.1	2.4	1.5	...	0.8	0.3	...	603	782	995	841	.230	.271	.501
Charwomen, janitors, and porters	48	100.0	4.1	12.7	32.7	27.9	14.6	6.0	3.5	0.9	0.6	...	...	...	...	466	651	810	665	.285	.242	.527
Cooks, exc. private household	57	100.0	6.0	23.5	26.6	23.2	10.4	5.5	2.9	1.1	0.6	0.3	...	...	...	362	554	763	601	.348	.376	.724
Housek'prs, stewards, exc. pr. hshld.	36	100.0	2.2	18.3	26.8	17.1	10.4	7.4	3.0	1.9	0.8	0.8	0.2	0.2	...	521	733	987	801	.289	.346	.635
Practical nurses and midwives	29	100.0	9.6	22.5	20.9	21.2	11.0	6.5	4.4	1.7	1.1	0.6	0.2	0.1	...	337	571	815	631	.411	.425	.836
Waitresses, bartenders, counter wkrs.	161	100.0	2.5	23.9	33.2	24.2	9.7	4.2	1.5	0.5	0.2	...	...	...	...	388	542	727	577	.284	.341	.625
Service wkrs., exc. pr. hshld.(n.e.c.)	93	100.0	5.2	28.5	31.7	24.7	6.9	2.1	0.7	0.2	0.1	...	...	...	...	339	503	678	526	.326	.347	.673

Source: Derived from *Sixteenth Decennial Census of the United States: 1940*, Vol. III, *The Labor Force*, Part 1, table 72. See Appendix A for description of the method used to estimate arithmetic mean.

TABLE C-5.—PERCENT OF AGGREGATE WAGE OR SALARY INCOME RECEIVED BY EACH FIFTH OF ALL WORKERS AND FULL-YEAR WORKERS IN SELECTED OCCUPATIONS, RANKED BY WAGE OR SALARY INCOME, BY SEX, FOR THE UNITED STATES: 1949 AND 1939

Occupation and sex	All workers												Full-year workers											
	1949						1939						1949						1939					
	Total	Lowest fifth	Second	Middle	Fourth	Highest fifth	Total	Lowest fifth	Second	Middle	Fourth	Highest fifth	Total	Lowest fifth	Second	Middle	Fourth	Highest fifth	Total	Lowest fifth	Second	Middle	Fourth	Highest fifth
MALE, EXPERIENCED CIVILIAN LABOR FORCE																								
Prof'l Techn'l, Kindred Wkrs.																								
Artists and art teachers	100.0	4.5	12.2	16.2	21.6	45.2	100.0	4.6	10.0	14.8	21.9	48.5	100.0	7.9	12.6	15.8	20.2	43.2	100.0	6.6	10.9	15.2	21.8	45.3
Authors, editors, and reporters	100.0	4.6	11.5	16.1	21.0	46.5	100.0	4.8	9.9	14.5	23.0	47.5	100.0	7.1	12.2	16.1	20.0	44.3	100.0	6.3	10.6	14.9	22.5	45.4
Chemists	100.0	7.5	13.9	17.4	22.2	38.9	100.0	6.5	12.2	15.9	21.9	43.9	100.0	10.2	14.0	17.1	21.1	37.4	100.0	8.8	12.3	13.5	21.8	41.3
Clergymen	100.0	5.6	12.1	18.8	24.6	38.7	100.0	6.6	11.6	16.5	23.8	43.7	100.0	6.4	14.0	17.7	24.1	37.5	100.0	6.6	12.2	15.5	21.7	42.7
Coll. pres., prof'rs, instr's (n.e.c.)	100.0	4.9	13.1	18.2	23.2	40.3	100.0	5.9	12.0	17.5	23.0	41.3	100.0	7.6	14.0	17.7	21.8	38.7	100.0	7.4	12.2	15.0	20.0	41.8
Designers and draftsmen	100.0	8.5	15.9	19.2	22.7	33.4	100.0	7.4	13.9	18.3	22.7	37.3	100.0	11.6	15.8	18.7	22.0	31.7	100.0	7.6	14.9	18.1	21.5	35.3
Engineers, civil	100.0	8.0	14.5	18.2	22.0	37.0	100.0	8.4	13.7	16.4	24.0	37.2	100.0	10.2	15.0	17.9	21.1	35.5	100.0	9.9	13.7	16.1	21.9	36.3
Engineers, electrical	100.0	8.2	14.3	17.9	22.0	37.3	100.0	7.5	12.5	15.9	24.1	38.8	100.0	10.4	14.6	17.9	21.1	35.8	100.0	8.8	12.5	16.9	22.8	38.7
Engineers, mechanical	100.0	8.4	14.5	17.3	22.3	38.5	100.0	7.2	12.2	15.7	24.2	40.4	100.0	10.4	14.1	17.4	21.0	37.4	100.0	8.8	12.2	16.9	21.8	40.1
Musicians and music teachers	100.0	3.1	9.5	15.8	22.3	49.0	100.0	4.3	8.9	14.0	20.5	52.0	100.0	4.6	10.9	15.5	22.5	47.7	100.0	5.6	10.2	13.6	19.6	50.7
Pharmacists	100.0	7.6	15.6	19.4	23.3	33.9	100.0	8.2	14.8	18.8	22.3	35.7	100.0	10.2	16.0	19.1	21.5	31.9	100.0	10.6	15.0	18.5	21.6	34.1
Social, welfare, and recreation wkrs	100.0	5.2	13.5	18.1	23.0	39.8	100.0	6.9	12.9	16.8	21.1	42.0	100.0	9.4	14.4	17.8	21.5	36.6	100.0	9.4	13.1	16.2	20.5	41.4
Sports instr's, athletes, entertainers	100.0	4.1	11.0	17.9	23.3	43.4	100.0	4.4	9.6	14.9	22.2	48.6	100.0	7.1	13.5	17.4	21.4	40.3	100.0	6.1	11.1	14.7	20.5	47.4
Teachers (n.e.c.)	100.0	7.2	15.2	19.8	23.7	33.9	100.0	6.6	11.8	16.9	22.7	41.8	100.0	9.9	15.9	18.9	22.7	32.3	100.0	7.6	13.0	16.9	21.5	40.7
Salaried Managers and Officials																								
Conductors, railroad	100.0	12.6	17.4	19.9	23.0	26.8	100.0	11.5	17.1	18.4	22.0	30.8	100.0	13.8	17.7	19.5	22.6	26.0	100.0	13.0	17.0	18.5	20.8	30.4
Postmasters, and misc. govt. officials	100.0	7.3	14.2	17.6	21.7	38.9	100.0	6.3	12.4	16.3	21.7	43.2	100.0	9.0	14.4	17.6	21.1	37.7	100.0	7.5	12.6	16.1	21.9	41.7
Managers and officials:																								
Manufacturing	100.0	6.6	10.6	13.9	19.9	48.7	100.0	5.7	9.8	15.8	27.2	41.3	100.0	7.3	10.1	14.7	19.6	48.3	100.0	6.2	10.1	15.9	27.5	40.0
Trans., commun., & other pub. util.	100.0	9.0	13.6	16.6	20.2	40.2	100.0	7.4	11.3	15.8	21.5	41.5	100.0	9.5	13.7	16.6	20.2	39.8	100.0	7.9	11.9	16.0	22.6	41.3
Wholesale trade	100.0	6.5	10.9	13.8	19.1	49.4	100.0	4.9	9.4	13.5	21.9	50.0	100.0	7.5	10.9	14.2	19.0	48.4	100.0	5.6	9.7	13.5	21.8	49.1
Eating and drinking places	100.0	5.5	13.1	18.2	22.8	40.1	100.0	5.5	11.2	15.4	19.9	46.8	100.0	8.8	14.1	17.9	21.7	37.3	100.0	6.7	13.5	15.0	20.7	45.3
Retail trade, exc. eating & drinking	100.0	6.9	12.4	15.3	20.0	45.0	100.0	5.9	11.0	15.1	20.4	47.6	100.0	8.0	12.4	15.4	19.5	44.2	100.0	6.9	12.5	15.0	19.8	46.8
Finance, insur., and real estate	100.0	7.0	11.2	14.6	19.4	47.5	100.0	6.2	11.0	15.9	24.1	42.8	100.0	7.6	11.4	14.7	19.5	46.5	100.0	6.6	10.1	16.1	25.0	42.0
Business and repair services	100.0	6.5	11.9	14.3	21.7	48.4	100.0	6.2	11.0	14.3	19.7	48.6	100.0	7.5	11.4	14.2	19.2	47.2	100.0	7.2	10.4	14.6	19.0	47.8
Personal services	100.0	5.6	11.9	16.1	20.7	45.5	100.0	5.0	10.0	14.0	20.1	50.7	100.0	7.7	12.7	15.8	20.3	43.3	100.0	6.0	10.4	14.2	19.8	49.3
Clerical, Sales, and Kindred Workers																								
Baggagemen, exp. mess., rwy. mail clk.	100.0	11.5	17.8	20.5	23.0	26.8	100.0	10.4	18.0	21.1	22.4	27.8	100.0	13.5	17.7	20.4	22.3	25.9	100.0	12.2	18.5	20.3	22.0	26.8
Bookk'prs, accs., cashs., ticket agts.	100.0	7.6	14.6	18.4	22.3	37.1	100.0	6.8	12.8	17.1	21.7	37.4	100.0	10.2	15.1	17.7	21.4	35.6	100.0	8.9	13.1	16.9	21.0	40.2
Mail carriers	100.0	10.9	18.3	21.3	23.7	25.6	100.0	8.1	17.8	17.8	23.4	27.2	100.0	13.1	18.3	21.0	22.8	24.5	100.0	10.1	18.8	22.4	22.4	26.0
Messengers, except express	100.0	3.3	8.9	18.1	26.5	42.7	100.0	6.3	11.3	17.8	24.1	40.6	100.0	6.8	14.5	18.9	24.2	35.4	100.0	9.4	14.7	19.2	23.1	35.6
Shipping and receiving clerks	100.0	8.6	16.5	20.3	23.7	30.7	100.0	8.2	15.0	20.0	24.1	32.4	100.0	12.5	16.7	19.3	22.6	28.7	100.0	11.7	16.1	19.2	22.1	30.6
Stenographers, typists, and secys.	100.0	5.5	12.0	15.5	20.5	46.3	100.0	5.4	11.4	15.7	21.0	46.2	100.0	8.2	12.1	15.3	19.7	44.4	100.0	8.0	12.1	15.4	19.9	44.4

TABLE C-5.—PERCENT OF AGGREGATE WAGE OR SALARY INCOME RECEIVED BY EACH FIFTH OF ALL WORKERS AND FULL-YEAR WORKERS IN SELECTED OCCUPATIONS, RANKED BY WAGE OR SALARY INCOME, BY SEX, FOR THE UNITED STATES: 1949 AND 1939—Cont.

Occupation and sex	All workers												Full-year workers											
	1949						1939						1949						1939					
	Total	Lowest fifth	Second	Middle	Fourth	Highest fifth	Total	Lowest fifth	Second	Middle	Fourth	Highest fifth	Total	Lowest fifth	Second	Middle	Fourth	Highest fifth	Total	Lowest fifth	Second	Middle	Fourth	Highest fifth
MALE.—Con.																								
Clerical, Sales, & Kind. Wkrs.—Con.																								
Telegraph operators	100.0	10.3	18.6	19.9	22.6	28.4	100.0	9.7	17.6	20.2	23.0	29.2	100.0	14.0	18.6	19.0	21.5	26.6	100.0	12.5	18.2	18.7	22.6	27.8
Newsboys	100.0	9.2	9.2	9.2	9.2	62.8	100.0	6.9	6.9	12.9	17.9	55.1	100.0	7.6	7.6	7.6	10.6	66.3	100.0	5.6	7.7	11.2	21.5	53.7
Insurance agents and brokers	100.0	7.1	14.0	17.5	22.3	38.9	100.0	5.9	11.5	16.8	21.6	43.9	100.0	9.1	14.3	17.5	21.5	37.4	100.0	7.2	12.2	16.7	22.1	42.4
Real estate agents and brokers	100.0	4.1	10.9	15.9	22.3	46.8	100.0	4.4	9.5	13.5	20.3	51.8	100.0	6.2	11.9	15.9	21.4	44.6	100.0	5.4	10.6	14.0	20.2	50.2
Salesmen and sales clerks (n.e.c.)	100.0	4.7	12.2	17.2	22.1	43.6	100.0	5.2	10.8	15.6	21.8	46.3	100.0	7.7	13.0	16.7	21.1	41.2	100.0	7.1	11.9	15.3	21.4	44.0
Craftsmen, Foremen, & Kindred Wkrs.																								
Bakers	100.0	8.3	16.0	20.5	24.0	30.9	100.0	7.6	14.6	19.3	23.5	34.8	100.0	11.3	16.6	20.1	22.7	29.0	100.0	10.2	15.6	19.0	22.7	32.2
Blacksmiths, forgemen, and hammermen	100.0	7.9	16.2	20.4	23.8	31.5	100.0	5.8	12.6	19.4	23.6	36.8	100.0	10.7	16.5	20.1	22.6	30.0	100.0	7.2	15.2	19.8	24.3	33.2
Boilermakers	100.0	9.8	17.1	20.0	23.4	29.4	100.0	7.6	15.2	19.8	24.4	32.6	100.0	12.9	17.6	19.6	22.0	27.8	100.0	12.2	16.4	20.2	22.1	28.8
Cabinetmakers and patternmakers	100.0	7.7	15.3	20.1	23.9	32.8	100.0	7.3	13.8	18.7	24.8	35.1	100.0	10.8	16.1	19.7	22.7	30.5	100.0	9.8	15.3	18.5	23.1	32.8
Carpenters	100.0	5.8	13.8	19.8	25.4	35.0	100.0	6.0	11.8	17.7	24.8	39.4	100.0	9.2	15.9	19.9	23.1	31.6	100.0	8.2	14.5	18.9	23.3	34.8
Compositors and typesetters	100.0	8.3	15.3	19.5	23.9	32.7	100.0	6.9	13.4	18.5	24.7	36.3	100.0	10.3	15.7	19.6	23.8	31.0	100.0	9.0	14.1	18.3	23.8	34.5
Electricians	100.0	9.2	16.7	19.7	23.1	31.0	100.0	7.1	14.4	19.5	24.1	34.6	100.0	11.6	16.7	19.2	22.5	29.7	100.0	10.5	15.3	19.1	23.8	32.1
Foremen (n.e.c.):																								
Construction	100.0	8.9	15.0	19.0	23.4	33.4	100.0	7.2	13.8	18.6	23.5	36.8	100.0	10.3	15.3	18.5	22.8	32.8	100.0	10.1	15.6	18.6	22.5	33.5
Manufacturing	100.0	11.0	16.0	19.0	22.7	31.1	100.0	9.5	14.9	18.5	22.4	34.5	100.0	12.0	16.5	18.7	22.4	30.8	100.0	10.8	15.3	18.5	21.6	33.4
Trans., commun., & other pub. util.	100.0	12.5	16.3	18.9	22.5	29.6	100.0	10.7	15.4	17.8	22.0	33.8	100.0	13.3	16.0	18.9	22.2	29.3	100.0	11.5	15.4	17.7	21.6	33.4
Inspectors (n.e.c.)	100.0	11.2	17.2	19.7	22.6	29.0	100.0	9.9	16.4	19.5	22.9	30.7	100.0	12.8	17.4	19.6	21.9	28.0	100.0	12.5	17.2	17.9	22.4	29.7
Linemen & servicemen, t'graph, etc	100.0	10.3	16.1	19.6	23.8	30.1	100.0	8.1	15.0	19.6	22.9	33.4	100.0	11.9	16.4	19.3	22.4	29.1	100.0	10.6	15.7	19.4	24.6	31.6
Locomotive engineers	100.0	12.4	17.3	19.7	23.0	27.3	100.0	9.7	16.0	19.0	24.4	30.7	100.0	13.5	17.2	19.6	22.4	27.1	100.0	11.3	15.9	18.8	24.6	29.1
Locomotive firemen	100.0	9.6	17.0	20.3	23.5	29.3	100.0	7.2	14.4	20.2	25.2	32.6	100.0	12.6	17.5	19.8	22.3	27.4	100.0	11.2	17.0	20.4	22.2	28.9
Machinists, millwrights, & toolmakers	100.0	10.6	17.3	19.7	22.9	29.2	100.0	8.3	15.5	19.4	24.3	32.5	100.0	13.2	17.5	19.8	21.9	27.8	100.0	11.5	16.2	19.5	22.2	30.1
Masons, tile setters, & stone cutters	100.0	6.0	13.7	19.7	25.1	35.2	100.0	6.1	12.2	17.8	24.8	38.8	100.0	8.8	14.9	19.3	24.0	32.7	100.0	8.0	14.0	18.0	24.0	35.7
Mechanics & repairmen, & loom fixers	100.0	8.3	16.1	20.2	23.7	31.3	100.0	7.1	14.1	19.4	24.8	34.8	100.0	12.4	16.5	19.3	21.9	29.9	100.0	9.7	15.2	19.2	24.0	31.8
Molders, metal	100.0	9.3	16.9	20.2	23.7	29.7	100.0	7.9	14.1	19.9	24.3	34.3	100.0	12.4	17.5	20.0	21.9	27.9	100.0	11.6	16.3	19.1	22.7	30.1
Painters (const.), paperhgrs., glaziers	100.0	5.6	13.5	20.3	25.1	35.2	100.0	6.2	12.2	17.5	24.3	39.2	100.0	10.2	16.2	19.8	21.9	30.8	100.0	8.9	14.8	19.1	22.7	33.7
Plasterers and cement finishers	100.0	5.9	13.6	19.3	25.1	35.8	100.0	6.4	11.8	17.9	24.5	39.1	100.0	9.1	16.2	19.8	23.9	30.2	100.0	8.0	14.8	18.2	23.3	36.4
Plumbers and pipe fitters	100.0	8.0	15.4	20.1	24.0	32.2	100.0	6.7	13.4	19.0	24.2	36.4	100.0	10.4	16.3	19.3	23.2	30.5	100.0	9.9	15.4	19.0	22.5	32.8
Print. craft., exc. compos. & typeset.	100.0	8.2	14.8	19.0	23.9	33.8	100.0	7.1	13.6	18.6	24.2	37.5	100.0	9.8	14.7	17.0	22.9	32.9	100.0	9.8	14.1	18.6	22.5	36.3
Rollers and roll hands, metal	100.0	9.8	15.5	18.0	20.9	35.6	100.0	7.1	13.6	17.7	22.1	39.2	100.0	11.3	14.7	17.0	19.7	37.0	100.0	10.7	14.1	16.9	20.7	37.4
Roofers and sheet metal workers	100.0	7.5	15.7	20.5	24.0	32.1	100.0	6.7	12.7	17.8	24.3	38.6	100.0	11.3	15.0	19.3	23.1	29.4	100.0	10.7	14.1	16.9	20.7	37.4
Shoemakers & repairers, exc. factory	100.0	5.2	13.0	19.6	25.6	36.5	100.0	6.4	12.7	17.8	24.3	38.6	100.0	7.4	15.0	19.7	24.2	33.6	100.0	7.8	13.5	18.9	23.6	36.0
Stat. engineers, cranemen, hoistmen	100.0	9.5	15.6	19.0	22.6	33.1	100.0	8.1	13.0	18.8	23.1	34.6	100.0	12.3	16.6	18.7	22.7	33.1	100.0	10.4	15.8	19.2	21.6	32.1
Structural metal workers	100.0	9.0	16.1	19.4	23.5	31.8	100.0	6.6	13.1	18.5	24.4	37.2	100.0	12.3	15.9	18.7	22.5	29.5	100.0	10.4	15.8	18.4	22.5	33.3
Tailors and furriers	100.0	7.8	14.8	19.4	22.9	34.9	100.0	7.0	13.0	18.2	23.2	38.3	100.0	10.4	15.4	18.9	21.9	33.2	100.0	8.8	14.4	17.9	22.0	36.7

TABLE C-5.—PERCENT OF AGGREGATE WAGE OR SALARY INCOME RECEIVED BY EACH FIFTH OF ALL WORKERS AND FULL-YEAR WORKERS IN SELECTED OCCUPATIONS, RANKED BY WAGE OR SALARY INCOME, BY SEX, FOR THE UNITED STATES: 1949 AND 1939—Cont.

Occupation and sex	All workers												Full-year workers											
	1949						1939						1949						1939					
	Total	Lowest fifth	Second	Middle	Fourth	Highest fifth	Total	Lowest fifth	Second	Middle	Fourth	Highest fifth	Total	Lowest fifth	Second	Middle	Fourth	Highest fifth	Total	Lowest fifth	Second	Middle	Fourth	Highest fifth
MALE.—Con.																								
Operatives and Kindred Workers																								
Apprentices	100.0	5.8	14.5	20.5	24.8	34.1	100.0	6.3	11.7	18.4	26.0	37.3	100.0	10.1	16.5	19.2	23.0	31.0	100.0	9.8	15.1	19.3	23.8	31.7
Attendants, auto service and parking	100.0	4.5	11.8	19.7	25.9	37.7	100.0	4.8	12.6	18.8	25.4	36.6	100.0	7.9	15.5	20.0	23.8	32.6	100.0	8.9	14.8	19.1	24.3	32.6
Brakemen and switchmen, railroad	100.0	10.5	17.4	20.4	23.3	28.1	100.0	8.0	15.5	20.7	25.3	30.2	100.0	13.2	17.7	20.0	22.1	26.7	100.0	12.0	17.5	20.5	22.4	27.3
Drivers, bus, taxi, truck, & del men	100.0	6.2	14.5	19.6	24.7	34.7	100.0	6.0	12.0	18.6	25.1	38.0	100.0	9.3	15.6	19.8	23.3	31.8	100.0	8.2	14.9	19.1	24.1	34.1
Stationary firemen	100.0	8.9	15.9	20.1	24.0	30.8	100.0	6.7	14.0	20.1	24.5	33.8	100.0	11.4	16.7	19.9	23.0	28.8	100.0	10.1	15.7	19.6	23.5	30.9
Mine operatives (n.e.c.)	100.0	6.9	15.6	19.2	23.8	34.2	100.0	6.8	13.1	18.4	24.7	36.9	100.0	9.5	15.4	18.9	23.0	32.4	100.0	8.3	14.9	19.7	24.2	32.7
Motormen, rwy., mine, factory, etc.	100.0	11.8	17.0	20.0	22.2	28.2	100.0	9.9	16.2	20.1	24.6	29.2	100.0	14.2	18.8	19.9	21.8	25.9	100.0	13.9	17.7	20.9	20.6	26.9
Painters, exc. constr. & maintenance	100.0	7.9	15.7	19.3	24.2	31.6	100.0	7.4	14.7	19.3	24.8	33.9	100.0	11.3	16.7	19.9	22.3	29.6	100.0	10.9	16.0	19.4	22.6	30.9
Sailors and deck hands	100.0	6.2	13.7	19.3	25.1	35.5	100.0	6.9	12.7	17.3	22.9	40.0	100.0	9.4	15.7	19.5	22.8	32.8	100.0	9.3	14.0	18.3	22.4	35.8
Welders and flame-cutters	100.0	9.4	16.6	20.5	22.9	30.3	100.0	7.7	14.9	19.9	22.6	32.6	100.0	12.6	17.4	19.0	22.0	28.8	100.0	11.3	16.4	19.7	22.2	30.1
Operatives & kindred workers (n.e.c.):																								
Food and kindred products	100.0	6.6	15.7	20.1	24.6	32.7	100.0	6.6	14.0	19.4	24.3	35.4	100.0	10.8	16.4	19.8	22.9	29.9	100.0	10.3	15.8	19.1	22.4	32.2
Knitting mills	100.0	6.5	13.5	18.1	24.7	36.9	100.0	7.2	12.8	18.0	24.4	37.4	100.0	9.5	14.4	18.4	23.4	34.1	100.0	9.9	13.2	18.1	21.7	34.8
Text. mill prod., exc. knit. mills	100.0	8.4	16.2	20.0	23.4	31.8	100.0	9.0	15.3	17.9	23.8	34.3	100.0	12.0	17.3	18.8	22.3	29.8	100.0	13.0	14.7	18.3	22.7	32.0
Apparel & other fabric text. prod.	100.0	6.8	14.4	18.2	24.0	36.8	100.0	6.8	12.3	17.9	23.8	38.9	100.0	9.2	14.8	18.3	22.3	35.6	100.0	9.0	13.7	17.5	22.8	36.7
Furniture, and lumber and wood prod.	100.0	5.4	12.5	19.4	25.9	36.5	100.0	7.3	13.8	18.5	24.4	35.8	100.0	8.1	14.7	18.9	25.0	32.1	100.0	10.5	14.8	19.1	23.3	32.1
Paper, paper prod., and printing	100.0	8.2	16.1	20.1	23.8	31.5	100.0	7.9	14.7	19.1	24.6	34.6	100.0	11.3	16.0	19.5	22.8	29.5	100.0	11.3	16.0	18.6	21.8	32.0
Chemicals & petrol., & coal prod.	100.0	9.0	16.6	20.5	23.5	30.1	100.0	7.8	15.5	20.1	24.5	31.8	100.0	11.8	16.6	19.4	22.8	28.4	100.0	11.7	16.4	19.3	21.8	29.0
Rubber products	100.0	10.3	17.2	20.5	22.9	28.8	100.0	7.9	15.3	20.1	24.5	31.2	100.0	12.1	17.2	20.1	22.2	27.3	100.0	12.1	16.1	19.1	23.2	29.3
Footwear industries, exc. rubber	100.0	7.8	15.3	20.2	24.0	32.5	100.0	8.2	14.7	19.2	24.0	33.7	100.0	11.7	16.5	19.1	22.6	30.0	100.0	11.4	15.7	19.3	22.3	31.1
Leather & leath. prod.,exc. footwear	100.0	7.8	16.0	20.3	24.6	31.0	100.0	7.4	14.7	19.6	24.0	34.0	100.0	12.3	16.6	19.1	22.5	28.6	100.0	11.7	16.5	19.1	21.9	30.6
Stone, clay, and glass products	100.0	8.7	15.9	19.7	23.2	32.2	100.0	7.7	14.5	19.7	24.3	34.3	100.0	11.6	16.3	19.3	21.8	31.5	100.0	11.2	16.0	19.3	22.2	31.5
Iron & steel, & not spec. metal ind.	100.0	9.0	16.4	20.2	23.6	30.5	100.0	7.4	14.4	19.7	23.8	34.4	100.0	12.6	17.1	19.6	21.8	28.7	100.0	11.8	16.2	18.8	22.3	30.6
Nonferrous metals & their products	100.0	8.3	16.5	20.5	24.0	30.5	100.0	7.4	14.4	19.7	24.0	33.2	100.0	12.7	17.1	19.6	21.6	28.1	100.0	12.0	16.5	19.1	22.3	30.4
Machinery	100.0	8.5	17.0	21.1	23.3	30.6	100.0	7.1	14.4	19.6	24.0	34.4	100.0	12.8	17.2	20.1	21.6	27.9	100.0	11.9	16.3	19.1	22.6	29.8
Motor vehicles & mtr. vehicle equip.	100.0	9.7	17.7	21.1	22.7	28.6	100.0	8.3	16.3	20.5	24.0	30.7	100.0	13.7	18.2	19.6	21.5	26.8	100.0	11.9	17.1	19.3	23.1	28.3
Trans. equip., exc. motor vehicle	100.0	9.3	17.2	20.5	23.0	29.7	100.0	6.4	13.7	19.2	24.9	35.9	100.0	13.7	17.2	19.6	21.5	27.7	100.0	11.5	16.3	18.9	22.3	30.7
Service Workers																								
Private household workers	100.0	3.8	10.5	17.6	25.3	42.6	100.0	6.1	11.1	15.9	23.7	43.0	100.0	6.2	12.9	18.2	24.1	38.3	100.0	7.1	11.2	17.4	24.1	40.0
Firemen, fire protection	100.0	12.8	17.5	19.7	21.7	28.1	100.0	11.6	17.5	19.3	21.7	29.8	100.0	15.1	17.6	19.4	20.5	27.4	100.0	12.7	16.2	19.5	20.4	31.0
Guards and watchmen	100.0	8.0	16.2	20.1	24.1	31.5	100.0	7.6	14.7	19.3	24.3	33.5	100.0	11.1	16.6	20.1	23.0	29.5	100.0	10.1	15.8	19.5	22.9	31.5
Policemen, sheriffs, and marshalls	100.0	10.7	16.5	20.1	23.5	29.3	100.0	8.7	15.6	19.2	23.7	32.8	100.0	11.1	16.6	20.0	23.0	28.5	100.0	10.2	14.5	19.1	21.6	33.3
Barbers, beauticians, & manicurists	100.0	6.5	13.8	19.4	23.9	36.2	100.0	7.5	13.1	19.1	23.7	36.6	100.0	9.4	14.5	19.8	21.8	32.9	100.0	9.6	14.5	19.1	22.6	34.1
Charmen, janitors, and porters	100.0	5.7	14.4	20.0	24.8	34.9	100.0	6.5	13.1	18.3	25.3	36.6	100.0	8.7	15.8	20.0	23.2	32.0	100.0	8.1	14.0	18.9	24.9	33.9
Cooks, exc. private household	100.0	6.3	13.5	19.1	24.8	36.0	100.0	6.7	12.7	17.7	24.4	38.2	100.0	9.7	15.6	19.0	23.0	32.4	100.0	8.4	13.9	18.6	23.3	35.6

TABLE C-5.—PERCENT OF AGGREGATE WAGE OR SALARY INCOME RECEIVED BY EACH FIFTH OF ALL WORKERS AND FULL-YEAR WORKERS IN SELECTED OCCUPATIONS, RANKED BY WAGE OR SALARY INCOME, BY SEX, FOR THE UNITED STATES: 1949 AND 1939—Cont.

Occupation and sex	All workers 1949						All workers 1939						Full-year workers 1949						Full-year workers 1939					
	Total	Low-est fifth	Sec-ond	Mid-dle	Fourth	High-est fifth	Total	Low-est fifth	Sec-ond	Mid-dle	Fourth	High-est fifth	Total	Low-est fifth	Sec-ond	Mid-dle	Fourth	High-est fifth	Total	Low-est fifth	Sec-ond	Mid-dle	Fourth	High-est fifth
MALE—Con.																								
Service Workers—Con.																								
Elevator operators	100.0	8.3	16.3	21.3	23.9	30.1	100.0	8.5	15.5	20.3	24.4	31.1	100.0	12.0	17.4	19.2	23.1	28.1	100.0	11.2	16.3	20.0	23.4	28.8
Waiters, bartenders, & counter wkrs.	100.0	4.9	13.3	20.0	25.3	36.4	100.0	6.3	13.0	18.2	24.7	37.6	100.0	8.6	16.1	19.2	23.9	31.6	100.0	8.6	14.4	19.3	23.9	33.5
Service wkrs., exc. pr. hshld.(n.e.c.)	100.0	3.9	10.9	18.3	26.1	40.6	100.0	7.5	12.5	18.6	24.6	36.6	100.0	8.0	14.6	19.1	24.4	33.7	100.0	8.9	14.7	18.9	23.4	33.8
Laborers, Except Farm and Mine																								
Fishermen and oystermen	100.0	4.2	9.6	16.2	24.2	45.5	100.0	6.3	9.3	15.1	23.1	46.0	100.0	5.9	11.4	16.9	24.5	41.1	100.0	5.6	9.7	15.3	23.8	45.4
Longshoremen and stevedores	100.0	6.8	14.4	19.9	25.1	33.5	100.0	6.3	12.0	17.7	24.7	39.1	100.0	9.5	16.2	16.9	23.1	31.0	100.0	8.3	14.5	18.5	23.8	34.7
Lumbermen, raftsmen, & woodchoppers	100.0	3.4	10.2	15.5	23.9	46.7	100.0	7.1	10.9	15.9	22.6	43.1	100.0	5.3	11.7	16.2	23.5	43.1	100.0	7.7	11.3	16.0	22.2	42.5
Laborers (n.e.c.):																								
Manufacturing industries:																								
Food and kindred products	100.0	6.2	14.4	20.5	25.4	33.2	100.0	6.0	12.8	18.9	26.3	35.7	100.0	10.5	16.8	20.1	23.5	28.9	100.0	9.8	16.0	20.2	23.7	30.2
Textiles, text. prod., & apparel	100.0	7.4	15.7	19.3	23.5	33.8	100.0	7.7	14.7	19.4	23.4	34.2	100.0	11.8	15.6	19.8	21.6	30.9	100.0	11.8	16.4	17.7	22.8	31.0
Furniture, and lumber & wood prod.	100.0	5.3	11.8	17.9	24.8	39.9	100.0	8.1	11.8	17.4	23.6	38.9	100.0	7.8	14.1	18.4	24.3	35.2	100.0	9.2	14.1	19.0	21.8	35.7
Paper, paper prod., & printing	100.0	7.2	16.5	19.7	23.2	32.5	100.0	7.4	14.5	19.9	25.0	33.0	100.0	11.7	17.2	19.6	22.5	28.7	100.0	11.1	16.6	20.4	22.7	29.0
Chemicals & petrol., & coal prod.	100.0	6.8	15.8	20.4	25.2	31.5	100.0	5.8	14.5	19.3	26.4	33.9	100.0	11.7	16.7	20.3	22.5	28.7	100.0	10.9	16.3	20.5	23.8	29.9
Stone, clay, and glass products	100.0	7.5	15.5	20.3	24.3	32.2	100.0	7.5	14.1	19.3	24.9	33.8	100.0	11.2	17.4	20.0	22.5	28.7	100.0	10.8	15.7	20.5	23.2	29.9
Iron & steel & not spec. metal ind.	100.0	8.8	17.1	19.7	23.9	30.5	100.0	7.1	13.7	20.2	25.3	33.5	100.0	13.6	18.9	19.9	22.1	27.9	100.0	11.8	17.1	19.8	23.2	30.0
Nonferrous metals and their prod.	100.0	8.4	17.1	19.7	23.9	29.9	100.0	7.1	14.0	20.8	25.1	31.5	100.0	13.6	17.2	19.9	22.1	27.4	100.0	11.8	17.0	20.3	21.8	29.1
Machinery	100.0	7.4	16.7	20.4	24.1	31.2	100.0	7.0	14.1	20.3	25.1	32.5	100.0	12.6	16.6	19.8	22.3	28.5	100.0	11.9	17.0	19.6	22.4	28.9
Motor vehicles & mtr. veh. equip.	100.0	8.8	17.1	20.9	24.3	29.6	100.0	7.0	14.6	20.3	25.4	32.5	100.0	13.0	17.8	20.3	22.3	26.9	100.0	11.9	17.0	20.1	22.5	28.1
Trans. equipment, exc. motor veh.	100.0	7.4	16.7	20.1	24.3	31.2	100.0	6.6	13.3	19.0	26.1	34.8	100.0	12.9	16.8	20.0	21.4	28.7	100.0	11.3	17.1	20.1	22.5	28.7
Nonmanufacturing industries:																								
Construction	100.0	5.1	11.9	18.6	25.5	38.7	100.0	7.2	11.0	16.8	24.2	40.6	100.0	8.2	15.3	18.9	23.8	33.5	100.0	8.6	14.2	18.0	24.8	34.1
Railroads & rwy. express service	100.0	7.8	16.5	20.8	24.5	30.1	100.0	8.0	14.8	19.5	24.0	33.5	100.0	12.4	17.9	20.0	21.9	27.6	100.0	11.9	16.3	18.9	22.6	30.1
Transportation, exc. railroad	100.0	4.9	14.5	20.2	25.0	35.1	100.0	6.0	10.8	17.9	26.4	38.7	100.0	9.7	16.5	20.1	23.7	29.7	100.0	8.3	14.5	19.9	24.9	32.1
Telecomm. & util. & sanitary serv.	100.0	6.9	14.8	20.6	24.9	32.5	100.0	6.5	13.1	19.5	25.9	34.7	100.0	10.5	16.7	19.8	23.4	29.3	100.0	9.5	16.1	20.2	23.5	30.5
Wholesale and retail trade	100.0	4.0	11.6	19.5	26.9	37.8	100.0	6.5	11.7	17.7	25.2	38.7	100.0	7.8	15.1	20.1	24.4	32.4	100.0	8.4	14.3	18.4	24.8	33.9
FEMALE, EXPERIENCED CIVILIAN LABOR FORCE																								
Profess'l, Techn'l, Kindred Wkrs.																								
Librarians	100.0	3.6	11.7	19.5	27.2	37.7	100.0	5.5	12.9	19.0	25.0	37.4	100.0	5.7	15.0	20.2	25.4	33.4	100.0	7.5	14.2	19.0	23.7	35.4
Musicians and music teachers	100.0	2.8	7.0	15.6	27.6	46.7	100.0	5.0	8.9	14.9	23.3	47.6	100.0	2.9	8.9	17.6	25.9	44.6	100.0	4.9	9.5	15.1	22.0	48.2
Social, welfare, and recreation wkrs.	100.0	6.1	15.9	19.7	24.2	33.9	100.0	7.5	14.9	18.9	23.4	35.0	100.0	10.5	15.5	19.3	22.6	31.4	100.0	10.3	15.5	18.2	22.3	33.4
Teachers (n.e.c.)	100.0	5.7	14.5	19.7	25.0	34.5	100.0	6.0	13.1	16.4	24.1	41.1	100.0	7.1	15.5	20.1	22.9	32.9	100.0	7.5	12.6	17.6	22.3	40.1
Nurses, professional & student prof.	100.0	4.5	13.3	21.1	25.7	35.2	100.0	6.4	13.5	18.7	24.3	36.8	100.0	9.1	17.2	19.5	23.1	30.9	100.0	8.6	14.7	18.6	23.6	34.3

TABLE C-5.—PERCENT OF AGGREGATE WAGE OR SALARY INCOME RECEIVED BY EACH FIFTH OF ALL WORKERS AND FULL-YEAR WORKERS IN SELECTED OCCUPATIONS, RANKED BY WAGE OR SALARY INCOME, BY SEX, FOR THE UNITED STATES: 1949 AND 1939—Cont.

Occupation and sex	All workers												Full-year workers											
	1949						1939						1949						1939					
	Total	Lowest fifth	Second	Middle	Fourth	Highest fifth	Total	Lowest fifth	Second	Middle	Fourth	Highest fifth	Total	Lowest fifth	Second	Middle	Fourth	Highest fifth	Total	Lowest fifth	Second	Middle	Fourth	Highest fifth
FEMALE.—Con.																								
Clerical, Sales, and Kindred Workers																								
Bookk'prs, accts, cashs, ticket agts.	100.0	6.4	15.1	19.8	24.0	34.7	100.0	7.4	14.3	19.0	24.1	35.0	100.0	10.8	15.6	20.0	22.4	31.2	100.0	10.6	15.0	18.6	22.5	33.0
Office machine operators	100.0	8.2	16.7	21.2	23.8	30.6	100.0	8.8	16.7	20.5	24.0	29.8	100.0	13.6	17.6	19.3	22.0	27.3	100.0	13.7	16.9	19.1	22.6	27.4
Stenographers, typists, and secys.	100.0	7.2	15.8	20.6	23.8	32.3	100.0	7.6	14.9	19.1	23.5	34.6	100.0	12.3	16.7	18.8	22.5	29.4	100.0	11.1	15.7	18.8	22.5	31.9
Telephone operators	100.0	7.3	16.0	21.0	23.6	31.9	100.0	7.5	15.2	20.0	24.6	32.5	100.0	11.9	17.0	19.9	22.3	28.7	100.0	10.4	15.8	19.6	23.3	30.6
Saleswomen and sales clerks (n.e.c.)	100.0	3.8	10.5	18.9	25.6	41.0	100.0	6.7	13.0	19.6	23.5	36.9	100.0	9.1	14.7	19.5	22.8	33.6	100.0	10.5	16.5	17.5	22.3	33.1
Operatives and Kindred Workers																								
Dressmakers & seamstr., exc. factory	100.0	5.1	13.9	19.5	24.9	36.4	100.0	6.8	11.8	18.4	24.3	38.5	100.0	10.4	15.3	19.7	23.2	31.2	100.0	8.0	15.2	18.0	23.7	34.8
Operatives & kindred wkrs. (n.e.c.):																								
Food and kindred products	100.0	4.3	11.8	19.7	27.3	36.6	100.0	7.5	12.0	19.1	25.5	35.7	100.0	10.4	17.2	20.0	22.7	29.4	100.0	11.2	17.7	19.1	22.8	29.1
Tobacco manufactures	100.0	6.5	14.7	20.1	24.3	34.2	100.0	8.9	15.2	18.4	24.1	33.1	100.0	12.0	17.1	19.3	23.6	27.8	100.0	12.5	17.0	18.8	22.6	28.8
Knitting mills	100.0	6.5	14.4	19.0	24.2	35.7	100.0	8.5	15.4	19.9	23.1	32.8	100.0	12.0	16.2	18.6	23.2	29.8	100.0	13.0	17.9	17.9	22.3	28.6
Textile mill prod., exc. knit. mills	100.0	7.0	15.5	21.0	25.0	31.4	100.0	8.7	15.5	20.0	24.2	31.3	100.0	13.0	17.2	20.1	22.1	27.4	100.0	14.1	18.5	18.5	21.0	27.6
Apparel & other fabric text. prod.	100.0	6.7	14.7	18.9	24.4	35.1	100.0	8.7	13.8	17.7	24.7	34.8	100.0	11.8	15.7	18.9	22.8	30.6	100.0	11.9	17.0	18.1	21.5	31.0
Furniture, and lumber and wood prod.	100.0	4.9	13.1	19.4	25.8	36.6	100.0	8.0	14.1	19.7	24.2	33.8	100.0	11.8	16.0	19.7	21.8	30.4	100.0	12.1	17.6	19.0	21.5	29.4
Paper, paper prod., and printing	100.0	6.2	15.3	20.4	24.1	34.0	100.0	7.7	14.1	21.1	24.2	32.1	100.0	12.4	16.9	19.9	21.8	28.9	100.0	13.6	16.7	19.6	21.5	29.0
Chemicals & petrol., & coal prod.	100.0	6.8	15.9	20.5	24.1	32.5	100.0	7.4	15.8	20.1	24.6	32.0	100.0	12.6	16.8	19.9	22.5	27.6	100.0	13.5	16.2	19.6	21.9	28.5
Footwear industries, exc. rubber	100.0	6.9	15.7	19.5	23.4	34.3	100.0	9.0	14.9	18.3	25.1	32.0	100.0	12.6	16.4	19.2	22.5	29.1	100.0	12.5	18.0	18.7	21.7	28.8
Leather & leath. prod., exc. footwear	100.0	6.6	14.0	19.0	24.9	35.4	100.0	8.6	13.6	18.3	25.4	33.9	100.0	12.4	17.0	19.0	23.3	28.0	100.0	12.6	18.0	18.0	22.7	28.5
Stone, clay, and glass products	100.0	6.2	14.4	21.2	24.9	32.1	100.0	7.5	15.1	20.7	24.4	33.0	100.0	13.0	16.6	20.1	21.4	28.6	100.0	13.5	16.5	19.6	21.8	28.4
Metal industries and machinery	100.0	5.8	15.5	21.2	24.9	32.3	100.0	7.1	15.1	19.5	25.0	33.0	100.0	13.2	16.2	19.8	22.0	26.8	100.0	13.6	16.2	19.7	22.7	27.6
Transportation equipment	100.0	7.5	17.3	20.8	24.9	29.2	100.0	7.6	15.0	20.5	25.0	31.7	100.0	13.4	17.3	21.0	21.6	26.4	100.0	12.3	16.7	20.3	22.3	28.2
Service Workers																								
Private household workers	100.0	7.0	7.0	15.8	22.7	47.1	100.0	8.5	12.0	17.0	22.9	39.3	100.0	5.4	11.9	16.4	24.1	42.0	100.0	7.6	13.9	15.2	24.6	38.4
Barbers, beauticians, & manicurists.	100.0	5.0	12.2	19.0	25.1	38.5	100.0	6.9	12.3	19.1	23.8	36.7	100.0	8.8	14.2	17.9	24.9	35.2	100.0	9.9	15.5	18.4	22.4	33.6
Charwomen, janitors, and porters	100.0	3.9	11.6	18.9	25.2	40.4	100.0	7.8	13.9	19.1	23.7	35.3	100.0	6.9	14.2	18.5	24.9	35.5	100.0	9.0	15.0	20.5	22.7	32.5
Cooks, exc. private household	100.0	4.4	11.8	16.5	24.6	42.5	100.0	7.8	11.6	18.5	24.4	37.5	100.0	8.1	13.9	17.7	23.9	36.2	100.0	8.4	13.4	17.9	23.4	36.5
Housek'prs, stewards, exc. pr. hshld.	100.0	6.4	13.0	18.8	25.4	36.1	100.0	7.0	12.8	18.4	24.4	38.0	100.0	8.3	14.7	17.7	23.9	33.5	100.0	8.6	14.1	17.7	23.4	35.7
Practical nurses and midwives	100.0	4.1	10.1	16.6	24.8	44.1	100.0	6.4	11.6	16.4	24.4	41.2	100.0	7.0	14.4	18.2	24.0	36.4	100.0	7.2	12.0	18.0	24.2	38.6
Waitresses, bartenders, counter wkrs.	100.0	4.9	10.9	16.2	25.1	43.0	100.0	8.1	12.7	18.3	24.0	36.6	100.0	8.9	14.4	18.0	24.4	34.1	100.0	9.7	15.1	17.4	24.0	33.4
Service wkrs., exc. pr. hshld. (n.e.c.)	100.0	4.9	12.7	17.4	25.0	39.8	100.0	8.6	13.0	18.8	24.3	34.9	100.0	9.1	13.8	19.4	24.5	33.1	100.0	9.9	13.8	19.0	24.5	32.7

Source: Derived from tables C-1 to C-4.

TABLE C-6.—SELECTED ESTIMATES FOR WAGE OR SALARY WORKERS IN SELECTED OCCUPATIONS, BY SEX, FOR THE UNITED STATES: 1949 AND 1939

Occupation and sex	Percent distribution of all wage or salary workers by occupation		Proportion of full-year workers by occupation			Percent change, 1939 to 1949							
						Increase in median income		Decrease in relative dispersion $(Q_3-Q_1)/Q_2$ [+ = increase]		Decrease in share of aggregate received by highest-paid fifth [+ = increase]			
	1949	1939	1949	1939	Percent change [- = decrease]	All workers	Full-year workers	All workers	Full-year workers	All workers	Full-year workers
MALE											
Experienced civ. labor force...	100.0	100.0	...	...	...	...	...	...	...	...	...
Profess'l, Techn'l, Kindred Wkrs.											
Artists and art teachers...	0.1	0.1	68.4	66.2	3.3	119	104	26.3	28.9	6.8	4.6
Authors, editors, and reporters...	0.2	0.2	77.8	82.2	-5.4	107	107	27.1	34.5	2.1	2.4
Chemists...	0.3	0.3	80.7	83.6	-3.5	103	98	19.0	23.4	11.4	9.4
Clergymen...	0.5	0.6	84.9	90.2	-5.9	83	88	+4.6	+0.9	11.4	12.2
Coll. pres., prof'rs, instr's (n.e.c.)...	0.4	0.3	56.0	51.8	8.1	48	42	14.5	23.2	2.4	7.4
Designers and draftsmen...	0.6	0.5	79.1	78.9	0.3	96	90	22.7	22.1	10.5	11.2
Engineers, civil...	0.5	0.4	80.8	85.9	-5.9	82	82	26.3	33.4	0.5	2.2
Engineers, electrical...	0.4	0.3	83.4	89.7	-7.0	74	73	33.6	36.6	6.3	7.5
Engineers, mechanical...	0.8	0.4	81.8	87.2	-6.2	73	72	35.5	36.1	6.6	6.7
Musicians and music teachers...	0.2	0.3	42.3	39.1	8.2	150	87	2.0	7.6	6.8	5.9
Pharmacists...	0.2	0.2	78.1	83.1	-6.0	134	134	0.2	6.0	5.0	6.5
Social, welfare, and recreation wkrs...	0.1	0.1	73.5	82.2	-10.6	91	97	+0.9	9.3	5.2	11.6
Sports instr't's, athletes, entertainers	0.2	0.1	46.2	40.1	15.2	138	139	18.3	34.5	10.7	15.0
Teachers (n.e.c.)...	1.1	1.3	48.7	29.9	62.9	122	85	33.1	34.3	18.9	20.6
Salaried Managers and Officials											
Conductors, railroad...	0.2	0.2	69.9	74.7	-6.4	79	78	6.8	4.6	13.0	14.5
Postmasters, and misc. govt. officials	0.8	1.0	85.2	88.8	-4.1	73	72	21.5	24.8	10.0	9.6
Managers and officials:											
Manufacturing...	1.5	1.4	87.7	92.7	-5.4	73	67	28.9	31.1	+17.9	+20.8
Trans., commun., & other pub. util...	0.6	0.6	90.0	94.1	-4.4	73	70	40.8	42.1	3.1	3.6
Wholesale trade...	0.5	0.5	88.5	91.0	-2.7	88	85	38.3	38.5	1.2	1.4
Eating and drinking places...	0.2	0.2	75.4	79.3	-4.9	131	135	19.4	27.3	14.3	17.7
Retail trade, exc. eating & drinking	1.4	2.0	86.6	89.3	-3.0	129	124	16.0	13.6	5.5	5.6
Finance, insur., and real estate...	0.6	0.7	88.7	94.5	-6.1	62	59	32.0	32.9	+11.0	+10.7
Business and repair services...	0.2	0.1	85.3	88.6	-3.7	125	120	+1.1	3.0	0.4	1.3
Personal services...	0.1	0.2	78.7	84.0	-6.3	100	94	22.5	23.7	10.3	12.2
Clerical, Sales, and Kindred Workers											
Baggagemen, exp. mess., rwy. mail clk.	0.1	0.1	82.2	88.2	-6.8	62	64	9.5	6.0	3.6	3.4
Bookk'prs, accs., cashs., ticket agts.	2.2	2.3	80.8	84.8	-4.7	107	102	20.5	22.7	10.4	11.4
Mail carriers...	0.7	0.6	84.6	88.4	-4.3	62	63	13.2	9.0	5.9	5.8
Messengers, except express...	0.2	0.3	56.4	57.1	-1.2	135	155	+36.0	+5.8	+5.2	0.6
Shipping and receiving clerks...	1.2	1.1	72.3	71.7	0.8	131	123	19.4	11.1	5.2	6.2
Stenographers, typists, and secys...	0.3	0.4	79.6	79.4	0.3	124	118	6.8	2.7	+0.2	...

TABLE C–6.—SELECTED ESTIMATES FOR WAGE OR SALARY WORKERS IN SELECTED OCCUPATIONS, BY SEX, FOR THE UNITED STATES: 1949 AND 1939—Cont.

Occupation and sex	Percent distribution of all wage or salary workers by occupation		Proportion of full-year workers by occupation			Percent change, 1939 to 1949					
						Increase in median income		Decrease in relative dispersion $\frac{q_3-q_1}{q_2}$ [+ = increase]		Decrease in share of aggregate received by highest-paid fifth [+ = increase]	
	1949	1939	1949	1939	Percent change [– = decrease]	All workers	Full-year workers	All workers	Full-year workers	All workers	Full-year workers
MALE.—Con.											
Clerical, Sales, & Kind. Wkrs.—Con.											
Telegraph operators	0.1	0.2	76.9	79.0	-2.7	85	82	27.1	31.5	2.7	4.3
Newsboys	0.3	0.1	56.6	59.4	-4.7	23	2	22.1	35.3	+14.0	+23.5
Insurance agents and brokers	0.9	0.9	80.7	86.5	-6.7	87	83	22.9	26.4	11.4	11.8
Real estate agents and brokers	0.2	0.2	70.2	80.7	-13.0	112	114	9.8	13.9	9.7	11.2
Salesmen and sales clerks (n.e.c.)	7.3	8.3	73.3	76.5	-4.2	132	130	17.2	20.8	5.8	6.4
Craftsmen, Foremen, & Kindred Wkrs.											
Bakers	0.4	0.5	72.3	73.7	-1.9	136	131	18.4	9.7	11.2	9.9
Blacksmiths, forgemen, and hammermen	0.2	0.3	58.8	53.3	10.3	157	132	39.5	31.8	14.4	9.6
Boilermakers	0.2	0.2	55.7	54.5	2.2	128	108	29.7	17.2	9.8	3.5
Cabinetmakers and patternmakers	0.4	0.4	61.7	56.7	8.8	135	120	21.8	23.4	6.6	7.0
Carpenters	3.2	2.7	40.0	28.3	41.3	171	127	19.1	17.8	11.2	9.2
Compositors and typesetters	0.6	0.7	79.6	70.5	12.9	140	123	25.0	21.0	9.9	10.1
Electricians	1.2	1.0	67.4	63.9	5.5	126	109	29.1	22.0	10.4	7.5
Foremen (n.e.c.):											
Construction	0.2	0.3	68.5	59.0	16.1	155	133	19.2	0.9	9.2	2.1
Manufacturing	1.9	1.4	85.7	84.5	1.4	118	111	18.7	14.2	9.9	7.8
Trans., commun., & other pub. util.	0.5	0.5	87.3	90.5	-3.5	96	95	17.8	17.5	12.4	12.3
Inspectors (n.e.c.)	0.4	0.4	71.7	79.1	-9.4	88	89	13.1	12.5	5.5	5.7
Linemen & servicemen, t'lgraph, etc.	0.9	0.9	85.4	85.0	0.5	75	68	18.2	18.2	9.9	7.9
Locomotive engineers	0.3	0.4	68.4	72.3	-5.4	83	82	28.2	36.8	11.1	6.9
Locomotive firemen	0.2	0.2	56.9	52.8	7.8	119	97	36.5	18.1	10.1	5.2
Machinists, millwrights, & toolmakers	3.1	3.2	70.3	62.8	11.9	129	115	33.9	30.3	10.2	7.6
Masons, tile setters, & stone cutters	0.6	0.6	37.2	20.6	80.6	175	127	13.9	13.0	9.3	8.4
Mechanics & repairmen, & loom fixers	6.7	4.1	72.3	68.1	6.2	137	126	26.2	19.9	10.1	6.0
Molders, metal	0.2	0.4	56.9	43.0	32.3	147	122	32.0	26.2	10.5	7.3
Painters (const.), paperhgrs., glaziers	1.2	1.5	40.8	26.2	55.7	179	131	16.7	19.0	10.2	8.6
Plasterers and cement finishers	0.3	0.3	35.8	18.4	94.6	199	164	12.1	13.6	8.4	10.2
Plumbers and pipe fitters	1.0	0.8	61.6	52.0	18.5	151	128	21.6	4.9	11.5	7.0
Print. craft., exc. compos. & typeset.	0.4	0.3	80.6	70.3	14.7	122	106	17.3	11.7	9.9	9.4
Rollers and roll hands, metal	0.1	0.1	34.4	39.0	-11.8	119	103	35.1	32.0	9.2	1.1
Roofers and sheet metal workers	0.6	0.5	56.9	45.5	25.1	154	124	27.7	25.1	10.8	10.4
Shoemakers & repairers, exc. factory	0.1	0.1	66.1	71.4	-7.4	149	146	3.2	12.2	5.4	6.9
Stat. engineers, cranemen, hoistmen	1.8	1.6	67.6	67.5	0.1	123	112	16.5	1.0	4.3	+3.1
Structural metal workers	0.2	0.2	46.2	32.8	40.9	163	130	34.6	22.6	14.5	11.4
Tailors and furriers	0.2	0.4	58.2	43.9	32.6	164	133	24.8	18.5	8.9	9.5

TABLE C–6.—SELECTED ESTIMATES FOR WAGE OR SALARY WORKERS IN SELECTED OCCUPATIONS, BY SEX, FOR THE UNITED STATES: 1949 AND 1939—Cont.

Occupation and sex	Percent distribution of all wage or salary workers by occupation		Proportion of full-year workers by occupation			Percent change, 1939 to 1949					
						Increase in median income		Decrease in relative dispersion $\frac{Q_3-Q_1}{Q_2}$ [+ = increase]		Decrease in share of aggregate received by highest-paid fifth [+ = increase]	
	1949	1939	1949	1939	Percent change [E = decrease]	All workers	Full-year workers	All workers	Full-year workers	All workers	Full-year workers
MALE—Con.											
Operatives and Kindred Workers											
Apprentices	0.5	0.4	56.9	46.6	22.1	214	164	25.7	18.4	8.6	2.2
Attendants, auto service and parking	0.9	1.0	58.5	64.2	-8.9	146	148	+0.7	7.9	+3.0	...
Brakemen and switchmen, railroad	0.6	0.6	61.8	57.4	7.7	104	91	32.7	17.2	7.0	2.2
Drivers, bus, taxi, & truck, & del'men	7.3	7.3	65.7	63.5	3.5	155	132	21.0	22.6	8.7	6.7
Stationary firemen	0.5	0.6	71.6	66.9	7.0	140	124	27.4	12.2	8.9	6.8
Mine operatives & laborers (n.e.c.)	2.4	3.6	26.4	18.8	40.4	178	135	24.4	12.7	7.3	0.9
Motormen, rwy., mine, factory, etc.	0.2	0.3	52.3	61.4	-14.8	104	96	26.3	15.3	3.4	3.7
Painters, exc. constr., & maintenance.	0.4	0.4	62.2	49.1	26.7	163	144	24.5	17.5	6.8	4.2
Sailors and deck hands	0.2	0.2	33.2	34.7	-4.3	192	166	6.9	22.6	11.3	8.4
Welders and flame-cutters	1.0	0.6	57.8	50.6	14.2	134	114	30.4	24.8	7.1	4.3
Operatives & kindred workers (n.e.c.):											
Food and kindred products	1.3	1.1	66.1	64.7	2.2	130	123	10.9	5.0	7.6	7.1
Knitting mills	0.2	0.3	57.3	37.5	52.8	175	172	3.7	8.1	1.3	2.0
Text. mill prod., exc. knit, mills	1.5	1.9	61.8	44.0	40.5	205	186	12.9	21.5	7.3	6.9
Apparel & other fabric text. prod.	0.7	0.8	43.1	29.8	44.6	170	139	14.0	11.2	5.4	3.0
Furniture, and lumber and wood prod.	1.1	0.7	52.3	47.2	10.8	131	125	+12.2	+12.8	+2.0	...
Paper, paper prod., and printing	0.8	0.7	71.1	60.8	16.9	151	141	13.8	6.6	9.0	7.8
Chemicals & petrol., & coal prod.	0.8	0.6	75.9	71.8	5.7	132	121	16.4	9.6	5.3	2.1
Rubber products	0.4	0.3	67.0	55.8	20.1	139	120	38.2	28.3	11.7	6.8
Footwear industries, exc. rubber	0.4	0.6	53.0	31.4	68.8	168	134	12.0	7.6	3.6	3.5
Leather & leath. prod.,exc. footwear	0.2	0.2	56.9	46.8	21.6	144	132	9.8	+1.6	8.8	6.5
Stone, clay, and glass products	0.6	0.5	62.7	45.9	35.9	145	126	21.1	1.0	6.1	4.4
Iron & steel, & not spec. metal ind.	1.6	1.4	49.9	46.8	6.6	141	123	28.3	14.5	11.3	6.2
Nonferrous metals & their products	0.3	0.3	57.0	53.3	6.9	139	128	21.9	10.4	8.1	7.6
Machinery	1.9	1.0	63.2	52.5	20.4	148	127	31.6	25.5	11.0	6.4
Motor vehicles & mtr. vehicle equip.	1.2	1.0	45.7	21.5	112.6	139	115	29.1	31.1	6.8	5.3
Trans. equip., exc. motor vehicle	0.4	0.3	64.9	49.7	30.6	177	130	47.5	26.8	17.3	9.8
Service Workers											
Private household workers	0.3	0.7	57.5	64.5	-10.9	164	168	+2.4	11.0	0.9	4.3
Firemen, fire protection	0.5	0.4	90.6	94.5	-4.1	57	56	12.1	14.1	11.9	11.6
Guards and watchmen	1.0	1.1	73.8	75.3	-2.0	137	131	15.4	14.0	7.1	7.9
Policemen, sheriffs, and marshalls	0.9	0.9	86.2	90.2	-4.4	61	59	24.9	23.4	5.1	14.4
Barbers, beauticians, & manicurists	0.4	0.5	68.2	79.3	-14.0	131	133	+3.5	7.2	1.4	3.5
Charmen, janitors, and porters	2.5	2.5	68.0	74.2	-8.4	138	129	21.1	28.2	4.6	5.6
Cooks, exc. private household	0.8	0.9	58.9	60.7	-3.0	177	159	13.9	21.9	5.8	9.0

TABLE C-6.—SELECTED ESTIMATES FOR WAGE OR SALARY WORKERS IN SELECTED OCCUPATIONS, BY SEX, FOR THE UNITED STATES: 1949 AND 1939—Cont.

Occupation and sex	Percent distribution of all wage or salary workers by occupation		Proportion of full-year workers by occupation			Percent change, 1939 to 1949					
						Increase in median income		Decrease in relative dispersion $\frac{Q_3-Q_1}{Q_2}$ [+ = increase]		Decrease in share of aggregate received by highest-paid fifth [+ = increase]	
	1949	1939	1949	1939	Percent change [E = decrease]	All workers	Full-year workers	All workers	Full-year workers	All workers	Full-year workers
MALE--Con.											
Service Workers--Con.											
Elevator operators..............	0.3	0.3	72.8	78.6	-7.4	116	111	13.8	15.2	3.2	2.4
Waiters, bartenders, & counter wkrs...	1.3	1.4	57.0	60.3	-5.5	165	150	5.9	15.0	3.2	5.7
Service wkrs, exc. pr. hshld.(n.e.c.)..	0.8	0.7	47.9	60.4	-20.7	122	152	+25.9	1.6	+10.9	0.3
Laborers, Except Farm and Mine											
Fishermen and oystermen..............	0.1	0.1	29.4	26.5	10.9	243	220	+1.9	16.5	1.1	9.5
Longshoremen and stevedores..........	0.3	0.3	37.7	28.4	32.7	177	131	23.6	24.6	14.3	10.7
Lumbermen, raftsmen, & woodchoppers...	0.6	0.7	29.4	21.6	36.1	162	152	+16.7	+15.9	+7.9	+1.4
Laborers (n.e.c.):											
Manufacturing industries:											
Food and kindred products.........	0.6	0.8	58.1	51.8	12.2	169	130	22.1	9.2	7.0	4.3
Textiles, text, prod., & apparel..	0.3	0.4	59.1	44.8	31.9	190	175	13.6	19.6	1.2	0.3
Furniture, and lumber & wood prod.	0.7	1.3	46.0	38.9	18.3	181	164	+14.9	+13.4	+2.6	1.7
Paper, paper prod., & printing....	0.2	0.3	64.5	54.5	18.3	167	139	20.0	7.2	1.5	1.0
Chemicals & petrol., & coal prod..	0.4	0.6	66.9	55.5	20.5	183	137	33.4	16.2	12.0	4.0
Stone, clay, and glass products...	0.3	0.5	57.5	40.1	43.4	186	148	22.7	23.7	5.0	4.3
Iron & steel & not spec.metal ind.	1.0	1.5	37.9	37.7	0.5	156	117	36.0	+3.2	9.0	4.1
Nonferrous metals and their prod.	0.1	0.2	52.4	50.8	3.1	131	120	23.2	+8.6	5.1	2.6
Machinery.........................	0.3	0.3	54.7	47.4	15.4	151	129	24.2	3.8	6.9	1.4
Motor vehicles & mtr. veh. equip..	0.2	0.3	45.2	23.3	94.0	147	119	33.1	28.9	8.9	4.3
Trans. equipment, exc. motor veh..	0.1	0.2	59.3	44.0	34.8	179	122	39.4	19.2	10.3	...
Nonmanufacturing industries:											
Construction......................	2.8	3.2	36.9	24.7	49.4	220	166	8.1	18.3	4.7	1.8
Railroads & rwy. express service..	1.1	1.2	59.2	55.2	7.2	178	160	19.4	25.8	10.1	8.3
Transportation, exc. railroad.....	0.4	0.4	54.4	48.9	11.2	202	144	27.6	29.3	9.3	7.5
Telecomm. & util.& sanitary serv..	0.5	0.5	67.8	65.5	3.5	111	92	17.7	8.7	6.3	3.9
Wholesale and retail trade........	1.2	1.0	54.8	52.9	3.6	164	156	+0.4	12.7	2.3	4.4
FEMALE											
Experienced civ. labor force....	100.0	100.0	...	...	...	...	...	...	...	...	...
Profess'l, Techn'l, Kindred Wkrs.											
Librarians.......................	0.5	0.4	61.0	68.3	-10.7	75	84	+25.4	+4.2	+0.8	5.6
Musicians and music teachers.....	0.4	0.4	29.6	32.5	-8.9	101	130	+30.8	+13.7	1.9	7.5
Social, welfare, and recreation wkrs..	0.6	0.6	70.1	77.9	-10.0	80	86	+2.6	+5.8	3.1	6.0
Teachers (n.e.c.)................	7.8	10.0	21.7	16.1	34.8	126	85	25.6	34.1	16.1	18.0
Nurses, professional & student prof...	3.6	3.3	53.5	55.1	-2.9	125	126	+7.5	30.2	4.3	10.0

TABLE C-6.—SELECTED ESTIMATES FOR WAGE OR SALARY WORKERS IN SELECTED OCCUPATIONS, BY SEX, FOR THE UNITED STATES: 1949 AND 1939—Cont.

Occupation and sex	Percent distribution of all wage or salary workers by occupation		Proportion of full-year workers by occupation			Percent change, 1939 to 1949					
						Increase in median income		Decrease in relative dispersion $(Q_3-Q_1)/(Q_2)$ [+ = increase]		Decrease in share of aggregate received by highest-paid fifth [+ = increase]	
	1949	1939	1949	1939	Percent change [- = decrease]	All workers	Full-year workers	All workers	Full-year workers	All workers	Full-year workers
FEMALE—Con.											
Clerical, Sales, and Kindred Workers											
Book'prs, accts., cashs., ticket agts.	7.7	5.8	71.4	79.1	-9.7	112	115	3.9	13.6	0.9	5.5
Office machine operators	1.2	0.7	71.6	75.7	-5.4	106	102	6.9	9.3	2.7	0.4
Stenographers, typists, and secys	15.0	13.4	71.9	78.2	-8.1	108	105	13.2	14.1	6.6	7.8
Telephone operators	3.5	2.5	72.4	79.4	-8.8	121	118	20.5	22.7	1.8	6.2
Saleswomen and sales clerks (n.e.c.)	10.4	8.4	52.1	61.1	-14.7	89	118	42.7	24.8	11.1	1.5
Operatives and Kindred Workers											
Dressmakers & seamstr., exc. factory	0.9	1.0	51.2	46.1	11.1	148	136	9.0	15.4	5.5	10.3
Operatives & kindred wkrs. (n.e.c.):											
Food and kindred products	2.0	1.6	41.3	39.0	5.9	150	156	+15.0	+1.2	+2.5	+1.0
Tobacco manufactures	0.5	0.8	48.1	39.8	20.9	166	151	+6.5	+3.4	+3.3	+3.5
Knitting mills	1.1	1.6	43.8	33.5	30.7	137	144	+18.7	+25.0	+8.8	+4.2
Textile mill prod., exc. knit. mills	3.6	4.2	47.6	34.0	40.0	192	179	+2.7	+24.0	+0.3	+0.7
Apparel & other fabric text. prod.	6.7	6.2	37.4	29.1	28.5	168	149	2.8	+17.8	+0.9	+1.3
Furniture, and lumber and wood prod.	0.4	0.3	43.5	40.9	6.4	135	146	+26.7	+26.5	+8.3	+3.4
Paper, paper prod., and printing	1.2	1.1	57.0	47.4	20.3	160	153	1.1	-1.6	+3.1	+0.3
Chemicals & petrol., & coal prod.	0.5	0.4	58.9	53.5	10.1	159	152	3.2	2.2	+1.6	+3.2
Footwear industries, exc. rubber	1.1	1.2	44.4	26.4	68.1	172	145	9.5	+17.9	+5.2	+1.0
Leather & leath. prod.,exc. footwear	0.3	0.4	36.0	28.1	28.1	163	143	+2.9	+13.9	+4.4	+1.8
Stone, clay, and glass products	0.4	0.3	47.5	41.3	15.0	147	151	+6.0	6.2	+4.4	-0.7
Metal industries and machinery	3.3	2.0	48.1	45.3	6.2	167	154	4.8	20.4	2.1	2.9
Transportation equipment	0.7	0.4	42.7	20.7	106.3	189	154	25.7	23.5	7.9	6.4
Service Workers											
Private household workers	12.2	20.7	47.3	66.5	-28.9	82	132	+33.8	+6.8	+19.8	+9.4
Barbers, beauticians, & manicurists	0.9	1.6	55.3	64.8	-14.7	119	134	+20.9	+14.0	+4.9	+4.8
Charwomen, janitors, and porters	1.3	1.0	63.0	70.0	-10.0	103	112	+40.2	+42.2	+13.6	+8.6
Cooks, exc. private household	2.2	1.4	43.0	59.3	-27.5	105	148	+17.8	1.1	+13.3	0.8
Housek'prs, stewards, exc. pr. hshld	0.8	0.8	62.7	68.1	-7.9	110	120	+8.3	+0.5	4.7	6.2
Practical nurses and midwives	1.1	1.0	42.5	41.4	2.7	138	163	+11.2	16.7	+7.0	5.7
Waitresses, bartenders, counter wkrs.	5.4	4.3	39.4	51.9	-24.1	106	142	+31.0	+9.0	+16.4	+2.1
Service wkrs., exc. pr. hshld.(n.e.c.)	2.9	2.0	50.8	63.8	-20.4	117	147	+21.7	+3.0	+14.0	+1.2

Source: Derived from tables C–1 to C–5.

INDEX